WOMEN
of
ILLUSION

ALSO BY
DONNALEE FREGA

Speaking in Hunger:
Gender, Discourse, and Consumption in 'Clarissa'

WOMEN

of

ILLUSION

A Circus Family's Story

Donnalee Frega

palgrave

for St. Martin's Press

WOMEN OF ILLUSION
© Frega Creative Enterprises, Inc., 2001

First published 2001 by
PALGRAVE
175 Fifth Avenue, New York, N.Y.10010 and
Houndmills, Basingstoke, Hampshire RG21 6XS.
Companies and representatives throughout the world

PALGRAVE is the new global publishing imprint of St. Martin's Press LLC Scholarly and Reference Division and Palgrave Publishers Ltd (formerly Macmillan Press Ltd).

ISBN 0-312-17718-6 hardback

Library of Congress Cataloging-in-Publication Data

Frega, Donnalee, 1956-
    Women of illusion : a circus family's story / Donnalee Frega.
        p. cm.
    Includes bibliographical references and index.
    ISBN 0-312-17718-6
        1. Huber family. 2. Women circus performers—United States—Biography. 3. Circus performers—United States—Biography. 4. Circus—United States. I. Title: Circus family's story. II. Title.

GV1811.A1 F74 2000
791.3'092'273—dc21
[B]   00-040438

A catalogue record for this book is available
from the British Library.

Design by Acme Art, Inc.

First edition: May, 2000
10 9 8 7 6 5 4 3 2 1

Printed in the United States of America.

This book is dedicated,

in loving memory,

to Charlie Lucas, Jr.,

our dear friend and "adopted grandpa"

CONTENTS

ACKNOWLEDGMENTS

Writing this book has been a remarkable journey for me. Of course I could not have done it—it would not exist—without the extraordinary gift of time and memories from the Huber family. My thanks to Betty, Fritzi, and Bobby Huber for the many interviews that they provided between 1996 and 1998. I have interwoven both my own reactions to their experiences and my friendship with them into this tale. I hope that, for the reader, this adds a useful counterpoint to the story.

Many others contributed to this effort. I am extremely grateful to William Parr, Betty's nephew, and to Anne Roberts, her sister, for their candid interviews. Charlie Lucas and his friends, Grace and Ruby Zeigler ("Charlie's angels"), drove for eight hours in order to be interviewed. I will never forget their warmth, laughter, and encouragement during the wonderful afternoon that we spent together in Betty's home. I treasure the memory of Charlie's friendship from that day until his death. I deeply appreciate the courtesy and kindness of Anthony Liebel, a skilled circus performer who braved confrontation in order to grant a valuable interview to an "outsider." He showed me what being "circus" truly means.

I want to acknowledge my gratitude to Duke University for an appointment as a visiting scholar to the English Department that facilitated the preparation of this book for publication. I am thankful, too, for the financial support provided by a Regional Artists Project Grant from the Arts Council of the Lower Cape Fear and the North Carolina Arts Council. I would also like to thank The University of Georgia Press for permission to reprint Kathleen Halme's "A World Without Words." Of the many secondary texts that I consulted in researching the book, I am particularly indebted to John Culhane's excellent study, *The American Circus: An Illustrated Display*. I am also grateful to Erin Foley, Archivist at the Circus World Museum in Baraboo, Wisconsin, for providing helpful information and sending wonderful pictures.

It is a genuine pleasure to acknowledge the friends who have helped bring this project to completion. My editor at Palgrave, Michael Flamini, is all that an editor should be, and I have enjoyed working with him. I am extremely grateful to Heather Florence, not only for her skillful, page-by-page legal review of the manuscript but for her kindness and contagious good humor. Heartfelt thanks to Debbie Manette, my copy editor, for her thorough reading and intelligent questions, and to Sonia Wilson, my superb proofreader, for her thoughtful queries and skillful suggestions for revision. These two women humbled an English professor with their attention to minute detail and nuance, and helped to craft this book with exquisite care. Dr. Melton McLaurin critiqued the manuscript in progress with unfailing energy and enthusiasm. Sandra Ihly provided a thoughtful reading and much appreciated reassurance. Rick Mobbs read with compassion and offered his services with the selflessness of a true friend. Patricia Coughlin revised numerous drafts, offering constant encouragement and sound advice; I consider her intelligent friendship a precious treasure. Above all, my family has stunned me with their love. My parents, Donald and Georgetta Wells, have been, as usual, boundless in their support. My three children have shared their mommy with a demanding project for several years, refreshing me daily with hugs; I am very proud of them. My husband, Alvin, is my best adviser, my lover, and my dearest friend.

A WORLD WITHOUT WORDS

A set of fresh lovers meets for the first
time out of bed at a cafe. They made some
love without words or used a few
words that took shape from their coupling.
Hear them turn their love, a piece
of cake on a plate, placed here between them. They devour
the whorls they put out the night before. Now
in fear of words they have to lean back
and find fast names for the whole dark ordeal.

The first snow is always the one we go out
just to be in, to have snow surround us
on its way down, and on the ground
we move as slowly as the word *elephant*—obsessed
and wanting for once to have snow
tell us without words about snow. As if
what we said meant anything at all. A thick trunk
pointing to an approximation of what we hope
we mean by tromping through unsigned snow.

Maybe this is why we can become so fond
of the afterevent—the grounds after
the circus has pulled up, the rock
overturned, the morning past a private event
taking shape beneath our bungalow. When everything is
final, vulnerable, then we can call it names.

—Kathleen Halme,
The Everlasting Universe of Things

INTRODUCTION

"Join the circus, . . . Run away," sings the master of ceremonies in the closing number of a Disney "Sing-A-Long" videocassette entitled *Let's Go to the Circus*. In this popular children's video, a group of youngsters visit the Ringling Bros. and Barnum & Bailey Circus (conveniently unaccompanied by adults) and are temporarily transformed by a clown's magic into circus entertainers themselves. Although the children's metamorphosis is portrayed as a fantasy, the accompanying lyrics voice the timeless assumption that joining a circus represents a "straying" from home rather than a deliberate choice of a profession. This assumption has followed circuses since their earliest days, centuries ago, when acrobats and animal trainers wandered across Europe in caravans of small wagons, cooking over fires, performing in town squares, and protecting one another from villagers whose inviolable work ethic and ties to the land often caused them to view such "eccentric" nomads with mistrust or hostility.

The lure of the circus, and its myth, is its promise of an alternative to the "normal" life of adult responsibility and social obligation. The circus has long been portrayed as a world of never-ending fun, wonder, and magic; a life of constant mobility; a "family" without constraints or authority. "You'll never go home again," sings the ringmaster, echoing the irresistible calls of Peter Pan and the Pied Piper.

Running away from home has been a fantasy of every child who ever protested a chore, and literature throughout the ages teems with the adventures of Tom Sawyers and lads running off to sea. While these young protagonists are quickly matured and sobered by the difficulties of the adult worlds they encounter, children who run away to the circus are often portrayed as being trapped or frozen, like Peter Pan and the "Lost Boys" of Never-Never Land, in a clownish world of childhood from which they never can grow up. In a culture that relies on a serious, long-term commitment to land, family, and community, the circus's seductive call to "children of *all* ages" suggests both an escape from and an inherent threat to adult responsibility.

The attraction of the circus is grounded on its ability to undermine the accountability and apprehension that adults must usually shoulder: Dangerous beasts and potentially deadly feats of skill are presented for amusement; the disabled and unusual may be showcased willingly as "sideshow freaks," and one can stare to one's heart's content without shame or impropriety; performers entertain in the scanty, sequined costumes normally associated with strippers but the intensely sensual nature of the performance is diffused by its address to children too young to recognize sexuality beneath the glitter. Although numerous circus entertainers have been mauled, hurt, or killed over the decades while practicing or performing their acts, the illusion that they are indestructible has been carefully and proudly crafted. The process of obscuring danger is fascinating and seldom open to "outsiders," yet it can be accomplished only by drawing on the misconceptions and desires of the outside world.

My interest with the world of illusion and the people who live in it began when I met the Hubers, a family whose members have, for generations, owned circuses, performed in circuses, run away from circuses, hidden in circuses, and raised "circus children." Their stories effectively shredded my understanding of circus life as a carefree alternative to the "normal" world, revealing instead rigid distinctions, hard work, intense loyalties, and an earnest regard for perfection. They spoke of a well-developed culture where histories could be instantly erased or reinvented, nationalities and names changed at will; a way of life in which children fearlessly swing from trapezes and ride elephants but are necessarily mistrustful of the delighted children whom they entertain; a "family" as worldwide as a religion but as private as a cult.

As the Hubers have "assimilated" into the "normal" world, gravitating naturally toward the movie industry with its emphasis on spectacle, illusion, and constant change, they have had to negotiate the demands of two very different cultures and have done so with remarkable humor and creativity. I have been constantly struck by their unique discernment that all social practices and beliefs are constructs, however deeply they may be valued. In recording their stories, I have found myself questioning the boundaries of concepts that I have always taken for granted: family, childhood, history, danger, and normalcy.

My experience with the Hubers has been a rich discovery of the processes by which we learn both to accept the illusory and to question the invisible. Together, the Hubers have slowly unraveled the tightly knit blanket of mystery, silence, and constant reinvention that conceals their family history. They have revealed the passion and exuberance, cruelty and fortitude, excesses and silences that accompany life in the world of illusion.

PREPARATIONS

In the dimly lit tank of rubber organs, one of the Living Liquid Ladies was apparently drowning. Betty Patrick had been trying for almost half a minute to eat a banana underwater. Mush oozed from her full mouth and drifted serenely through the prenatal landscape of Salvador Dalí's "Dream of Venus," swirling around the exploding giraffes and adhering to the anthropomorphic seaweed. Her fellow manic mermaids played piano, milked the cow, and warmed their hands at the aquafire with a calmness appropriate to lovely maidens of the subconscious realm, but the bubbly mess rising from the half-naked new girl was thwarting surrealism as mercilessly as Hitler was crushing Czech nationalism on the other side of the globe.

The great Dalí was fuming even before he stomped through the giant open legs at the entrance to the pavilion, saw the struggling mermaid with the stuffed mouth and swollen cheeks, and roared, "Get that minnow out of my tank!" Betty did not read the papers and had no idea that the "savior of modern art" was still smarting from a night in jail in protest of the exploitation of his genius. She had not seen the surrealist giant almost decapitated as water and glass shards rained down on him from the window he had broken at trendy Bonwit Teller. An artist with temperament has the right to defend his work, Judge Brodsky had pronounced, sympathizing with Dalí's dramatic rage after the store's managers had sabotaged his "Day" and "Night" window exhibits, replacing cobweb-covered "Ophelia" mannequins with conventional dummies in smart suits.[1]

Now it was all happening again. The World's Fair committee was blocking the Dalínian vision at every turn. After months of compromise and postponement, the "Dream of Venus" had opened to hundreds of thousands of visitors, heralded by a press release entitled "Is Dali Insane?" Dalí complained that he soon would go insane. The philistines had forbidden him to erect a woman with the head of a fish on the exterior of his pavilion. Such things were "impossible," they claimed. Dalí threatened to resign.[2] Even with the Gestapo marching through its cities with lists in their hands, Europe seemed more welcoming than New York's World of Tomorrow.

Twenty-two-year-old Betty had no idea that surrealism was under attack, nor that the world was on the brink of war. She knew only that the thundering man with the exaggerated handlebar mustache was the boss and that she had lost another job. Fortunately, the World's Fair of 1939 had more dazzling jobs than there were stars in the sky. The perky young acrobat scrambled out of the tank, shook her dripping dark curls at the artist, and marched across the vast Amusement Area with its multicolored array of flags, columns, pylons, pavilions, and statuary. She would audition for Billy Rose's Aquacade. Rose didn't expect his girls to eat underwater.

∼

Betty Patrick (also Barbara Schutz, Liazeed, Cristiani, Parroff, Kay, Huber, and others) is still perky and easily dazzled. At eighty-one, she has lost numerous jobs, kept even more, and remembers each one fondly. Lost in thought, she sits at her dining room table sorting piles of colored felt, seed beads, sequins, and faux gems, sips killer coffee, and deliberately ignores the hearing aid lying at her elbow. I can come in unnoticed and watch her for a minute before I announce that it is time to record another interview. With her white curls bouncing as her hands fly between piles, she reminds me of a cheerful, busy Christmas elf. Her small brick home in Wilmington, North Carolina, is decorated with five hundred dolls, many wearing replicas of the sequined costumes that she designed for circus performers and strippers. Strings of blinking Betty Boop Christmas lights hang across a doorway. A giant puzzle clock ticks on one wall. Miniature toys, gadgets, decorations, and memorabilia blanket windowsills and countertops. Life in a circus trailer has taught my hostess that every inch of space is valuable.

Dozens of framed photographs line the cluttered bookshelves and tables. On the mantel, in a place of honor, are photographs of Betty and her iron-bodied third husband clowning on the high wire in snappy dinner attire, an act that they performed with circuses across the country. The antique piano is heaped with dolls and toys, along with several faded black-and-whites of Betty's mother Babette, "The World's Strongest Woman," and of the Parroff Trio performing Roman Ladders, the precarious aerial act that Betty's acrobat father designed and forced her to perform.

I met Betty several years ago at the opening of an art exhibit. My husband and I had come to view an annual nonjuried show of local artwork hung in a downtown "alternative space"—more of a track-lighted warehouse than an art gallery. As a writer married to a sculptor, I often find myself wandering about such exhibits, my pencil tucked behind my ear so that my hands are free to hold a plate of crackers and melon balls or a Dixie cup of punch. On that particular evening, though, I was interested only in quitting the affair as soon as I decently could. My stomach twisted with queasiness whenever I approached the buffet table, and the amplified sounds that pounded through the industrial corridors throbbed in the delicate nerves behind my eyeballs. Feeling bulbous in a bland maternity smock that I had dug out of my closet for a third pregnancy, I waddled in hormonal misery through crowds of chain-smoking, tattooed, orange- and purple-haired youngsters with rings in their noses and navels and more energy than I was sure I would ever feel again. I had just collapsed gratefully onto a chair when I heard an infectious laugh and found myself staring into the face of a lovely white-haired woman—the classic image of a grandmother. Her eyes swept my body, and she announced cheerfully, "You're going to have a girl."

Hours later Betty and I stood grazing at the buffet table, scraping the last smudges of spinach dip with wilted carrot sticks. We had talked so hard that we had made ourselves hungry. Plates and napkins were long gone, but we gobbled the crumbled remains of cake with our fingers and drank the dregs from the punch bowl. Betty had shown me her entry in the exhibit, a cardboard box in which she had constructed a tiny circus scene, complete with painted animals, intricate rigging, refreshment booths, and joyful children. Pointing to a couple of clowns suspended from the high wire, she said, laughing, "That's me and my husband. We were the 'top' performers, weren't we?" Baby-sickness forgotten, I listened in ever-growing amazement as she chatted on and on, telling me stories of a world without physical limitations, stories that I knew I would have to repeat.

When the exhibit hall closed down, my husband came to find me, accompanied by Fritzi Huber, a striking woman with curly brown hair pulled tightly into a ponytail and sparkling eyes. I had long admired her work in handmade paper and wished to meet her. Fritzi took one look at the crumbs strewn across our chests and said, "Well, Mom, you've found another good listener, haven't you?" I left my new friends with a promise that we would get together again soon. Instinctively I knew that they were to become an important part of my life and that I wanted to learn more about their fascinating histories—much more.

That spring evening seems long ago now—almost part of another lifetime. On the next full moon, I gave birth to a little girl, exactly as Betty had predicted, and named her Emma. As I looked into my tiny daughter's infant-wise eyes, I felt a powerful stirring, something much deeper than happiness. For the first time ever, I felt at peace with history. I had no idea that I would soon be called on to defend that certitude, that I was about to undergo a test of character so exacting that I, too, would feel newborn when it was finished. Nor did I understand how necessary to the process my friendship with the Hubers would become.

I can now look back on the challenges that followed Emma's birth and feel grateful for the transition they so painfully wrought, but at the time I understood only that I was being wrenched from my comfortable life and attitudes by an almost uncanny series of misfortunes. Strangely, "Grandma" Betty and "Tante" Fritzi moved into my world right along with Emma, as if these women had somehow been sent together to ease my passage. The first blow came in the mail—a formal notice that I had not been granted tenure at the small university where I taught southern literature. Behind closed doors, a coldly corporate dean informed me that I ought to have concentrated on producing publications rather than a baby. Stunned, I discovered how thoroughly I had always relied on my profession to define myself. Teaching was my vocation.

The Hubers were my closest friends during that disastrous postpartum period in which my world seemed to be crumbling. Paychecks vanished; insurance could no longer be taken for granted. My husband woke at night to help with the baby, then staggered off each morning to the double load of contracts he had taken on to make up for my lost income and the added expenses of a new child. We hardly saw each other and were exhausted when we did. I was treated for postpartum hemorrhaging with doses of hormones that made my hair fall out and caused me to cry without reason. Worst of all, my books, treasured over decades, and the thick files of teaching and reading notes that I had carefully collected and lovingly shelved in my office at the university, had to be crammed into cardboard boxes and laundry baskets, brought home, and then wedged into closets, under beds, behind chairs. Having lost my job, I seemed also to have lost an important part of myself.

I turned my attention to home, comforting myself with the thought that I finally had time to enjoy the lovely log house on seven acres of woods that we had purchased the year before. Betty began to keep Emma each Tuesday, giving me precious hours to rest. Entranced, Emma would gape while Betty dangled endless sparkling toys and played music boxes, and I found that my body was getting stronger and my mind clearer with each free afternoon. The slow summer was delightfully sensual. The muggy southern days turned into steamy nights as I lulled my baby and nursed my healing body. Fritzi brought me exotic books—magnificent hardbound volumes with gorgeous pictures. I was astonished by the depth and range of her private studies. Together we pored over Islamic calligraphy and Indian Tantric designs, the harems of the Sultan Suleiman, and the *Tao Te Ching*. I lent Fritzi novels by my favorite southern authors, and she found in them the same magic realism that had drawn her to the art of Mexico. Soon I had embarked on a new course of study— Mexican circuses, Freida Kahlo's diaries, and D. H. Lawrence's journeys through Oaxaca.

Our conversations were exhilarating—the first truly reciprocal teaching I had ever enjoyed. I relished these journeys of the mind that did not need to be charted on a résumé or validated in academic journals. Suddenly my old job seemed like a prison to which I had been shackled for too many years, my former colleagues musty and unadventurous. Emma began to sleep through the night, her tiny fingers curled in my hair, her little lips sucking a dream bottle. I decided that I wanted to write again—perhaps a creative work about awakenings and coping with change.

When that sweltering August came to an end and the university opened for the fall semester—an event that I had been dreading—my days were not empty and defeated as I had feared. I was able to rejoice at not having to return to the English Department, and I envisioned an autumn spent reading on the porch.

Air-conditioned schools opened to thousands of relieved children but they closed again almost immediately, the children arriving home late in the morning with written warnings to their parents to prepare for a catastrophe. The torpid weather had churned into an ominous tropical storm that hung off the coast of North Carolina. Hurricane Bertha struck Wilmington just as frightened crowds began to mob grocery stores for batteries and bottled water. Before dazed families could find new boards for their shattered windows, Hurricane Fran slammed into the already battered coast the next month with even greater fury, leaving Wilmington ravaged—its roofless homes and powerless stores exposed and defenseless.

It seemed like the end of the world. Tornadoes followed the hurricane's winds. Rivers rose over stretches of Interstate I-40 while copperheads and water moccasins took refuge from the rising floods on porches. Downed power lines twitched and seethed like nests of angry serpents over unearthed streets and sidewalks crusted with shattered glass. The air filled with a sickeningly sweet vinegar stench as thousands of downed trees rotted in the heat and rain. Swarms of mosquitoes began to breed in the standing water. In a neighboring county, a small child became the first to contract mosquito-borne encephalitis.

In the aftermath of the tempest, a career transition seemed a nuisance not to be confused with life's true catastrophes. Our thick log walls had withstood the storm, keeping us safe in the sticky darkness while the forest crashed down around us. Three years later, we are still cutting and burning the giant trunks of mammoth trees that fell like pickup sticks, their exposed root systems standing twelve feet in the air. We thankfully ate cold canned soup and dry cereal, bathed in tepid water collected in a canoe, and listened to the radio with the same attention its first listeners must have offered in the days before television, when the sound of a human voice from beyond the walls of one's home seemed a miracle and a lifeline.

Betty weathered the storm like a trooper, although we all mourned the loss of a giant pecan tree in her yard that had provided many a fine pie. Fritzi's studio and artwork were destroyed in the winds and flooding that tore down most of the buildings on Topsail Island. Sand-filled boats lay in homes whose walls had washed away. When the National Guard finally allowed dazed residents to return to the homes from which they had been evacuated in the worst-hit zones along the coastline, the friend who had rekindled my joy in learning found her studio sopping with ocean water and her precious paper-making equipment buried under crab-covered mounds of mud and decaying fish. She scarcely gave herself time to cry. She dumped Clorox, sponges, garbage bags, and a bottle of drinking water into the back of her car, sloshed through the muddy debris, and set to the spine-wrenching work of digging and mopping.

We didn't talk much during those first hellish weeks of recovery—we were all too busy—but I remember the look in Fritzi's eyes as she handed me a tiny fragment of painted paper torn from a ruined work of art. She was bruised and weary, her almost girlish body overwhelmed by what the goliath forces of destruction had wrought, but she was not defeated. There was a determination and an acceptance in her eyes that almost shocked me when I remembered how, only months earlier, I had cried over books neatly boxed in corners of clean rooms. She seemed resigned to the inevitability of abrupt endings and fresh beginnings.

Eventually the crews of tired emergency workers and insurance agents left town, the new homeless abandoned their cots in school gymnasiums and found shelter with relatives, power was restored and shelves restocked, and the endless caravans of gawking sight-seers disappeared. Normal routines resumed as if nothing had happened, and yet everything seemed changed. On a cool morning in October, Fritzi and I sat together at Leon's Ogden Restaurant, laughing at each other's exhausted faces and worn work clothes. Over fried eggs and grits, we took inventory. Each of us wanted to get back to more fulfilling work, but first we had to take stock of what we had to work with.

"This is the first time in my life that I haven't gone back to school in September," I mused. "My colleagues and I used to joke about leaving academia and going out into the 'real world,' but this feels unreal to me. I do the same errands and chores each day, the same dull work. Last night one of the kids pressed the 'pause' button on the VCR and the screen froze. I thought to myself, That's me—I'm on pause. Books aren't enough anymore. I want a new challenge, but there are dishes to wash and diapers to change and bills to pay. I'm busy all the time, and yet I feel so, so . . . unused."

"You've lost your comfort zone." Fritzi chuckled and then leaned forward, her tone suddenly quiet and serious. "People always cling to comfort zones—to the extent of trying to freeze them into cultures. That's how we define ourselves. We tell ourselves that how we are living is 'normal,' that we have found the 'right' job, the 'right' place, the 'right' life. But comfort zones disintegrate all the time and then we feel lost. You'll just have to reinvent yourself. It's not as hard as you might think."

I stared. This was the sort of language I had heard in study groups of critical theorists at the university. I thought of the intellectual jargon for pedagogical growth that we had thrown about so glibly: "collapsing naturalized assumptions," "interrogating interpretive communities," "realizing empowerment strategies." We had never discussed how such concepts might apply to our own personal lives, perhaps because tenure guaranteed that the same group of aging colleagues would continue the same theoretical conversations endlessly. "Comfort zone" was a very appropriate term, indeed.

"Easy for you to say," I answered sharply, surprising myself. I had not been ready for the rush of exhilaration I had felt at the idea of leaping unfettered into an uncharted future. "You don't have kids. A lost job may be a fresh plain of possibility for you, but I carry responsibilities. Children need a consistent, dependable home. I must maintain that. I love them. And they don't want me reinvented. They like the mom they have." I stabbed impatiently at the yolks of my eggs. "How?" I whispered finally. "How do you reinvent yourself? How do you do it without being selfish? Without hurting anyone?"

Fritzi stared past me for a moment, as if weighing what she was about to say, then reached for the bill and stood up. "You don't have to hurt anyone, necessarily," she mused. "You should talk to my mother. She has stories you won't believe. Every culture she passes through seems to disappear behind her. I guess it's a gift." We both laughed, but she quickly took my hand. "There's no single answer. Maybe what worked for us wouldn't work for you—maybe it won't work for us much longer. And there's a price. When you've heard her story, come back to me, and I'll tell you mine. Then you can choose your own way. You said that you wanted to write, didn't you? Why not focus your unused energies that way? Take a pencil."

Her advice contained a warning, but I listened only to part of it. If Fritzi had meant to motivate me, stir me from my sluggishness and push me back into doing what I love to do, she could not have chosen a more captivating and seductive project. I visited her mother the next morning, was given a tour of her home, and with Betty's encouragement, left with my mind racing through plans for a full-fledged book.

A month later I invited Fritzi to drive with me to Savannah, where I was to attend the annual South Atlantic Modern Language Association Conference—a three-day schedule of academic presentations, literary readings, and book fairs. Fritzi wanted to visit friends in Savannah and gladly agreed. After meeting Fritzi's friends for dinner and spending the next afternoon wandering through the city's wonderful old cemetery, thoughtfully reading stones and willing ourselves back in time, I could no longer ignore my own conference plans. Fritzi had brought along a box of family circus photographs; we circled our hotel's grand hall where the book exhibits had been set up, and where I hoped to find an editor interested in supporting a book about a circus family. By late afternoon we were sipping cocktails in the lounge while the directors of several university presses clustered about us, eyeing each other and gasping over the photographs. I received contract offers that very evening, and Fritzi and I celebrated with song and laughter all the way home. By December, senior editors and directors of numerous publishing houses were calling me daily, and I found myself in the enviable position of being able to choose and negotiate.

It was a thrilling turnabout, and I called everyone I knew, celebrated with my friends. I could not wait to start my new project. It took a few weeks for the glow to wear off, and then I had to ask myself what I had done. I had never written a biographical work, and I was beginning to realize that Betty would not be a simple subject.

~

Listening to Betty, watching her work, I realize that her sense of history relies on impressions woven into an intricate pattern that she has designed herself using colorful memories in the same way that she uses beads and thread. "So why did Dalí fire you?" I ask when she finally looks up from her embroidery. She picks up her story from the day before, as if I had casually stepped out of the room for only a moment.

"I couldn't eat that banana underwater." She chuckles. "When the other girls came back from lunch, I asked them, 'How *did* you eat bananas in the tank?' and they cried, 'You got in the tank? We're not supposed to get into the water!'" When Betty insisted that she had watched them eating underwater, the first shift explained that they had merely been sitting *behind* the aquarium eating their lunches; cooling fans set up behind the exhibit had apparently blown their hair about, contributing to her mistaken impression that they were submerged. Betty had been raised in an era of mass unemployment, eviction notices, and bread lines, and had learned never to ask questions when a job was at stake. Undaunted, she had assumed that whatever others could do, she would do as well.

As I enjoy Betty's stories, I am reminded of the *Young Indiana Jones Chronicles,* one of the many series, movies, and specials filmed in Wilmington in which one can catch a sight of Betty with her toothless, drooling Chihuahua cradled in one arm or tucked discreetly on her lap. Episodes always begin with a deceptively ordinary old man recounting to children a chance encounter in his youth with Albert Schweitzer, Pancho Villa, T. E. Lawrence, or Lenin. Flipping through her photo albums, Betty pauses over autographed pictures of Billie Holiday, Sophie Tucker, Billy Rose, Red Skelton, a yellowed Christmas postcard of the Kaiser's family. People she remembers. People she worked with. People she passed by. People from another world.

The World's Fair of 1939 had a theme: Building the World of Tomorrow. For months before its opening on April 30, its "Dawn of a New Day" slogan was heard at fund-raisers and preparatory celebrations, flashed on electric signs, and splashed across bus stops and train stations. Gershwin's song with the same name played endlessly. After the sour years of the Depression, as Europe prepared for another world war, the slogan must have appealed tremendously to a nation hungry for a future that was progressive and relaxed. Twenty-five million fairgoers waited in line, eager for a chance to examine the tiny screen called television. DuPont displayed a new type of thread called nylon that would soon become crucial for parachutes. For miles around, New Yorkers could see the breathtaking Perisphere theme center. Seemingly suspended in space by gushing fountains of misty, multicolored water, the eighteen-story-high globe was brilliantly lit at night. Inside, two revolving balconies carried unending lines of people around Democracity, a model future city of skyscrapers and interstate superhighways in which 250 million people would live in peace and prosperity by 2039. Building the future could be fun, the fair seemed to insist. When King George VI came to America to visit the fair, President Roosevelt fed him a picnic lunch of hot dogs.

For Betty, the Dawn of a New Day must have seemed a promise of glorious potential. Fun was a new concept. Her past had included only personal wars and a private depression. She could dimly remember the foster homes in which she had spent her first eight years—the hunger, the sexual molestation. There had been no caresses or lullabies in Betty's infancy, only strangers who fed her sour milk and seldom changed her reeking diapers. While her performing parents traveled with famous circuses, she was bounced from one foster home to another, never receiving the toys and chocolates lovingly shipped from Chicago or New York or Havana by her mother. When Betty amazed her visiting father by eating orange peels and sausage casings, having been taught by her foster family that the best parts of the fruit and meat he sent each week were inedible, Harry Schutz realized why his little daughter was suffering from rickets. He brought her home and for weeks carried her about the house on a pillow. When she had healed, he decided to pack Betty and her two brothers off to Germany to "visit" the family from whom he had run away as a boy. Unfooled, her mother pleaded with him, "Harry, bring me home one of my babies. Please don't leave them all," but the "strongest woman alive" was no match for her husband's stubbornness. Weighing over two hundred pounds, Babette Tyana could easily lift a young elephant in her act, but she could not keep her husband from giving away her children.

It is late afternoon when Betty unwraps a crumbling leather album with a handpainted American Indian head on the cover. Sprawled on the floor with our heads together, we gingerly examine the photographs that once were Babette's. The passport photograph of three tunnel-eyed children about to be abandoned on a strange continent must have wrenched her heart. Betty is eight, Harry Jr. is ten. Charlie is only four and his little face is dark with fright. Harry Jr.'s eyes are haunting, as if the epileptic child were anticipating the beatings that would result in irreparable brain damage and the experimental medical treatment that would lead to early death. Betty's eyes are vacant. She had already learned the trick she has used to survive horror all her life. "You ask me what I thought about during those dark days," she confides in a low tone. "The truth is, a lot of the time, I didn't think at all. Even now, I try not to think too much."

Harry took the children first to their Uncle Joseph's handsome home in Munich, but his brother's wife, Mary, was struggling with stomach cancer and refused to care for somebody else's cast-off children. Undaunted, the glib performer managed to convince his aging parents that the boys would be a help to them, but the couple could see no promise in a scrawny little girl with too-short bangs and clenched fists. When the handsome acrobat boarded the ocean liner for New York, he was once again a hard-drinking, high-rolling bachelor, conveniently unimpeded by his stout wife and three unwanted offspring. He had left his tiny daughter behind high convent walls where, he told her, she would receive a European education and become a lady.

The quiet afternoon sunlight flickers gently over the photograph Betty shows me of her convent life. A verdant lawn and shaded path is dotted with fairy children in ivory frocks, each tending a tiny doll carriage. The elegance of a private European establishment for young ladies combined with the peaceful sanctuary of a Catholic retreat is deeply, achingly familiar; shocked, I realize that the photograph represents a longed-for world I once experienced almost sensually through cherished books—*A Little Princess, The Portrait of a Lady, Emma.* "You lived there?" I whisper, half jealously.

Betty stares intently at the photograph. "That was the first convent." She sighs, and I suddenly recall that the heroine of each of the books I loved was forced from her pristine refuge into a reality whose harshness was all the more cruel for being unexpected. "It was very expensive," she continues. "I had to have white linen, a white nightgown, white slippers—all my toiletry was white—my combs and brushes and hairpins. We had pressed uniforms and were treated like ladies. Sometimes we would walk into town in long lines to see the *Glockenspiel.* People would point to us and smile. I stayed there for about two years."

"Did you have friends?" I urge, remembering my girlhood fantasies of sharing midnight confidences with wonderful, exotic girlfriends in the dormitory of some prestigious foreign boarding school. She whisks the question away, her eyes shining with proud independence. "No. I studied almost all the time. I wanted to excel. They would pass you in the middle of a term—if you were exceptional. Then you were given a red stripe on your hat to show that you had risen another grade. By the end of the first two years, I had three red ribbons and was ready for high school. I was a very quick learner, and the teachers spoke English. I was great in arithmetic and history. Of course, history over there was all about Germany—only Germany. When I came home to the states, a teacher asked me, 'Who discovered America?' and I said, 'Wasn't it here all the time?' I didn't know about the Pilgrims or anything. You know, they say a 'European' education is the finest you can have, but it wasn't very helpful in America. I had to learn all over again in America."

She is far ahead of me now, already turning the page of the album, about to flip to another decade while my imagination is still captivated by a glimpse of children playing in a secret garden. My imagination has always been a pampered and fairly reliable friend—a distinct difference between Betty and myself, it seems. "You said that was the *first* convent," I remind her quickly, forcing my subject once again to abandon her pleasant train of associations and return to events that she has worked to forget.

Now that relating Betty's story has become my new work, I find myself increasingly exasperated by the sealed closets in her memory.

There is no prying them; I have to lead her to each locked door and insist that she produce the key. All too often, she simply blinks and selects something brighter to show me, something easier to divulge. I want to find some sort of common ground with my subject, to resist the impulse to impose an agenda on her narrative, but her associative ramblings undermine my notion of what constitutes even a nonlinear "story" or "narrative." I am trying hard not to infantilize or dominate her as she glides playfully across time, but when I ask a curious question that causes her face to crumple, I feel exactly like a child abuser.

Betty shakes her head quickly, a gesture that I am unable to interpret. "The second convent was different," she says, flat-voiced, as she gently runs her fingers back and forth over the muscles in her arm. I feel old anger filling the room, as unsettling as a change in temperature, as potent as a strong odor. She has apparently accepted my challenge and wrested open a sealed door. The initial blast of long-checked memories (a phenomena I will eventually learn to anticipate) lasts only seconds. I hold my breath as bitter sentences shatter into fragments: "'too expensive,' he said," "like an orphanage," "disgusting," "and he didn't want to know." A deliberate, stone-cold silence follows this rush of words, and my stomach twists as I begin to realize what is happening—what I have done.

This is no simple recollection that I am witnessing but an emotion so overwhelming in its immediacy that it practically transforms my hostess. Betty is still speaking with the calm voice of a woman, but her blue-gray eyes have narrowed into those of a wary, preadolescent girl. A woman-child whose face is contorted with impotent indignation. A furious child too distant to comfort. It is hard to determine where the familiar personality of my eighty-one-year-old hostess ends and this miserable child begins.

She tells me that her name was changed to Ancilla by the new nuns to whom Uncle Joseph entrusted her after he had determined that her beloved first convent was no longer financially feasible. He left her buried alive behind the ancient stone walls of a vast estate that had been left to the holy order by a long-dead baron. She remembers drab children who scoured massive floors with heavy brushes and scrubbed piles of coarse laundry with burning, blue-knuckled hands. Her voice trembling with disgust, she tells me of the most detested task—of deep baskets crammed with knitted pads that were stiff with women's clotted brown blood. These were to be hand-washed until each woolen cushion was fresh and white. Ancilla did not ask why Jesus Christ made the black-robed sisters bleed.

Escape was not impossible, only useless. My narrator recalls that a fellow girl once escaped through the darkness and implored kind-hearted villagers to help her to find her never-seen parents. She was returned to the nuns after a single night, her hair freshly washed and braided, her thin body amazingly attired in a child's colorful frock. Betty explains carefully what happened next. "They took her nice clothes away, then they made us stand in a circle around her and told us to spit at her. I couldn't do that, but her 'angel' did."

In this long-disappeared cloistered world, it seems that each child was assigned an "angel"—another child to act as guardian and friend so that the nuns would not be distracted unnecessarily from their spiritual calm. Ancilla's angel was a quiet girl. One cool autumn morning, Ancilla could not awaken her angel for mass. The frustrated nun to whom she appealed for help shook the seemingly lazy sleeper until her loose hair fell away from her face, revealing a thin hair ribbon knotted tightly around a swollen little neck. "They hurried us all into the dining hall," Betty relates softly. "There was no fuss. They told her parents that she had died of pneumonia."

I swallow hard. I know that I have heard this awful story before—decades ago. I can even remember exactly where and when: on a slumberless winter night in Buffalo as I sprawled in my pajamas with my Catholic girlfriends on a mattress in a friend's creepy basement. We had lit candles and levitated each other, asked the Ouija Board to tell us whom we would marry, and held an ineffectual seance before one of the girls produced *Jane Eyre* and began to read aloud Charlotte Brontë's spellbinding tale of two children who discover that they are soulmates in brutal Lowood Boarding School. For many nights afterward, I lay in bed staring at the snow-heavy roofs outside my window and thinking of the lonely Jane, who climbs into her beloved Helen's bed one icy night for an earnest talk but awakens to discover lifeless young limbs wrapped about her neck in a final embrace.

Betty has probably never read *Jane Eyre*, but she is an accomplished storyteller. Maybe, I think at first, she once saw one of the many movie versions and incorporated the famous scene of Helen

Burn's pitiful death into her own remembered past, perhaps so long ago that it now seems real to her. I look down at the yellowed photographs spread across the table, then at Betty's face. Her eyes tell me more forcefully than the photos that this incident was not borrowed from a book or movie but is absolutely true. The world that Charlotte Brontë describes so convincingly, I recall, was one that she knew from experience. Children lived in such places—boarding schools, orphanages, convents, concentration camps. Children like my own thoughtful sons and my precious daughter Emma.

Betty is still talking and I am grateful that my cassette player is recording her because I cannot listen. I am imagining my tow-haired, freckled ten-year-old son surrounded by a spitting mob of children or snuggled against a corpse—my sensitive little Kurt, who worries about whether his dog is lonely when he is at school. I have to change her train of thought or I will start to cry. My children are my secret vulnerability. When I am exhausted or emotionally shaken, I often torture myself with imagining the ills that can—perhaps will—befall them. These nightmarish imaginings are as addictive as a drug, and I wonder if all mothers struggle against anticipating the unthinkable. I cannot let myself go down this slippery path.

Betty knows that I was also educated in a convent school. The nuns whom I remember, however, wore knee-length skirts, filled their classrooms with straw flowers and posters of sunny landscapes, played the guitar and sang beautifully. At mass each morning, I would grip the back of a pew with both hands as their voices rose in eight-part harmony, filling the private chapel of Mount Saint Mary's Academy. "Did they sing?" I interrupt hastily. "Did your nuns sing?"

She pauses politely, thinks a moment. "Yes, we sang—only religious songs, of course. I had a good voice, so they put me in the choir. My job was to hold the melody. They would say, 'You are the leader. Let the others sing around you.' I wanted so badly to harmonize but they never let me. I should have just done it." We smile at each other and suddenly we are both relaxed. In fact, the whole room seems to have breathed a sigh of relief. "Let me tell you something funny." She grins. My Betty is back.

"You know, the other girls thought that I was a millionaire because I was an American. Uncle Joseph never came to see me; he just sent fruit or candy instead. We had to share everything. You'd think they would have liked me for sharing but they didn't. They thought that I was pampered. Once one of the girls stole my pencil and laughed because the rich American girl couldn't do her assignments. That's how I knew who to get even with. We weren't allowed to hit, so I had to be creative."

Betty is grinning wickedly as she relates the story of her revenge, and it strikes me that she was probably never the helpless child whom I have been imagining. She explains that each girl had a small potty under her bed—for tinkle only, and she had to empty it herself in the morning. Betty waited until hers was full, then crawled from her cot, lifted her enemy's covers, and quickly poured the contents into her bed. Her victim screamed and sprang from the sopping mat, grabbed Betty by the hair, and was tussling with her when an exasperated nun burst into the dormitory.

Betty knew that the nuns could devise grotesque punishments. Without hesitating, she stretched her arms out to the moon and shuffled toward a window, astonishing her outraged adversary and scaring the sister. "Don't touch her. She's sleepwalking," the anxious woman warned the girls, gently leading Betty back to bed and tucking her in. "There now, go to sleep."

I grin at her and she grins back. "Why, you were an actress even then, you clever thing." I laugh, astonished that a child could execute such a snap performance under pressure. She must have been sharp.

"Nope. I giggled. I couldn't help myself. It was so easy and so silly. I giggled and then she knew that I wasn't sleeping. The next day they beat me across the hands with a broomstick. I didn't care. I'd had my revenge. No one picked on me after that. They stayed out of my way."

Suddenly Betty pushes her face close to mine and glares, as if she is challenging me to choose a side in this long-ago conflict. Shaken, I force a smile and suggest that we stop for lunch. I catch my breath as I watch her eyes—or are they the eyes of Ancilla?—refocus and Betty's calm, grandmotherly countenance return.

I try to transcribe tapes as soon as possible after interviews, while I can still remember all the gestures, expressions, and impressions that cannot be recorded on a cassette. Playing back my last conversation with Betty, I ask myself if any of what I recall actually happened. Did her face really change? Did I feel her anger in the room or simply a strong dose of my own growing impatience for an unguarded story? Back in my quiet living room, surrounded by friendly books, far from the eyes of costumed dolls and painted clown puppets, I wonder if the bizarre afternoon that kept me tossing last night was not merely the product of a desire to give my book a gothic flavor.

~

I am so relieved when Fritzi answers the phone that I almost thank her. I can be blunt. "Your mother is giving me nightmares. What is it that she does to me? Is it my imagination or do I need some sort of protection during these interviews?" The laughter on the other end of the line tells me that she knows exactly what I am talking about. What she says makes sense.

"Remember, Mom is a storyteller, not a historian. She's a professional performer, and so she is uniquely aware of her audience. She's watching you as closely as you are watching her. Haven't you felt that? Performance is interactive. She's telling you the truth, but how she presents those facts—and how you receive them—is an active collaboration between you. It's like lovemaking, you know? The act itself is pretty standard, but it will be colored moment by moment by whatever subtle emotions the participants are bringing to it—maybe even by the time of day or cast of the light. That's the rationale behind romance, isn't it? You create the right mood and voilá!" We both laugh.

"Seriously, Mom is the most immediate person you will ever meet. She can reach down deeper than most mystics and bring all of that emotion right to the surface—with the pure magical openness of a child, but she isn't a child. She has anger that you don't want to touch—that *she's* never touched because she knows that it's too much to deal with now. You've heard what her life has been like. She has had to bury so much in order to get through it. I'm amazed at how eager she is to talk about things that she has never wanted to bring up before. She's getting older, and she wants to tell her story. You are negotiating that story between you—do you understand? How much can she give—how much can you take?"

"Fritzi, I'm not a therapist!" I cry. "I wanted to record an oral history. I am not qualified to play the role of grief counselor or psychologist. I don't want her transferring her anger onto me. Yesterday she practically snapped my head off because I asked a question about rigging. She told me to pay attention in a tone that I wouldn't use with my most recalcitrant students. I almost left, but then I looked at her and—I was furious but I couldn't focus my anger back at her. It just simmered all night."

"I know. She's good, isn't she? That's how she got by." Fritzi chuckles. "She reads you. And if she doesn't like what she's feeling, she spanks your brain."

Unsettled, I hang up the phone and sit for a long time. I have a Ph.D. from Duke University with a specialty in narrative theory. I understand the dynamics of reader reception, have written articles on how to help students to achieve self-determination through language awareness. I have lectured to writing classes on the importance of knowing one's audience, of addressing a specific audience with a rhetorical strategy, of designing that strategy around the assumptions that members of interpretive communities bring to texts. I have designed courses on women's literature, examined the necessity of helping women to overcome patriarchal silencing, to discover their voices. Why isn't this background helping me to claim a place for myself within this writing process?

In the library, I comb through the wealth of recent, critical academic research on the writing of biography and autobiography but find appallingly little practical discussion concerning how to deal productively and tactfully with living subjects. The field is a rich and currently popular one, but before long, the essays begin to sound the same. All address the problems implicit in writing a life story—problems of control and authority over the narrative, of the dangers of displacement, subjectivity, voyeurism, conflicting perspective, editorial imposition; uniformly the literature assumes that these issues are controlled primarily by the writer rather than by the subject. Although some readings do address the complicated ways in which a subject can manipulate her biographer, dismantling her authority, undermining her sense of worthiness as a recipient, it is customarily assumed that the editor can immediately regain her authoritative ground during the recomposition process by editing and organizing the subject's story as she pleases.

This possibility seems to posit the subject and hearer as well-meaning adversaries of a sort. Scholar Jean Humez, for example, explains:

> These oral-historical autobiographies are the result of an invisible process of negotiation between two people: a specific interviewer, at a particular moment of her life, engaged in a friendly contest of wills with a specific woman, also of course at a particular moment in a very different life. The contest is over final control of the meaning of the life story they are generating together. The interviewer's interests, questions, assumptions, and physical presence as an auditor stimulate the woman being interviewed to tell some stories and not others, and to interpret those stories she does tell in ways that she might not have done, had she been telling them to beloved contemporaries or to polite strangers, or even had she been thinking with a pen in her hand, alone in a room of her own, contemplating a faceless public.[3]

A "friendly contest of wills," I think; it seems like an oxymoron. What site does one occupy when one locates oneself midway between beloved contemporaries and polite strangers? This is surely a precarious ground on which neither the social amenities reserved for strangers nor the considerate affection granted to loved ones applies. What I am experiencing is an uncharted intimacy for which there exists no etiquette, only a shared resolve.

Scholars acknowledge that modern biographies, especially those concerned with the private lives of women, differ substantially from the personal success stories generally told about famous public men in that they are necessarily far more intimate. Feminist theorist Linda Wagner-Martin writes, in *Telling Women's Lives: The New Biography*, "Women's biography is more often based on private events . . . purposely kept secret by the subject (such as sexual abuse, dislike for parents, dislike by parents, or other unfortunate childhood or adolescent happenings)." The biographer's challenge, I read, is to present a vivid account of the "tightly woven mesh of public and private events" that make up the subject's selfhood, to reflect with insight and integrity on her complex interior life—her motivations and conflicts—and to discuss the choices she has made in terms of the times in which she made them. "Good biography," Wagner-Martin insists, "attempts to unearth the hidden, more interior self."[4]

Of course, this challenge presents unprecedented difficulties for the individual who must poke and pry for those inner conflicts and intimate recollections while still, somehow, maintaining a courteous regard for personal privacy—and while guarding her own peace of mind. What if the subject's interior life is dangerous, a field pulsing with alarming currents? I visualize Betty's anger as a live wire deceptively motionless under quiet water and myself the well-meaning writer who tries to pick it up for a closer look.

Eventually I uncover candid warnings that the process of hearing and repeating a life can be exhausting and nerve-wracking, quite simply because the dynamics and ethics involved are indeterminate, particular to each teller/listener, and subject to continual change. Wagner-Martin cautions that women who tell their own lives can assume disguises, can romanticize or sentimentalize their stories as they tell them, can take their biographers on a roller-coaster ride of conflicting stories, conflicting emotions, guessing, flirting, skirting, concealing. This I have already discovered, and it feels good to see my experience acknowledged by someone else. "Biography can be a double-edged sword," she admits. "Portraying a woman's life faithfully and explicitly is sometimes dangerous."[5]

"We do not have much choice about lies and silences. They accrue whether we will it or not," muses scholar Victoria Glendinning, in her essay in *The Troubled Face of Biography*. "The biographer brings to her task her own essential but dangerous imagination. Without imagination and intuition her portrait will be lifeless, but she should be careful not to novelize unintentionally, and not to project her own personality unknowingly on to her subject, in an act of identification."[6]

How to identify with and detach myself from a subject simultaneously is a feat that no book can teach me, although several writers warn of the temptation to hero worship and of the possibility of self-loss implicit in the process. "The writing of biography is more than a discovery of another person. It is a matter of self-discovery. . . . The writer goes through a painful process of immersion in another's life, a baptism by research," warns biography scholar Andrew Sinclair.[7] Glendinning refers to this process of immersion as a challenging "game," yet also admits that "You do get uniquely close to a person, studying full-time a career, a set of relationships and ideas, a family heritage, a social milieu. You do have to struggle to preserve detachment."[8] Choose a subject who seems to have some kind of special gift, Wagner-Martin urges. Write about a subject for whom you have value yourself and paint her as you see her, not simply as she sees herself. Make your own choices and let your conviction direct the narrative. Let the reader understand why you care.[9]

I put the books down, feeling encouraged and empowered but still apprehensive. I care a great deal about Betty, and I can be honest and thoughtful about what I am hearing, but can I be as discerning about the complex emotions that she engenders in me? None of these books have told me how to deal with getting my brain spanked.

~

"I prayed that they would all die," Betty tells me matter-of-factly. "I didn't want the nuns to die—they didn't mean anything to me. My family had to die so that my father would be forced to return for us. Children's prayers are extremely powerful. Uncle Joseph came to the convent one morning and told me that Aunt Mary wasn't suffering anymore, but he didn't invite me home for the funeral. Grandfather died next. Grandma wrote to my father then, telling him that she couldn't care for two boys by herself, that he should come for them. She was dead before he could resolve to ignore her letter. I had gotten what I had prayed for. I was going home."

Harry Schutz returned to Germany in 1930, when his daughter was thirteen. He found Charlie and Harry Jr., now nine and fifteen respectively, living in their grandparents' empty downstairs apartment. The Schpeckels, a young couple who rented the upstairs portion of the house, had been washing the boys' laundry and cooking their suppers. These generous tenants had sent a tender message of condolence to their new landlord after his mother's death. Realizing that he could now sell his parents' house, Harry had hurried to Europe.

When her handsome father arrived at the convent in his dark suit and cashmere coat, carrying a huge box for her, Betty wondered if perhaps she were, indeed, a millionaire's daughter. Carefully folded in layers of crispy tissue paper were two exquisitely beaded silk dresses which Babette had lovingly chosen for a daughter whom she barely knew. Giddy with joy and beautifully attired, Betty walked through the convent's massive outer gates with her head held high, deliciously indifferent to the farewells of the suddenly obsequious sisters, determined to convince the distinguished gentleman from America that his daughter was now a lady. "Imagine me sitting at the Schpeckels' dinner table that evening, cutting meat in an elegant silk dress," Betty urges, watching me intently.

"You must have been ecstatic," I say with a smile.

She closes her eyes for just a moment, then looks away from me and begins to talk quickly. "I was terribly nervous. I was certain that my father wasn't pleased with me. He was drinking heavily and watched me constantly. I was trying to cut my meat like a lady but I could barely hold the knife steady. I pushed too hard and the entire plate flipped over into my lap. My lovely dress was ruined."

Around the table conversation stopped and hands froze in midair. The Schpeckels locked eyes in alarm, Harry Jr. made a small sound like a puppy, little Charlie giggled nervously. When Harry's fist slammed down on the table, everyone jumped. With a loud curse, the children's baffling parent sprang to his feet, overturning his chair. He grabbed his sobbing daughter by the hair, yanked her up hard, and flung her across the room. She slammed heavily against the wall and crumbled to the floor in a mess of gravy and broken plate. "You are going back to the convent," he screamed. "I am not taking you to America."

"I had hardly ever seen a man much less learned how to handle a drunken one," Betty recalls, "but I was terrified that my father wouldn't take me back to my mother. Mrs. Schpeckel told me what to do. The next morning, after my father had slept and eaten breakfast, I fixed myself up pretty, got down on the floor, and crawled to him on my hands and knees. I begged him for forgiveness." Harry stared at the prostrate young girl for a long while before he murmured, "I'll think about it."

The last days in Germany passed slowly, heavy with the weight of uncertainty. Betty began to believe that Harry had forgotten his threat when he bustled all three children into the city to be examined for visas. Before they could leave the country, a physician had to certify that they were free of parasites and disease. "Can you imagine? They discovered that I had lice!" Betty tells me in mock horror. "I had never had lice at the convent, but we had been playing in the straw outside my grandparents' house. It must have been full of them." Nurses hastily cut her hair and doused her head with kerosene, then wrapped the stinking mess in tight rags. For the next twenty-four hours—the necessary waiting period before her head could be washed—Betty consoled herself with the thought that her stinging scalp meant that Harry intended to take her home.

She tried to avoid her unpredictable parent as much as possible. If the Schpeckels were receiving visitors and a playful gentleman happened to pinch her freckled cheeks, she could be certain of a hard slap from her father after the guests had left. "You're nothing but a little whore!" Harry would yell at the tearful daughter whose budding beauty may well have caused them both torment.

Betty was beginning to know the two brothers with whom she now shared a bed. Harry Jr. was intelligent, timid, and easily pleased. The frail teenager could not attend school. His unexpected epileptic seizures twisted him into such violent spasms that three adults were often insufficient to hold him down and force a belt between his jaws so that he would not bite off his tongue. He loved to spend his days drawing pictures of Betty and Charlie in a notebook. "You're a good boy, Harry," Betty would croon as she stroked his head. The two siblings would hide in their bedroom whenever they heard their father's rough laughter beyond the kitchen door. Harry seemed almost as disappointed in his eldest son as in his daughter, although he never struck the fragile boy.

There were two bedrooms in the downstairs apartment. Betty slept in one room with her brothers, Harry in the other with whichever pretty "cousin" was visiting for the night. "I had no idea that we had so many cousins"—Betty grins—"but I figured that they must be from one family because they all had the same red hair." Harry was seldom at home during the day, dividing his time between the attractive new relatives he seemed always to be meeting and the dark-eyed, street-smart Charlie, whom he seemed to adore.

Charlie was a loner. At age nine he stayed on the streets from dawn until dusk, avoiding the meals that so terrorized his sister. He associated with his awkward brother as little as possible, sometimes went fishing with local boys, and occasionally spent a rainy afternoon playing upstairs with the daughter of the Schpeckels, who was about his age. Harry was obviously amused by his intrepid son. He bought him gifts and sometimes took him along on his rambles. Betty saw her younger brother only at night when he would crawl into bed, wedge his dirty little body between those of his two siblings, and fall asleep tightly cocooned in their arms.

Harry's parents' large brick home sold for 15,000 Marks—a great deal of money at that time. He walked up the gangplank of the grand ocean liner with his three children with the air of a wealthy sultan sauntering into his harem. They barely saw him for the rest of the journey. Charlie also disappeared as soon as they had gotten under way. Betty cannot remember how he ate or where he stayed. Harry Jr. hid in their stateroom for most of the trip, terrified of the hordes of immigrants on board; the swarthy men and ragged women reminded him of the gypsies who had once helped his grandmother to exorcise his "demon-infested" head with heavy clubs taken from the fireplace. Afraid that he could have a seizure on deck, Betty guarded him carefully. With his sister close by, Harry Jr. was always calm. The days at sea passed uneventfully.

New York City crept up on them overnight. A sharp, unfamiliar winter wind slapped hard against gray water as the Schutz children pushed their way through boisterous crowds on deck and grasped the dripping railings. They stared in wonder at a city of towering castles whose steel spires sliced through the rapidly disintegrating haze. Even Harry felt exhilarated. Standing behind them, watching their dazzled faces, he laughed out loud. When Betty's unbecoming, too-broad hat blew off her head and into the churning ocean, she instinctively tensed to receive his punishment, but her suddenly youthful-looking father simply grinned and muttered, "Thank God."

Home was a modest upstairs apartment on the East Side; their mother, Babette, a huge woman with a dark face and warm smile. Her massive body hidden under a softly flowing gown and her neck glittering with exquisite rubies and other jewels, the circus strong woman wrapped arms of concrete about her children and searched their tired eyes for the years that had disappeared. She looked quickly away from Harry Jr.'s vulnerable face. Charlie gazed steadfastly at the glittering points of light on his mother's breast. Only Betty stared straight back into eyes that reflected her own fears. Babette asked in German if Betty had met any of the family. When Betty replied that they had met at least fifteen cousins, her heavy mother shook her head. "Yah, yah. So many cousins," she whispered, looking sadly at Harry. Without a word to his wife, Harry poured himself a drink and put his coat back on.

Betty had imagined that they all would return to a comfortable, easy home in magical America, but New York City could offer no spell for turning five strangers into a family. Betty watched in horror as her father struck Babette with the same brutal impatience she had thought reserved for herself alone. Her muscled mother accepted the blows wordlessly while her pursed lips warned her narrow-eyed daughter to keep silent.

Betty now studied her father's moods and habits with urgency, as if he were a dangerous creature whose attack could be avoided with the right precautions, but it would take years before she would begin to understand his seemingly conflicting tendencies. Harry's cruelest gestures were often masked as generosity. One evening, during a dinner party, Betty watched as a guest complimented an expensive silk scarf that Babette had cleverly twisted around her thick neck. With a courtly flourish, Harry reached over the table, grabbed hold of the feathery fabric, and pulled hard. He presented the gorgeous cloth to its admirer as if he were a knight paying homage to a noble damsel. "I'll buy Babette another one," he bragged, as his silent wife held a trembling hand to her neck.

"One night he gave a party," Betty recalls coldly. "He was so drunk that he stumbled over to one of our neighbors and grabbed her breasts. There he stood in our living room juggling her breasts in his hands, saying 'Man, you sure have got big ones,' and no one did anything—just laughed at him! I thought of how hard I had wanted to become a lady for my father."

When the guests finally staggered to the door, Harry stood next to Betty as each tipsy friend lavished kisses on him, then hugged his daughter. No sooner had the door closed than his heavy hand crashed down on her head. Babette whimpered and begged ineffectually as her husband struck the girl again and again. "Did you see her kissing them all?" he raged. "I told you! She's going to be a whore if I don't stop her."

The following morning Harry sent a bruised Betty to return a small leather purse to a Hungarian widow who had left it behind. "She looked at my purple cheeks and puffy eyes with an expression that I had never seen in a woman's face before," Betty relates thoughtfully. "I told her that I had a cold but she shook her head—*'nein.'* She knew exactly what had happened. Understand—people liked my father. He could be witty and charming. When he talked to people, you could watch their faces just open up with pleasure. I had thought that there was something wrong with me—with us. It was a shameful, hateful secret. This woman told me, 'We always knew that down deep Harry was a brute, but we had no idea that he was so bad.' People knew! It was a revelation to me. She washed my face and took care of me. She knew what to do—another surprise. My mother never knew what to do. Mama would hold me and ask, 'Did he hurt you, baby?' I always lied and said 'no,' but of course it hurt. I don't know why she never stood up to him."

At night Harry Jr. slept on the floor of the one large room that served as a living, dining, kitchen area, his father's cot close to him in case he needed assistance. In the single, windowless bedroom at the back of the apartment, Babette had pushed four mammoth trunks together and topped them with a thin mattress. She shared this makeshift bed with her two younger children. "Charlie would tickle my toes and make me laugh," Betty recalls, "but if my father heard us, he would get mad. He would drag me downstairs into the dark backyard and force me to do exercises on the patio until the sun came up. That was his punishment because he said that I obviously didn't need any sleep. My mother would beg, 'Please don't hurt her, Harry,' but he would shout up to her, 'Another word and you will join her.'"

Betty's dreams of a happy family dulled each time her passive mother accepted a fresh insult, but they died completely when her brothers both disappeared. Harry Jr.'s fits had frightened the neighbors. Even the bull-size Babette could not hold him as he thrashed against walls and slammed into furniture. In response to anonymous complaints, Harry was taken from his parents and made a ward of the state. He was placed in a state institution where doctors treated his epilepsy as a form of insanity. His skull was opened and surgically fitted with a steel plate. When he died at twenty-three, an autopsy revealed to his shocked family that he had been beaten to death.

Charlie was a stunningly handsome child. Moody and deeply troubled, he refused to speak about his years in Germany and broke a teacher's jaw before Harry removed him from the public schools. No one knew where he wandered during the days, returning only to sleep or to command an occasional meal from a mother who seemed almost as frightened of him as of his father. Betty cannot tell me how the brilliant little urchin learned enough English to invent the heart-wrenching lies that he used for both currency and safety.

There are no pictures of Charlie's adolescence in Betty's albums. He seems magically to have grown without transition from a wide-eyed little boy into a startlingly attractive man. "Where did he go? How did he live?" I ask my hostess, deeply touched at the thought that the impressionable child had suddenly lost his grandparents, home, school, and friends in Germany, then had found himself stranded in America, unable to speak the language and forced to live among angry strangers who called themselves his family. Betty's abrupt reply—"I have no idea; Charlie was a spoiled snob"—tells me that this is a door that has been deliberately wedged shut and that my interest will only wedge it more tightly. I cannot help being fascinated, however, with the younger brother whom I know had less of a childhood than Betty, yet eventually made his way to Hollywood, became a millionaire, and died in a bizarre murder suicide. "He wasn't there," Betty tells me rather defensively. "That's all I can remember." I let it drop.

She begins to talk again but I interrupt. "Wait a moment, I'm still confused."

Betty purses her lips and looks at me closely. "Well?"

"So, did your parents have money or didn't they? You said that Babette had sent you silk dresses and was wearing genuine rubies— and yet there wasn't a real bed in the apartment? That doesn't make sense to me."

Betty looks startled, then falls into an urgent explanation. "You have to understand—there was money but it was always disappearing. Mama worked for Ringling Brothers and Billy Rose. At one point she owned a boardinghouse and a restaurant, but my father drank and gambled everything away. She learned to put all of her money into goods that could be worn or hidden. When she worked in Cuba, for instance, she bought yards of valuable lace and sewed it onto her slip so that she wouldn't have to pay duty. That was smart because Harry would have just squandered her pay, but we couldn't live on lace, you know? Before she died, she showed me a loose tile beneath the bathroom sink. She had stashed some of her jewelry behind it, tied to the plumbing inside the wall. Mama knew that Harry and Charlie would steal everything. She wanted me to have her jewels. They ransacked the house after she died, but only I knew where to look."

She pauses for a moment to let this sink in. If I don't ask a question now, she will pick up the story where she just left it—at the time of her mother's death. I want to keep her focused on her youth. "So you had nice clothes, at least?" I offer gently, imagining a smartly dressed mother and daughter scouring fashionable New York City stores in the 1930s, intent on exhausting a large paycheck on "portable commodities."

"You're not listening," she snaps. "I just told you—there wasn't any money!" I lean forward and try to look very attentive and concerned. "I never shopped in a store until I was an adult," Betty is confessing in a voice that sounds slightly irritated. "There was a neighborhood policeman, a big man almost as burly as Mama was, and his wife would come to our door with boxes of kids' outgrown clothing. My mother knew lots of people in the industry who had children. Everyone liked her and wanted to help us. We had clothes." I nod. I remember how cruel children can be to kids whose clothes are not fashionably competitive. I sigh and she looks at me quickly, mistrusting my ability to pay attention.

~

"She has moods," I tell Fritzi dismally, then realize how funny the understatement sounds. I hear laughter on the other end of the phone.

"Yup. She has moods."

In the conversation that follows, I struggle to articulate what I have been feeling for several months while listening to Fritzi's mother. I hate having to hide my thoughts while Betty speaks. It strikes me that there is nothing reciprocal about this process. How I wish that we could return to that first night at the art exhibit when Betty's stories seemed magical and uplifting, when the personal feelings that her stories evoked could be indulged, when I felt that I was on the brink of a friendship with a grandmotherly someone who could teach me to enjoy life more.

Betty expects me to write her story, but I resent having to take control of her narrative, demand explanations, probe her secrets, and listen to dark, private confidences that I do not necessarily want to hear. It seems a terrible burden to impose on a valued relationship. Betty has told me of the many writers who have offered to document her story and then backed out. I can understand why they quit. This project started out as a gift—to her, to myself. It does not feel like that anymore.

"She notices everything—the tone of my voice, the way I look at her, how I respond," I tell Fritzi. "I have to be so careful. I have been trying to explore what might be common ground for us both—the experience of daughterhood or motherhood, for example, but common ground is the most dangerous. If I let myself drift into my own thoughts for even a moment, I am vulnerable."

"You're an isolated audience member and she's reading you," Fritzi responds. "She had that old gypsy training growing up. Did she tell you how her mother trained her to read the cards?"

"No. She refuses to show me the cards."

"Well, there's something to it, but the cards are largely prompts to reading people. First, you get photos of people—just their heads. You look at their faces, and you start learning to read a face. Then you get photos of full bodies."

"You ask your subjects to bring photos?" I interrupt.

"No, no." My friend laughs, half exasperated. "They did this between them, Mom and Grandma Babette. When they were alone together."

Babette would lay a photograph of a stranger on the table, perhaps an advertisement or a publicity shot, then guide her daughter as she studied individual features. "Yes," she would hint, "and what about the eyes? What do you see there? No, look again. You're missing something in the eyes. Look at the way he's holding his chin. What does that say to you?" When Betty had become adept at reading photographs, Babette led her to the window, then out onto the streets of New York City. Betty became skilled in the silent art of watching, noticing dress, posture, minute mannerisms, the length of time that a stranger would hold her gaze before looking away.

Babette's tarot cards were small, a German deck with tiny cups and pentacles, the elegant writing in four languages—three of which neither woman understood. "Here is the dark ace," Babette would explain in German. "Everyone will say 'Oh! The death card!' but it doesn't necessarily mean that. There will be death somewhere—perhaps the close of an activity, the cessation of love, the changing of a lifelong goal. And death of any sort can also mean birth—new possibilities, fresh chances, different paths to follow. Read the person and ask yourself, Where do I sense a death?"

"It's not a skill that you can learn from a book," Fritzi stresses. "It just kills me when people say that they've learned to read cards from a manual." "You know"—she laughs—"there was this one man we knew who had learned from a book and was charging people 50 dollars for a reading! Mom was aghast. He used to challenge her constantly to read his fortune. Mom hates to read for men but finally she agreed. The poor guy was in a cold sweat the whole time. He couldn't hide from her. She barely looked at the cards. She just stared at him and told him everything—his weak points and strengths, things he had done that had not been successful, things he could do that might be successful, things at which he would certainly fail. Every now and then she would throw out a card for a trigger point, glance at it, turn back to him. He told me afterward, 'Your mother is damn good,' but he stayed away from her after that.

"She stopped reading when she was a young person. You can lose friends quickly reading fortunes. Mom would predict something and her subject would stomp away furious, then when the prediction came true, that person would return and beg for another reading."

"But she isn't reading the future, she's predicting," I remind my friend.

"Yes, that's right. She's making an informed prediction, based on what she knows and senses about her subject. During interviews, when you are alone with her, all of that intense scrutiny is focused on you. You may raise your eyebrow and that means something to her. It may be that you are thinking about Kurt being sick or your cousin's surgery or meeting your husband for lunch, but if you break focus for even a moment, she will read it as something that's happened between the two of you."

"God"—I gasp—"and I'm so worn out in the mornings to begin with."

"Go in the afternoon," Fritzi advises. "Mornings are your worst time because Emma keeps you awake at night. Mom's fresh in the morning."

"I like having her tell stories when she's fresh; she's ready to talk then."

"I know," my friend cautions, "but remember, that's her strongest time and she will be reading you like crazy."

∼

I hear a car crawling down the dirt driveway as I am pounding out the final pages of a long, difficult interview, and I immediately start to shake. Our house is isolated, surrounded by fields and woods, and I am alone here.

My heart starts beating again when I see Fritzi smiling through the panes of the front door. She tramps into my kitchen wearing overalls and plops a big picnic basket on the table. "Turn off the computer," she instructs, and produces a bottle of French wine. I hesitate, but the basket is full of amazing gifts—a little flannel shirt with a dainty white collar for Emma, fire-hot cinnamon toothpicks for Al, see-through gadgets for the boys, herbal soap and chamomile tea for me. By the time my family get home, we girls are both a bit tipsy. Fritzi stays for dinner, the normal routine goes out the window, the kids tease us into letting them stay up late, we eat cake in the living room while we all make fun of goofy television shows. "When I talked to you on the phone at lunchtime, you sounded so washed out. Don't forget—you have to be present to win," Fritzi reminds me, laughing as she quotes her favorite motto.

So this is what having a sister is like, I think, after she has driven away to the kids' frantic handwaving and I have collapsed on my bed, refreshed by laughter and the enervating sense that my lifestyle can change instantly whenever I decide to let it: friendship that feels like family, family that feels like friendship.

~

Without the supportive family for which she longed, Betty tells me that she determined to make her own way in America. Her single year in school was very difficult. Free from the convent, she seemed weird and otherworldly to her classmates, rebellious and unteachable to her teachers—impressions that were, no doubt, reinforced by the fact that Betty was no longer fluent in English. Harry stubbornly refused to speak the language to his children at home. Although Babette would beg him to "talk American," he preferred to retain English as a private tongue to be used when he did not want the children to understand what he was saying to their mother. "She'll learn at school," he would insist, unconcerned that his daughter could not read, write, or speak to her classmates. Fortunately, they were living in New York City, where English was spoken with every accent imaginable. Few of her classmates had parents who could speak English fluently—if at all. In a port city in 1930, one might be ridiculed for one's clothing, hair, or manners, but rarely would the children of immigrants tease one another for lacking language proficiency.

On her first day at school, thirteen-year-old Betty Schutz stood at the front of a long, narrow schoolroom, staring helplessly at the overworked teacher who asked questions with thinly veiled impatience. Betty would shake her head as the battery of foreign sounds was repeated over and over, each time more slowly and a little more loudly. Finally the exasperated teacher grunted and pointed to a desk in a far corner where her new pupil would have the least chance of learning.

Betty had already closed her mind tightly and was rigid with defensive indifference when a slight hand reached across the aisle and touched her arm. "Home," whispered the girl with the dark braids and pretty, ruffled frock. Betty stared as the child deftly drew a map of the city, enlarging a house and trees on one street. *"Heim?"* Betty repeated with sudden understanding, as the knot in her head began to unravel. After school, sisters Vira and Jeannie Coco each took an arm and steered the new girl across bustling New York City streets to a lively Italian neighborhood where large brick houses rang with children's voices and smelled of tomatoes stewing. Her education had begun.

Mrs. Coco was not a woman to be refused when she decided that a child needed to be fattened. As their buxom, aproned mama heaped a plate with steaming spaghetti and sauce, and buttered huge slabs of hot homebaked garlic bread, Vira and Jeannie began lessons. They pointed to cups, utensils, food, and body parts, enunciating the words in careful English and making Betty teach them the same words in German. "Italian," they would say, pointing to themselves. "German," and they would hug Betty. "English. America!" as they pirouetted about the kitchen, arms spread wide in glee. Mama Coco would laugh.

Betty practically lived with the Cocos for the next year. The clever girls taught her to speak and write English, to play poker, skinny-dip, flirt, and enjoy life for the first time. Even Babette began to grow less timid as her teenage daughter taught her, in turn, how to feel "American."

In the evenings mother and daughter would pore over the comics, relishing hard-earned laughter when they finally understood the jokes. Betty was content simply to be snuggled against her mother's warm shoulder—she had never had trouble learning—but Babette's determination to grasp American culture sprang from a long-suppressed dream that now seemed possible. Babette was not yet an American citizen.

Language was her primary barrier. Adults were less tolerant of immigrants than were children, and Babette soon discovered that women from sheltered backgrounds who spoke broken English were amusing victims for any practical jokester. Betty mimics her mother's heavy accent with precision as she relates that one day Babette cornered her in the hallway and pleaded, "Vhy do dose boys ask me do I have nice cherry? I tell dem, 'Yah, I have da nice cherry und banana und apple for eating. Dey laugh at me.'"

Betty wrapped her arms around her mother's massive shoulders, realizing that similar jokes lay in store for her unless she could master the language quickly. "'Cherry' means *'pflaume,'* [plum or maidenhead], Mama," she explained.

Babette snorted wildly. "Oh, Jesus! Dose *Schwein!*"

"Pigs, Mama, say pigs," her daughter prodded.

"My mother was very naive about her body," Betty tells me. "When I got my first period, I didn't know what it was. Mama told me that she had eaten soap to kill herself when she got hers. She didn't know either." Reaching across the table, Betty clamps a wizened hand over my arm and leans toward me confidentially. "I'll tell you a story." She pauses to sip her coffee and shakes her head slowly. "Mama was gullible. She never learned. I remember one time, she was playing the Hippodrome for Billy Rose. I think they were rehearsing *Jumbo*."

I take a quick breath. These are the sort of show business stories that I have been waiting for her to tell me, glimpses into a dazzling world of vaudeville and musical revues that vanished forever before I was born. I have begun to study the shows of this era, and *Jumbo* is one of the most fascinating. In 1935, with the country barely out of the Depression, a spunky Billy Rose spent over $340,000 to gut the orchestra level of the old Hippodrome and rebuild it to resemble a huge circus tent. The show was plagued with delays and cost Rose thousands in lost expenditures, but when it opened, after half a year of rehearsals, it was an unprecedented extravaganza. The opening number was a spectacular circus parade that included an entire orchestra in blue and gold uniforms, dozens of the world's most famous clowns, a horse-drawn calliope wagon, and hundreds of skilled circus performers. From the rear of the stage, an exploding cannon would shoot a showgirl into the arms of her partner, who would leap out of the audience and catch her just in the nick of time. As the parade reeled around the ring, Tiny Klein stopped hearts with her three-hundred-foot slide for life from the top balcony of the theater to the stage floor, hanging all the way by her teeth.

Jumbo apparently cost more than money. One of the Kimris brothers broke his back when he plunged 150 feet from a small plane that whizzed around the dome. His wife and brother continued the act without a safety net, hanging from the plane by their feet. An acrobatic aerialist fell from a high wire stretched over an open cage of tigers and was fiercely mauled when the cage door stuck. In spite of these accidents, the fast-talking Rose was able to convince Jimmy Durante to lie on the stage floor while Jumbo the elephant held his mammoth foot over the comedian's head. *Jumbo* took Broadway by storm and launched Rose's career. The show's main songs, "The Most Beautiful Girl in the World," "Little Girl Blue," and "The Circus is on Parade," were instant popular hits. The reviewers raved.[10]

I lean forward. "Please tell me about *Jumbo*. Did you see the show?" I plead. "Did people really get hurt? Was it wonderful?"

Betty falls silent, and her eyes shine with faraway memories of Broadway theater lights reflected in giant gold and white mirrors, of cashmere-coated men with glimmering ladies on their arms, of Babette, billed as "Tyana the Strong Woman," clowning with her daughter and fellow performers after the heavy velvet curtain had dropped and backstage had erupted into frenzied, giddy festivity. The glow fades as she remembers her story, and she sighs heavily. "Billy Rose loved my mother," she continues. "They all did: Donald Novis, Jimmy Durante. 'Schnoz' Durante used to call her 'the tiny lady.' Ha! Mama could have thrown him across the theater with one hand. Well, you know, the razorbacks [chorus boys] were always after Mama. They would ask her, 'How's your twat?' and Mama would answer, 'My twat is very goot, tank you.' She tried so hard to be good-natured. She was always naive. Mama never understood why they teased her. She was funny because she didn't understand but pretended that she did."

I smother a smile. I have noticed how Betty pretends to hear when people talk to her and the hearing aid is not working. I suspect that it is not only good nature or naïveté that prompts such mild deceptions, but rather a profound sense that there are some contests that you simply must let go by. This must have been particularly true for women such as Babette. In an alien culture, one probably must choose one's lessons and emotional battles carefully, especially when one is without allies.

Babette had been without an ally for most of her life, but she was growing closer to the lively daughter who had been lost to her almost from birth. The strong woman had lived her entire life in the circus and naturally tended to see everything in terms of circus norms and values. With a growing network of teenage friends—all intent on enjoying their lives in golden America—Betty was becoming a cultural guide to her sheltered parent, a teacher who could help Babette to understand the perplexing culture beyond circus boundaries.

When Babette accepted an offer to perform during the opening festivities of a huge regional conference of the Ku Klux Klan, for example, she returned from her engagement thoroughly bewildered and appealed to her daughter. Betty had to resort to the German language to make her mother understand the ideology of the KKK. With her imperfect English, Babette had thought that she had been invited to perform at a benefit for an organization of retired clowns— the "Ku Klux Klown"—and she could not understand why all the clowns wore the same costume and refused to do tricks. "Dey only just sat dere. Dey vere none of dem funny at all," she told her daughter, thoroughly confounded. Babette was aghast when her daughter enlightened her. She had not thought that supremacist organizations could exist in America.

As Betty tells me of this one magical year at home, I can almost see the two women in the kitchen of the new house on Fifty-Third Street that Babette had purchased with her earnings, teasing one another and sharing their feelings in the language that Harry had hoped to reserve exclusively for his own purposes. I can see them huddled over books and papers, weaving a private world around themselves, determined to be in control of their lives. Mother and daughter.

"Tell me about the good times—this whole story has become so dark," I plead. "You are always telling me about beatings—did you and your mother ever have any fun? Can't you remember anything nice?" It is the kind of request that could easily backfire on me—I have never been so blunt before—but her face softens and I am treated to some unexpectedly delightful stories.

On bath night, Betty confides, Babette would bring her mandolin into the bathroom and playfully serenade her daughter while she soaked in the tub. Their favorite song was "Over the Waves." Babette would belt out the words, stumbling over consonants, while Betty tilted her dripping face upward and gargled along. On Mondays, Betty would give her tired mother a quarter and send her out to see a movie while she cleaned the house and made spaghetti. "Mama could never understand how I got the floors so shiny," she relates, her eyes sparkling. "One time she came home early and found out. There I sat on the waxy floor—wiggling myself around to polish it with my butt. Mama plopped right down next to me and we slid and wriggled around the kitchen laughing our heads off. When it came time to get up, she couldn't get back up to her feet—she was a heavy woman and the floor was slippery. She had to roll over and push up against a wall. She fussed at me to help her but I couldn't stop laughing—and then she would start laughing and slide right back down again. We ended up eating our spaghetti picnic-style on the floor!"

Betty laughs and shakes her head. "One night—I was a little older then—we went to a nightclub together," she whispers, leaning toward me like a conspirator. "Neither one of us had ever had a drink, so we told the waiter to pick something for us, and he brought us Manhattans. Well, we had one apiece and ended up dancing together on the dance floor, stepping on each other's toes and giggling like crazy fools. When the manager discreetly led us to a quiet table and asked if he could call us a taxi, we just about died. We knew that we couldn't be drunk because we had seen Papa drunk. Drunk meant angry and falling down, not giggling and dancing. Drunk meant spending the night vomiting in a police cell and being retrieved by your wife in the morning, not piling into a cab and singing on the way home. The management must have found us amusing because they called us a taxi and escorted us out very discreetly and kindly. When we got back home, we could barely make it up the stairs. We fell asleep in our clothes, and the last thing I remember is my mother mumbling 'Are we drunk, baby?'"

Betty grins mischievously and lifts her chin. "In 1930 my mother became a citizen and we celebrated," she tells me triumphantly. "My father had told her that she was too stupid, but she studied hard. She wanted us all to be an American family. It wasn't easy for her. She memorized the questions. She could remember the answers only if the examiners asked her the questions exactly as they were worded in the book. The fellow who gave her the exam was very patient and fortunately not very talkative. She answered every question correctly until the last one. The book read, 'Who freed the slaves?' but he looked up at her and asked, 'The slaves—who freed them?'"

As Betty tells me of her mother's slick solution to a naturalization nightmare, I cannot help remembering her own split-second decision to feign sleepwalking in the convent. "Do you know who did dat?" Babette asked the examiner. "Of course," he responded. "Den I don't need to tell you," she shot back, and clasped her hands sedately on her huge lap. "He thought she was so cute that he gave her her papers." Betty grins. "So she came home and said, 'I am American, Harry! Now your turn it is.' You know, it took my father three tries before he could pass. Mama would huff and say, 'Und I am schdupid?' but she would never say it to him. He wanted to go back to Germany, but Mama would tell him, 'Dis is my country now.'"

"Can you remember any nice things about your father?" I ask, remembering the young parent who once carried his daughter about on a pillow while she recovered from rickets. "You remember the bad things so forcefully. Tell me some good memories."

Betty's happy face darkens instantly, but she dutifully stares at the table and thinks hard. I wait for what seems a long time before she looks up in triumph and offers, "When we were working the fairs in the 1940s, he used to buy me coffee and a hard roll with butter in the morning. I loved those hard rolls."

"Anything else?" I ask in my best come-on-I-know-that-you-can-do-this tone.

Her head flies up and she gives me a look of half indignation at my persistent manner and half amazement at her own emptiness. "There's nothing else," she finally whispers.

"But your mother married him," I urge, "and she stayed with him. She must have loved him for some reason. Did she ever tell you why?"

Betty shakes her head slowly. We stare at each other in wordless dismay—and suddenly, for the first time since beginning our conversations, I sense that we are genuine partners confronting a very perplexing history together.

~

Over the next few weeks, I ask Betty and Fritzi to share with me whatever they can find of the family's history before Betty returned from the convent in 1930. They tell me that Babette Tyana Brumbach arrived in New York City from Europe in 1905 at the age of eighteen with only an address to guide her in the land of opportunity. Fortunately, the family of performers to whom Babette had been directed by circus friends in Germany were awed by the young girl who could lift a 500-pound baby elephant; they agreed to sign entry papers guaranteeing that she would have work in America. Within a few years she was performing with the Barnum & Bailey and Ringling Bros. Circuses.

Babette had been trained from birth to be a strong woman in her family's famous European circus, the Cirkus Brumbach. Her people had been wandering across borders in circus wagons for as long as anyone could remember, and the sixteen Brumbach siblings apparently had accepted unquestioningly the expectation that they would carry on the family tradition as jugglers, acrobats, animal trainers, and contortionists. Each year on her birthday, Babette's stern father, Xavier Brumbach, would formally present her with a new set of personalized weights that she was to lift with each hand while he counted out the number of years in her age. On her eighteenth birthday, he watched her hoist her 200-pound gift eighteen times with one arm, then ordered her to switch to her weaker arm, but Babette was tired and refused.

That night Babette tiptoed away from the family's mahogany-paneled traveling car with her head wrapped in bloody bandages, having resolved never again to see the cruel father who had struck her so hard with an elephant hook that his blow would leave a permanent dent in her head. She followed a group of itinerant performers to the next circus on their circuit and became friends with the Grunatho sisters, a traveling troupe of acrobats who would later work for Ringling Bros., performing fascinating feats of tumbling and contortion in elaborate, floor-length evening gowns. When Elvira Grunatho married an Arab named Haji Liazeed and started a new life in America, Babette decided to come to America, too. "My mother broke with her family completely," Betty admits, "and so even though I had this huge network of aunts and uncles and cousins in Europe, we were considered outcasts."

Betty has shown me photographs of Babette's siblings and parents, but it is Babette's mother—Betty's grandmother—who most interests me, perhaps because I have been able to "see" her in the 1953 movie *Man on a Tightrope*. Teresa Brumbach plays herself in Elia Kazan's moving film reenactment of the Cirkus Brumbach's daring escape across the Iron Curtain to free Europe. In his journals, Kazan later claimed that this "event in history" had redeemed for him the dark days of the McCarthy era.[11]

The family's escape was spectacular, even by Hollywood standards, and Kazan tried hard to portray the daring and determination with which each performer approached a stunt more dangerous than any circus feat. When the colorful little circus straggled up to the wired barricades separating them from freedom, the heavily armed guards patrolling the border of Communist Czechoslovakia assumed that they were desperate for business and meant only to entertain the troops with tricks and clowning. The tunnel-eyed sentries stared, incredulous, as the hand-painted musical wagons and gaily costumed performers paraded through the dirty snow, past the dark guard towers and frozen barbed wire, waving merrily. They could not leave their posts, but they stomped their cold-numbed feet in their heavy boots and watched the clowns' antics with growing appreciation. As the eight alluring Brumbach sisters rode by on a garish wagon, flaunting their sequined legs and flashing prewar smiles, the caution that had held the duty-deadened men rigidly alert gusted away like powdered snow. Rifles were lowered. Stiff shoulders relaxed. Startled smiles appeared on suddenly younger faces.

They were not expecting the wolves. When the beasts were sprung from their cages, bristling with unexpected freedom and the scent of crowds, the terrified guards turned and ran, virtually ignoring the finest performance the Cirkus Brumbach had ever given. Against a background of blaring sirens and frenzied gunfire, the entire entourage of performers executed a perfectly planned feat of skill and daring: Together they crashed through the border barricades and over an icy river, escaping unharmed to free Germany—wagons, performers, animals, and all.

"Typical propaganda stuff," spit director Elia Kazan when producer Darryl Zanuck showed him Robert Sherwood's script for *Man on a Tightrope*. In his autobiography, Kazan recalls his initial disdain, his refusal to accept Zanuck's enthusiastic insistence that the story would make "one hell of a picture." Kazan considered the script only because he was under pressure as a suspected communist sympathizer and needed to make an anticommunist film—one that would soothe American distrust but could not be discredited.

Unconvinced, the director arrived in the rubble heap that had been Munich with only a few sketchy newspaper clippings and little desire to make a movie. He discovered more truth than he had bargained for. The Cirkus Brumbach existed. "They'd broken across the border, they'd risked their lives. I was not dealing with a faulty scenario; I was dealing with an event in history," Kazan wrote excitedly, but added that the once-fabulous circus had been reduced to "an impoverished group of humans, grinding out a living at an old trade." Like everything else in postwar Munich, it was "run down" and "second-rate," but it was quite decidedly there. "They were simply going on with their professional lives," he marveled.[12]

Kazan felt himself to be "a demoralized man in a ruined city," yet he seized on the tattered circus's war-time story instantly. Struggling with his own ties to the Soviet Union, Kazan realized that no words can express the painful process by which one is forced to disassociate oneself from a place or a culture. Today narratives of displacement and diaspora are the subject of countless books and articles; however, Kazan came to the conclusion that "Circus people [are] outsiders in any society—freaks, in fact."[13] He immediately set about making the film not for others but for himself, as proof of his comparable identity as an "outsider."

Even as a fellow "outsider," Elia Kazan might never have understood the courage that characterized this tenacious band of performers had the Cirkus Brumbach not received a threat of oppression against which his experience of being professionally blacklisted paled. It was the first day of production. Kazan had decided to assemble an all-German crew and to cast the Cirkus Brumbach as itself, using only the authentic artists and equipment together with a supporting cast of American actors. He relates that as the production equipment and circus wagons pulled into position for the opening shot,

> all of a sudden, everything stopped. The crew was gathered around a small radio, listening to a broadcast. It was in German, but I could tell that it was a list of names, pronounced in a manner that reminded me of broadcasts from Radio Leipzig, the official East German station, and that it was a warning. The list of names was the roll call of our crew, and they were being ordered to quit our film. Then came the names of the circus members, warning them of revenge without limit if they went on working with me. Gerd [Gerd Oswald, associate producer] told me that the members of the circus and some of the crew had relatives in East Germany. When the broadcast was

over, the crew and the circus people all went back to work; they did not heed the warning, they did not respond to the threat.[14]

Kazan was stunned by the resiliency and energy of the escaped circus. "Although the official Communist radio would warn them repeatedly and threaten them with loss of property and the abuse of relatives in the east, they carried on," he marveled. "My questions as to where they stood on the issue that had split me in half seemed ridiculous to them." The famous director came to admire the "freaks" who carried so much fortitude within. They had an unshakable sense of themselves that did not depend on circumstances or associations. Embracing their concept of "home" as his own, he confessed, "I made the circus my home . . . and was accepted as a member."[15]

As I think about Kazan's meeting with the Brumbach family, I cannot help but wonder how a Brumbach daughter, having displayed the independence and courage that had so captivated Kazan in leaving her family, could end up submitting to Harry's abuse of herself and her children. I wish that I knew more about Babette's mother, a woman who apparently also allowed her daughter to be beaten by her husband. When I try to imagine the weight of mothering sixteen children while wandering through war-shattered countries, my mind closes protectively and refuses all reflection. The sturdy woman who appears in Kazan's movie has inexorable toughness in her posture and in every feature.

∿

"I did meet my grandmother once when I was a child in Europe—did I tell you about that?" Betty offers when I return her video of *Man on a Tightrope*. I want to shake her. She is always doing this to me— casually adding some really important element to a story that she has already told. Listening to her history is like participating in a scavenger hunt in which the captain refuses to tell you what is on the list. Have fun with it, I remind myself. Try to think of it as a journey.

Betty explains that the wizened circus matriarch appeared at the convent one day and demanded to meet the daughter of Babette Brumbach. Betty had not known that she had a maternal grandmother. Dizzy with hope, she followed a silent, draped nun along unfamiliar corridors to the ornate front parlor reserved for the reception of the convent's more important visitors. "My grandmother was not warm," Betty remembers. "She told me to hold out my arm, then she felt my muscles, shook her head, and said that I was too skinny— that I would be worthless in the circus. She held my hand for a long time, turning it over and examining the bruises, then she asked if I could have pocket money and opened her purse. It was full of beautiful twinkling stones. I told her that we were allowed to have money but that the nuns kept it locked up until we needed it. When she heard that, she snapped her purse shut and left me." Years later, when Betty told her mother of this disappointing visit, Babette merely huffed and clasped her daughter to her iron chest. "Those were real diamonds in her purse, baby," she whispered in Betty's ear.

Babette carried with her her family's determination and pride. She made the acquaintance of Harry Schutz in a rehearsal hall in New York in 1908 in a manner that might seem extremely peculiar to anyone but a circus performer. The handsome trapeze artist had been watching her intently as she stretched and worked her famous muscles. Finally he strolled over and asked casually, "Do you think that you could hold me over your head?" With a shrug of her shoulders, twenty-one-year-old Babette replied, "Yah, if you vant," and casually hoisted the young man into the air, allowing him to execute a perfect one-handed handstand as he gripped her solid wrist. When she had set him on the floor again, Harry asked if they could try the same trick using a perch (a fifteen-foot pole balanced on the holder's shoulder). The perch was not uncommon in acrobatic routines, but a woman working the "bottom" of a perch act was a novelty. Harry scrambled up the pole and the pair spent the rest of the morning experimenting with tricks, then decided to work as partners.

Harry and Babette had only two things in common: Both were circus performers—which meant that they were accustomed to mobility, excruciating work, and pride in performing well—and both were runaways from German-speaking families. Born in 1887 to a farming family in Perlach, Germany, Heinrich (Harry) Schutz had been restless and ambitious from the time that he could walk. He claimed to have abandoned his parents and two sisters as soon as a traveling circus came within running distance of the town. No one knows how the young farmboy learned acrobatic and aerial work, but his performances were always breathtaking and impeccably executed. Although she hated her father, Betty used his widely respected name with pride at auditions and was always hired without a tryout because of it. "If Harry taught you, you must be good," the bosses would tell her.

Had he stayed in Germany, Harry would most certainly have become part of the kaiser's military machine. With his boundless energy and pitiless discipline, the man who mastered painful tricks by exercising merciless control over his own muscles and limbs would have made a fierce soldier. Instead, he and a fellow performer put together a hodgepodge act that involved gymnastics, acrobatics on flying rings, strong-arm feats, and comedy, and billed themselves on the American vaudeville and burlesque circuit as "acrobatic eccentriques," apparently never intending to return to Europe when their engagements were over. They called themselves the Parroffs.

The reviews of the original Parroffs (Harry used the name with different partners and acts throughout his life) are carefully pasted into one of Babette's deteriorating leather albums along with announcements and reviews of her own first American appearances. "Just give me all of it. I'll be really careful," I tell Fritzi, although part of me is shocked that she is even considering handing over her family's century-old papers and precious scrapbooks. I leave her house with my arms full and drive home cautiously as if hitting a bump will somehow wound the yellowed papers and crumbling leather binders stacked in my daughter's padded car seat.

At home, I wash my hands and carefully lay out these treasures on my dining room table. The vaudeville memorabilia and reviews in Babette's notebooks are truly valuable. I must admit that I love this part of my research—the little glimpses into the past which I can now view from an insider's perspective. How I wish that I could thank Babette for having kept such wonderful scrapbooks of the family's acts over the decades. These are a great help to me—even though many do not have dates. Without them, I probably would be unable to trace the performers' professional lives because they changed their stage names so often. I like to imagine that Babette cut out the clippings about the Parroffs and pasted them into her book because she was developing an interest in a certain somebody. It is a touching thought.

I practically jump out of my chair when I come across a review for the New Bijou Theater that provides a complete description of the Parroffs' act. It reads:

> The Parroffs, comedy ring artists, have wonderful muscles and accomplish some marvelous acts on swinging rings. One of the duo is dressed up as a clown and injects considerable humor into the act. Muscles of the teeth, neck, arms, and lower limbs are all brought into active play by these agile performers. Hanging by his feet, one of the gymnasts swings his partner on a trapeze holding the ropes in his teeth.

No one remembers the name of Harry's first partner or how he was gotten rid of when Harry decided to use Babette, but reviewers found his work on the rings a superb counterpart to Harry's questionable comedy. Babette once told Betty that Harry was a good acrobat but that audiences never thought him very funny, so I assume that he was the clown in the act. A critique of the Parroffs' performance at someplace called Hammerstein's is harsh: "The comedian is also a good ring performer, but falls off some in the comedy. He has one or two new wrinkles that are funny, but he is not a natural comedian."

More interesting to me than reviewers' critiques are the quoted commentaries about the artists' personal lives that often accompany them. These provide a splendid glimpse of the sort of cockamamie stories performers routinely feed to eager and gullible journalists. I slap my thigh when I read a review that states, "It is rather an interesting fact that many turns of this sort [acrobatic acts] come from Germany, where there are duly accredited schools for acrobats. The two Parroffs, who are playing at the Orpheum this week, are graduates of a Berlin school and both have served their time as gymnastic instructors in the Kaiser's army."

"All rubbish," Betty laughs when I read this to her. Her eyes gloss over a bit, though, when I merrily quote another write-up that has the runaway farmboys "recently returned from appearances in the principal European cities." "Of course," she says matter-of-factly. "We let them believe whatever they will believe." It seems almost a good-natured warning. I cannot help but wonder if she considers me one of "them."

Babette's reviews are more provocative than Harry's. Billed as Mlle. Tyana, "The Earth's Strongest Woman," she did an act that consisted of bending steel bars and driving nails with her bare hands through thick boards, lifting as many as ten men seated on a board with her feet, and hoisting a baby elephant weighing 500-plus pounds several inches off the floor. To do this, according to Fritzi, she would stand on a platform above the animal and use a harness that passed under the elephant's belly and across her hips to lift it in a leg press. Reviewers consistently call her act the "high point" of every show, referring to her as "the beauty with muscles of steel."

I find it intriguing that Babette's reviewers constantly comment that her act is free of "packaging" and that her skill is its own remarkable advertisement. "There is no press agentry about the statement that Mlle. Tyana lifts a live elephant weighing over one ton clear off the stage," exclaims an enthusiastic reviewer for the Gayety. "She does it 'in harness,' to be sure, but still she does it." "When a little bit more showmanship is used, this act will be a knockout," writes a reviewer for the Capitol Theatre, and I have to smile when I think of hefty Babette stomping onto the stage in her black boots, tights, and leotard, a huge feather fluttering over her head and a satin cape dragging behind her. I have seen pictures of her in costume. She was no Marilyn Monroe but the lady could deliver. "The marvel of two continents," the papers all declare of Mlle. Tyana, and I suspect that this was absolutely true.

It is hard to know how much of Babette's interviews is based on truth. Harry Jr. died in 1938, yet in one lengthy 1939 article, Babette tells reporters that she once traveled throughout Europe, South America, and Australia with her family's circus and that she currently has two sons and a daughter who are all acrobats. How interesting that she apparently felt a private need to include both of her sons in her fictional history.

By the end of this article, the reporters seem well aware that they are being taken for a ride. Babette gets increasingly silly, swearing that she practices daily in the soft dirt outside her house by swinging two obliging male neighbors "around like a merry-go-round." She treats them to a dubious story of her arrival in America: "I come off the *schneilldampfer*—the steam-boat—on Twenty-third Street and my trunk, with 200 pounds in it and my mandolin and hat box with my wooden shoes on, I carry on my head to Seventeenth Street." The article ends with her sober pledge that "I leave everybody for Billy Rose [whenever he might need her again for a show]."

When I show the article to Betty, she chokes on her glee. "Wooden shoes! Can you imagine her telling such nonsense? Mama was having fun, but that part about Billy Rose—that's absolutely true. Mama loved Rose—and he loved her, too."

Babette and Harry were married in 1915. "Harry went out with every girl that he could find, but he always came back to my mother," Betty tells me. "Mama never said a word to him, but she would corner those other girls and threaten to bend them like steel bars if they didn't stay away from her man."

Obviously, Babette was neither helpless nor oblivious to Harry's philandering, so I cannot help wondering why she decided that Harry was "her man." I am starting to discern that circus partnerships can carry unspoken assumptions, though. "One day Harry came to my mother and told her that they should get married because they were good partners," Betty explains nonchalantly, as if this arrangement should be the clearest in the world for me to understand. "When he proposed, Harry said, 'I think that I could love you,' and Mama replied, 'Yah, I know dat you do.'"

There are no wedding pictures or mementos of a marriage in Babette's notebooks, only performance reviews. Mlle. Tyana and Mr. Parroff changed their stage names to "Patrick" after a manager at the Hippodrome named Fitzpatrick counseled them to find a different name, suggesting a variation of his own. A typical review of their act for Ringling Bros. Circus reads: "An extraordinary demonstration of great physical development is presented by the Two Patricks. It is unusual in character and has aroused favorable comment everywhere. The woman is a phenomenon and undoubtedly the strongest of her sex that has ever appeared at the Hippodrome." The "principal headliner" of Sam McCracken's American Circus is listed as "the Patricks, formerly with the Ringling Brothers Circus, with Miss Babette, the strong woman, featuring." Harry obviously had found himself a profitable act with a featured partner, but I wonder if he resented being upstaged by his wife. Every review tells me that Babette did not need Harry. He must have known this.

I had not considered why two performers would abandon names that commanded instant recognition and respect in their field until I came across a tiny newspaper clipping wedged into a corner of Babette's show album. At first I was tempted to skip over it—a rumpled, poorly cut column of impossible-to-read print about American soldiers advancing across European battlefields—but then the sheer improbability of its being pasted into the album along with flashy circus headlines struck me. I looked more closely and noticed that Babette had marked several passages along the margins with dark ink.

The article is entitled "Cordial to America." A heavily marked section reads: "From a fortified hill overlooking the battlefield of St. Mihiel, I saw General Pershing's army advance into the salient while more than 2,000 big guns silenced the German artillery." Babette has drawn a huge question mark next to the line that describes a "festival of thanksgiving" for their "deliverance" that the people of St. Mihiel held the day following the battle. Other marked sections report that the French and Americans have "opened a new attack" across the entire front "stretching to the Channel." "The stream of German prisoners and the captured war materiel told of the rout of the enemy," I read next to a shaky pencil line at the bottom of the column.

Betty assures me that circus is an apolitical realm removed from threats of war or depression and that her parents married and changed their professional names casually—without caring about international politics. This is a pleasant idea but one that is difficult to accept. I do not think Harry or Babette could possibly have been as oblivious to impending world war in 1915 as their American-born daughter was in 1939. In May of 1915, German U-20 submarines torpedoed and sank the British liner *Lusitania* off the coast of Ireland. Most of the 1,251 passengers (of whom 124 were American) and 650 crew members were lost. The sinking of a commercial liner carrying citizens of neutral nations through neutral waters aroused passionate national outrage; Theodore Roosevelt called it "an act of piracy." Within two years, growing resentment would lead America to declare war against the kaiser's Germany. For two circus artists without the rights of citizenship (Harry was probably not in America legally), German names would have been a professional and personal liability.

The words "the enemy" must have had strong meaning for a German woman who was not an American citizen. How difficult it must have been for Babette to read that boys from her new home were waging one of the most devastating wars in history against young men in the home of her childhood. She had left eight army-eligible brothers behind in Germany. Perhaps the German-born Harry was the closest thing Babette could find to home at a time when General Pershing was leading the American Expeditionary Forces across war-blasted Europe. Perhaps he also read the papers carefully and watched the newsreels in sickened silence.

Whatever Babette's motives may have been, Harry may well have decided that marrying and producing an American-born child would ensure his right to remain in America while the kaiser was rounding up able-bodied German men to defend gas-filled trenches. None of the dazzling and ambitious young showgirls of whom he was so fond would have been eager to become pregnant, I suspect. Babette was his partner, his compatriot, and had a loving heart. They married and became parents in 1915.

The presence of a single marked war report in Babette's little album opens some further tantalizing questions about how I should be researching her belongings. From what I have been able to gather, Babette's entire life revolved around her work. Other than the Grunathos, she apparently had no particular friendships in the United States outside of the general camaraderie that develops among members of a show. Her only hobby was embroidery—less of an artistic pursuit than a relaxing time-filler. Given her complete involvement in her work and separation from her family, Babette may have seen her album as a journal rather than as a mere scrapbook—a single private place for reflection or comment for a woman who lived an intensely public life with little opportunity for emotional confidences. If this is true, then I have to learn to read her choices of clippings, visual imagery, and marginalia as carefully as I would normally search text for clues to a writer's personal thoughts. What I really want to know is whether Babette and Harry were always the heroine and villain that they have become in Betty's memory. I am looking for some human dimension.

Babette's album of her 1925 tour of Cuba with Robinson's Circus is a blatantly personal keepsake. On page after page she has designed colorful collages of fellow performers' pictures, reviews, stickers, and drawings and has collected their poetry and personal messages in half a dozen languages. There is no writing of her own in the book, perhaps because her command of English was limited at this time, yet what is written to her reveals a great deal about her personality and her life with Harry. On a page that Babette has decorated with foil angels from valentines and little glittering leprechaun stickers, for example, there is a publicity photo of a debonair young man with slick dark hair and a carefully penned poem: "I'll never forget, as I used to hear, a crash above my head / While I would sit in my dressing room, and think someone was dead / But, my partner would say to me, it was just the Patrick act / Where Mrs. Pat throws Pat in the air, and of course, he has to come back—Success to You, Clark Morrell, Feb. '25." Another performer's poem reads, "Mr. Patrick 'says' he can lick his wife / But we have our doubts about that / For the way she handles him in the act / We think she could knock him flat."

The album spans the years from 1925 through 1933—the period during which Babette's children resided in Europe until their return during the Great Depression. The Patricks apparently had a wonderful time—many performers refer in their little notes to parties, spaghetti dinners, and good times never to be forgotten, but Babette was obviously worrying about her children in Germany and of her own uncertain position as a German masquerading as an Irishwoman in America. The stickers that she has pasted on every page are without exception Irish shamrocks or leprechauns; American eagles, flags, or landmarks; and babies, bare-bottomed cupids, or happy little children singing Christmas carols.

"To you and your little family—may you find the happiness that you deserve—Dorothy Taylor," I read under a small picture of a quiet-looking young woman—the type of woman in whom I can imagine Babette confiding (and to whom she evidently did confide) that she was not happy. By 1929 the messages reveal that Babette wanted to be known as a mother who missed her children. There are no mentions of Harry, and every message is addressed to Babette alone. A barely legible script beneath one photo of a white-haired gentleman in spectacles reads: "Here is hoping that you will have a very prosperous year and soon be reunited with your children." Obviously Babette and Betty were harboring the same dreams of a happy domestic life while they were an ocean apart. Once reunited, the two women strove to realize their dream. It is hard to place Harry within this history, however. He seems a mere impediment to the hope for domestic happiness that both his wife and daughter cherished, yet neither woman ever thought to oppose him.

∼

Harry must have been surprised by the relationship that was developing between his wife and daughter. Perhaps it was the change in Babette that prompted him to separate them once again. Accustomed to his alcoholic binges, she could usually be trusted to stand placidly by his side as he threw dishes or linen out of the windows. In the morning, while he slept, his long-suffering wife would plod through snowbanks to retrieve her possessions. One wintry night, after a particularly invigorating English lesson with her daughter, Babette stood up as her drunken husband lurched toward the window with armfuls of her clothing. Crossing her Herculean arms, she warned him, "You trow dem out, you vill out vit dem go, after." Betty stared, incredulous, as her father meekly turned and stumbled back into the bedroom. Moments later he was snoring.

If Babette was starting to stand up to her husband, Betty was learning to go around him. The six Coco children had a wonderful life and the kind of home that Betty had dreamed about during the dark years of entombment in the convent. Their parents loved her and welcomed her as another daughter. The saucy sisters, Vira and Jeannie, adored escapades and weekend adventures. On Sundays, dressed sedately for a novena that they had no intention of attending, the girls and their friends would squat in the bushes behind the church, intent on a hot game of poker. One morning Betty saw a pair of spit-shined men's shoes beside her and heard a deep male voice whisper, "Deal me in, ladies." Squinting up into the sunlight, she invited the man to take a seat. Instead, her irate father grabbed her collar and dragged her home. The game was finished. School was discontinued. Childhood was over.

While his independent daughter and newly liberated wife had been perfecting their English, Harry had apparently been busy making plans. Babette was working solo again on the New York City nightclub circuit, and he must have felt alarmingly dispensable. Soon after the churchyard incident, he bought a van and started a moving service. Babette proved handy at lifting pianos and furniture, and did not have to be paid. With a flexible schedule and income to spend, Harry began to frequent clubs and coffeehouses about town, cultivating friendships with the performers and artists who congregated to nurse hangovers, trade professional gossip, and borrow money.

It was at a coffeehouse in 1932 that Harry met the Pichiani Troupe, a team of eight acrobats who needed both a mover and a fill-in acrobat. Harry thought quickly, offered to move their furniture, and casually mentioned that he had a lovely daughter who could perform all the usual acrobatic maneuvers as well as exquisite leaps from a teeterboard. He returned home that afternoon having come to an agreement with the Pichianis. Although Betty had never even seen a somersault, Harry was determined that he could train his daughter to perform as an acrobat. She had six days to learn.

The gym was a solid concrete pad behind their house. Betty would stand with her legs spread apart and arms level, her limbs crisscrossed with welts. Harry gave instructions only once. If they were not followed exactly, he would strike bare legs and exposed arms with a slender stick that could cut through even a hardened will. Around her waist, he fastened a belt and cord as a makeshift mechanic to pull her into position or yank her up from the cold cement whenever she fell. She learned flip-flops, somersaults, standing back flips. Fear was an efficient teacher. Betty performed admirably with the Pichianis until their regular partner returned. Her earnings were paid directly to her father.

Harry had discovered that his daughter had a natural talent for gymnastics, perhaps a legacy from the generations of circus performers who made up her mother's side of the family. When her gig with the Pichianis ended, he began to train her in earnest. Betty soon realized that her father's indifference had been a blessing compared to his new interest in her. They practiced each day until even a beating could not force her legs to support another cartwheel. Underneath her tights, her thighs were stained with black and purple bruises, but her performances were flawless. The sixteen-year-old with the angry eyes could fling herself from a table, twist backward in the air, bounce off of her hands into a series of backward flips, and finish with a pretty bow. Harry quickly sold the house on the East Side and moved the family to Fiftieth and Eighth Avenue, effectively fooling the school system. Neither Betty nor Charlie were enrolled in the new district. No one bothered to trace them. Harry's daughter was finally his to command.

Harry ran into Haji Liazeed in a Broadway coffee shop in 1933. Over rich foreign coffees, the handsome gambler and the balding acrobat—husband to the former Elvira Grunatho—spoke of the friendship their wives still harbored, of the war that seemed inevitable in Europe, of the shoddy new generation of circus performers, of Harry's efforts to teach his daughter the grace and precision that performers had cultivated in the old days. When Harry deftly took advantage of the intimate conversation to mention that he was short on cash, Haji produced his wallet and good-naturedly counted out one hundred dollars. Nonplussed, Harry promised that his daughter would begin working off his debt in the morning.

The week before Betty left to go on the road with the Liazeeds must have sped by for Babette. Never again would her daughter brew coffee in the evenings before reading her mother the comics or teaching her the words of some naughty show tune. Once again she would sit alone through the empty hours of winter nights waiting for Harry to return. No matter. Her precious daughter would be far from Harry's reach, her skin once again unscarred, her career in the hands of Haji and dear Elvira.

Babette no doubt understood that Betty had to escape her cruel father before he destroyed her spirit. While Harry ran the girl through exhaustive exercises and rehearsals, her clever mother expertly pieced together a flowing satin costume in which her daughter could twist and leap without catching her limbs in material or exposing too much flesh to the audience. Knowing that her husband would squander the child's earnings, Babette climbed to the attic and found the box in which her oldest costumes lay folded in layers of tissue. Sitting on the dusty rafters piled with pigeon dropping, she ripped open the silken double hems in which she had hidden her emergency savings and emerald earrings.

As a child, Babette had learned the ancient precautions that allow circus nomads to travel across borders and through foreign lands. Decades later she would confide to Betty that in the deepest corner of her mind there lingered an early memory of a border crossing, perhaps somewhere in Russia. A little girl hid, numb with cold, in the secret space beneath the floor of a circus wagon. Through a crack in the plank siding, she saw bearded, hairy men stomping their heavy boots in the muddy snow. She heard the women's screams as rough hands tore apart their braided hair and ravaged through the trunks and baskets they carried. Blouses were ripped open and skirts lifted, but the wolfish guards never thought to check the tightly sewn hems of the circus costumes—the garish petticoats, fur-lined cloaks, and immense feathered hats in which each performer had hidden a life's fortune. They did not realize that each artist had anticipated the inevitable fall from the wire or accident in the bear cage, the restless nights in a foreign hospital after the circus had left him or her behind, the hands of strangers searching through one's pockets. Gems that had been neatly sewn into padded buttons or rich laces layered between cotton linings of a skillfully constructed costume could support an acrobat long after his leg had been amputated or help a homeless girl to raise an unwanted child. Betty would learn the ways of circus women.

The Liazeeds were a large troupe but they welcomed the new girl warmly. Haji and Elvira had been joined by Elvira's sister Frieda—a former Grunatho sister, and they had picked up the rest of the troupe in Morocco. Handsome, dark-skinned boys and feisty women, they watched Betty carefully during rehearsals and were impressed by her exacting standards and willingness to practice a new trick until it seemed effortless. Lachader, Mohammed, Abdulah, Abdrahamed, Amzal, Mustapha, Bashia, Hadu, Adolf, Peggy, Evelyn, Frieda, and Moses were now her family. "Papa" Haji and Elvira were tender and parental with their young charges—and particularly watchful of the girls. Betty quickly learned to love them. Many years later the aging couple would play the role of grandparents to her own two children.

Life with the Liazeeds proved a new sort of education for Betty, who was, in many ways, far more naive than her mother. Her nomadic blood boiled with restless joy each time the train pulled into the grand, vaulted stations in Chicago or Detroit or Minneapolis. As the boys juggled boxes and shouted to her to stay with the group, she dove into the swift currents of travelers and tried to lose herself in the pulse of the city streets. There were rented rooms in boardinghouses for long engagements in the cities and small tents to camp in during the summer season on the fairground circuit.

Broadway was no longer the unknown world where Babette worked. The Liazeeds played the Roxy, the Palace, the Apollo, the New York Paramount, and Loews theaters. When their call came up, Betty would race down the iron staircase from their top-floor dressing room, pausing in the wings to rosin her slippers while Sophie Tucker sizzled the audience with a hot number. The "Red Hot Mama" was a treat to hear. Only a year earlier, in 1932, Tucker had mesmerized audiences at the Palace by refusing to flee the stage after a spark from a faulty switchboard ignited the stage curtain. While flames shot up the curtain and showers of cinders blew over the orchestra pit, Tucker stood bravely in center stage, brilliant in a highly combustible evening gown, and continued to belt out her song until the asbestos fire curtain was lowered. On Broadway, Betty discovered that the performance pride for which her parents were respected professionally was valued above all else. Familiar names became familiar faces, then friendly faces: Milton Berle, Red Skelton, Jack Benny, Bob Hope.

Clad in satin and sequins, Betty could execute stunning leaps onto a teeterboard or hold her own gracefully in a four-person pyramid, but outside of the gilded theater walls, she was simply a trusting sixteen-year-old without a home. "That little girlie don't know a thing about nothing," Haji would warn the others. "Take good care of her." Papa Haji insisted that Frieda never leave the convent-bred child alone, an arrangement that caused both girls distress whenever Frieda had a date.

The concept of dating was new to Betty. The Coco girls had often taken her to the beach on weekends where they would meet male cousins and their friends, but the young people had never paired off into couples. Flirting had been a group affair—innocent, silly, and adolescent. Always obliging but completely baffled, Betty now had to walk a discreet ten paces behind Frieda and the earnest young men who invited her to stroll the parks and shopping districts in St. Louis or Pittsburgh or Buffalo. After one poor beau got a bill that was more than he had bargained for and did not call again, Frieda insisted that Betty order only soup or a salad when she tagged along on dinner dates. "You're just a third wheel," she complained. Betty shrugged. She had thought that the nice young man had invited both girls to dinner.

If Frieda was exasperated at having to play guardian to her wide-eyed partner, she seldom showed it. All the troupe loved Papa Haji and obeyed him without question, but Frieda genuinely liked the odd little German girl as well. Not only could she be counted on to stand still in the pyramid and keep smiling when the next jumper accidentally bent her ears backward as he slammed down onto her shoulders, but she was an unobtrusive, uncomplaining companion in their tiny tent. On summer nights, when the last of the crowds had straggled off the fairground and the surrounding fields rang with the music of bullfrogs and whippoorwills, the two girls would sprawl on their stomachs under a single bulb that they had strung over their cots with clothesline, their heads pressed together over the latest issue of *True Romances*. Frieda allowed herself the luxurious hope that her true love would magically appear backstage one night and sweep her away to Hollywood, but romance seemed as distant a possibility to Betty as paternal affection. Betty just wanted a chance to make her own way.

Opportunities to explore how others lived were never lacking. In Decatur, Iowa, a farm girl stole from the 4-H tent each evening to watch the acrobats rehearse on the field. One night her overalled father cornered Papa Haji and asked if the little acrobat with the curly hair could come home with his lonely daughter for the weekend. Hoping that Betty would enjoy a glimpse of "normal" life, Haji agreed, on the condition that the family return her one hour before each afternoon performance so that she could warm up with the troupe.

∾

Betty settles back in her chair and grins at me. "That's how I got the nickname 'tafunis'"—she chuckles—"and I don't know how to spell it. It means 'cow' in Arabic. Those stinkers worked me! I got up at five every morning and fed chickens and pigs and milked the cow. By the time I got to the fairgrounds, all I wanted to do was sleep. The boys called me 'little cow' ever after. I stuck to our own kind after that."

Her face darkens for a moment as she watches squirrels race across the hurricane-downed pecan tree in the yard outside her window. "That's not true." She turns away from me, a sure sign that

I am about to hear something absolutely truthful. "I was very naive then. I couldn't always tell who were our kind and who weren't." She pauses, then continues quickly. "Peggy and Evelyn were allowed to go out, but I wasn't allowed to go anywhere without Frieda. If I suggested that she and her date leave me somewhere, she would say, 'Oh no. Papa Haji says I have to be with you all the time.' One night I woke up and found myself sitting on top of Frieda, choking her! After that Papa Haji decided that I should try to make friends with other girls—and Frieda made me sleep on the floor.

"I had been invited to attend a local dance. Was it in Milwaukee? I don't remember. A lady teacher there told Papa Haji that she would drive me to the dance and bring me home. We had shows the next day, but she promised that she would have me back by twelve at the latest. Well, she met some guy and forgot all about me. The dance finished, and I couldn't find them anywhere. I thought, 'Oh my God, how am I going to get to the fairgrounds?' I ran around asking everybody who was left where the fairgrounds were. One of the boys told me that he was a reporter and that his friend was a photographer. They offered to take me home. I was so relieved. I got in the car. I didn't know that they had been drinking. They were chewing gum. I thought they were our kind."

Betty stares hard at the fallen tree, forcing herself to remember this early instance of the only sin she does not forgive: betrayal. "We drove out of town. They were laughing. I told them, 'Stop. I think you're going the wrong way. This isn't the way I came,' and they said, 'We're just going to have a little fun, and then we'll take you home.' I knew I'd gotten into something bad. I asked, 'What are you going to do?' They kept laughing, 'You'll find out.'"

She tells me of a terrifying ride, of her fear as the car careened around curves on a road that skirted the water. Her companions had wedged her between them in the front seat, so she could not leap out of the car before it missed a sharp curve and sped off the road, sideswiped a tree, and spun over into a ditch. When Betty regained consciousness, she found herself trapped under broken glass. One side of her face was cold, her swollen lips throbbed, and her mouth filled with blood every time she tried to call out. A bleeding head slumped onto her right shoulder, shards of glass protruding from the flesh at wild angles. Neither of her companions was moving.

When I envision Betty climbing out of that car through the broken windshield, I think of a baby chick pecking a passage through the shell of an egg, jerking and stretching its trembling body until it forces itself free of its prison. When Betty fell into the ditch and raised her battered face, she saw a scrawny old man sitting above her, spitting tobacco into the ditch. She lapses into an unexpected drawl as she tries to impress upon me the sort of person to whom she had to appeal for help, and I have to laugh. "So youse finely moved," he croaked.

"Why didn't you help us?" Betty mumbled through mangled lips.

"Thought 'cha wuz ded," the odd man replied. "I'll go sind fer the sheriff now."

Oh boy, thought Papa Haji's littlest girl.

Hospital X rays determined that Betty's arm had been fractured. "But I have to use my arm," Betty insisted when the doctors told her that she would not be able to work her acrobatic routine for at least several weeks. "I'm part of a troupe. We perform tomorrow." She didn't explain her fear that if she could not work, Haji might be tempted to return her to Harry.

When she was presented with a bill for five dollars, Betty was at a loss. She had left the fairgrounds to attend a dance; her purse held only a comb and a handkerchief. The hospital offered to keep her in the charity ward overnight and to send for Papa Haji in the morning, but Betty insisted that she felt fine. Terrified that she would be sent back to New York City, she lied about her age and convinced the staff to release her and to hold her purse until she could return with the money. "Where's the fair?" she demanded. "Down the hill" came the reply.

Betty's head throbbed as she staggered down the hill toward the dark fields and silent carnival wagons. The high-wire fence and metal grating surrounding the fairgrounds was locked securely for the night. Even with one arm bandaged, Betty managed to writhe to the top of the fence and throw herself over. After springing up from the wet ground, she raced wildly through the amusement area with its phantom towers and monstrous dark shapes toward the tents. Frieda never moved as Betty rummaged through her cardboard box of belongings and darted back into the darkness, the five dollars for the hospital clenched between her torn lips. She scaled the fence twice more that night. By the time she had paid her bill, reclaimed her purse, returned to her tent, and collapsed into sleep, dawn was streaking the eastern sky and the carnies were rolling out of their sleeping bags and lighting cigarettes.

The Liazeeds always practiced before breakfast. Their fast-paced tumbling act was impossible to perform on a full stomach. Papa Haji stood before Betty's tent the next morning in deep concern. The girl was usually awake before any of the others, desperate for the bitter coffee she loved. This morning Frieda had come to the kitchen tent first, explaining that she could not rouse Betty. The sun rose higher and the troupe washed, had coffee, and finally gathered on the flat grassy playing field to rehearse, but still the little one did not appear. Haji banged on the canvas with the flat of his hand and shouted, "C'mon, girlie. Get on out here, or there'll be no more dances for you."

No one said a word when Betty crawled groggily from the tent wearing dark glasses and cradling one hand tenderly over her mouth. "What's wrong, girlie?" "Nothing, I'm just sleepy," Betty muttered. The boys laughed. Practice usually began with good-natured wrestling. Hadu threw a heavy arm around Betty's neck and lifted her into the air. "Wake up, Tafunis!" The glasses flew off her face and her body crumpled.

Fists began to clench and eyes burned as Betty pulled herself up from the dust. Her eyes were black with angry bruises, the stitches were torn where her swollen lips had rubbed against her pillow as she wrestled with unmedicated pain. Her bandaged arm hung awkwardly at her side, the fingers cold and bleached. Beads of sweat stood out on her forehead despite the cold morning air. "My God, who did this to you? We will kill him!" the boys shrieked, but Haji simply stared in shock at his littlest angel. "Girlie, girlie, what am I going to do with you?"

Betty worked that day. Layered with makeup, she somersaulted and flip-flopped with one hand, threw herself into the air, and landed on her feet with furious determination. When the boys pulled her into the pyramid, she bit her tongue to keep from sobbing but smiled proudly as soon as she was placed. Even Frieda was too impressed to scold. While Haji paced his tent, the young people silently watched Betty whip through her act with a steel-like pride that they had never imagined so young a performer could possess.

Haji was furious. He walked up the hill to the hospital and inquired after the two newspapermen who had kidnapped Betty.

Both had been discharged and had left hurriedly for Chicago without mentioning their passenger. Once home, the reporter and photographer explained their injuries with journalistic flair. The Chicago radio station reported that two local boys had been involved in a terrible automobile accident, the result of their having offered a ride to a drunken showgirl named Miss Barbara Schutz. Harry started receiving phone calls from friends in Chicago almost immediately.

When a messenger arrived with a telegram from Harry, the Liazeeds crowded around Haji's tent in silence. Haji emerged with stricken eyes but put on a reassuring smile before he crawled into the tent where Betty lay exhausted after three performances, no longer able to hide her misery. "Your father loves you, girlie," he whispered. "You stay with us." Betty shut her eyes in relief and instantly fell into a hard-earned sleep. While she slept, blissfully deceived, Elvira showed Harry's telegram to her sister in disgust. Frieda realized that a mistaken trust in Harry could be dangerous, and as soon as Betty had rested, she repeated a message that closed the girl's heart to her father forever: "If Betty is badly hurt, send her home. If not, the hell with her."

Betty's accident came as a stark awakening. She had thought herself independent and beyond her father's control, but now she realized that her liberty could vanish with a single fall, a foolish twist of an ankle or wrist. It had never occurred to her that her work was worth money. Betty assumed that she was working without pay in order to gain experience in the profession. She received no paycheck, and her meals, lodging, and personal items were always discreetly provided. She began to understand that she needed financial security.

The Liazeeds kept Betty for well over a year, perhaps fearful that if she were returned to Harry, he might use her to repay debts in darker ways. Betty was in no hurry to return to her abusive parent. Harry had told her that she was fortunate to "get a break in showbiz" and that the Liazeeds offered a valuable opportunity to learn new material.

It was by accident that Betty finally learned of Harry's arrangement with Haji. The Liazeeds were playing New York City once again, and she was savoring the delicious opportunity to practice in a well-furnished rehearsal hall. Betty tells me that, as she spun high in the air, she was spotted by a scout for the U.S. Olympic games. He immediately invited the teenager to join his team of Olympic hopefuls. In spite of her full work schedule, Betty managed to attend the whirlwind training session each day. Her superb form and expert skills surprised and delighted the American team's coach, who assured her that a gold medal was a goal that she could achieve.

Betty finally had a fantasy to relish. She secretly dreamed of handing her mother the golden prize. She imagined Mama Coco's tears of joy as the American national anthem played for the little girl she had fed. An Olympic star would be welcome in every home in America; she would never need to enter her father's home again.

One afternoon, as she was quietly beginning her stretching exercises, Betty saw her coach running across the waxed gym floor in forbidden street shoes, his face contorted in fury. He had been speaking with Haji. Although she had never received money for her work, Betty had worked in lieu of money and was therefore ineligible to compete in the Olympics as a nonprofessional athlete. He announced this news to his protégée with tears in his eyes.

Betty listened in silence. In a single moment, her hope of competing in the 1936 Olympics had been dashed, but she fiercely forced her disappointment to the back of her mind where it could wait until she had sufficient privacy to confront it. When the coach finished speaking, it was an adult who looked into his face and stunned him with the graciousness of her warm thanks for his wasted efforts and asked him to carry her love and encouragement to her teammates. Although she wasn't sure what she would do next, Betty was now a professional; she had learned to hold her head high and leave her audience satisfied.

~

I have been growing cold as I listen to Betty's compelling tale of blasted childhood and forced maturity. We have been taping interviews for months. I could not rest last night. I fell into a troubled sleep in the early hours of the morning and dreamed that I was climbing fences with bloody hands while I held the pages of a heavy manuscript between my teeth, gagging as the paper disintegrated and clogged my throat.

Betty pauses suddenly, as if she has read my mind, and looks intently at my face, then rises quickly and picks up my empty coffee mug. I rise, too, and click off the recorder. Listening to her stories exhausts my emotions, but I am ashamed to admit this. I could say that I have errands to run and leave early, but Betty is sharp enough to detect a lie by the tiniest tremor in my voice. I decide to tell the truth. "I'm tired. Aren't you?"

At first, I assume that she has not heard. The hearing aid is still lying on the table in the dining room, and we have moved into the kitchen to microwave more water for coffee. I would probably get through these sessions more calmly, I think, if I did not try to drink her extra-strength coffee.

"Yes, I'm tired." Her hand reaches for mine. "You're so young. Don't you see, I'm a good performer. Isn't that what we all do? We perform all our lives. We want people to see us at our best, to imagine us with longing and remember us with tenderness." Betty sighs and looks across the room at the elaborate shrine she has constructed on her deceased dog Nikki's little bed, still lying on the floor next to the warm oven. I cannot help smiling. Nikki was not a friendly dog. She snapped with her gums after her teeth were gone. In the end, the toothless Chihuahua could barely keep her head up. Betty cradled the tiny dog in her hand and fed her milk-sopped bread.

After the dog died, Betty lovingly placed on a little cushion a painted plaster Chihuahua, an empty bowl, and pictures of her beloved pet. The little shrine has always struck me as charming. I know that she keeps a book in which she writes about Nikki—words to fill a need too deep to share with an audience.

"And when you're alone?" I ask mercilessly, glancing down at the plaster dog. Betty places her hands firmly on my shoulders and jolts me from my depression with a sharp slap of professional pride. "Then you fantasize. You imagine who you want to be. You are a writer. If you want to write a grand performance, you'd better be prepared to come backstage. You'd better be ready to see the show without lights or scenery, without costumes or music or makeup. Before all that, there's work. And even before the work, there's yourself, just yourself, without any audience at all."

We carry our cups back into the dining room and sit down. Betty fits her hearing aid into her ear. I reach over and press the "record" button, then discreetly push my cup to one side. I am not going to drink her coffee, but I am going to finish writing my story.

THREE

INITIATIONS

The Depression years were difficult ones for performers. Circus historian John Culhane points out that with millions of workers unemployed or working only part time, few Americans could afford to go to the circus. When the stock market collapsed in 1929, it brought an end to what had been an unprecedented decade of prosperity in circus history—an era of "superstars performing super-feats."[1] No one in the ever-precarious and unpredictable world of circus could have realized during the 1920s that a period of glorious record-breaking and global recognition of circus artistry would end so soon or so pitilessly, crushed by economic collapse, world war, and high-tech entertainment. Even if they had, circus performers had no language for discouragement, much less surrender. In private life as well as in their work, they were used to risk taking and dream making.

Risk taking had generally paid off for the big circuses in the two decades before the Depression. Babette and Harry could not have picked a better time to have worked in America as performers. In his superb, comprehensive history, Culhane writes that in 1917, when the United States entered the first world war, dozens of small to midsize circuses were flourishing, and both Ringling Bros. Circus and Barnum & Bailey Circus were traveling with hundreds of horses, enough exotic animals to fill a zoo, and over a thousand employees apiece.

Ringling Bros. Circus needed ninety-two railroad cars to carry its acts, equipment, and menagerie across the country.

When war broke out, both Ringling Bros. and Barnum & Bailey lost practically every able-bodied man to the armed forces, obliging elderly helpers, women of the circus families, and even the stars themselves to handle the crushing labor that had formerly been done by hundreds of grooms and hostlers, canvasmen and property men. The demands of wartime shipping made it impossible for the railroads to accommodate the needs of the two huge traveling circuses owned by Ringling Brothers. The Ringling family determined to exploit their legendary circus ingenuity and business savvy to save their two shows without compromising talent. The results could not have been more fortunate for New York audiences.

In 1919 New Yorkers were treated to the opening of the combined Ringling Brothers and Barnum & Bailey Circus—the "world's first super-circus," featuring an all-star cast of performers. Culhane records that audiences could watch "Poodles" Hanneford's world-record-breaking running leaps onto horseback, Tiny Klein's giant revolutions on the swinging trapeze, Bird Millman's tantalizing dances and tricks on the wire, and young May Wirth's breathtaking back-backward somersault on horseback—a perilous and exacting trick accomplished while the horse is galloping forward and the equestrienne is catapulting backward. In midair, Wirth could twist around so that she would land facing forward on her steed. Although few audiences were able to understand just how dangerous her act was, other performers crowded the ring openings to watch her and to marvel at one of their own.

By the mid-1920s, The Greatest Show on Earth was boasting circus-royalty billing. New York audiences in the 1920s were used to seeing such "immortals" as Lillian Leitzel, "the World's Most Daring Aerial Star," and her lover Alfredo Codona, "the King of the Flying Trapeze"; May Wirth, "the Greatest Bareback Rider of All Time"; and Con Colleano, "the Wizard of the Silver Thread." Colleano had become a circus legend by driving himself to perfect the first feet-to-feet forward somersault, a perilous trick that no other wire walker had ever dared to attempt. Culhane explains that unlike the relatively routine backward somersault that can be executed using the body's natural reflexes and momentum, the forward somersault whirls the wire walker's feet forward ahead of his head, forcing him to place his feet on the wire before he can actually see it. Only split-second timing and impeccable coordination can save the walker from spinning past the wire. Like May Wirth, Colleano performed for audiences that did not always understand the full extent of his daring, but those who did—especially his fellow performers—were stunned into speechless admiration.

Circus stars of the Jazz Age captivated the public in much the way that rock stars and television and movie celebrities would later come to dominate a culture's imagination. Although they seemed larger than life, their amazing feats could be watched live, and their private lives were even more spectacular and bizarre than their acts. Perhaps the most fabulous and tragic performer of the age was Lillian Leitzel, a ninety-four-pound fairylike aerialist who mesmerized her audiences by turning herself into a human airplane propeller, throwing her tiny body over and over in a series of rapid one-armed "planges" as she clung to a single loop of rope attached to a swivel high above their heads. Thousands of voices would count together as the drums rolled and the spotlighted Leitzel continued past the one hundredth plange.

Like Babette, Leitzel had been born into an ancient circus family and despised her brutal father. She also had taken advantage of vaudeville and the theater circuit before her daring allowed her to command from Ringling Bros. the astronomical salary of $500 a week and her own circus car, complete with electricity—a previously unheard-of luxury for any performer. Such luxuries would soon become not only possible but routine for the most talented in the field.

In his detailed account of Leitzel's tragic love for Alfredo Codona, Culhane notes that the pair seemed almost a metaphor for the decade itself. At the height of their glamour and appeal, the two were the most famous stars of the world's most famous circus. Alfredo was the only trapeze artist who had ever been able consistently to execute the "somersault of death"—a triple back somersault at a speed of sixty-two miles an hour into the hands of a catcher. In 1927 the two superstars culminated their famous love affair in marriage, and Codona suddenly found himself the consort of the "Queen of the Circus," an awkward position for one who was a king in his own right. Their tumultuous and jealousy-ridden marriage ended in separation in 1930. A few months later, during her performance at the Valencia Music Hall in Copenhagen, the brass swivel ring from which Leitzel was hanging while throwing her famous planges suddenly crystallized from friction and snapped. The tiny star plunged twenty feet to the circus floor, landing on her head. Although she begged to be allowed to finish her act, Leitzel was carried to a hospital where she convinced her terrified husband that he should leave her side and honor his commitment to perform at the Winter Garden in Berlin. He obeyed her, and she died of unexpected complications the next morning.

So famous was this young circus girl that a hockey match at Madison Square Garden several days after her death was delayed while a crowd stood to sing "Auld Lang Syne" in her memory. News of her accident spread around the world. In his grief, Codona lost the concentration that had always characterized his brilliantly graceful flying. He became reckless, taking risks that shocked his fellow performers. Soon after Leitzel's death, he fell from the trapeze, wounding his muscles irreparably. Codona lived on the fringes of the circus for a few tortured years, then fatally shot his second wife, equestrienne Vera Bruce, before shooting himself. His life had ended, colleagues agreed, when he and Leitzel had fallen from the sky.

~

These old circus stories always seem a bit exaggerated to me, particularly those of the postwar Jazz Age in which practically everything must have emerged as alternately romantic or tragic. Their tenacious appeal, however, is proof that Babette and Harry moved through a culture that was far more seductive and celebrated than we can appreciate today—when circus is generally considered to be a "disappearing culture." For Babette especially, who had never known life outside of the circus, the dark days of the Depression must have seemed particularly threatening.

When the stock market crashed in October 1929, most of the smaller circuses were crushed. The Gentry Bros. Circus closed before the end of the year. Christy Bros. Circus collapsed in 1930 along with Floyd King's Cole Bros. Circus. By 1931 Miller Bros. Circus, Miller Bros. 101 Ranch Wild West Show, and Robbins Bros. Circus had all fallen apart. Atterbury Bros., Mighty Haag Circus, and Orton Bros. managed to stay on the road only as little truck shows. The mighty

John Ringling resigned authority over his circus while pledging all of his personal assets toward paying its debts.[2]

The circus has always been remarkably resilient, and a comeback was right around the corner—but no one knew it then.

By 1935 Americans would see the birth of the impressive new Cole Bros. and Clyde Beatty Combined Circus featuring such unforgettable performers as lion trainer Clyde Beatty, beloved clowns Emmett Kelly and Otto Griebling, and the strikingly beautiful bareback rider Harriet Hodgini, whose fairy-tale marriage to millionaire Harold Van Orman would thrill a romance-hungry nation. By 1937 Clyde Beatty would be featured on the cover of *Time* magazine, but during the early days of the Depression, circuses were struggling and jobs were scarce. Most performers preferred to work at any job in the industry rather than to leave it for more secure work, and Babette and Harry were no exception, but times were hard. In quiet resignation, skilled artists sought work outside the only culture they had ever known while despairing outsiders struggled to get in on any terms. "Geeks"—carnival performers whose acts generally included biting the heads off live chickens or snakes—suddenly became common on carnival grounds as desperate men and women agreed to perform any bizarre act, exploit any deformity, or embrace any danger simply to earn a buck.

∾

I have often wondered if the hardships of those few dark years of the early 1930s might not account for the obsession with finding work that Betty remembers as having been such an integral part of her family's life. Had Harry pulled her from school and forced her into acrobatics during a time of relative security and prosperity, there would be no redeeming explanation for his cruelty, but I wonder whether, in 1932, when scores of banks and factories had closed, farmers had been evicted from their lands, and entire families were living in tarpaper shacks and scavenging food from the city dumps, Harry might have thought that he was doing his daughter a favor by helping her to find work as a performer. He and Babette were working as furniture movers and cooks. No one in the family, however, claims to remember his ever having done a single thing out of goodwill alone.

Babette and Harry left the circus and opened Schultz Bavarian Restaurant and Hall at 326 West Forty-Eighth Street in 1933. Babette was a marvelous cook and could fill a plate with steaming old-world sauerbraten, schnitzel, or kartoffel knödel (potato dumplings). How and where the strong woman had learned to cook, Betty cannot tell me, but she remembers an almost gourmet menu. "My father would bring home the finest smoked herring fillets, and Mama would 'milk' them [soak them in milk to remove the salt]," Betty recalls. "Mama made the most wonderful rollmops [herring marinated in vinegar and spices, rolled with onions and secured with a sliver of wood]." Betty laughs when she tells me that her father so loved Babette's fried pastries that he would hide them. The restaurant was a favorite haunt of performers because it boasted a large rehearsal hall and gymnasium in the back. It could have been the start of a stereotypical "American" entrepreneurial success story for Harry and of domestic peace for Babette—if they had been just a bit more savvy and if Harry had stayed just a bit more sober.

One other obstacle to his success may have been that Harry had decided to use his real name although the world was once again watching Germany with fear. He added an "l" to Schutz (making it "Schultz") so that it would sound better when pronounced by English speakers. (The proper pronunciation of Harry "Schutz" in English sounds embarrassingly like Harry "Shits.") It is hard to know how aware Harry might have been of nationalist public sentiment at this time. His restaurant opened soon after Hitler was declared German chancellor—an event that struck dread throughout the international community. Germany's new leader immediately adjourned the Reichstag (the German parliament), thus securing for himself almost dictatorial power. In March 1933 the Nazis opened the first concentration camp in Dachau and began to fill it with intellectuals, scientists, gypsies, homosexuals, and cultural leaders accused of possessing an "un-German ideology." Books were burned and school curricula revised to include "race science." By Hitler's order, Jews were legally banned from participating in business, education, or other professions, and the chancellor promised a shocked world that "Treason toward the nation and the people shall in future be stamped out with ruthless barbarity."

Whatever his sense of American sentiment might have been, Harry evidently was not oblivious to German politics. After Hitler passed the German law for the "perfection of the Aryan race" that ordered all men, women, and minors suffering from epilepsy, mental retardation, schizophrenia, depression, chorea, or "physical weaknesses" such as blindness or deafness to present themselves for surgical sterilization, Harry marched himself down to the federal building and applied for American citizenship. He failed the test twice before passing, but on June 5, 1933, he became a citizen of the United States. The father of an epileptic son no longer told Babette that he wanted to return to Germany.

Harry and Babette's restaurant opened at an opportune time—just as the Eighteenth Amendment was repealed, ending thirteen years of prohibition. Depression-weary Americans craved entertainment and fine liquor. Restaurants, lounges, nightclubs, and theaters were springing up daily on every New York City street. Across town, Radio City Music Hall opened with six thousand seats. Schultz Bavarian Restaurant had a large clientele eager to eat Babette's cooking and drink the night away. The only problem was that Harry could not obtain a license to serve hard liquor because the restaurant was located across the street from a church and an elementary school. "It wasn't a problem," Betty tries to convince me. "People knew that they could bring in a paper bag." I assume, however, that most New Yorkers were tired of sneaking forbidden liquor around in paper bags and wanted to celebrate the end of prohibition properly—by choosing from a wide selection of exotic drinks mixed openly and legally by a licensed bartender in a comfortable club. Harry could offer only beer or a clean glass.

During these difficult times, Harry enjoyed the companionship of many loyal fellow performers who came to drown their sorrows and to gossip around his tables. "Harry simply drank up all the profits," Betty admits, shaking her head sadly. "For a while, Mama and I kept everything floating. The Liazeeds weren't booked and I was back at home. At night, after she had finished cooking and serving, Mama and I would leave my father drinking with the patrons while we visited other lounges around town doing 'standel.' After midnight, it wasn't hard to find bars full of tipsy men who were feeling good-natured and generous. We entertained them."

"How?" I gasp, shocked by the unlikely images that leap to my mind. I do not want to think about how a young girl and her mother entertained a bar full of soused men, but the picture Betty paints for me is proof that I am completely ignorant of the flavor of the 1930s New York nightlife she remembers or of the practical attitudes that career performers had about their work.

"I went first." Betty giggles. "I did some acrobatic tricks and then Mama would pass the hat around, promising that she was going to bend steel next. She teased and taunted the men, and they filled the hat. If someone only gave a quarter or was stingy, she embarrassed him in front of all the others by saying 'Is dat all dis pretty young girl is vert to you?' After the hat had gone around, Mama would tell me to sneak out and hail a taxi; she would bend a nail and then pretend to step out to get her steel bars. She never came back. I was waiting in the taxi when she came rushing out of the back door."

"You hustled them?" I exclaim, and Betty instantly rises to her mother's defense.

"We didn't cheat anybody. We gave them a good show—and my mother did bend steel. Not one man could have done what she did. They got what they paid for." Her blue eyes are flashing, but I am not going to be intimidated.

"Wasn't it dangerous for two women to be running around to bars in the middle of the night?" I ask, immediately aware of how judgmental my question sounds—but these were, after all, two women who could not tell when they themselves were drunk.

Betty's face softens, as if she is suddenly seeing in me a convent-bred child grown into a university-sheltered woman. "They weren't bars like the ones you see today," she explains gently. "People socialized in bars back then—you could buy food or see a floor show. Remember the movie *White Christmas* with Rosemary Clooney and Bing Crosby? Remember the nightclubs they sang in? People went out to lounges to have a good time, to talk and dine and dance. Times were different then. We had fun."

~

As I am replaying her last interview, I get a sudden impulse to call Betty and suggest that we get together—not to tape interviews and watch each other's eyes, but just to have fun. Our relationship seems to have become far too focused on this project—far too centered on production. I do not explain to her that I feel this way; I merely invite her to have lunch with me the next day—Friday—at Wilmington's annual Greek festival. This year I have no responsibilities to keep me from heaping a plate with moussaka and baklava and enjoying an afternoon outdoors.

Betty and I arrive just as the festival opens and the band is warming up. The food is fresh and steaming hot, and columns of people have already formed at the entrance to a huge, colorful tent under which dozens of picnic tables have been set up. Greek music fills the warm afternoon as long lines of lunchtime visitors begin to move slowly past counters of spicy baked dishes and rich, buttery pastries stuffed with sugary nut paste. As the music heats up, I sway slightly to the rhythm and notice that a few other uninhibited souls in the crowd are tapping their feet or moving unobtrusively. Suddenly Betty is dancing beside me—arms above her head in Latin poise, hips swaying and feet hopping. Her hip smacks into mine and I swing my arms up and bump her right back. What the hell, I think. The crowd is watching us—some with delighted smiles, others in uneasy dismay. As my white-haired companion and I merrily cavort our way across the lawn toward the concession stands, caught up in the irresistible throb of music and inhibition-melting aromas, I remember Fritzi telling me to reinvent myself and laugh. I have just been waiting for an attractive invitation.

～

Schultz Bavarian Restaurant did not last long. Harry discovered that he could leave Babette at the restaurant and take Betty around to bars himself. Instead of passing a hat and coming home with money, Harry let his daughter entertain for free drinks. "Show them what you just learned," he would urge her in his not-to-be-argued-with voice, and Betty would do a flip for her father's performer friends, then settle quietly into a chair to wait while the men enjoyed another round. "I hated it," she fumes. "His friends were nice men but they ignored me. I had to sit there until three or four in the morning. Mama was always threatening to lock us out. We came home at five A.M. one morning and, sure enough, the door was locked.

"There was a fence around our house—about eight feet high," Betty recalls with an impish grin. "My father climbed the fence in the dark—remember that he was an acrobat—and tried to leap for an open window. The windows on the second floor were almost level with the top of the fence. He was stinking drunk, though, and never even made it over. When he fell, his pants hooked on the top of the fence and there he hung, cursing his head off."

Across the street was the fashionable Belvedere Hotel where the dashing Ritz Brothers lived when they were in New York. "They knew our family," Betty explains, "so when they heard shouting and saw a man trying to break into our home, they grabbed a BB gun, opened their front window, and started shooting. I was rolling on the ground, laughing like crazy. Pellets were flying past my father, and he was hanging upside down screaming bloody murder: 'Jesus Christ! It's me, Harry. Babette, help!' My mother finally came to the window and shouted that she was coming down. When she got to the yard, she yanked him off that fence so hard that his pants ripped apart. Then she slung him over her shoulder like a sack of potatoes and hauled him into the house. Mama told him, 'Now you know vat I do if you don't come home.' My father was just as meek as a lamb."

Harry had been watching Betty as she flip-flopped in the bars. He knew that she was worth more than free drinks. Not long after his humiliating adventure with the locked door, he decided that it was time to return to a world that he understood—the world of performance, the world of risk taking and dream making. In late 1933, he closed the restaurant, hired five pretty girls who swore that they were acrobats, rented some stripper costumes from a costume warehouse, packed Betty and the girls into his car, and took the show on the road.

"It was a rotten act." Betty sighs, rolling her eyes. "My father was a terrific performer but a lousy organizer. We opened at a club in Boston, but the club manager canceled our dates once he had seen our routine. The contract called for us to bring our own music, curtain drop, and scenery, and to retain the original performers [the five girls hired in New York]. My father had forgotten the music and didn't have a backdrop. He just used whatever he could find around the theater—marching music with tropical sets, Latin music with oriental sets. The costumes were made out of that sheer material that shower curtains are made from—far too flimsy to wear. After one of the girls quit, my father hired another, but she knew the manager and confessed that she was a replacement. That was a breach of contract. It was a mess."

"What did you do, exactly?" I prompt her. I have noticed that Betty seldom describes her acts to me. She will say "I did acrobatic," and assume that I understand exactly what this entails. This time I am pleasantly surprised.

"I did jackley drops while the other girls did acrobatic around me," she responds. "I guess you wouldn't know what that means, would you? You start on a table about fourteen feet above the floor, do a backbend, drop backward to land on your hands on the floor, push up and do a jack-knife up onto another table, and then a series of flip-flops across the stage." I watch as she illustrates the moves by slapping a pencil across the table, breaking its point. "I was the only woman doing jackley drops. My father would break my fall with his arms, but it was very dangerous and I hated it. The Liazeeds never allowed me to do that trick."

The show apparently got more laughs than acclaim. "I did the hard tricks and the others got hurt." Betty chuckles. "The first night one girl did a simple stunt, fell on her head, and just stayed upside down. She actually stood on her head throughout the rest of the routine! She claimed that she had fainted, but wouldn't she have fallen over then?" I nod vigorously and we both laugh. "The manager told my father that he couldn't use us any more, so we all came home."

In 1934 Harry put together another show, and this time he threw in everything that he could think of, although Babette was conspicuously missing. In addition to Betty and the acrobatic girls, he hired a male cast of jugglers, comedians, dancers, and singers. "He put me in the back of the chorus line because I was a lousy dancer," Betty confesses, and I smile, remembering her exuberant and contagious dancing across the church lawn. "We opened in Troy, New Jersey," she recalls, "but after the third day there was hardly any business. It wasn't our fault. They didn't have a movie screen—just the show."

Try as he might, Harry had been unable to book the sort of upscale engagements that Betty had used to perform with the Liazeeds. The Arabs had played the finest theaters and clubs on the East Coast, and Betty knew firsthand what discerning people expected for their money. An afternoon or evening at the Roxy or the

Palace, for instance, typically began with a movie and a newsreel, followed by a full show featuring a wide range of professional acts. "I could sit on the side of the stage behind the curtain and watch the movie," Betty remembers. "The bodies looked kind of long, but that didn't bother me."

The best theaters boasted lovely dressing rooms with couches, showers, makeup lights, and tables. Stagehands ran errands and announced visitors. "Sometimes we'd run across the street to the automatic [Automat]—you're too young to remember that," Betty explains. "There were lots of little windows—one with soup, another with pie. You could put in a quarter and get what you wanted. Elvira and Frieda sometimes brought food and coffee, but of course we couldn't eat until after the last show—and by then everything tasted so good. The stagehands were always very respectful; they treated us like artists. It was a lovely life."

The establishment into which Harry had booked his new show was nothing like the theaters that Betty remembers so fondly. There was no movie and only one small, dumpy room backstage for dressing. After they had played for three days to an almost empty house, the manager approached Harry and confessed that he could not afford to keep the act for their predetermined fee. He offered to let them perform for a percentage of the house take. Harry quit instantly, stranding his large cast of performers without enough money to get home.

"My father called Mama and told her to come to New Jersey on the train and to bring all the money that she had," Betty tells me. "She came, but she didn't bring any money. She knew better. For the next three days, Mama and I did ten shows a night at different bars. I did acrobatic and she pounded nails through a board with her fist. She collected enough money to send all of the kids home, then she got our scenery back."

Betty explains that the theater had held all of their props because Harry had refused to finish out the week on renegotiated terms. When hefty Babette arrived at the stage door in work clothes well after midnight, mentioned the manager's name, and told the night watchman that she had been instructed to haul out the old scenery so that a new show could set up in the morning, he simply shrugged and watched as she tramped back and forth to the car with costumes and backdrops.

"Your mother was sharp, wasn't she?" I ask Betty.

"Oh, yes," she admits enthusiastically, "but my father never gave her any credit for it."

Suddenly I am struck by a nagging question. "Where was Charlie while the rest of you were in New Jersey?" Betty shrugs her shoulders, uninterested, but I am not going to let the subject drop so easily this time. "If this was early 1934, then Charlie was only about twelve years old—that is not very old, you know. My Kurt is eleven. Who was watching him while the rest of the family was traveling? Surely your mother did not leave a child of that age alone in New York City without money or anyone to care for him?"

Betty sits very still, her eyes fixed on the table. When she raises them and meets my gaze, I detect genuine confusion. "I don't know. He was my brother but we were almost strangers," she admits softly, and then, in a smaller voice than I have ever heard her use before, "It never bothered me. I never cared. I was always working." As we stare blankly at each other, I wish fervently that I knew what to ask next. The silence grows strained and I realize that our interview is probably over. Charlie has become a gaping hole in this narrative, and neither one of us wants to be the first to test its depth.

～

Betty's career as a solo performer began in 1935, after her father had aborted his efforts to star her in a show of his own and had decided to become her agent instead. "I wanted to be a singer, but my father said that singers were a dime a dozen." She smiles wistfully. "I was a very good acrobat because I have big bones. I can throw my body weight onto my wrists and ankles without fracturing them. Everybody said that I tumbled like a man." For a female performer whose work was extremely athletic, this was a treasured compliment indeed.

Harry booked his daughter into some of the most popular cosmopolitan nightclubs—the Red Mill, the Silver Dollar, the High Hat in Brooklyn, and Frank Daly's Meadowbrook Farm. In these lavish establishments, patrons danced to the latest big-band hits or popular love songs before returning to tables set with candles and flowers, and to a fresh round of expensive drinks. When the tuxedoed emcee announced Miss Betty Patrick, Harry would sprint onto the polished dance floor to set up her table and position himself to break her fall, and Betty would instruct the orchestra to break into something snazzy. In her hand-sewn, tiny black skirt and sequined blouse, she gave the house a show that impressed even the crustiest managers and reviewers.

"There were two shows each night—one at eight P.M. and one at eleven P.M.," Betty recalls. "By two A.M. the last floor show had ended, and I could relax and enjoy a meal on the house. They fed the performers well—filet mignon, oysters, whatever we wanted. I loved to have a thick steak." She pauses and looks at me closely. "In addition to my meals, I got two dollars a week. My father collected the pay and gave me my share after the booking agent got his. That seemed like a lot of money to me then."

"How much did the booking agent get?" I ask innocently. Immediately I feel the room filling with anger and realize that I have opened another can of worms.

"Sometimes I'd see my father talking with our agent in the club," Betty muses. "I knew his name. About a month after we had closed at the Red Mill, my father got angry about something—I can't even remember now—and he punched me in the eye. I suppose he thought that I would take it quietly, as usual, but I didn't. I had my own act. I told him that he was fired, that I could handle my own affairs. He stopped talking to me then. At home, we each acted as though the other were invisible."

Betty explains that she went back to the Red Mill and asked the management for the address of the agent with whom she had seen her father talking. The next morning she dressed as elegantly as possible, took the bus to the agent's offices, and explained to him that she had separated from her father and would be negotiating her own contracts in the future. "My agent was extremely businesslike and treated me very professionally and courteously," Betty recalls. "He told me that the Red Mill had liked me and would take me back if I could add a third number to my usual fast and slow acts. [A slow act consists of splits, cartwheels, kicks and dancing without difficult acrobatics.] He offered me forty dollars a week for two weeks and assured me that, with a third act, I could work year round. When I heard those figures, I just about died. I had assumed that Harry was pocketing some of my money when he gave me two dollars a week, but I had guessed that he was keeping only two or three dollars and giving the agent the rest. I signed a new contract and came home with my head very high. I was finally working on my own."

"What did you do for your third act?" I ask, imagining that there are probably just so many acrobatic tricks that one can do in a single night.

Betty grins sheepishly. "You know how I love Latin music. My mother had a pair of castanets and I borrowed them, then I got a Carmen Miranda-type outfit from the costume rental place. It had lots of colorful ruffles and a long train. When my number came up, I asked the band to play something fast—something Latin-sounding." Betty illustrates with a little clapping dance while she hums a lively tune that I have always associated with cartoons about Mexican mice. "When the curtain came up, there I stood, in my gorgeous costume, with my arms poised over my head like a flamenco dancer. The orchestra broke into a fiery introduction and I tried to clack my castanets, but I had never played them before. They're not easy. All that I could manage was one pitiful 'clop-clop.' The audience started to murmur, so I nodded to the band leader and he launched into my introduction once more. I held my hands high over my head and tried again—clop-clop. I could feel my face getting red."

Betty explains that she tried to ignore the loud snickers and titterings in the audience. She decided to forget the castanets, dance about the stage as charmingly as possible, and throw a few cartwheels. "I raised my arms and tried to do a Spanish twist, but when I kicked up my skirt with my heel, that darned trail caught on my shoe. I fell flat on my face." Betty chuckles. The audience laughed out loud, and in a desperate attempt to regain her stage presence, Betty smiled at the patrons and quipped, "That wasn't in the act!" As she turned to make a gracious exit, her train twisted around her legs and she tripped again. "I fell right on my face. The audience was howling," Betty recounts sadly, and I think that I have never felt closer to her during an interview.

"What did you do for your act after that?" I ask, intrigued, but Betty shakes her head hurriedly. "My face was bruised. The manager sent back a big steak—the crowd was roaring and he was delighted, but I was terribly embarrassed. I left the theater without speaking to anybody and took a taxi home. The next day I went back up to the agent's office and left four dollars—I figured that I owed him ten percent of my week's pay—along with a message that I wouldn't be coming back.

"I guess that down deep I wasn't quite sure if I had behaved appropriately," Betty muses, "because I ended up telling my father that I had quit. He was livid, of course. I remember shouting, 'If you're worried about the thirty-six dollars I made, you can have it,' and my father actually gagged. 'You fool,' he roared. 'You were doing three acts for forty dollars a week? He was paying three hundred fifty dollars a week for two acts when I handled your contract.' When I heard that, I packed my bags and left.

"I left home and went to Chicago," Betty says crisply, holding her head up with the same defiance that she must have felt as she boarded the bus for what she hoped would be an independent professional life far from her father. "I was only seventeen years old but I knew some people there. They worked on the Ringling show, and I think that they were partly cousins—somehow related through my mother's parents. I didn't call. I just showed up in town and they took me in. Performers are always like that. *Babes in Toyland* was opening in Chicago, and they took me right up to their agent for an audition. I signed a contract that very afternoon for two hundred fifty dollars! I couldn't wait to surprise my mother. I was going to be on Broadway!"

When Betty called home that evening, she could hardly contain her exhilaration. Charlie answered the phone and listened quietly as his breathless sister revealed that she was now a well-paid actress who would soon be performing on Broadway. When she had finished speaking, Charlie told her that she had to come home immediately because Babette was sick—very sick.

"I dropped the phone," Betty confesses. "Everything disappeared—my joy, my revenge, my hope. All that I could think about was being near my mama. Mama was a Christian Scientist and did not believe in doctors or hospitals. I knew that she needed me—that she had no one to depend on but me. I called the producer and told him that I had to cancel my contract and leave for New York instantly. He didn't believe what I was telling him. It was a huge Broadway show, and the pay was fabulous for those days. I said good-bye to my friends and raced back to the bus station."

"What was the matter with your mother?" I gasp.

Betty gives me a chilling look that I have never seen before. "She had a little cold."

~

I could not work much today—did not want to talk to Betty. I have finished with Babette's journals and want to give them back to Fritzi. It is weeks since I have seen her—months since we have spent much time together. Whenever I talk to her on the telephone now, she explains how busy she is. I know this is true; however, this time last year, we were meeting for breakfast at Leon's practically every morning. The waitresses knew us so well that they didn't even have to ask for our orders.

As Fritzi has grown increasingly dear to me, I realize that I could not have imagined a more perfect sister. Our similarities are uncanny and our differences seem complementary. Fritzi loves parties, is a chic dresser, and is known for dancing a night away. I am a studious and domestic person, seldom seen without books or a child in my arms, not flashy, always the designated driver for an evening out. We mystify the local crowd who cannot imagine on what foundation two such seemingly different women might build a friendship. When a bewildered acquaintance asked Fritzi what the two of us could possibly have in common, she laughed and responded, "We both love our husbands."

The deeper truth is that we share a commitment to lifelong learning and, for a while, enjoyed participating in one another's studies. Fritzi spent a weekend helping me with meticulous research for a book on eating disorders, and together we combed the archives of the Rare Book Collection at Duke University for material on early paper-bleaching techniques that she hoped to present at an international conference on papermaking in Australia. We did not distinguish between her work and mine.

We seemed to be siblings of a sort. As my children began to call Betty "Grandma Betty" and to invite her to their school activities, I started to call her "Mom," a name she encourages, and joked with Fritzi that we fuss about our "mother" just as two sisters might. When

Fritzi traveled out of town, I accompanied Betty to her doctor's appointment and ran her errands—just as I do for my own mother when we are together. On their last birthday (February 7), I threw Betty and Fritzi a mother-daughter party to celebrate their mutual special day. We invited several other mothers and their daughters, I cooked a meal, and we celebrated like a family.

My children know Fritzi as the fairy-tale aunt who has taught them to crab off a dock, can draw realistic tattoos on their arms, and has a witchlike ability to cure anything from acne to cold sores with homemade remedies. Last year, after consulting with my husband, I asked Fritzi if she would accept guardianship of our children in the event that we should ever die together. She and her husband considered my request and ultimately agreed. Al and I selected their lawyer to draw up a will and left them unconditionally all of our property and life insurance. It was the most crucial decision of my life.

Shortly after our return from the conference in Savannah last fall, Fritzi's husband, a property master in the film industry, decided to take time off from work, and my friend suddenly disappeared. She never left town; she simply stopped calling, stopped seeing me. During those long months, as I struggled with contract offers and big decisions, I found myself alternately confused, hurt, and frustrated by her sudden disregard. In the spring, her husband returned to work, and Fritzi called to explain that she had been "cocooning," a personal ritual that requires physical and emotional withdrawal from the world into seclusion, in order to reaffirm the romance of their marriage of five years.

I was stunned. I wondered how Fritzi would reaffirm her marriage if she were raising my children and suddenly decided that my perceptive, generous, intelligent friend had no idea what a demanding, full-time job parenting is. I also realized that she had no sense of how large a project I had taken on and how discouraged I was at having to pursue it alone. "It's your work," Fritzi insisted. "I can make time, but you'll have to give me notice. I'm very busy now." I didn't recognize my friend anymore. Had she "reinvented" herself, I wondered, recalling our conversation after the hurricane? She seemed to have become as much of a chameleon as her mother. I remembered how calmly Betty claimed to have been "too busy working" to think about her younger brother, and felt cold fear rising.

I complained to Fritzi one day that without academic support—clerical help and an office—I felt overwhelmed and could not juggle my family's needs and still get in the kind of workdays I needed to meet my contract deadline. "You have to train your family better," she counseled. I hung up the phone and fumed. I felt that she had left me dangling.

"Don't take it personally," my husband would soothe. "Fritzi doesn't think like you. She isn't used to working on a dozen things at once. She's probably like her mother—immediate, absorbed in whatever needs to be accomplished today. That can be a strength. It's what you liked about her, remember? She may think that you're too busy to see her." I shook my head. I felt betrayed, angry. I missed our friendship. "Just finish the book and everything will probably go back to normal," my husband urged. "Keep working."

$\sim$

In 1935 Harry returned to circus life with the Parroff Trio performing Roman Ladders. The act was a precarious one that Harry had designed himself. Atop a slim pole roughly ninety feet in the air, Harry had erected a small platform on which he would perch holding a free-standing ladder with each hand. With Harry acting as a brace, two partners would climb the ladders and perform acrobatic tricks while hanging from wrist or ankle braces—trusting their lives to Harry's sense of balance. The breathtaking finale involved a series of daring stunts done on a revolving ladder annexed to the two Roman ladders. The entire act was performed over the heads of a crowd several times each night without a net or any safety devices whatsoever.

"There were two other men in the act—Alex and Herman, both elderly," Betty explains.

"On the ladders! How elderly were they?" I ask, dismayed, and have to choke down my laughter when she replies, "Late twenties or early thirties." Betty was eighteen when her father took her and Charlie on the road, and I am apparently going to hear this story from an eighteen-year-old's point of view.

"I did my acrobatic act when we traveled. Charlie did nothing. We all lived in the car and Charlie and I slept in it."

"He must have hated that," I interrupt, thrilled that the forbidden subject is finally on the table. "Without school or work or friends—what an awful life for a child."

"He got everything he wanted." Betty pouts, and I decide to let her finish her story, but not until I whisper "Except love."

"He never talked," she explains. "Sometimes we would argue, but never in front of my father. Guess how we resolved all our disagreements? We would climb up the rigging and play cards on the platform. Whoever won the game won the argument."

"That was very civilized of you," I blurt out, impressed. My little brother and I employed far less mature strategies for conflict resolution.

Betty merely shrugs. "My father never thought of looking for us way up there. When he wasn't performing, he was drinking, and no one cared where we were. Harry never figured it out."

Quietly I make a note. In her conversations with me, Betty seldom calls Harry "Papa" or "Dad" although she always refers to Babette as "Mama." She tends to use "my father" when she is relating incidents from her childhood, "Harry" when she is speaking of her adult life. That she has just used both appellations in one breath suggests that she may regard this time in her life as transitional.

"How did you cook if you were living in the car? Surely you didn't eat out all the time?" I prompt her.

She stifles a grunt and looks at me as if I am a simpleton. "We didn't eat. Harry bought us a bottle of milk and a loaf of bread each morning. We had to live on that for the rest of the day while he went off to the bars and drank with his friends. We stole potatoes out of the fields and ate them raw—we were that hungry. We would find a cornfield and eat the corn raw. Charlie would go down one row and I would run down the next because you can get lost easily in a cornfield. The corn tasted good—full of juice. One time we gorged ourselves in a strawberry field and both broke out all over in little spots." She grins for a moment, then her face grows dark.

"When we weren't looking for food, my brother wandered about the fairgrounds or played cards with me. We didn't talk much. Charlie read everything that he could get his hands on—murder books, mysteries, promotional flyers. I sat in the car and embroidered things for my mother—pillow cases, table linens. They had taught me to embroider in the convent, and to crochet lace borders around hand-kerchiefs. I didn't see Charlie very often, but he seemed to know whenever Harry was coming and would always show up to warn me. We usually made it up the rigging before our father could find us, then we just waited until he'd gone away."

"Where did Charlie learn to read English?" I ask. Betty shrugs.

"Where was your mother?"

"Mama was playing clubs in the big northeastern cities that year," Betty recalls, her face softening. "We were at a fairground in Selins-grove, P.A., and Mama had just finished working in Philadelphia. She decided to visit us." Betty pauses and gives me a perplexed look. "I never asked how she got there."

"That's all right," I respond gently. "What happened when your mother saw how you were living?"

Betty thinks for a second. "Mama had taken a room in a board-inghouse. She found my father and asked where we were, and he told her that we were probably playing on the fairgrounds. Well, she came looking and there we were, curled up on the back car seat. We had half a loaf of bread left and were dividing it carefully. When Mama asked if we would like to go someplace to eat, we practically flew out of that car. She took us back to the boardinghouse for supper."

When Betty stops talking I look up quickly. Her face is filled with emotion—joy, pain, I cannot tell which. "Oh, Donna, that table was covered with food! The woman who owned the boardinghouse had fixed everything that she had for us—meat and potatoes and hot vegetables, fruit and bread and desserts. We were beside ourselves. We went at that meal like it was the last food on earth. Mama sobbed while she watched us. She turned on my father and cried, "Harry, they're hungry! They're starving!" but my father told her that children didn't need much food or they got fat. Mama insisted that she wanted us home but my father had three weeks of bookings left. He wouldn't let her take either one of us. When she went back to New York, she left us alone with Harry. Alone again with Harry."

Betty glares at me angrily. "I'll tell you what was the worst. You know, back then they didn't have Kotex. I had to ask my father for rags—he would save them for me. I had to go find him in the bar and he would holler after me, 'I've got lots of rags in the back of the truck for when you've got your business.' He would make sure every guy in the bar heard him. I was mortified. Once I was about a week late. I never counted the days but my father did. He slapped me and screamed that I was a whore. What had I been doing? When I got it a week later, he gave me a nickel to buy ice cream. That was my big reward for being a good girl." She glares indignantly, then seems to see me and softens her voice. "I tried to be happy, but he hated everything about me. No matter what I did, it was wrong, and he let me know, too—with black eyes and swollen lips. And you wonder why I don't try to make a good man out of a bad one?"

Betty leans back in her chair. I can tell that she is tired. It has been a difficult interview, and I have begun to gather my notes when she brings up Charlie unexpectedly, almost urgently. "You know, he was a spoiled brat. My father gave him everything. After Mama left, my father bought him a motorcycle and started giving him thirty-five dollars a week! I got nothing. Charlie stayed in nice hotel rooms while I had to sleep in the car. I had to carry Charlie's bags up to his room." Her voice is high-pitched with anger. I say nothing, but my stomach twists. I think about Harry's arrangement with the Liazeeds to pay off his debts with Betty's services. Charlie was a stunningly handsome boy who would later be hired to impersonate Superman. Reviewers would call him a "modern Atlas." I do not want to think about why Harry rented hotel rooms for his comely thirteen-year-old son and paid him large sums of money; it seems highly unlikely that he did so out of fatherly affection—or for nothing.

~

Fritzi's voice is flat when she answers the phone. She says that her back is out again. My maternal, protective instinct is instantly triggered. I urge my friend to do something nice for herself, and she admits that she has made an appointment to get a massage and is going out to dinner with friends tonight. "Good, good. You take care of yourself, girl. Call me when you've had some rest."

I hang up the phone and lean back against the kitchen counter. I feel guilty that I have been pushing her for interview time. I mentally will my friend to relax. If she were not going out, I would invite her over for dinner. I imagine Fritzi treading barefoot through her clean, contemporary home. I visualize the skylights that shine onto her off-white furniture, glass-topped tables, reachable fine artwork. Suddenly my body is shaking and I realize that I am—what? Furious? Jealous? Sad?

The screen saver on my computer is spitting stars at me. Behind me on the floor, a pile of laundry seems for a moment to be wriggling. The kids will be home from school soon. I am tired. Why did I call Fritzi? I start to push the laundry toward the washing machine with my foot, then suddenly grab the phone back up and peck out a long-distance number. My mom answers. "Oh, it's you, honey! I was just thinking about you. How's the book coming? How are my kids?" I swallow my tears and we talk.

~

Betty has a selection of tea bags laid out on the counter and my cup filled before I can get indoors and set down the tape recorder. We have fallen into a comfortable routine. We will record for a few hours, then she is going to make me one of her two proudest lunches— chicken à la king over macaroni, or hot tomato and cheese sandwiches pressed in her electric sandwich machine. "Nineteen thirty-five," I remind her as she clears a place for my cup on the cluttered dining room table. I wonder if I will be able to relate the events of single years from my youth when I am eighty-one years old. I doubt if I could do it now. You have to love her.

Betty hits the ground running—right where we left off last week. "Mama was working again when we got home," she tells me. "Billy Rose had opened 'Small Time Cavalcade' and Mama loved working for Rose. He always called her 'Tiny.' Isn't that funny?"

I nod, smiling. "And where were you working?" I ask. I have decided that Betty's life story will need to be woven from tales of jobs found, lost, quit, or sought after; work is the most important and cohesive factor in her life. It would be easy to construct her story like a typical man's biography of accomplishments, easy to miss reading the signals that jobs seem to function as signposts for Betty, signals that relationships may have become dysfunctional or valuable, clues to what her own unexplored needs might be.

"My father had booked me into Frank Daly's Meadowbrook Farm again."

"Did you do a Latin dance?" I tease, and she shakes her head, smiling.

"No—worse than that. The first night, he told me, 'Put the new trick in.' He wanted me to do a jackley drop to the dance floor. I was terrified but I knew better than to argue. You know how in a normal flip-flop you go up, turn over, bounce off of your hands, and come down on your feet?"

I don't, but I nod anyway, and she buys it.

"Well, I was trying to turn full circle without bouncing off of my hands first. I should have landed on my feet but I came down on my knee. Knocked it right out. My father had to carry me off the stage and I lost the engagement." She pulls up her cotton housedress and traces a long scar that winds around her kneecap.

"I hope your father felt like hell," I murmur, and Betty practically leaps out of her chair.

"Humph! He wouldn't even take me to a doctor. He soaked and bandaged my leg himself, and all the while he was crying 'Years of training and you blow it in one night! Thanks a lot!' He told my mother, 'See, she's no good. She's not worth training.' All he could think about was how much money he had lost."

Several nights after Betty's accident, Harry told his daughter that he was going downtown to pick up her mother at the theater. Babette waited for him on the dark steps outside the stage door, but he never showed up. "He disappeared completely," Betty recalls. "Days went by. Mama was worried sick. She had to go to work each night, not knowing whether her husband was alive or dead. Sophie Tucker told everyone how impressed she was that my mama could perform flawlessly when she had so much emotional pain to bear." Betty looks up at me and grins. "I guess that she'd never met my father." I chuckle and she continues in rare good humor: "Charlie was home with me when a man came to the door asking if we knew a Harry Schutz." I throw Betty a look and we shout in unison, "Never heard of him!" then fall back in our chairs, laughing. Cool weather has finally arrived and we are both feeling rather flippant. "We should have. I wish we had"—she snickers—"but we were good children. We called Mama and she raced right over to Bellevue Hospital."

Harry had left the house to pick up his wife wearing his "downtown" clothes. "He always dressed to pick up Mama," Betty explains. "When the police found him, he had been beaten over the head and robbed of his wallet, camel-hair coat, buffed shoes, and cashmere socks. He was drunk and delirious. They took him to the ward where they keep people who are going to die." Again, we look at each other and pull a face, "Awwww!" but Betty suddenly grows serious and launches into a muddled story about a foreign doctor who was convinced that Harry was on the brink of death and gave him a syringe of something experimental that cured him.

"Come on, now," I reason. "Harry was only drunk; he wasn't dying. And how could he have known what they gave him?"

"My father heard them talking," Betty insists, suddenly petulant. "He heard the doctor say 'He'll be dead soon, so why not try it.' And he was not just drunk, he was crazy."

I do not point out that a crazy person's memories are seldom to be trusted. This is obviously one of those hand-me-down stories in families that one does not question. "How crazy?" I mutter.

Betty gives me a big smirk. "He thought Mama was a whore." We both burst into choking laughter.

When Babette came to his bedside and tenderly took his hand, murmuring "It's me, Harry. I'm here now," Harry pushed his wife away.

"Look at you! You've been out prostituting again, you whore!" he ranted in his heavy accent, and the doctors and nurses must have struggled to hide their amusement. With her massive shoulders and muscled arms, Babette could probably have passed for a member of the vice squad more easily than as a prostitute, but her stricken face must have hinted that she was a better wife than the foul-mouthed man in the bed deserved.

"Where've you been all this time?" Harry shouted at his wife. "You went out whoring and left me here to die!" A disgusted doctor jumped to Babette's aid, explaining that no one had known if Harry's ravings could be trusted. Harry had been identified only because a patient in the next bed had heard him mutter an address and had asked his son to investigate. Harry pouted and was quiet.

"Mama came to get my father with a baby carriage and wheeled him home," Betty tells me, and at first I assume that she is pulling my leg. Babette used the buggy in numerous cities over the course of several decades. "When she would show up at the jail with her cute accent and baby carriage, the police would fall all over themselves to help her. She would tell them, 'Oh, sir, I am so ashamed. He has never done dis before. He has on his mind so many problems,' and they would let Harry go with a warning. Mama would plop him in the carriage and take him home for a bath." Betty laughs, but I cannot join her. The imagery is too sobering.

～

Betty started 1936, at the age of nineteen, determined to resume her work, in spite of her injury. Babette was busy rehearsing *Jumbo* and had a frantic schedule; Harry avoided the daughter who, he said, had "ruined" a career for which he had dedicated himself to her training. A German neighbor, Hans Schroeder, had just opened a restaurant with a rehearsal hall behind it, complete with a hanging trapeze; although the hall usually rented by the hour, Schroeder allowed Harry's daughter to practice all day whenever she wished. She began slowly, nursing her swollen knee, unsure of whether the best strategy would be to nurture it until it healed or to toughen it with immediate exercise. A troupe of Hungarian acrobats rented the hall while she was practicing one afternoon and watched her routine carefully. One of the tumblers approached her shyly with a rubber kneecap. "I loved performing. I could work pretty good when I was wearing it." Betty smiles. "Nobody needed to know that I had been hurt."

It was Babette who found Betty her next job. "A new show was looking for girls to take to England," Betty tells me, and I feel her excitement throbbing almost tangibly around us as she recalls the offer. "The manager's daughter had worked with my mother in Cuba, so she asked Mama if I was available. Mama wanted me away from my father. All he ever talked about was how I had destroyed his life by getting hurt. He said that I was born to be a whore. Mama had so many problems with him that whenever I tried to talk to her, I always ended up listening to her problems instead. She never explained anything to me about men. Maybe she didn't understand them either."

The girls played in the States in 1936, then traveled to England in 1937. Betty looks radiant in her passport photograph, suave in a dark high-necked sweater and a wavy, clingy hairdo. The troupe performed at the Brighton Hippodrome, then to a packed house at the London Palladium. "We had to dye our hair blond." Betty snickers. "When I sent my mother home a photograph, she thought that I looked like a gangster's moll."

"Did you make friends with the other girls?" I ask quickly, wondering if Betty could have gotten through the years of her late adolescence with only her mother as a girlfriend.

"There were three others," Betty slowly recounts. "One was the boss's lesbian girlfriend—they sort of stayed to themselves—one was nice but got drunk all the time, and the third was very quiet—not like me."

I laugh. "No, you're not quiet. That's for sure."

"But there was a boy," she offers in a hushed voice, and suddenly we are both speaking softly, as if we are talking about a child who died.

His name was Pip and he played in the band at the Hippodrome. One night he went backstage and asked if he might take Miss Patrick out after the show. "He picked me up every night after that." Betty sighs. "We would dance or just walk under the lights. He never tried to kiss me—he was very respectful—but he told me that he loved me." She looks at me sadly.

"Well? What happened to him?" I prod eagerly.

"You know, British theaters are just like American ones, except the Palladium had a slanted stage," Betty begins; I have to stifle the urge to interrupt her, but it turns out that she knows exactly where her circuitous story is going.

"There was a comedy act on before us and they had to spill a glass of water," Betty explains hurriedly. "A stagehand was supposed to mop it up between the acts, but the water ran down the stage and he missed some."

When the curtain opened again, Betty had to dance onto the stage with a cane that she would suddenly tilt, balance on, then flip over. Three months into their British tour, the girls lost their best acrobat when Betty set her cane down in the puddle and it slipped out from under her as she tried to somersault over it. "I was supposed to land on my feet, but I came down on my back with my knee bent under me," Betty recalls, wincing at the memory. "My bad knee."

"You could have sued," I insist, and Betty shakes her head.

"I know that now, but back then I didn't know anything. The boss was terrified, though, that if I sued the theater, agents wouldn't book the act any more. She made me sign some kind of a waiver and then packed me off on the next boat to America."

"Did you see Pip again?" I ask quickly, uncertain if she still remembers the purpose of her story, and she chuckles at my impatience.

"Oh, yes. He came to the train station when I left and asked if he could kiss me. I thought, well, it's about time. You know, he kissed me on the forehead! He said that he would be seeing me again soon, but that didn't seem very likely.

"When I got back home, we moved to Woodside, Long Island," Betty continues quickly, and I decide simply to let this frustrating story take its own course. "There was a family on the next block that I visited sometimes, and below them lived a nice young truck driver named Moe.* He was dark-haired and handsome. One day he cornered me on the sidewalk and asked if I was the girl from the theater that his neighbors were always talking about, and he asked me out."

"Where did he take you?" I ask, hoping for a story of 1930s romance, and she laughs at my earnestness.

"Home, silly—for three months the only place he ever took me was home. His parents must have been dead because his brothers were still living in their house. They were all builders—nice boys. They would cook big dinners and make me darn all their socks!"

"I cannot imagine you darning socks." I laugh, and she shakes her head furiously.

"Nope, it wasn't for me. I had to think of some way to break our engagement."

I stare, then realize that my mouth is open and shut it fast. "You were engaged?"

"Of course, I had five or six engagement rings at one time and had to remember which one to wear whenever I went out." Betty laughs. I search every inch of her face for signs that she is teasing me, but I do not see any of the usual telltale twitches or twinkles.

"You had better tell me about them in order," I murmur, quickly scribbling a new topic on my notepad: "Lovers."

"Later, if you're good," Betty teases. "I couldn't work with my knee out and I didn't want to live with my father any more, so marrying Moe seemed like a pretty fine idea. I just didn't want to marry his whole family. After a while, I started to see other boys, so I told Moe that I had to work out of town. I would write him a letter, stick it in the envelope, and enclose it in another envelope along with a note to the manager of a hotel in another city. I'd stayed in so many boardinghouses and hotels with the Liazeeds that I had a long list of addresses. In my note to the manager, I'd say, 'Please give this letter to Mr. [name omitted] when he stops on May 5. If he does not stop, kindly forward to the address on the envelope.' Moe would get a letter from me postmarked from another city and I'd be dating other guys."

Betty chuckles smugly as she relates this complicated stratagem, and I find myself starting to feel vaguely uncomfortable. "Why didn't you just break the engagement?" I ask, genuinely perplexed. "Why not just be honest?" Betty instantly stops smiling and stares at me; I can see that she considers my question a sign of naïveté at best and moral righteousness at worst. She does not answer my question—a potentially bad sign.

The topic of lovers is a juicy one, however, and she soon resumes her story with relish. "Want to know how I finally got rid of Moe? His brother took him out with another girl once when I was supposedly out of town. I heard about it. I confronted him and accused him of having cheated on me while I was working. I said, 'You couldn't have missed me much. You said that you loved me.' That was the end of Moe."

In the silence that follows, Betty beams at me with self-satisfaction, and I glance quickly over my notes for any other topic to which I can lead her.

"Did you ever hear from Pip again?" I ask softly. Her face clouds over. "I had figured that I would never see him again, but I was sitting in my mother's kitchen with Moe one day when who showed up at the door but Pip. He said, 'I've come for you,' and Moe told him, 'Well, too bad. She's engaged to me.' Pip had actually come to America to ask me to marry him! He went back to England before I could talk to him again. He never wrote. Tough, huh?" Betty smiles darkly, and I suddenly understand that Moe and the Palladium accident have relevance to her now only as signposts to a lost opportunity. This story has been about Pip all along.

~

The afternoon has been growing dark while we have been talking, and rain begins to patter on Betty's roof before I rise and turn off the recorder, then settle back down for what I hope will be a conversation between two women. I know that Betty considers me a sheltered girl, too entrenched in my eighteen-year marriage, motherly duties, and intellectual pursuits to be able to understand her romantic and sexual escapades. Jobs have been easy to talk about. We are both hard workers in fields that we love, and we share a strong sense of professional integrity. Betty knows that I have just lost a career position for reasons that we both consider shallow and unfair. Because my professional history includes scars like hers, in her view, I am a confederate who has earned a certain amount of trust.

My love life, on the other hand, has been pleasantly mild with no major upheavals—not to be compared with Betty's many loves, engagements, and marriages. Betty and her two children have had nine marriages between them, putting me at a distinct disadvantage as a family biographer who is perceived to be something of an "outsider" anyway because I do not share a circus background.

It is important to me that Betty be able to discuss her relationships openly, that she trust my ability to depict this important side of her being. Silence about sexuality has been a tradition of women's autobiography, according to Wagner-Martin, largely because the complex sexuality of the unconventional, venturesome woman often opens her story to negative judgments.[3] While Betty does not consider herself promiscuous, she is all too aware that others might define her in this way. "My father always said that I must be a whore because apples never fall far from the tree," she tells me, referring sarcastically to Harry's pride in his own constant marital infidelities, and I remind myself that I must be very careful with my portrayal of this woman whose innocence, daring, and independence must have been in continual conflict throughout her life.

It is the first woman-to-woman talk that we have had, and I can tell that she is impatient with it, but I am determined to experiment. I know that she does not want to hear too much about me, prefers to talk about herself. The audience is not supposed to ask the storyteller to sit down and listen, after all. I tell her of my past boyfriends, especially of a young Frenchman I met while studying in England twenty years ago. He was a divinity student at Cambridge, philosophically witty and darkly handsome, and I fell head over heels. Our friendship had just reached the stage of what I hoped was romantic promise when he disappeared. British authorities had deported him to France where he was wanted for having refused mandatory national military service. In a letter sent from prison, he told me of his affection, of how we would share a bottle of wine in Paris when he obtained his freedom.

I determined that I would follow him. I studied so intensely for the next six months that I was awarded a scholarship to spend a semester in France. Letters told me that he had been released into the custody of his family, that he had been allowed to substitute community work for military service, that he was eager to see me again.

I was living in a crowded house with a family of six in Grenoble when I received the envelope that should have contained the time and place of our meeting. I read the letter quickly, then threw it away. Over the next few months, I made my way across Europe to Africa, met many new friends, had wonderful adventures, but could not escape the sense that something crucial had been amputated from my being and had left a hungry pain in its place.

I tell Betty this story, and others. There has been no violence in my past, no horror or devastation, but perhaps enough disappointment and frustrated hope to convince her that I understand these universal and timeless feelings.

The following evening Fritzi calls. "Mom says that you told her yesterday about all the times that you didn't get laid," she quips, laughing heartily. I hang up the phone and wrestle with nameless, complicated feelings. By morning I have determined to stop trying to be the perfect scholarly biographer, the selfless daughterly confidante, the pliable friend giving sisterly advice. I will simply present Betty's story as she tells it, along with whatever feelings it creates in me. I will trust my instincts as a writer and claim control over my own project.

~

"In 1937 I went up to Frank Wirth's office [an agent] looking for work, and a comedian happened to be there at the same time. His name was Don,*" Betty relates, and I breathe a sigh of relief. Today we are evidently going to talk about jobs. "My knee was bad, but I didn't intend to let that stop me from working. Don pulled me aside and told me that he needed an acrobatic partner. No hard tricks—I just had to do a cartwheel with him." She notices the quizzical look on my face and pauses. "He'd do a headstand, I'd hold his feet, he'd grab my waist, and we'd go over together. Can you picture that?" I nod sheepishly, and she resumes her story. "There was a dog in the act, too. The dog would roll itself into a carpet and I was supposed to try to get her out. In the end, the dog got a steak and I got a bone." Betty smiles, and I wish once again that I could somehow go back in time and watch her on stage.

On the road with Don, Betty got a new taste of how much fun a performer's life could be. The Liazeeds had been very protective of her while they traveled, and Betty had seldom been able to socialize outside of her own troupe. "They weren't paying me but they didn't want to lose me," Betty muses. "If Papa Haji caught me speaking with other acrobats, he would command, 'Girlie, get in the dressing room!' Heck, we were just talking. He'd tell me, 'That troupe needs another girl in the act. They'll offer you good money, but you'll never see any of it.' What could I do but believe him?"

Eventually Haji ordered Betty to pretend that she was an Arab and could not speak English at all. When the other performers would ask her, "Why is your skin so white?" Betty would answer in exotic Arabic, "Good morning. How are you?" Because Elvira was German, it was assumed that fair-skinned Betty Liazeed was her non-English-speaking daughter. "Elvira had miscarried her only child and could never have another one." Betty sighs. "Maybe that's why she loved me and my children so much."

At age twenty Betty Patrick was no longer part of a troupe and could talk with anyone she pleased. "I met some great people," she tells me as we flip through her yellowing scrapbooks of autographed headshots. "Bob Hope was around then, but he was still a small fish. Fanny Brice was working that circuit, and Buddy Rogers, and Olive and George—they were midgets. I used to give them massages between shows. Joe Penner was a nice guy." I shake my head and she laughs. "Wanna buy a duck? That was his line. I worked with Xavier Cugat at the Detroit Hippodrome. He was a band leader who played fabulous Cuban music. I still have some records. I got along well with his first wife, Carmen Castillo. Jack Benny was a pain in the neck. He tried to get into everybody's act. Dorothy Lamour was very beautiful, but she never talked to us. We were beneath her, I guess. I worked with Eleanor Holm back when she was married to Art Garrett. He was a band leader, you know. She divorced him to marry Billy Rose." I smile. Betty is still an avid reader of celebrity news. These were big stories once.

Betty browses through the scrapbook casually, occasionally pausing wistfully over a photograph of a dapper young fellow or a red-lipped woman in a sizzling gown. She recites the names of people who must have been famous in her own day but mean nothing to me. She lingers a long time over a picture of three handsome men with slicked back hair. "Those were the Ritz Brothers." She sighs.

"The neighbors who shot at your father?" I ask.

"Yes"—she chuckles—"but there was more to it than that."

Harry Ritz was in his thirties when seventeen-year-old Betty first joined the performance circuit. It must have been as obvious to him that the dark-haired teenager had a crush on him as it was to Babette. When he invited Betty over to sunbathe on his roof, normally tolerant Babette flatly insisted that Betty stay home. "I never quite got over that." Betty laughs. The Liazeeds knew how much Betty liked the eldest Ritz Brother, as well. In her innocence, she had confided her hopes to Elvira and Haji. They played a trick that taught Betty to be particularly cautious about sharing secrets of the heart.

The Liazeeds were playing the Roxy Theatre in New York, and Betty was able to live with her parents and take a bus to the theater each morning for rehearsals. "I used to stop at Walgreens every morning for coffee and a doughnut, then go up to the dressing rooms," Betty remembers. "One morning Elvira met me as I was shuffling in and cried, 'Oh, good—you're in! You've still got time to catch him.

Harry Ritz was just here a minute ago asking for you. He wants to take you to breakfast. We told him that you were probably at Walgreens.'"

Betty's heart was pounding as she tumbled down the three flights of theater stairs and raced down the street. She flew into Walgreens and frantically searched the diner for the young man who would soon become a movie star, but only a few elderly gentlemen still sat at the counter sipping coffee. When Betty breathlessly questioned the boy behind the counter, she was assured that Harry Ritz had had breakfast sent to his hotel room—as usual.

Betty trudged slowly back to the theater where her dismal face caused a roomful of Liazeeds to break into open laughter. It was April Fool's Day. "I cried," Betty murmurs softly. "It wasn't funny to me. I wrote Mr. Ritz nice polite letters when I was out of town but he never answered them, so I stopped. I didn't tell Elvira about those letters. No one needed to know about them but me."

Betty starts to flip through the rest of the album rather quickly, but I lay my hand across hers when I spy a glossy shot of an extremely youthful Red Skelton. Betty grins from ear to ear. "Boy, did he pull one on me." She chuckles. "I was working with Don. Red and his wife, Georgia, were booked with us, and they were good friends with Wally Brown, who did an act with a midget named Annette. One morning Wally and Red decided to go golfing and asked me to come along. I'd never golfed, but Georgia said, 'Go, Betty. You'll have a good time and get some sun.'"

When they arrived at the club, Red told Betty that the first thing that she needed to learn was how to balance the bags and identify the clubs. Eighteen holes later, she was still lugging both bags. "If I complained, they would tell me, 'When you've learned the clubs, you can hit the ball.'" She laughs. "By the time we had to leave for the theater, I was exhausted and I still had to do two acrobatic acts that night.

"Georgia came to my dressing room and asked how I had enjoyed the game," Betty recalls, and gives me a wry grin. "I told her, 'I'm tired! It took me so long to learn the clubs and how to carry the bags that we didn't have time to play another game.' Georgia stared and then burst into laughter. 'Betty, those stinkers made a caddy out of you. They usually hire a boy to carry their bags.'" Betty gives me a wicked look. "That's how our feud began. Everybody in the theater knew that I was out to get Red and Wally. The trouble was that we thought alike. One time all three of us jumped out of our dressing rooms into the hall shooting squirt guns at the same time. Boy, what brains we had—we'd come up with the same corny idea! Georgia decided to help me out. She placed a cup of water above their door and I kept Red talking as we came up the stairs after the show. When he reached his room, he was forced to back in while he finished answering me. Splash! He told me, 'I'll get you, kiddo.' The next morning the entire crew was laughing when I came out of my room and found a Kotex pad hanging from the doorknob. I was mortified. The stagehands howled when Red put his arm around me and said, 'Isn't it your time, kid? Just wanted to be a gentleman and help you out.'"

"I'd have killed him." I laugh, and Betty smiles.

"Oh, Red strutted like a peacock after that. He knew that he'd won. I was a teaser, too," Betty assures me. "Harry Richmond worked with us in Canada. He played the piano and kept to himself. Everyday he would play solitaire. I told the stagehands not to tell him that I had slipped one card out of the deck. For a whole week he tried to win a game and couldn't. Everybody could see how frustrated he was getting. On the last day of our engagement, I shook his hand shyly and said, 'It's been nice working with you, Mr. Richmond.' Then I handed back his card and ran. He didn't say a word. The stagehands said that he just stood there staring at the card while everyone laughed.

"The hardest audiences are in Boston. They never laugh at anything," Betty mumbles, then looks up proudly and says, "but they laughed at me. I was funnier than I knew. Clowning around is just my nature, you know?" I nod, grinning. She *is* funny. "One night those Hungarian acrobats were on the same bill with us—remember my friends who gave me the kneecap at Schroeder's rehearsal hall? They came backstage and told Don that they had never laughed so hard in their lives—that I was hilarious." Betty grows quiet suddenly. "Don fired me right then and there," she whispers, and I pause in midsip and put down my teacup. "He told me, 'The act has only one comedian and that's me!' He paid for my bus fare back to New York City and there I was—at home all over again, with my mother and Harry."

The room is still. I understand now why Fritzi told me to consult her mother on how to cope with abrupt endings. Throughout months of interviews, not one story that I have heard has included any sort of closure. Her relationships merely broke, her opportunities shattered one after another. "I had just come home when we heard that my brother Harry had died. He was twenty-three years old," Betty relates quietly. "I tried not to think about it, but somehow, that changed things. I decided to have my knee operated on." She rubs her leg gently, and I feel anger swelling. "I went to that hospital where the athletes go. They opened the wrong side and took the cartilage out." She pauses, gauges my shock. "When it still bothered me after a few months, I went back for an examination and they admitted that they had made a mistake. They wanted to open the other side then and take out more cartilage. Can you imagine? I wasn't going to take another chance. I went back to Schroeder's and started to rehearse right away, before my leg could get any stiffer. I decided that nothing was going to get in my way any more. By the time the 1939 World's Fair opened, I could tumble pretty well. That's when my father started speaking to me again. It seemed like a good chance to make a fresh start."

～

New Yorkers called it the greatest peacetime migration in history. Millions streamed to the World's Fair of 1939 to enjoy the newest scientific discoveries, the most advanced industrial techniques, and the most progressive social and educational ideas, all dedicated to a single theme: the building of a peaceful, enlightened "World of Tomorrow." The very existence of the fair seemed proof that miracles might be accomplished through visionary planning, imaginative financing, and a strong dose of good will. In selecting a site, city officials and fair planners had taken the long view; they had chosen Flushing Meadows, a vast, 1,216-acre, debris-filled bog of stagnant pools and evil odors, and transformed it into a brilliantly engineered and romantically beautiful municipal park.

In his fine study *1939: The Lost World of the Fair*, writer David Gelernter recalls the majestic park in glorious detail.[4] From the theme center, with its pure white Trylon tower, avenues stretched away like spokes of a wheel, each with its own progression of gradually deepening tones of primary colors culminating in a burst of brilliant red, gold, or blue. At night, the multicolored lights drenching the sky over the fair were visible for miles. On the Lagoon of Nations, 1,400 water nozzles, 400 gas jets, and hundreds of fireworks containers produced a stupendous play of super fountains, soaring flames, and pyrotechnics, synchronized with music and special color effects from giant searchlights. The "inferno" display over Fountain Lake was even more staggering. Each night, to the cacophonous accompaniment of a symphony orchestra, searchlights brightened colored smoke produced by titanium tetrachloride and bursting rockets; huge gas burners shot colored flames 150 feet into the air, and brilliant fireworks sprinkled the sky with red, green, blue, and silver diamonds.

To restless Betty Schultz, fresh from another abortive venture and living at home once more, the World's Fair must have seemed like a fabulous, enchanting dream. The Amusement Area alone covered 280 acres and boasted a fantastic array of eye-dazzling, quarter-luring open-air rides, exotic shows, zoos, music festivals, fireworks, and aqua shows. The *1939 Official Guide Book* invited fairgoers to wander through the crooked streets and village greens of "Merrie England," enjoy Punch and Judy shows, listen to Welsh choral singing, or experience Shakespearean drama in a replica of the Globe Theatre. They could drink beer beneath the windmill of "Heineken's Dutch Tavern on the Zuider Zee," hurtle at stomach-jolting, ninety-degree angles on the bobsled ride, or take a daring parachute jump. They could visit the deep southern polar region, with its live penguins and albatross, view Admiral Byrd's Antarctic trail camp and personal team of Eskimo huskies. A quarter allowed the inquisitive guest to explore the splendor of a Manchu dynasty emperor's palace with its treasured Gautama Buddha; watch the "Cavalcade of Centaurs" as they performed stellar feats of horsemanship on some of the handsomest mounts in the world; and invade dark forests of Central Africa full of man-eating giant cats and gorgeously plumed birds, meet Ubangi tribesmen, giraffe-necked women, headhunters, and tribal phantoms.

Children could enjoy an exhibition of more than thirty thousand wild animals and birds, with its famed rare sea creatures and giant panda. While their offspring were enjoying the exhibits in "Children's World," adults might visit the "Congress of World's Beauties," gawk at "Nature's Mistakes," climb the two-hundred-foot "Sky Ride," or explore the cosmos in the "Theatre of Time and Space." In the tauntingly suggestive walk-through spectacles along the Great White Way, scantily clad Amazon princesses performed feats of gladiation before bulb-eyed male patrons. The Arctic girl allowed herself to be entombed in 1,400 pounds of solid ice, protecting herself from its frigid sting through self-hypnosis. Lovely diving girls revealed the secrets of Salvador Dalí's hidden dreams. In the mammoth Aquacade Amphitheater, 10,000 people at a time watched the magnificent water pageantry for which Billy Rose was famous.

~

"I could have worked the burlesque. You didn't have to take off your clothes—just prance around in little outfits," Betty explains. "They offered me $350 for thirty-two weeks, but my father wouldn't let me take that. He said that those girls were whores." She shakes her head at the irony of Harry passing moral judgment on showgirls. "My father arranged a job for forty dollars a week. I worked from eight A.M. until three or four in the afternoon. There was a show every five minutes."

Betty had no idea what an Amazon was when she presented herself at the "Amazon's in No-Man's Land" exhibit. The official guidebook described the walk-through show as a Grecian spectacle of ancient design, performed by "athletic women whose sole purpose is to display the harmony and beauty of the perfect feminine physique in action." From behind a high glass wall, quarter-paying customers viewed a stage on which the large-bosomed Amazon queen lounged, clad only in a rhinestone G-string, while young girls in tiny mesh panties and nude-colored mesh bras sported about her, performing temple rituals, wrestling, dancing, and competing in various gymnastic contests involving conspicuous frontal bouncing. "The queen would demand someone's head, and two of the discus throwers would bring her a head on a platter and then dance for her," Betty remembers. "I didn't understand the story. They didn't teach us about the Amazons in the convent."

The boss met the new girl behind the stage and handed her a pair of flesh-colored panties and a tiny triangle of mesh to string over her breasts. "You do somersaults and cartwheels," he told her. The dark-curled beauty stared at the ball of mesh in her hand, then slowly shook her head and held out the costume. Blushing, she explained, "I can't do acrobatic in this. I'll fall out when I turn over." "Then turn fast," the boss muttered, shoving the scraps of cloth back at her. "Your father signed a contract. Now put that on and get to work."

Betty pranced and shot arrows all day, one of dozens of anonymous girls amusing hundreds of thousands of unknown eyes. When her shift ended, she charged back to the tiny dressing room and stuffed her sopping costume into her purse. That night she and Babette sat on their bed, sorting through piles of buttons and fake gems. "I sewed rhinestones onto every inch of that costume so that no one would think that I was naked." Betty smiles. "It was so sheer. You could see the hair line! I was glad when they closed that show."

"What do you mean, 'they closed the show'?" I ask. "Did it shut down before the fair ended?"

Betty smirks and shakes her head. "You really kill me. The police closed it down. These were girlie shows. They got raided all the time. Do you understand now?"

"But I thought that the fair was a family exhibition," I reply.

"Well, yes, but people knew which exhibits were for children and which ones weren't. If there was a chain of bally girls out front, it obviously was going to be an adult show. The police were always raiding. There was supposed to be a big strip show at NTG one night, but the cops were there before they could even start it."

It was a good time to be young and comely. Betty quickly found herself another job as a bally girl for the "Enchanted Forest" miniature illusion show. Her task was to stand outside the gate and beckon to passersby, urging them to visit the nymphs within. For a quarter, the curious customer could peer through a telescopic eyehole and behold tiny girls dancing merrily, clad only in three strategically positioned gardenias. "They were supposed to drop the gardenias on the top at the end of their routine"—Betty smiles—"but the girls always dropped the one on the bottom, too. It was a thrill. That show got raided all the time."

One afternoon Betty returned from a pleasant lunch to find a paddy wagon pulled up outside the show gate and the nymphs being herded onto its rough benches for a ride to the precinct headquarters. Before Betty could open her mouth, a gardenia-clad showgirl called out, "If you see Betty Patrick, tell her that we're all in jail." "And who are you?" the arresting officer demanded. When Betty responded meekly that she was Betty Patrick's sister, that her sibling was ill and had sent Betty for her clothes, the officer grunted, "Lucky her," and slammed the wagon door closed.

"The boss would bail them out and they would be back in an hour." Betty shrugs. "He would warn them not to drop that last gardenia, but they always did. I left that job. The cops kept raiding. It was just a matter of time until my luck ran out."

Betty wandered the vast Amusement Area, presenting herself to proprietors and bosses, asking hopefully if they could use an acrobat. She auditioned for the "Old New York" show, a gay-1890s entertainment program staged in the gas-lighted replica of a village from a bygone era, complete with hansom cabs, organ grinders, Bowery newspaper boys, a tattooing parlor, an old blacksmith's shop, and a night court. The stage show featured impersonations of such former "toasts of the town" as Lillian Russell, Elfie Fay, and Lily Langtry. Betty performed the comedy acrobatic act perfectly—until it came time for her to end in a split. She only managed an awkward squat. "All of our girls do splits," the boss informed her gruffly, so she swallowed her disappointment and headed back out onto the strollway.

At the NTG "Congress of World's Beauties" show, featuring stripper Sally Rand, the boss was not particular about splits. In a huge outdoor enclosure, sixty gorgeous "devotees of health through sunshine" performed six shows daily. Betty was handed a G-string and told to turn somersaults in the fake outdoor garden adjoining the stage. This time she wisely said nothing, quietly walked back to the dressing room, and donned the black sequined top and satin skating skirt in which she had performed at the Red Mill. Late that afternoon, the manager noticed a conspicuously covered girl frolicking in the sun and screamed, "What is that weed doing in my garden?" Betty was instructed to finish the day and get out.

"I had gotten smart by that time and joined AFA [the entertainers' union]," Betty explains happily. "When Dalí fired me, I couldn't collect any pay because he had let me go on the spot. The NTG boss made a big mistake when he told me to finish out the day. I reported him to AFA. I had worked more than half a day and my work had been satisfactory, so he had to pay me two weeks' severance pay."

Suddenly work-smart, confronted with hundreds of job opportunities for the asking, Betty was finally able to indulge the long-yearned-for luxury of standing up for herself. When an unscrupulous vendor instructed her to sell weighted darts to throngs of young fellows eager to win plush animals for their girls, Betty consistently sold only the three unweighted sample darts that she had been told to keep in her hand in case someone got suspicious. She lost that job as quickly as the vendor lost his inventory. In a booth where the rings were slightly too narrow to fit over prize-tied posts, Betty sold the larger sample rings and lost most of the inventory in a single morning. She enjoyed yelling "You cheat people" as she stomped away from the irate owner before the crucial half-day limit had been reached.

Babette was working as a shiller in the Amusement Area, allowing mother and daughter to converse, plot, and collaborate as they maneuvered from one new opportunity to another. "Mama was hilarious as a shiller." Betty laughs. "She would strut outside the girlie shows in her heavy housedress scolding the men and warning the women 'Ach! Dose girls in dere are all neked! I am shocked! shocked! Do not go in dere to see dose shameless girls vit no close.' Of course, the men would rush right in."

While Babette was fussing outside, Betty worked for a show in which she had to roll backward and forward in a giant wheel, her hands and feet secured to the flat rim with straps. She did not know how to stop the wheel, so she had a boy push her on to the stage and another catch her at the other side. When the strap broke and she fell out, there was a general outcry, and Babette rushed into the show to find her daughter sprawled on the ground. Later that day the show-wise mother gave her exhausted daughter some plain advice. "Dey all get time off but you," she huffed. "Fool! Next time dat tink breaks, you don't so fast get up. Lie dere!"

Betty remembered her mother's advice well. When she fell from the wheel again, several men could not drag her seemingly dead weight across the stage. Babette rushed to her daughter's side and balled her fist under Betty's thick hair. "Vat a lump! Feel dat lump!" she screamed. Betty limped out of the door in her mother's arms as the frantic manager implored her to take two weeks off with pay to recuperate. When they got to the subway platform, Babette laughed. "Now you can valk."

Babette was protective of her perky daughter, eager to help her to find work, quick to pull her from a job that seemed threatening. She warned her daughter of the newspaper reporters and photographers who showed up regularly at the shower stalls, promising that they could make starlets of girls willing to pose in the nude. "Those pictures ended up on playing cards within a week." Betty smiles. "Not a few girls had to keep their boyfriends away from the concession stands for fear of what they would find there."

It was Babette who introduced Betty to the emcee of the "Arctic Girl's Tomb of Ice" show. Betty remembers this job quite fondly. A huge coffin of ice lay on a platform surrounded by stunned viewers. Betty would walk past a line of smiling bally girls and show the audience that she did not have cream or plastic on her body. "I wore a G-string and a little bra," she admits, "but I had sewn a lining in so you couldn't see through the material."

Four men were necessary to lift the top off of the giant freezing coffin. Betty lay down ceremoniously on a thick towel and was slid into the frosty prison from the top, carefully compressing her limbs so that they did not touch the burning ice. "They covered the top with ice and slush so that it was supposedly airtight, but I got plenty of air," she recalls. "It was wonderfully refreshing in there on a hot day. I generally stayed three minutes entombed. I could hear the people outside but they couldn't hear me. Once in a while, I would move my finger or blink my eye so that they knew I was alive, but I never turned my head. That would have been a good way to take the skin off of my nose. We did twenty or thirty shows a day, one every few minutes."

When Betty came out of the ice, she was supposed to faint or scream, but she simply could not fake a violent withdrawal from supposed self-hypnosis. "I always giggled"—she laughs—"and the emcee would tell the audience that I was hysterical." Voluntary entombment was an easy act that paid forty dollars a week, and Babette approved of the chilly charade until she discovered that the emcee's wife was a former "arctic girl" who had been crippled by the ice. "She wasn't cautious. She stayed five full minutes in the block and let her arms and legs press against the ice walls," Betty tells me. "She ended up paralyzed. When Mama heard about that, she told me to give notice, but first she informed the emcee that I had just had an operation. He let me leave with two weeks' pay."

"I am surprised that your mother did not try to get you a job with Billy Rose," I offer, and Betty chokes on her coffee.

"Oh, I didn't tell you about that, did I? She took me to audition for the Aquacade when the show opened." I can tell by her face that the audition is a sore memory. Jobs might come and go, but Betty was not used to failing auditions.

"Billy Rose's Aquacade," starring Olympic champion Eleanor Holm, was one of the highlights of the World's Fair. The huge amphitheater looked out over the water toward a three-hundred-foot-wide stage while between the two a filmy curtain of colored cascading water delighted the crowds. Eight thousand gallons of water a minute poured into the forty-foot-high cascades as four mammoth pumps worked to keep the misty cataract suspended. Hundreds of lights illuminated the shimmering fountains. When the cascade subsided, audiences were treated to the pageantry of graceful aqua dancers and Olympic diving champions. Rose had searched worldwide for the most graceful and beautiful women, the most accomplished swimmers.

Rose watched, amused, as Babette came forward eagerly with her embarrassed daughter. Betty had pleaded to her mother that she could not swim, but practical Babette had snapped, "Vit all dos girls, no one vill notice you. Just float."

"Rose loved my mother." Betty laughs. "When she came to him and said, 'I've brought my dotter, Mr. Rose,' he beamed at her and replied, 'She's beautiful, Tiny, just beautiful.' Then he took me aside and asked me seriously if I could swim. It looked easy enough, so I said that I could swim. He asked if I could dive. That looked pretty easy, too. I said that I could. 'Go on up and dive,' he ordered."

On the first dive of her life, Betty executed a graceful swan from the fifteen-foot-high platform and held herself in that position until her stomach slammed flatly onto the water's surface. Shaken, she managed to crawl out of the water. "How can you stand this pain every time you dive?" she asked the stunned swimmers who had just witnessed her spectacular belly flop. They explained that one was supposed to put one's hands together and tuck in before hitting the water. Rose merely shook his head. "What should I tell your mother?" he asked Betty kindly, when the dripping girl returned to his side. Betty thought carefully and fed him his lines. "She's wonderful, Tiny," Rose shouted across the platform to proud Babette. "I have all the girls I need right now, but as soon as one leaves, I'll take her."

"He winked at me when I left." Betty smiles. "I never had the heart to tell Mama."

The summer and autumn of 1939 passed happily away while Betty and Babette enjoyed the fair during the day and curled up on the lawns to watch firework-splattered skies at night. Although the main exhibit area of the fair closed at ten P.M., the Amusement Area stayed open until two o'clock each morning, allowing restless Betty plenty of time to roam and make new friends. In the Cuban village, she could rhumba, and there was a dance every night in "Morris Gest's Miracle Town," as well. The 36,000-square-foot miniature village had been brought from Europe on a specially chartered ship and was complete in every detail, right down to a diminutive organ in the small church. The 125 midgets who lived in the tiny town had their own restaurants, city hall, theater, art gallery, and railroad station. There was a midget circus, motion picture studio, garage, radio station, ballroom, guard barracks, and toy and doll factory. Best of all, there was the nightly festival. "One of the midgets always asked me to dance," Betty relates gleefully. "We had a wonderful time."

Another favorite after-work haunt was the "Seminole Village," a reproduction of the Florida Everglades in which brown-skinned men dove into pools to wrestle with alligators. The guide brochure claims that the performers are a tribe of fifty aborigines who have "refused all efforts of the Indian Department of the United States to bring them under government control, so they are not Reservation Indians," but Betty was not interested in their backgrounds. "I liked Indians, so I went back to meet them," she says simply. "A concession woman had told me that they couldn't speak English. They were very quiet, very polite. They always invited me with gestures to eat with them. We ate with our hands. I often stayed until closing time playing cards with the women." She smiles wistfully. "You know, there was one guy I really liked. He was handsome and had a terrific body. I knew that he couldn't speak English, so I used to tell him all my problems and thoughts. One night I told him how attractive he was, how much I would love to go to bed with him. He just sat there."

Betty holds out her hand. On her finger is a massive silver bull's-head ring with turquoise eyes that I have often admired. "When the fairgrounds closed, he sent a boy scout to give me this. There was a note with it—in perfect English. He hadn't been permitted to speak, so he couldn't tell me that he liked me, too." Betty smiles sheepishly. "He was a college graduate."

≈

When the fair closed down, Betty sadly returned to the rehearsal hall, hoping that some new opportunity would present itself. The Liazeeds were auditioning for Billy Rose, and both Betty and Babette had high hopes that Rose would hire the acrobatic troupe for his next production. Haji's family performed three times, but Rose never saw the routine. "The first time they did their act, someone came to Rose with a costume problem and by the time he had finished dealing with that, the troupe had finished their routine," Betty explains. "Rose yelled, 'Let's see the Arabs,' so the Liazeeds plowed into the routine once more. Rose turned to talk to someone about music and missed the act again. He was interrupted on the third try, too." Betty relates that when Rose finally looked up in exasperation and hollered impatiently for the Arabs to begin their act, Haji staggered to the edge of the stage and announced that the troupe needed to rest. "Well, I can't hire tired old acrobats," Rose huffed, completely unaware that the panting tumblers had just performed their demanding routine three times in rapid succession.

Betty heard of this fiasco from Haji when she told him that she was leaving the troupe. She had been practicing alone in Schroeder's one afternoon when five coal-eyed Cristiani boys arrived to rehearse their famed four-high pyramid. Betty was impressed with their amazing workout and could not help noticing how handsome the celebrated acrobats were. The world-famous tumblers observed Betty closely while she whipped through her difficult stunts and talked quietly among themselves. When iron-chested Tripoli strolled over and asked if she would like to join their troupe, Betty felt a dizzying, delicious sensation sweep over her.

"Go on, girlie," Haji said, when she told him of the offer. "We're not going to get any more work. Take what you can get. But don't tell Elvira that I told you to go."

Betty Cristiani said good-bye to her mother with a feeling that she could not describe even to Babette. When she thought of the young acrobat, Tripoli, her body seemed suddenly weightless. She joined the boys at the train station, clutching a single bag, hardly daring to hope that her World of Tomorrow had finally begun.

FOUR

REHEARSALS

"She read the entire book in one night," Fritzi warns me over the phone. "She's pretty excited. You might want to talk to her today."

I had just finished—and passed on to Betty—Richard Hubler's biography *The Cristianis*. I fairly gobbled his account of this fiercely close-knit family whose daring equestrian and acrobatic skills had earned them the homage due circus royalty. Halfway through the volume, I began to notice a strange similarity between the tales of childhood hardship and professional pride that Betty had been telling me and the romanticized, almost sensationally poignant story of Chita Cristiani. Chita's account of her subservience to her father and brothers, her determination to shine as a performer, her frustrated loves and lost opportunities rang all too familiar, yet somehow seemed more calculated than the vibrant oral history I had been recording for months. I wondered how Betty would react to this biography of her rival.

Hubler tries hard to mythicize a family known for its tight loyalty. He writes: "Bound up in a group, conceived within an institution . . . [the Cristianis are] as mystic as a cult and as isolated as a bay at the moon. . . . They have the unique capacity of scratching upward through their own ashes and rising only a little less glorious than before."[1] Betty had known the members of the famous clan not as mystical beings or as reborn phoenixes, but rather as individuals with both strengths and faults. I suspected that the book would annoy her.

When Betty joined the Cristiani troupe, they already were acclaimed. Papa Ernesto's family had been performing across Europe for over a century and had recently been lured to America by Pat Valdo, the Ringling talent scout. By 1938 the Cristianis were a featured act in the Greatest Show on Earth. Their bitter rivalry with the show's other equestrians, the Loyal-Repenskys, had begun to take on the status of legend. The extended Cristiani family was able to support several troupes, however, and in 1939 Tripoli, Remo, Pilade, Aldo, and Benito were traveling the nightclub circuit while their cousins finished a contract with the Ringling show.

I imagine that if a young singer had met the Beatles in a recording studio and been invited to join them as a vocalist, she might have experienced the same sensations that motivated twenty-two-year-old Betty Patrick to leave the Liazeeds and join her new "family." Betty had watched the Cristianis the winter before at Madison Square Garden, had turned to her mother during their performance and exclaimed, "Now there's an act that I would love to work with!" The Cristiani boys were especially famed for their tumbling; Tripoli could hurl himself over the backs of five elephants and land lightly on his feet. Betty's world must have spun when the young star casually asked if she would replace a sister who had just eloped.

The Cristianis' dazzling performance was demanding, but Betty's training had equipped her to shine in a routine few acrobats could have managed. Hubler describes the four-high pyramid as a very hard stunt indeed:

> At the impact of each man landing, the column becomes rigid, muscles and bones locked, breaths held. No shoulder pads are used because of the necessity to feel the tiniest movement below and above. The leeway for mistakes is slight. The third man may sway six inches to right or left, a foot forward or back but that is all. If the timing of the top-stander is off, all their fates are in the hands of the under-stander [the person on the bottom]. . . . He can move a single slow step in buffalo-skin slippers, either forward or backward.[2]

The act wowed audiences up and down the East Coast. A review for the *Cincinnati Times-Star* in 1940 describes the routine as a "lulu," calling particular attention to the new girl in the act: "The lady of the company, whom you might think capable of only light tasks, is at the bottom of many of the piles, so to speak, and she deserves a sentence to herself for this display of brawn." Decades later Lucio Cristiani would confide to Fritzi, "Your mother was a terrific tumbler—one of the best. She could have done anything."

They opened in Chicago, then Cincinnati, performed at the Palace in New York, moved through New Jersey to St. Louis, played Shrine dates in Georgia, and ended a year and a half run in Jacksonville, Florida. They were a large touring family; Pilade's wife, Carmen, Aldo's wife, Nina, and baby Henrietta traveled with the troupe. "Sometimes we would rent an entire house. It would be full of children running and women talking and men laughing. I learned to cook fabulous spaghetti," Betty recalls wistfully.

She pauses, remembering. "The boys had just come to America and had a lot to learn about how we do things here. For example, the prop boys got a salary, but usually you would tip them for good service. The Cristianis didn't know anything about tipping. We'd worked six weeks when the prop boys came to me—to me, mind you, complaining, 'Betty, they've never tipped us once. Be careful, because next show, we're going to do something to the teeterboard.' I said, 'No, please!' and told Pilade right away, 'You'd better give them a tip.' Nobody had ever told them. In the Ringling shows, you know, they were stars and everything was different."

It was the family for which she had always longed—large, devoted, professional, exciting. Betty was no longer the little "girlie" who tagged along behind Frieda's boyfriends. "There's a lot that's not in that book," she says with a huff, pushing it across the table back to me. Her face darkens. "I went with Tripoli for a long time but he didn't marry me. I loved him. He was with me, but then Chita would come to town and he'd disappear. I'd ask Remo, 'Why does he say that he loves me and then hurt me?' I couldn't figure him out."

Betty stares down at the book, lost in anger, still astonished that anyone in his right mind would refuse the miraculous gift of sincere affection. "In St. Louis, one of the cowboys invited me out for a nice evening with his parents. It was innocent enough, but I was trying to make a point. I came in at three o'clock in the morning ready to crawl into bed, but there was Tripoli, sitting up in the lobby, looking angry and miserable."

Betty admits almost proudly that when she saw her lover waiting, she danced over to him with a liveliness that was only half feigned. He stood heavily and blocked her way, uncertainty, displeasure, and fatigue battling in his face. "You happy?" he questioned.

"Yes! Oh, yes," Betty teased, warming to the opportunity to teach him a needed lesson, in sudden possession of a powerful antidote to the disturbing sense of vulnerability that had been building for so long.

Tripoli held her arm, pulled her up close, smelled her breath. "You no drunk. Why you go out?"

"Why not?" she shot back.

"I no like it."

Betty pretended to consider, then retorted, "Well, too bad."

As Betty recalls this confrontation, I can almost see the dark hotel lobby, the exasperated lovers facing off, testing and challenging one another with a desperation grounded in passion. "I tried to push past him but he wouldn't let me go," Betty tells me. "He pulled me upstairs, hurled me into our room but didn't trust himself. He locked me in, then went off to sleep with his brother. The next morning, he stomped into the dressing room, more upset than ever, and demanded, 'You go out again? You say me yes or no!'"

Betty stops speaking. She stares straight ahead, chin held high and lip trembling, once again confronting her adored, long-dead Tripoli, his angry face looming over her, sexual tension and defiance mounting between them.

"Why shouldn't I go out? You're not my brother, my fiancé, my husband," Betty shouted, forcing a point that any American man would certainly have recognized as a strong hint, but Tripoli only shouted back, "Answer me! Yes or no?" Her stricken face tells me that even now that moment of suspense sickens her. She had captured his attention, but she had also trapped them both in a perverse contest whose rules were in codes that neither understood. To a woman of his own culture, Tripoli's tortured fury might have suggested that he considered her his, regarded their relationship as one of obligation—

at least on her part—but Betty did not know how to soothe his wounded pride or to manipulate his possessiveness to her advantage. Cornered, not understanding how a half-playful lovers' quarrel had inexplicably thrown her into a fierce battle of wills with this man with whom she shared such intimacy, Betty looked him full in the face and answered mechanically, "Yes." There seemed to be no other choice but self-assertion for a girl whose mother had been beaten for her tolerance and passivity.

Tripoli's heavy blow landed on her upturned face. "He hit me the way my father would have," Betty explains, her voice small and tight, "but he wasn't my father. I threw a mirror after him as he rushed out. It hurt me. I loved him."

"How did you work with him after that?" I ask her, my own voice trembling. "You had the power to halt the act, didn't you?"

Betty shakes her head furiously. "Carmen told me, 'Don't you dare do the act—say that he hurt you too much,' but I couldn't punish the whole family. I dressed with tears running down my face. Remo saw me backstage and begged me, 'Why you cry? Why you cry, Betty?' but I didn't talk at all—just did my performance. Offstage, I wouldn't go near Tripoli or let him in our room. Remo came to me, finally, and asked me please to talk to Tripoli because he was making all of them miserable. 'For the family,' he begged."

It was a compelling plea, one that the Cristianis could resist no more than could Betty. "I was stupid." Betty smiles. "Stupid in love. I said 'okay' and went down and did the dishes."

Tripoli proposed when Betty least expected it. There was no dinner, no bouquet of roses, no ring—no recognizable symbolism to bridge the language barrier and cultural differences that separated them. He simply turned to her one day on the street, his face serious and weary, and remarked, "You get tired of work, I marry with you and we do the act."

"I didn't understand," Betty admits, still shocked that the dedication to their profession that she and her lover shared ended up separating rather than uniting them. "It sounded like he wanted me more as a performing partner than as a wife."

Betty had been exploited as a performer for most of her young life. "I prodded him," she insists. "I argued, 'What do you mean—if I get tired of work, I can marry you and work? That doesn't make sense.' He just got frustrated and didn't answer." She looks at me sadly. "If only he had said that he loved me. Maybe he did—in his own way. I don't know. I said, 'I don't want to marry you,' but he should have known it was a huge lie."

Jacksonville, Florida, was the Cristianis' last date. Pilade came to Betty one morning, head bowed, and explained that the Ringling show had closed and that Chita and Cosetta Cristiani were coming to join their cousins. He hated to tell her that she would not be needed in the act any more. "I knew what was happening," Betty says flatly. "Tripoli had started disappearing on me again. He'd tell me that he had to see his agent in New York. Oh, sure. I'd pack his suitcase. Before I dropped his toilet case in, I always opened the box of condoms he kept in there and poked a needle through every one. Served her right."

Betty fidgets for a moment. The story is becoming harder for her to tell. "I was packed to go and waiting to be taken to the train. The women were supposed to arrive later, but Chita and Cosetta had decided to come over early. They couldn't resist the chance to mock me. Chita rushed up and demanded, 'Congratulate me. I am married to Tripoli.' I couldn't answer. Her sister shoved her ring hand right in my face and laughed. 'And I am married to Remo. Congratulate me, too.' I stared at Remo and whispered, 'You got married, too?' My friend couldn't look at me. He turned his face away. I put on my best smile and wished both women all the bad luck in the world.

"Upstairs, Tripoli told me that he still loved me, insisted that the marriage had been arranged by his family. What was I supposed to think? He was a grown man. I said, 'You've made your choice. Leave me alone.'" Betty leans forward, her face practically glowing. "You want to know something that isn't in that book? Tripoli told me and it's the truth."

As I listen in amazement to her torrent of unguarded words, I know that I will not repeat the fascinating story that she is telling me. "You want me to print that?" I ask sharply. I lock eyes with her in silent challenge, but she lowers her gaze to the book that lies between us. I watch as she leafs through the pictures of the brilliant Cristiani family in later years, their children, their honors. "No," she decides, then smiles tenderly—a beautiful smile.

Betty sits quietly for a few moments, then shakes her head laughing, looks up at me brightly. "So guess what happened next?

Papa Cristiani comes and gives me $50. 'Don't tell the boys,' he says. Then Nina does the same thing. Then Remo. I got two weeks' salary and $350 extra because everyone of them gave me $50 privately—except the new brides, of course. It was a nice good-bye."

I sigh. Just this one time, I want the familiar abrupt ending to have some sort of resolution, some sense of coming to terms with human complexity and one's own identity. I want Betty to dismantle her formulaic tendency to frame each story around a job found and lost, to reflect on the sexual politics of her difficult life, to tell me what all of this means to her now. Betty is watching me closely. "The story doesn't end there," she says in a voice that I haven't heard before.

"I was back in New York and the Cristianis were in town, staying at the Hildona Court. That's where performers always stayed, you know. I wanted to see Carmen, so I stopped by on my way to the rehearsal hall. I walked into the lobby and there was Tripoli, just moping by the elevator, doing nothing. I went to him. He looked up—so glum. 'Betty, I not too happy.' I wasn't very kind. I said, 'Too bad.'

"I went upstairs and found Chita's mother with Carmen. Mama Emma was a huge woman. You know how big my mother was?" I nod. "Well, my mama used to walk right backstage at the Ringling Show because the prop boys always mistook her for Mama Cristiani. Then when Mama Emma would arrive, they'd be confused." Betty chuckles but sobers immediately. "When Mama Emma saw me, she exploded: 'You! You make my daughter unhappy. This is all your fault!' I wasn't going to be intimidated, though. I shot right back, 'Am I the one who married her?' Cosetta grabbed me by the arm—'I want to talk to you, too.' Carmen begged them, 'Please, no trouble, no problem,' and ran to find Remo. In a moment, I was surrounded. 'We are a family,' they shouted at me. 'What have you been saying about us?'

"I left in a hurry, but dumb me, I forgot my rehearsal bag and had to go back up there to get it. Chita was alone when I came in. She was furious. She told me, 'You are to give me back everything Tripoli ever gave you.' I guess she thought he'd given me presents." Betty grins at me—the same grin that she used when she told of having dumped her urine into a hated schoolmate's bed. "I walked straight over to her and slapped her hard across the face. 'There! Now you have what Tripoli gave me.'"

In the dimming light of a winter afternoon, Betty looks worn as she finishes her story and reaches for her cup of coffee, but her face is unusually calm. She pats my hand gently, her warm fingers brushing lightly over my wedding ring. "You know, it's funny how people change, how things turn out in ways you'd never imagine," she says, her voice so soft that I lean forward. "I saw Remo again when we played the Shrine dates. He told me, 'I loved you more than Tripoli did, but I couldn't cause family problems so I never made a move.' I liked him so much—maybe if I'd . . . Ah, well."

She pauses for a moment, lost in thought, and as she gazes down at her still-strong hands I can almost watch the years floating effortlessly past her, the easy drifting away of unclaimed possibilities. "I married my Fritz. I had two wonderful children. It must have been fifteen years before I saw them all again. Fritzi was—oh, maybe five and Bobby four. We were visiting the Fredisons at the Hildona Court when who should come running over to us but Chita and Cosetta. They actually hugged me and told Fritz, 'Betty is our best friend!' I wasn't sure what they were up to, but they were very kind to the children. They invited us to eat with them and gave Fritzi a little Pluto purse. As we were leaving, they hugged me once more. I couldn't help blurting out 'I don't understand.' They smiled. 'You won't, Betty, and we can't explain. But we do love you.'"

She shuts her eyes, keeps talking quietly. "Benito worked for Ringling and Tommy Hanneford. His wife fell from the rigging and died. Pilade and Aldo both died. Chita sent me a letter. She wrote, 'Betty, our lover boy is dead.' Last year Cosetta wrote to say that Chita is gone." She sighs. "In our world, you can find anybody if you need to."

~

I climb into my van still warm from a motherly embrace. Betty waits behind her back porch door as I load up the clunky recorder and extension cords, the canvas tote bag that holds cassettes, notebooks, Hubler's biography, a loaf of her homemade tomato bread. I slam the door, and as she waves through the cold glass, we both mouth "I love you" and blow a kiss.

The more beloved my subject grows, the more openly she shares the tensions and injustices that have shaped her life, the more difficult I am finding it to position myself outside of her narrative. She pulls me in. There seems to be no language for what is happening between us, although scholarly theories give me practically unlimited ways of analyzing our changing relationship: negotiating boundaries, exploring self-identities, discovering integrations and fissures, fusing, interrogating distancing strategies and solidarities. My heart tells me that we have adopted one another.

There was a time I could have shared my feelings with my closest friend, but I never see Fritzi now. I cannot quite put my finger on what has happened to our friendship, but I suspect that we may be caught in some kind of triangle. On Mother's Day I bought Betty a flower, then decided not to take it to her. How would you feel, I asked myself, if Fritzi were calling your mother "Mom," buying her presents, encouraging her children to think of your mother as their grandma? I hope that this analysis of appropriation and resentment is too simplistic. My friend surely knows as well as I do that we expand our sense of family over the course of our lives, proposing to those we love in ways that seem to make sense—with a loaf of bread, a hug, a deliberate forgetting.

Streetlights are blinking on, bleary dots to punctuate the day's-end procession of pickup trucks dragging along the city's edge. In the darkness, the van is filled with ghosts that I imagine have come from Betty's house along with me. I feel them settling in, erasing the boundaries between her life and mine, her current and my future memories. Someday, I think, the news of her death will also be sped along a circus network more efficient than the Internet and more private than a monastic chronicle. I try to imagine how it would feel to drive by Grandma Betty's house and not see her little brown car, her carefully trimmed grapevines, the flickering of a television behind drawn curtains. A dismal thought on a dismal evening.

She is elderly, her body fragile and mortal, I know—however vibrant her spirit. She is in remission from cancer. I force myself to confront these facts; I think to myself that I must hurry and write her a book, give her the gift of her story in print, not take the future for granted.

I think of my own aging mother, so far away, a lonely voice on the phone that can soothe parts of me that predate my own memory. A voice that tells me regularly of funerals attended, of masses offered for the dead, of my name written along with hers on condolence cards. Her entire generation is disappearing relentlessly; the helpless ache in her voice moves me to tears. My father, semideaf, takes the phone away from my mother, "Talk to me, too. Why don't you talk to me?" Will I look back on afternoons such as this one and regret that I did not spend them living differently when the people I love are gone?

I pull too sharply onto our dirt lane, swerve around shadowy ruts and muddy seasonal trenches, and arrive home in a mood darker than the woods around me. As I tramp slowly up the porch steps, I hear Emma's little voice behind the door, squealing, "Mommy's home! Here she comes! Mommy, Mommy, Mommy!" The cheerless tunnel into which I have ventured starts to twist inward and fade. I remember that time has multiple directions.

∾

My "once and future friend," as I have been calling Fritzi during the long postwinter months of fading chills and timorous budding, has once again come out of a season-long self-seclusion. She looks somewhat pale, thinner, determined to appear casual. Her husband has taken another job, will be on location until next Christmas. She hugs me with genuine welcome, but her smile is uncertain, her eyes somewhat wary. We linger in the kitchen, pretending that nothing has changed, waiting for the sense of unfamiliarity to wear off, but it seems to me that an unhealthy energy is building. I grow more wounded and indignant with the passing of each minute of pretense.

I have no idea what has happened between us, and I cannot hide my feelings. "I want to stay angry with you," I blurt out, and her entire body goes rigid. "I've been furious with you all winter. You left me hanging. You left me." I can almost see the layers of defensive armor slamming into place as Fritzi pulls herself up, faces me with a look that tells me that she has deeper reserves of wrath to draw on than I do.

"Yes I did," she says stiffly. "It's something we do. I am not going to apologize. Mom will tell you. We leave constantly—but we return."

My frustration mounts as she continues speaking, embracing what I consider an insulting rhetoric of exclusivity that labels me as an

outsider, tries to defend her personal choices as cultural and professional habits. "Don't give me that 'I'm from another culture' stuff.
We're talking about friendship and responsibility," I spout, too angry
to prioritize. "I need your interviews. I only have a few more months
to finish this book. I would never have touched this project if I had
known that you would pull out and leave me stranded. Do you know
how much work this is? I have a family. I want to get back to teaching."

"Well, I need to get back to my art," she snaps, chin up and eyes
flashing.

We stare at each other, shaken and silent. Perhaps she reads in
my eyes the same confusion that I see in her eyes. My anger wavers
and I know exactly what I want to tell this chosen sister whom I no
longer trust or understand. "I love you so much. You left without
saying good-bye. You never even said good-bye."

Her face twists and tears threaten. "I know. I'm sorry for not
understanding your needs. Next time I'll give you warning."

∼

It is early spring when I next interview Betty—a quiet afternoon. She
tells me that she did not let herself mourn the Cristianis. She found
a new job almost immediately. The New Major Bowes Unit, "the
Prize Winners of 1941," was not really the amateur show that it
proposed to be. "All of us were professionals," Betty admits. "In every
town, he'd hire on one local and showcase that kid for the week, then
leave him behind when we moved on."

The Major Bowes Unit of 1941 was an eclectic show. The master
of ceremonies did fair imitations of Eleanor Roosevelt and Charlie
McCarthy. There was a young ventriloquist with a smart-alecky
dummy, a pretty female whistler, a trio of tap-dancers, a tabletop roller
skater, a novelty act who played tunes on sweet potatoes and a bicycle
pump, and an acrobatic/contortionist act called the Three Graces.
Betty had been hired to replace one of the Graces.

"Zimmy was German, like me," Betty recalls. "Helen was Jewish.
We used to joke about two Germans and a Jew doing acrobatic
together. Helen would laugh, 'Well, now you've got me. What are you
going to do with me?' We certainly didn't care about any of that."

What a luxury for you, I think to myself, at a time when Londoners were huddled deep in subway tunnels as 190,000 tons of German Luftwaffe bombs shook the earth over their heads. I flip through her reviews, check the headlines: "Major Bowes' Amateurs Ride in New De Soto," "1941 Winners Dine at Miller's Waffle Shop," "Bowes' 6th Anniversary Revue in Person at the Palace with Rita Hayworth in her 1941-derful Hit." The pictures always show the group together—all young faces, cheerful and exuberant. "It was a really good group," Betty remembers, "but the show closed in the spring, so I didn't get much of a chance to know them. I did get engaged though. Want to hear about that?

"He was a violinist named Marcel,*" Betty begins. I quickly scan the reviews in front of me and read, "Marcel does more outlandish things with a violin than Rubinoff ever thought of. He plays it after the manner of a cello and a bull fiddle and he plays it with his bow held in his mouth."

"That was on stage." Betty laughs. "In his room, he played . . . oh, so beautifully. He never talked to anyone, though—just played his violin."

Betty relates that one of the troupe bet her fifty dollars that she could not get Marcel's attention. She accepted the wager, insisting that within three months, she would not only have the reclusive musician's attention but a proposal of marriage. "What was your strategy?" I laugh, this time careful not to show my distaste for those who trifle with others' affections. She responds almost gleefully.

"Okay, the bet was on. When he was on stage, I'd sit and watch him [she pantomimes rapt attention], then compliment him afterward [she gives me a wide-eyed flutter, what my sons would call a "clueless" look]. We went out and had coffee. He never romanced me. After the show, he always went straight to his hotel and practiced. Eventually, though, I was allowed to carry his violin. I didn't know that all his money was in there; he told me that when he broke the engagement." Betty grins. "When he asked me to marry him, I simply said, 'If that's what you'd like.' He answered, 'Well, you're so very nice to me.' I had won the bet. Then I had to figure out how to get rid of him."

She must read something in my face, my posture, the way I am gripping my pencil. She changes her tone slightly, becomes defensive. "He was very jealous, you know. We lived in hotels and he had the bellboys spy on me through the transoms to see if anybody was in the room with me. If I even spoke to the emcee, Marcel would get mad. He'd say, 'You're engaged to me!' One afternoon the cast decided to surprise him with a birthday cake. We thought we'd just knock at the door, fling it open, and yell, 'Surprise!' We surprised him, all right. I'd never seen him without his beautiful ruffled shirt on. He had dirty feet and dirty arms. I asked, 'Don't you ever take a bath?' He fumed, 'It's off! I can't marry you.'"

Suddenly Betty starts to speak quickly. I cannot follow the story, except to get a general impression that she is not at peace with it, that much is missing. "He kept one of my pictures but he called me a devil. . . . I have a letter he wrote to me after the show. He said that if it hadn't been for me, he wouldn't have had to go in the army. So that's why he proposed. He thought if he married . . . but he didn't go in the army anyway. He had flat feet." She sits back, almost breathless.

Over the decades, I figure that Betty has probably built up a formidable tolerance to caffeine, but this afternoon she is obviously nervous and coffee is not helping. I have heard multiple versions of favorite stories relating to this time in her life—stories that she has told over the years to anyone who would listen—but today she is sharing uneasy memories that I have not heard before, tales that she evidently has not practiced on audiences.

She brings up another suitor, one whose name she will not remember. "He was Colombian, almost black," she recalls uncomfortably. "He took me all over Boston. He wore a huge diamond ring. He said that he wanted me because I'd been raised in a convent and that meant I was a good girl as well as a good performer. When I went back to New York, he called my mother at the Diamond Horseshoe to ask her to arrange a wedding! My mother was astounded. She asked me, 'Vy do so many men vant you?' One night he called us at Rose's club and begged Mama, 'Tell me what I can give Betty to make her want me.' Mama told me what to tell him. I asked for fabulous presents—a thousand-dollar makeup kit I'd seen, five thousand dollars in cash. He hung up. I'd acted like a gold-digger so he'd be disgusted and leave me alone. He was too persistent." Betty actually shudders.

I am struck by Betty's strong reaction to this story. What would have happened, I think to myself, had the rich foreigner from a Roman

Catholic country married the "good little convent-bred" girl and discovered that she was not a virgin? How frustrating for Betty to have been pursued by a suitor who defined her in terms of her past association with the convent, who insisted on seeing only what he wished to possess. Perhaps it was easier for her to assume an unsavory role and disgust a man who had blindly magnified her virtue than to be stripped of that assumed virtue and shamed in her own eyes. I wonder if the process of narrating her life story for publication seems to Betty to invite the same appropriation, the same lack of full recognition, the same danger of disclosure.

As Grandma Betty fuses with my family, I know that it becomes both harder and more necessary for her to assert herself during our interviews. Our personal relationship has been built on the trust that develops between women who love one another's children. Our professional relationship, however, is grounded on the broad differences in our experiences—differences that are not transcended by an easy, uncritical bonding based on gender or goodwill. Storyteller and performer though she may be, Betty has never had to address her deepest feelings with her audience, never needed to reveal more of herself than a good story demanded.

I am expecting another recollection when she startles me with a rare reflection on herself. "I know that you think I'm pretty wild, but I get shy sometimes. It just comes over me. I don't know why it does. If someone has told their friends about me—how funny and lively I am—I get real shy when I meet them. I can act, but I can't make myself into a performance." Her frustration grows obvious as she struggles for words to make me understand. "I used to get the same feeling with the nuns. It's the way they look at you," she whispers. "They look into you. They know that you've been sinning."

"Where did you work after Bowes'?" I ask gently, thinking that questioning her about her work might be the surest way to ease her back into her narrative. She seems to be purging herself today, struggling to articulate thoughts that are private, unspeakable. Her telling of her life story has always been personal and immediate, but I am coming to realize that the child-woman of her earlier stories has a historical space of her own. She moves on the margins of Betty's present existence; however dehumanized or silenced she may have been, hers are the secret fears of an unwanted child, a pawn in the tangled plot of her parents' history. Her story cannot threaten Betty's current sense of herself because Betty will never again be that confused child, however keenly she may remember her pain.

Far, far harder to relate is the life of an angry, victimized adult woman whose bitterness and hopeful yearning still tear my subject apart, dictating her daily moods. Betty judges her past choices harshly even though she acknowledges that she was emotionally and physically dominated. It is hard for her to admit the roles that she played within an internalized oppressive system that demanded her collaboration. Her personal identity, so rich in the need for self-determination, has been firmly grounded in acts and attitudes that she cannot sanction, in feelings that even now intrude and overwhelm. She is forcing herself, I know, to look into a mirror of regrets.

"When the show closed, I went back to my father," she tells me, her voice already tight in anticipation of the unpleasant memories that she is about to review. She explains that in June of 1941 she joined Harry and Charlie in the Parroff Trio—"because my father wanted me for the act." For the next year the three toured the American Northeast and Canada, thrilling the crowds who gathered outdoors each evening to gaze up at the agile family whirling on their rigging, ten stories above the fairgrounds.

Betty brings out her scrapbooks and I flip quickly past the generic advertisements, searching for individual facial and full-body shots of the siblings. Charlie's publicity photos were featured large in local papers: tall and dark, muscled and handsome, the twenty-year-old posed dutifully in stereotypical "macho" poses. Headlines advertised him rather crudely as a "perfect specimen" of male strength. Betty's headshots no longer show the Cristiani-smitten, misty-eyed girl with flowers in her bobby-pinned curls and ruffles on a pink gown. Her look is harder, more sophisticated. Brows shaped, eyelids shaded, and lips colored, Betty lifts her chin defiantly in her pictures, holds herself almost boldly. They must have been an eye-catching family on the ground, too.

"God, he was gorgeous." I sigh, pointing to a full-length picture of Charlie.

Betty grins. "Yup. And he knew it. Men chased him as well as women. His agent sent him to audition for a major role in *The Robe*, but when he got up there, the guy made a pass at him. You don't think of men being auditioned on a casting couch, do you? Charlie rejected him and didn't get the part. He joined the act after that."

I flip through the album quietly, then start to chuckle. I point to a shot of the Parroff Trio; high in the air, Charlie's large frame straddles the platform, legs and arms akimbo as he holds the side ladders parallel to support Harry, who perches on his son's shoulders, with Betty standing atop her father's shoulders, her arms raised triumphantly. "You just liked being on top of things, didn't you?" I laugh, moving my finger across the album to similar photographs of Betty in a tiny-skirted swimsuit at the beach, balancing gleefully on the thighs and shoulders of her younger brother and a crowd of muscle-proud lifeguards. "So did you just walk up to all those good-looking boys and ask, 'Wanna make a pyramid?'" I tease.

She shakes with laughter. "That's about it. They were Charlie's friends. I liked lifeguards."

I point to another photograph: Betty snuggled close to her brother, her arms wrapped tightly around him, her head against his chest. He is wearing an American World War II uniform. "So you did have some good times?" I demand. "You've made Charlie into such a villain, but it looks as if you loved him once."

The laughter of a moment ago is gone instantly; her fury arrives with less warning than a tornado. "I had to look happy. I didn't want to be beaten up by my brother! And sure, he'd let me cuddle up for a picture, then he'd push me away. We got along all right when I had money to give him." Betty's anger grows wilder as she careens backward and forward in time. "Charlie never got a spanking his whole life. I got beaten all the time. He never got anything taken away from him. He was always 'my boy' or 'my son.' I didn't count. My other brother didn't count. Charlie always called Harry a drunk, but I wasn't a drunk, was I? He claimed that he had a miserable life. Ha! He got all the money and I did all the work. He told the rest of us what to do."

Betty is glaring at me. I know that I have upset her. "He couldn't have been very happy, though. Surely he knew that he wasn't loved?" I offer quietly.

"He was never home anyway. He was always out with his girlfriends," she snaps.

"That doesn't mean that he was happy. He didn't have the sort of love that you had with your mother."

"He never tried to get near my mother. He hated my mother."

"My mother," I note, not "our mother." Betty is glaring at me and breathing hard, but I keep pushing her backward in time, wondering if she will soften for the child that Charlie once was.

"Perhaps he wanted a different life. He must have hated starving as much as you did. Who knows what he was taught all those years. You had your mother for a guide. He had Harry. He was a smart little boy who was probably screwy as hell because he had only Harry teaching him."

Betty pauses, seems to falter. "That's true. That's true," she admits slowly. "Well, my father always told us, 'All women are whores,' so what did he expect? I guess they both looked at me as just another whore." She stops talking, searches my face, continues slowly. "You know, one time my father touched me—when he was drunk."

I tilt my head and look her in the eye, inviting the confidence. She has never spoken to me in detail about sexual abuse, only hinted enough to let me know that it happened.

Betty continues quickly, her voice low. "He was telling me what nice breasts I had. He was always looking at me and saying 'I'd better hide that bicycle pump.' He put his hands on them and I pulled away from him. My mother yelled, 'Harry!' Boy, did he crouch down! But I thought to myself, if he ever has the opportunity, this is what will happen. I was very well built—thirty-six–twenty-six–thirty-six. They said that I was perfect for a woman. My father used to grab women's breasts all the time. He'd say, 'Well, God damn it, that's what they're there for.'"

"Imagine a little boy growing up with a father like that," I suggest quickly. I can see that she is listening to me. "And he was a smart child, too, which probably made it worse."

I watch the wordless battle in Betty's face as she struggles to dismiss my words. "We went out together. That's all I know. If he wanted to date a girl, I had to go out with her brother, whether I liked him or not. If Charlie knew that I had cash, he'd 'borrow' whatever I had. He never paid any back. He always put me in jeopardy, too. You know that finale trick with the revolving ladder between the other two? Harry designed it. He came with these two broomsticks together. Charlie wouldn't try, so Harry and I did the revolve and it broke apart. That's why Charlie wouldn't do it. He could see it wasn't going to hold, so he made me try it first, see?"

She pauses, tired, and I corner her with one last question. "Can't you remember anything good about Charlie?"

I am expecting a simple, closing negative, but the story that rushes out astonishes me. Almost breathlessly, Betty relates, "He got a girl pregnant and he told me to get her an abortion, but I didn't. I took her to the doctor instead. I wanted that baby. I told the doctor to give her vitamins. I promised the girl that I'd take her on the road with me so her parents wouldn't find out about her pregnancy. Then, when her time came, I was going to check her into the hospital under my name so that the baby would be mine."

"Wouldn't it have looked very odd at the hospital if they had seen your name and your brother's together on the birth certificate? Isn't that illegal?" I offer feebly.

Betty gives me the look that she reserves for when I have not been paying enough attention. "And what names would those be? Charlie called himself 'Charles Parr III' throughout his life. I was Betty Patrick."

"So what happened to the baby?" I ask cautiously, unsure of what I am feeling but careful to appear detached.

"Charlie got in trouble and needed it himself. He had been working for a couple of men—brothers, who loved him and wanted to adopt him, but Charlie had been stealing thousands of dollars worth of fine jewelry from their store. His friend had stolen some Chanel #5. This was during the war when you couldn't buy it. They went down to Florida to sell the stuff, but Charlie left me a garage key and told me where his Cadillac was. I'd go to the garage every now and then and check on the car, run it, you know. Man, it smelled like tweed. Charlie loved tweed." Betty stops and sniffs appreciatively. I wonder what tweed smells like.

"What happened then?"

She pauses, collects her thoughts. I have seldom seen her so intent on getting facts ordered chronologically. Generally, we pass back and forth endlessly over the same story—my questions, her answers, until I have a firm idea of what probably happened. She is working hard to present this story thoroughly and accurately, as if she were a filing a police report rather than telling her life. "He was caught in Florida when he tried to sell the stolen jewelry. He was extradited to New York and Mama put up the house for bail. She told me, 'Go und vipe dat car off. It might have been shtolen too. If your prints on it dey find, dey'll take you, not Charlie. Go und do it.' So I went to the garage and wiped the inside and the handles with a towel. I never went back. Charlie wrote and asked me to send him the garage key, so I cut the middle out of a deck of playing cards and sent the key inside the cards." Pretty slick for a supposedly naive girl, I think.

Betty continues as if recounting a conversation that happened only yesterday. "When my brother came home, the first thing he said was 'Did you get rid of the car?'

"'No,' I told him. 'It's in the garage.'

"'Oh, shhhhit! I have to go there. Want to come with me?'

"'Mama said I should stay away from there. She made me wipe the car off.'

"'You wiped the car down?'

"'That's what Mama told me to do.'

"'Good! Now I don't have to go.'

"He had never told me that the car was stolen, and I wouldn't have known if Mama hadn't figured it out. Imagine if I'd been caught with it! They arrested him, finally, and took him to jail. Mama hired a lawyer."

Betty looks out the window, as if suddenly bored with the story. "It was his first offense. His lawyer told him, 'Too bad you aren't married with a pregnant wife. I could get you off.' So Charlie calls me and I confess that I didn't arrange the abortion. He takes the girl to court with him and says that she's his wife. She was showing by then. The lawyer got him off but he had to marry her, just in case they checked. He told her that he didn't love her. He wouldn't even sleep with her on their honeymoon. He came and slept in my bed instead."

I sit very still. "He slept with you?"

Betty looks at me quickly. "Well, he did that a couple of times. It wasn't a big deal. We had to get rooms in boardinghouses on the road." She smiles disarmingly. "This is a good story. Once in Pennsylvania we rented a room from an elderly couple who had a boardinghouse. Now, Charlie was dark, you know, and I wasn't. We told them that we were brother and sister and wanted two beds, but they didn't believe us. We came home after the show and there was only one bed." Betty giggles almost girlishly, remembering. "It worked out fine. I wore my long jumpsuit to bed and Charlie wore his trunks. One night my brother came in late and said, 'Sis, I'm going to jump over you,' and the bed collapsed. Of course the landlords came rushing upstairs in their nightgowns and just stared at us. 'Brother and sister, eh?' Their daughters had showered Charlie with coffees and cookies up until then, but after the bed broke, he didn't get nothing. He told me, 'You ruined it for me.'"

I frame my next question carefully. "Did Charlie ever touch you the way Harry did?"

"Oh, no," she replies, relaxing her voice and body. "My brother always had plenty of girls around him. I don't know what he thought of me. He did pick out all of my clothes, though. I'd take my shower, and when I'd come back in the room, he'd have left my outfit for the day all laid out on the bed. He'd say, 'Now you're wearing this brassiere with this shirt, and this garter belt with these stockings, or this slip and this dress.'"

"Why did you let him dress you, Betty?" I ask.

She shrugs her shoulders. "He had real good taste."

~

Charlie went into the service in 1942, several months after the Japanese bombing of Pearl Harbor, Betty tells me, and the Parroff Trio broke apart. She went straight back to New York and asked her agent, Frank Wirth, to hook her up with a new act. Wirth introduced her to Beth and Andy Starr,* "superior acrobatic dancers."

"They were a husband-wife team," Betty explains, "but they had hired a girl as a third. The 'Three Starrs' were booked to play the Silver Dollar in Boston, but their girl was sick and couldn't go, so they took me. They did a dance routine and I did acrobatic. They tried to teach me how to tap-dance, but the manager always begged me not to dance. I wasn't too good at that."

Betty's engagement with the Starrs was short, but she remembers it more vividly than many of her other jobs because it involved a baby and a near disaster. "They had a little girl," Betty tells me. "Her name was Andrea.* She couldn't have been more than two or three years old. When she was naughty, they'd hand the poor thing to me and tell her, 'You're going home with Betty. You can't stay with us any more.'

I'd make her chocolate milk and hug her. One time she got her little rabbit fur jacket dirty and I tried to wash it for her. Of course, it fell apart. I didn't know that you couldn't wash fur. I snuck out and bought her a new one." Betty chuckles to herself for a moment, then looks at me sharply. "You know, we performed at night, so they left that baby alone when we went to the nightclub to do the act."

Betty stares at me and grimaces, knowing absolutely that we share the same deep maternal need to guard small children from harm. She explains that the father, Andy, would leave first. Hoping to soften her fears, he would tell the child, "Daddy's just getting some coffee," and little Andrea's lip would quiver. She would whimper, "Baby no cry." A few minutes later, Beth would pretend that she was going to find Daddy. Again, Andrea's little voice would promise plaintively, "Baby no cry, Mommy." "Wait a few minutes, then tell her that you're going out to find Mommy and Daddy so she's not afraid," Beth always told Betty. "Then you leave, too, and she'll fall asleep."

Betty twists her face into a mask of pain as she admits that she followed her difficult instructions. "It hurt me to lie to a little child like that," she confesses. "I pretended that I was going to find her daddy and mommy and left." Betty winces as she remembers the tiny face staring up at her, wide-eyed, as she closed the heavy door, locking the little girl into the apartment alone. "Baby no cry, Betty. Baby no crrry."

The Starrs had rented rooms in Boston's midtown theater district, one block from the luxurious Cocoanut Grove Night Club, newly expanded to accommodate hundreds of soldiers, sailors and marines eager to drink and dance in style before shipping off to war-tortured countries. The Cocoanut Grove was nestled between Piedmont Street and Shawmut Avenue, and lavishly decorated with exotic artificial palm trees, clinging fronds, and creeping foliage laden with coconuts, writer Lee Davis relates in his study *Man-Made Catastrophes*.[3] The club offered a fantastic night of faux-tropical escape for newly uniformed men and bejeweled ladies intent on forgetting that in the flooded real jungles of Guadalcanal, American boys were trapped in a green hell of leeches, malaria, and snipers.

Davis recounts that on November 28, 1942, a fresh, sun-happy Saturday, Boston football fans witnessed Holy Cross's miraculous trouncing of Boston College and took their celebration into the streets. That evening the Melody Bar, a normally intimate ground-level lounge at the Cocoanut Grove Club, was crammed wall to wall with boisterous patrons. Well-groomed waiters practically had to elbow their way through the unprecedented crowd of over one hundred people who had descended the narrow staircase leading from the main foyer into smoky, jazz-filled darkness below.

As the evening progressed, the club's main dance hall and adjacent cocktail lounge upstairs filled to capacity, then to overflowing. The safety regulations concerning capacity limits that governed theaters at this time did not yet apply to nightclubs. It is estimated that between eight hundred and one thousand people were packed into the posh club, designed to hold a maximum of six hundred, all laughing over fine liquor and waiting for Mickey Alpert's band to open the 10 P.M. floor show, when shrieks of "Fire" flared above the sounds of merriment. Survivors would remember a blinding flash roaring across the ceiling, the glittering jungle suddenly ablaze, mass hysteria erupting as showering cinders leapt to life on clothes and hair.

It is now believed that a tiny spark from a discarded match began the catastrophe that sickened a city. Downstairs in the Melody Bar, where the conflagration was ignited, draping palms exploded into scalding light over patrons' heads, instantly trapping them in a fiery incinerator. The shrieking mob charged the narrow stairway that led up to the foyer, clawing and crawling over one another in the darkness. A few made it to the top, only to be trampled by the stampede of frantic, choking people attempting to escape from the main hall through the club's front revolving door, which instantly jammed. The auxiliary exit next to the revolving door was bolted. With the terrified crowd crushed against it, no one could release the bolt.

It was over in minutes. Firefighters watched helplessly as flames shot into the night sky through the collapsed roof of the highly flammable building. Four hundred ninety-one bodies were pulled from the smoldering wreckage. Over one hundred bodies were found piled against the single exit from the main cocktail lounge, which unfortunately opened inward. In the basement, employees who had tried to escape through the nightclub's kitchen had discovered that the employee exit was locked.

Boston mobilized with an efficiency worthy of wartime. When the city's 150 ambulances proved insufficient to transport the wounded, taxicabs were appropriated as makeshift ambulances. Hospitals for miles admitted burned and smoke-poisoned people throughout the night. Every available doctor and hundreds of nurses were called to duty from Boston and surrounding counties. The Red Cross organized five hundred disaster relief volunteers to aid emergency workers with the seemingly endless stream of wounded and dying. As medical supplies ran low, planes sped to Boston with replenishments from New York hospitals.

Martial law was declared in the early hours of the morning as police and servicemen fought to keep curious crowds from hampering emergency efforts. A group of sharp-witted sailors locked arms to form a human barricade against the crowds. Street blockades were pulled aside to allow trucks full of corpses to drive silently past. Sirens blared and lights flashed, firefighters repeatedly dove into the suffocating smoke and emerged carrying or dragging bodies, rescue workers and medical teams formed triage units, military police cordoned off the entire area.[4] The Three Starrs, returning home on Sunday morning after their last performance, found unimaginable chaos separating them from their little Andrea.

"They made me do the talking," Betty remembers grimly. "We were pushed away, ordered to leave. No one was being allowed through, but I had to make the police understand that we had left a child alone somewhere in all that smoke and screaming and death. The officer I told yelled at me, told me what a stupid, bad mother I was. She was their child but I got all the blame. I got all the blame." Betty picks at a crumb on the table with a shaking hand. "It took that fire to make them realize that we should never leave her alone again."

~

"I was twenty-six when I finally got close to my mother," Betty announces brightly as she shoves pencils and beads aside on the table to make room for unwrapping our McBreakfast burritos. The house is full of fluttering sunlight this morning. Betty has opened all the doors and windows to allow a fresh savory breeze to waft through the house. The curtains are rippling in the fragrant air, birds are singing, the morning is already warm. Huge, puffy clouds are passing overhead; a front is visibly building to the east but we are both in a spring mood.

"I called Mama my *goldstück*, my little gold piece." Betty laughs. "She loved miniature things—little surprises. When I traveled, I'd wrap presents for her in my clothes and hide them in my suitcase. Mama always unpacked my bags to find her gifts, like a child searching for them."

Betty leans comfortably on the table, absorbed in remembering her delight in pleasing a mother as lonely as she—and as grateful for affection. Suddenly she sits back and grins at me. "You know, once when we worked in Montana, they paid me off with one hundred silver dollars. I hid them in my purse and didn't tell Mama."

Betty relates that when her mother emptied the suitcases, she found nothing but clothes. She looked at her child sadly. "You vere busy, yah?"

"No," Betty replied nonchalantly, "I had lots of free time."

"You have no money?" Babette offered gloomily.

"I had plenty of money. Where did I put my purse?"

Tears ran down Babette's cheeks as she dutifully brought Betty's purse. "Here it is. Ach! Vat so heavy is?"

"Mama! This is for you—don't cry."

Babette sobbed as she emptied the glistening silver onto the bed. "She thought that I had forgotten her. It hurt her to be fooled," Betty remembers. "Her birthday was April Fool's Day, too."

Cloud shadows drift across the yard outside Betty's large side window, casting patterns over dangling toys and strings of tinkling trinkets hanging from the curtain rods. "She hated to be fooled," Betty repeats, her tone as unsteady as the shifting sunlight. She seems determined to wait until a particularly unpleasant memory has materialized completely. When she speaks again, her voice has gone flat. "My father had a girlfriend on the side. Rhonda.* She wrote him love letters: 'To Harry, my dear husband.' I still have the wedding ring he gave her so that everyone would think that they were married."

Rhonda had been hired to join Harry and Betty when they once again hit the road as the Parroff Trio. Babette knew that her husband was being unfaithful but no longer was in a position to threaten her rivals with a bar of steel. "Mama had retired by that time," Betty recalls. "She was a housewife. My father mocked her—called her fat—but we would come home and Mama would have made new pillow covers and curtains for the living room, lovely pastries and a nice dinner. Mama was a good woman."

Betty tells me that when Harry brazenly announced that he could not love two women and had chosen another, Babette had a friend write to Rhonda's mother, not trusting her own awkward English. The letter informed the woman that Rhonda was involved with a married man and begged her to remind her daughter that Harry and Babette had children. It was Rhonda who wrote back to Babette. "How dare you upset my mother!"

Betty's face grows darker as once again she feels herself twisted and entangled in her parents' bizarre story of passion and domination. "Rhonda said that she was eighteen but she was really thirty," she hisses. "Anything she wanted, my father gave her. She 'earned' eighty dollars a week but I got practically nothing. He bought her beautiful clothes and gifts while my mother stayed at home and did the cooking and washing. I told my father, 'Mama is alive. She's a wonderful woman,' but he claimed that he was in love with Rhonda. It made me sick. I called him Mr. Parroff in public. I wouldn't even walk down the same side of the street with him. In the act, we were on separate ladders and didn't have to talk. The other performers told me that I should be nicer to my father. As long as he was with her, I didn't have a father."

Rhonda is slim and svelte in the photographs that Betty shows me, perfect in tapered slacks, elegant in the tight satin panties and black fishnets that the girls wore in their act. Her short wavy hair is Marilyn Monroe blond. It was wartime, Betty explains, and Harry had found the perfect patsy for his newest racket—duping battle-bound servicemen who had money to spend and little reason to save it. Her next story is a twisted one, and I try to follow its sharp turns without disrupting the flow of outrage, still fresh after half a century.

The Parroffs were performing in Boston, and Rhonda had managed to ensnare both a sailor and the young owner of a motel, a boy who had been rejected by the military because he was lame. She had told each man that her mother desperately needed an operation that she could not afford. It was a complicated business, made worse by the fact that both "marks" had shown up with the money at the same time. Harry instructed Betty to distract the hotel owner while Rhonda took the sailor for two hundred dollars, then to entertain Rhonda's supposed fiancé, who had just arrived in town, while she collected five hundred dollars from the hotel owner. Betty cornered the lame owner in the lobby, took one look at the bills in his hand, and said, "Let's talk."

"I told him everything," she announces proudly. "I told him about the sailor who was being cheated of two hundred dollars. I told him about Rhonda's so-called fiancé. I told him that my job was to distract him while she talked to the others. He said, 'We're talking about Rhonda, right?' I let him see for himself."

Betty led her companion to a dark corner from which they could watch and hear her hated partner as she argued furiously with a uniformed man. He was insisting that she give him the name of her mother's doctor and hospital. When Rhonda rose in exasperation and stomped off, the hotel manager strode quickly to the table and sat down with the sailor. After an earnest conversation, they left together.

"Weren't you afraid to defy your father that way?" I ask.

Betty shakes her head resolutely. "It didn't matter. Nothing I did was ever all right with him."

Betty remembers exactly Harry's words: "You and your big mouth!"

"I didn't say nothing, Papa."

"Well then, you and your goddamned eyes. You're always talking with your eyes. You must have said something. We need Rhonda in the act." Betty shivers. "*I* didn't need her in the act."

Back in New York, Babette had had enough humiliation. When Betty next came home for a visit, the retired strong woman insisted, "I need you to get rid of Rhonda."

Shocked, Betty pleaded, "I can't do that, Mama," but Babette urged her with the passionate perseverance of a hurt child. "I don't care how you do it—just get rid of her." Sickened by her mother's pain, Betty promised, "Mama, I'm going to get my own act and you're coming to live with me. We will both leave Papa and I'll take care of you."

Babette had helped Betty to disentangle herself from unwanted lovers often enough, but because the two women had grounded their relationship on their mutual fear of Harry, they shared a companion- ship that did not posit Babette as a maternal authority figure. Babette was her daughter's beloved friend but seldom a source of security. As Betty became an increasingly independent adult, she assumed the role of a parental figure to her ineffective, loving, naive mother. This distortion in role allocation must have seemed as gratuitous to Babette as it did to her child.

The daughter who had refused to be manipulated through fear of her father succumbed easily to the manipulation of parental love. Caught between parents, a pawn of each, Betty determined to do away with her father's "other wife."

Several times I have played through the tapes of her passionate and muddled telling of the final showdown with Rhonda. It is not going to get any clearer. Ultimately, I suppose, the details are unimportant; the hatred, abandon, and desperation that characterized their final evening together are emphatic in her passionate narrative.

~

The scene was a lounge in Camden, New Jersey. Rhonda had acquired a husband, and the couple had joined Harry for some serious drinking, a common pastime when the Parroffs were not performing high above the ground. Betty apparently was no longer distancing herself from her father because she was the fourth member of the party. What I do not understand is why Betty and Rhonda's husband were present. Did this husband know about his wife's affair with Harry, and if so, did he care? Why was Betty socializing with these people whom she detested and mistrusted? Did she feel obligated to placate her father, or was she plotting mischief? Betty cannot understand why I keep asking questions about the subtleties of triangles and complexities of these relationships; she begins to snap at me, impatient to tell her story in her own way. What matters to her is what happened that night.

What happened, it seems, is that Betty acted as her father's parent as well as her mother's, for the first of what would become many times. She assumed responsibility for his behavior just as she had shouldered the blame for the Starrs' abandonment of their little daughter several months earlier in Boston. That evening found her sitting sober in a lounge as her stiff-faced, speech-slurring companions ordered round after round of cocktails. "We have to do the act tomorrow," she begged her raucous partners, knowing that when the sun rose again, her life would depend on their timing and dexterity.

"There's no hurry. Damn it, have a drink," Harry ordered. Only when the bar closed down did he rise unsteadily and lurch out onto the dark, quiet side street where he had parked their truck.

Swearing loudly, Harry clung to the wheel and jabbed his key against the shadowy dashboard while Rhonda's husband pulled himself into the back of the truck. Harry found the ignition and the truck lurched into wild motion. In the middle of the front seat, wedged between her reeking parent and his truculent, pretend "wife," Betty tried to shrink into Harry's shoulder as Rhonda lunged over her, half crying and half shouting obscenities at Harry.

"She called him a son of a bitch," Betty tells me, lowering her voice modestly when she says the B-word. "Well, he was that, but he was also my father. She wasn't going to call him those names right in front of me." Betty's slap must have carried the full weight of her accumulated hatred because it broke Rhonda's nose. Rhonda's shriek brought the truck careening to a halt. The complacent husband flew out of the back and into the street. Rhonda sprang from the vehicle, screeching bloody murder.

It was three o'clock in the morning. Rhonda's obscenities were soon directed at irate voices yelling down at her from bedroom windows. When the police arrived, she immediately began to sob and told them that she had been kidnapped.

"There I was, doing all the talking again," Betty mutters grimly. "I called the officer 'sir.' I told him that they were all drunk but that I was not. He dumped the other two into his car and told Papa and me to get back into our truck and *drive*," Betty remembers. "Papa started up the engine again, the officer yanked him out of the cab. 'Not you—*her*.' I'd never driven in my life, but when I opened my mouth to say so, Papa bellowed, 'You heard him. Drive!' I said, 'Yes, Papa,' and climbed into the driver's seat."

Driving turned out to be much easier than Betty had expected. "There was nothing to it." She chuckles, winking at me. "I didn't know that you had to put the clutch in. I just drove real slow and every now and then I would shift—I figured you were supposed to. I never pushed the clutch down. When we got home, I put it in park and went to bed. I was about to fall asleep when Papa burst into the room. He stomped over the bed and whacked me hard. 'So you don't know how to drive, eh? You lying whore.' I woke up the next morning to Papa's screams. 'Jesus Christ!' I'd burned out the clutch. Well, I'd told him that I didn't know how to drive. He was furious, of course. After that, I wasn't even allowed to sit in the cab; he made me ride in the back of the truck."

"And what happened to Rhonda?" I ask impatiently.

Betty grins broadly. "She quit."

~

Springtime seems to have vanished while we have been talking. As Betty ends her story, I notice that the birds have stopped singing; in fact, the morning has become ominously silent. The curtains hang very still and the sky has clouded over. The heavy air seems charged with electrical energy. I should go home and check my windows but we are on a journey that has not ended yet, and I want to see it through.

The expression on my face must scream my confusion because Betty laughs and assures me quickly, "It's all right. I told you, I have the letters that Rhonda wrote to my father—addressed to 'my dear husband.' Mama kept them all."

"Why would she save such hurtful things?"

Betty merely shrugs. "Marriage was important to Mama. Once you were married, that was your man—for better or worse."

"So how did Babette feel about your two divorces?" I ask.

Betty is quiet for a moment. "She didn't like my first husband," she says finally. "Mama thought that we were wrong for one another, that we were both too stupid to know what we wanted out of life. It was true. He was domineered by his family like I was by mine. But I knew that I wanted to get away from my father. Any act would have been better than the one I was in. It seemed like a good idea at the time."

She called him Romeo. His Italian family were renowned for their skillful bareback riding act. They were a large, loving family— probably the best inducement to marry that any beau could have offered Betty. In April 1943 they were booked for several weeks at the Chicago Stadium along with the Parroff Trio. It was all the chance that the young people needed. Betty explains nonchalantly, "We talked for a week, then he told me that he'd found a special place where they could process blood tests in one day, so I married him. I came home the next morning and told my father that I was a married woman. He didn't believe me, of course. He accused me of having slept with my Romeo and ordered me to get back to work. See, my father thought that you had to wait at least three days for a blood test. When I showed him my marriage license, he hollered, 'Oh, God! You really did it!' He let me keep my dog—that was my wedding present."

"Were you happy married?"

Again, Betty pauses to think, as though my question were an unusual one. "He made me wear high collars. I had to wear my hair straight up and no makeup. He'd say, 'You look too good.' I'd been domineered by my father all of my life and here was this husband controlling me in the same way. I wanted to be more free, you know?"

"What had you expected?" I ask gently.

Her answer is immediate but vague. "Something different."

Silence follows, and I offer a suggestion: "Were Haji and Elvira Liazeed a happy couple?"

Betty's generous affirmative tells me exactly what I need to know—she had a firm sense of what she wanted from marriage. "At any rate, we never got the time to try together."

After Chicago, Betty's husband's family moved on to Clifton, New Jersey, and the Parroff Trio went to Carlin's Park in Baltimore, Maryland, then joined the Spangles Ringling Show in Madison Square Garden. Apparently, neither new spouse questioned the necessity of finishing the season with his or her family's act. "We had to honor our contracts. Of course, we had planned to get together when the season ended, but the service took him just one month after our marriage," Betty explains. She grows quiet. She is deciding how much to tell me.

"I went home to my mother," Betty relates carefully. "We were playing in New York, and my husband came to see me. He wanted me to join his family's equestrian act. He wanted to train me to do somersaults from the back of a galloping horse. I was supposed to go backward and land on his horse, and he would somersault forward onto mine. We would have been the only act doing that stunt. It was his brother's idea. Romeo had great height and I was an acrobat so I had good bounce and timing. I didn't want to do the trick though. Equestrian work is hard—and dangerous. No one can really spot you and horses can lose their tempo. I was afraid that I would fall and land between the horses."

Betty suddenly is speaking hurriedly, whether out of frustration or determination, I cannot tell. "So when my husband came home, I gave him back the money that the service had sent me. He told me that he loved me, but I said that I didn't want him any more. I told him that I'd been sleeping with lots of men. It was a lie. He wanted to keep trying, so I hit him with a bigger lie—I said that I'd aborted his baby. I was very convincing. He cried, 'How could you do that?' Charlie came into the room and told him to take his money and get out."

"Not long after that, Romeo called to say that he needed an operation on his knee. He wanted me to send him money but my mother said 'No. Don't give him anytink.' I told her, 'Mama, he is my husband for better or worse,' but she wouldn't let me send much. He still thought that we could make a go of it. I figured that maybe I had been a rat."

"How long did you stay married?"

My question is followed by an uncomfortable silence. "I found out that I was divorced in May of 1944," she answers tentatively.

"You didn't know? What do you mean you 'found out'?"

The story that follows is one of the saddest that I have heard, perhaps because Betty firmly blames herself for having contributed to an unhappiness that affected both partners. Her husband had come to New York once again and had asked her to return to him, had assured her that they could work things out. Realizing that she had been guilty of several very cruel falsehoods, Betty resolved to give their marriage another chance. She gave her current show notice, met her husband in a hotel, and made love with him. "He carried my picture in his jacket," she tells me wistfully. "I thought that he must really love me if he still carried my picture after all the nasty lies I had told him. We were going to join his family. I was determined to be a good wife." Her face darkens. "When we had finished making love, he handed me a letter to read. Divorce papers. He had divorced me. He had waited until . . . I didn't know until afterward."

Betty's voice shakes as she recalls the chaotic thoughts, the turmoil in her mind. Her most insistent first thought was that she had just quit her job. She dashed from the hotel to find her boss, bare feet shoved into her shoes, leaving her suitcase behind. "When I returned about an hour later, I asked the desk clerk to ring his room. I was beginning to hope that this was some kind of joke—some kind of revenge. I knew that I'd hurt him, too. Maybe he was just teaching me a lesson."

Betty crumbled when the clerk told her that Romeo had checked out, then announced with a grin that he had left something behind for Betty. "The boy held up my stocking with my wedding ring tied in the middle," Betty remembers, her face twisting. "I broke down and cried. I felt like a prostitute. I had thought that I was with my husband. Had I hurt him so badly?"

Betty recalls that the desk clerk wanted to call the police, assured her that she could have her former husband arrested for rape. "I couldn't comprehend what had happened," she tells me. "Mama called him a *schwein*, but when I confessed about my lie—that I had aborted his baby, she groaned and looked at me hard. 'You told him vat? Oh, baby! It's over.' I knew then how much I had hurt him, too."

I sit quietly and watch Betty's face. A range of emotions plays over her features quickly, ending with the flicker of a smile that grows into a broad grin. "Of course we ran into one another again"—she laughs—"after I was married to Fritz. I told Fritz, 'Look, he's a nice guy. I want you to get along as friends.' Fritz took one look and said, 'You were married to that character?' and Romeo looked over Fritz and said, 'You married him?'" Betty chuckles, seems to relax. "They got along beautifully. They played chess together."

I shake my head in disbelief. "What happened to your first husband?"

"He married my cousin about a month after he divorced me, and don't ask how she's my cousin. I don't understand it myself. They live out west now. You know, his family never let me go. They all still call me Aunt Betty. Fritz and I and the kids used to winter with his sister's family. She and I always loved each other like sisters. So you see, it was all right in the end."

Cleansing rain spatters across the window beside us as Betty calmly reaches for her coffee cup. She watches the peaceful rivulets for a moment, then gives me a beatific smile—the kind of smile that surely must spring from age-earned wisdom. "It's funny how things work out. They do, though—if you let them."

~

I allow myself a week of living solely in my own present before I ask to interview Betty again. The rains have stopped but the low-lying streets of Wilmington are still flooded and clogged with debris, the sandy parks and lawns deeply puddled. We turn on the lights and Betty pulls a mammoth photo album from the huge pile of albums piled under her coffee table. We flip through the pictures almost playfully. I could label most of the pictures with only a little help. We have come a long way, I think. I groan silently when I see the fabulous headshots and signed photographs that Betty has "colorized" with Magic Markers, the original signatures that she has penned over to "bring them out." Suddenly Betty points to a small photograph of two tall, dark young women standing close to one another, both dressed in elegant, floor-length evening gowns. "That's me with my sister."

"Romeo's sister?" I ask casually.

"No! I told you. That's my sister!" Her voice goes high and sharp. "My *real* sister—Anne."

I shut my eyes. The ceiling seems to have wrenched open. I feel as if a huge slab of broken cement has slammed through my head and embedded itself in the cavity of my stomach. Betty is munching on a piece of banana bread. She is not going to give me time to recover— perhaps is not even aware that my precious, hard-earned sense of mastery over her history has just been decimated. I tell myself to breathe deeply and say nothing.

I realize what has happened. I have been deliberately offered prompts to keep me from asking questions. I resolved early on to abandon the standard interrogational interview format and let my subject follow her own nonlinear course. Betty has never mentioned Anne, I suppose, because Anne does not fit into any of the sequences that Betty has initiated: She is not a job, or a lover, or a costume. What in our recent conversations has caused Betty suddenly to point her out? She could easily have passed over this picture.

The answer comes almost immediately. I spend the rest of the morning listening to a long, bitter story. Almost as soon as she begins speaking, Betty lets me understand Anne's place in the sequence of triangulated betrayals and retrospective regrets we have been following. Like Charlie and Rhonda, Anne was a rival for Harry's affections. Like Romeo, Anne may also have represented to Babette a potential competitor for Betty's attention. At any rate, Anne was one more person whom Babette instructed Betty to eliminate, one more person whom Betty obediently determined to hurt.

She was Harry's illegitimate daughter, a love child who had been kept a secret. "Harry's mother paid the pregnant girl to stay away from my father," Betty admits, "but he always wondered about his child. When we went back to Germany, he must have looked for her. I know that he sold our grandmother's house for fifteen thousand marks but told Mama that he had only gotten ten thousand. Two days later Anne showed up on our doorstep. What do you think? He must have given her the money to come to America."

Harry's unexpected "daughter" was seven years older than Betty and probably the last person in the world Babette wanted to see. Betty recalls that their introduction did not go well. "Anne called my mother 'Mama,'" Betty tells me resentfully, "and then she did something incredible—outrageous! She asked if Mama would leave her money when she died. Can you imagine! Mama hated her from then on, and so did I."

Only Harry did not hate his long-lost daughter. Perhaps he felt guilty that he had abandoned her. Perhaps she represented for him a choice that he had not been allowed to make, or perhaps she seemed somehow to have been salvaged from a past that his recently deceased mother had evidently dictated. Betty remembers with vivid fury his tender preference for the newcomer, the same sort of preference that already had distanced her from little Charlie. "I made my own clothes, my own hats," she fumes. "Anne would come along and show my father her hat. Oh, wasn't Anne clever! Wasn't she smart! He praised her constantly. She was older than I was, you know. She didn't live with us but she used our shower after work. She had gotten a job as a waitress and she had a boyfriend—Eddie. One night he called. He was coming over to our house to pick her up. Mama told me to put on a tight dress and lots of makeup. She said, 'Dis is your chance. I vant you to take Eddie avay from Anne.'"

"And you did it?" I ask her.

"It was a cinch," she blurts, half triumphant, half ashamed. "I did whatever my mama told me."

I have to force myself to transcribe the long story of Betty's mother-fueled plot to steal Eddie from Anne. It is a story that reminds me of a teenage girl contending murderously over some young male, or of competitive mothers threatening mayhem if their daughters do not win a coveted spot on a cheerleading squad. The entire story—told in amazing detail (whom Eddie sat next to at the movies, what he said to each girl but did not tell the other, which one he kissed when the other was not looking, tidbits and teasing, plotting and fussing)—seems shallow, mean, and adolescent in the cruelest sense of the word.

What emerges from this story, however, is the intensity with which Betty pursued a man whom she did not particularly want, the zealous determination with which she plotted against her new sister, the seriousness with which she embraced a role dictated by her mother. Babette was apparently a woman far less naive and helpless than I have been led to believe.

"Your mother domineered you as much as your father did," I inform Betty. "You were her instrument against Anne, against Harry, against Rhonda. She never stood up for you, yet she used you, didn't she?"

"Yes," Betty acknowledges. We have reached the turning point where storytelling collides with unglossable truth. "Yes, she did," Betty repeats, "but I loved my mother. She could have been a much happier woman if Harry had loved her." So could you have been, I think.

Betty claims that she was wearing Eddie's class ring when she became engaged to Romeo in Chicago. She wrote him, "I have not dirtied your ring. I am married." When Eddie confronted Babette, the triumphant mother informed him that Betty had never loved him. "He went in the navy," Betty muses. "We both lost him. From 1943 until 1949, he was gone. My father would beg me, 'Make up with Anne,' but I wouldn't. I didn't talk to her again until 1950. Fritz and I were in New York, so I called her to tell her that I was pregnant. She told me, 'Eddie and I got married and I'm pregnant too!'"

Betty runs her hand over the tiny picture of two girls in evening dress. "When you're young, you don't realize how much you can hurt someone," she muses. "I didn't even know my sister, but I tried to hurt her. Now I understand that her life was hard too. Anne told me how terrible it was for her in Germany. She had to sleep on the floor. Her stepfather worked at night. Anne did all of the cooking and cleaning. Her mother hated her because of my father."

"They made life hell for everyone around them—all those angry parents," I suggest, but Betty stops me.

"No. I agreed to do what my mother wanted. I was very foolish when I was young. Maybe we all are. I hurt my sister—not physically, but mentally." She leans toward me, an older woman offering a younger woman strong advice. "When you realize the wrong you've done, you shouldn't just say that you're sorry. 'Sorry' is the sorriest word there is—it's not the right word. Anne and I are very close now. We have made it up in a different way. She loves my children."

≈

"I've already eaten," Betty tells me rather testily. I ignore the tone.

"So don't eat. Have some McCoffee and sit with me. Emma needs to burn off energy and I need to get out of this house."

Instantly her voice changes. "Okay. I'm ready."

I can tell that Betty has been alone with her thoughts too long. It has been awhile since I have called her. While I lean back against a life-size (life-size?) Ronald McDonald and watch my pigtailed toddler wriggling and pouncing in a netted cage of balls, Betty talks almost breathlessly, reeling off stories that I have heard many times before. She does not seem to need any response from me at all, so I let her chatter until she suddenly relaxes, looks around and notices the kids, asks me about myself. We keep an eye on Emma and gossip about the world until our coffee runs out.

I know that storytelling serves many complex purposes for Betty, but one is quite simply to "vent" when she has been shut up for too long. I have chosen a sedentary, contemplative profession, yet just sitting at my desk through a long afternoon makes me feel a bit crazy these days. I cannot imagine what it must be like for someone who has been active—moving constantly and surrounded by people always—to sit alone in a quiet house day after day, thinking about time and age, regrets and loss and inevitable change. I know that Betty wishes fervently that she had more options for distraction. When I returned from a short trip to London, she looked up from the stack of postcards and photographs that I had brought and lamented, "Wilmington is such a small town, isn't it?"

"Do you want me to take you home before or after I run my errands?" I ask craftily, and am not surprised when she piles back into the car with my kids, ready for a whirlwind scenic tour of the grocery store, video store, pharmacy, and gas station. As I watch Grandma Betty fumbling with a Happy Meal toy, almost as delighted with it as Emma, I decide that aging is neither a progression from childhood nor a regression from "maturity," as so many middle-age daughters like myself probably assume, but is perhaps a deliberate choosing, a revisioning of oneself.

Whenever I see the word "revision" in critical texts, I remember how it felt to be the mother of a curious toddler for the first time. Taking a bus to campus seemed suddenly a magical experience as I imagined how my young son would enjoy such a ride. I began to notice squirrels scampering across sidewalks, raindrops rippling puddles, colored banners strung across aisles in grocery stores—all the sensory stimulation that bombards us daily and that we learn to take for granted or merely ignore. I worked seriously to revision my world in an attempt to understand, appreciate, and share his new experience of it—to recapture the sensual immediacy and youthful wonder that I had both outgrown as an adult and altered in constructing myself intellectually for a community of professionals.

One afternoon I lost myself temporarily in play with my three-year-old ("Look at that funny bug. Do you think that trees have birthdays? Let's taste the sunshine.") and congratulated myself sincerely on having broadened my consciousness. This was not, however, an accomplishment that I could discuss safely with any of my colleagues—not even with those who were parents. What they might well have viewed as a deliberate regression into childishness, a loss of some sort, I recognized as flexibility, an expansion of awareness. Years earlier I had felt the same exhilaration as I awoke one morning and realized that I had dreamed in French.

Betty has this ability to slide back and forth—not only through time but across perceptual boundaries. I have witnessed the depths of hurt and fury to which her memories can lead her, the sensual immediacy of her unleashed adult pain, so I cannot help but marvel at how thoroughly she can retrieve pure playful joy as well. She can care for my children with the responsible loyalty of a seasoned, even cynical parent, yet she can also allow herself to slip into a state of immaculate, childlike innocence, an intoxicating release. I have always associated this state of excitement and receptiveness with childhood because it is natural to children. Never before have I met an adult who can retrieve it so fully at will, who can revision her world and herself so effortlessly and completely, apparently as a matter of choice.

The grocery store is transformed into a playland as Grandma Betty leads my children through the doors. ("Open, Sesame!") The whole gang is disappearing down aisles, peeking around corners: In the produce section, I notice that the mounds of shaved ice around the vegetables have recently been molded into little snowmen. Emma squeals from her cart as contorted faces start from behind displays. Betty is chief spokesperson on the subject of which treats should be in my basket and are not yet. At the checkout counter, however, I find her waiting for me sedately, a tiny baby cradled gently in her arms, the parents surprised at how instantly their infant has attached himself to a cooing, maternal stranger. It does not surprise me that they have simply handed their baby over to this elfin lady with the bobbing curls—as I once did.

I drive her home feeling both brightened and drained, as if I am simultaneously her child, her mother, and her friend; and yet also, somehow, still very much a stranger. How is it that she leads me so often to feelings and roles that defy definition?

~

"Here. I want you to read this!" The book Betty gives me to take home looks like a grade-B novel. I am intrigued. Betty's favorite reading consists of tabloids, but she will also thoughtfully devour any work of fiction or nonfiction that I pass on to her. I suppose that it is my turn to read on demand.

"What is this?" I ask.

"It was written by somebody I know. The names are changed but the people are all real. It will tell you what our life was like."

"Are you in it?"

"Nope."

The book is called *Flight into Fury*, a work of creative nonfiction about a young woman who puts together a trapeze act called Peaches' Sky Review and takes her girls on the road. Betty apparently substituted for one of the performers in the review for several weeks early in 1945. Peaches's memoir, thinly veiled as a novel, graphically details the logistics of life on the road. Reading it, I come to understand how hectic traveling for a season must have been for free agents like the Parroffs. Performers would finish their last act well after the sun had set, then immediately tear down and pack their rigging in the dark—often without having eaten or bathed. Each act wanted to get on the road quickly for the long drive to the next fairground on the route, perhaps several states away. Whoever got to the next site first hooked up closest to the electrical generators. The farther away one parked, the dimmer the lights would be. Toilets would be a long walk for stragglers. Laundry was a luxury reserved for the rare day off. Sleep could be indulged only after the rigging had been hauled up, perhaps between the noon and 7 P.M. shows. Some performers spent weeks at a time performing and moving almost daily.

The Texas dates—an eight- to twelve-week tour of major cities for which the Shriners put together a single circus each season—were coveted by many performers, Betty has told me. Because Shrine dates were well established and generally played in coliseums, performers were almost always guaranteed dressing rooms, water, lights—all the little perks that were too often missing from fairground or tent show engagements. Betty and Fritz, her third husband, were fortunate in their bookings during the 1950s, but I know that she crisscrossed the country over and over again during the 1940s, living out of a truck. It must have been very demanding.

Flight into Fury is enlightening and entertaining, but also disturbing, and I decide not to share with Betty my deepest impressions. Its plot centers on the girls' petty competition for boys whom they meet one summer. All of the relationships in the book seem rather silly to me—summer loves taken far too seriously by women old enough to know better. The main conflict occurs when the season ends and each character must decide whether to continue with his or her lover in the off-season world of more permanent obligations, responsibilities, and commitments, or simply to drop the romance along with the rigging and go home for the winter.

Long after I have returned Betty's book, I am haunted by the odd combination of carefree immediacy and paranoid urgency contained within its pages. It is the same uncanny mixture of apprehensive resolve and breezy indifference that underlies so many of Betty's stories. Entrenched as I am in the hard-wrought security of my home and long marriage, I realize that I am not immune to the seductive lure of the busy, sensual, whirlwind life that the book and my subject have described. The transient ties that bind the characters together during a fast-paced season allow them to concentrate almost fully on their own bodies, their daily feelings, their personal desires. Any sense of community involvement—neighborhood investments, civic responsibilities, social accountability for public property or organizations—is either absent or very fleeting. While work is very serious to each performer, the danger real, the sense of shared group pride in the show strong, each character knows that the dates will soon end and the company will disband. This is probably why Betty married Romeo so quickly, I tell myself. A nice long courtship on the porch swing simply was not an option.

I know very well that many circus performers purchase homes and lead dual lives over the course of a year—a busy professional life on the road during the season, and a private and settled life at "home" in the off season—but many of the stories of young, unmarried performers to which Betty has treated me seem almost antithetical to those I have heard about performing families. They are primarily stories of sustained emotional and physical abandon. Betty does not seem to associate this attitude with wartime apprehension, nor with her personal situation, nor even with the tendencies of youth. "This was our world," she tells me. Circus.

The temporal limitations that Betty associates with circus life are not unlike the artificial "semesters" and graduate school programs that I have come to know. Many professions bring people together for short, intense periods of time without condemning them to emotional superficiality. Try as I might, I cannot help feeling disturbed by the rationalized suggestion that this one particular profession necessitates a vacuous inner life. On the contrary, I have always assumed that being transient for any reason demands huge reserves of inner strength. Fast decisions necessitate a firm knowledge of oneself, a sense of long-term personal development that transcends temporary circumstance. Without mature self-understanding, spontaneity becomes impru-dence, sensual immediacy turns to thoughtless indiscretion. A casual boyfriend can become the unsteady basis of one's whole life and happiness. Peaches's self-absorbed book seems to suggest that achieving true love is as uncomplicated as finding the right person for your act and making sure that no one tampers with your rigging.

~

I can tell right away that it is going to be a difficult interview. Betty's voice is artificially cheerful when she greets me in the kitchen, her hug not as quite as generous as usual. Her mood probably has nothing to do with me; it may mean that she is worried about her family or has had an argument with someone at the senior center, or perhaps is a reflection of the stories that she has determined to explore this morning. I know all of this, and yet I still feel personally hurt by the inconsistency.

Betty relates what happened to Charlie's first wife in the coldest voice that I have heard her use. She tells me that the young wife moved into Babette's house. "We didn't have much to say to each other. I was mad. I wanted that baby." I say nothing. Betty grows agitated, begins to speak more quickly. "She slept all day, then when Charlie came home, she would complain to him that we had made her clean house. She was a slob. She used to throw the dirty diapers behind the couch! She was always made up at night when Charlie came home, though—her hair, her nails. We told him, you come home early one day and see what she really looks like. He took our advice and decided to get rid of her." Betty looks at me triumphantly.

Charlie spent only a short time in the service, according to Betty. He was stationed in Texarkana and never saw overseas duty. She insists that he was discharged as a sergeant of some sort. "He cross-dressed so they would let him out." She laughs. "He pretended that he was gay."

"Was he?"

My question elicits instant resentment. "That's what his first wife told their son," Betty huffs, "but it wasn't true." "They had another baby, after the boy—a little girl, Christine, but she died. I think that she died of too many laxatives or something. I got a nice letter from them: 'Our poor little angel is gone.' I called the mother once because I wanted my children to know their cousin. She told me that her lawyer wanted her to stay away from us people."

Betty pauses, then decides to tell me more. "You know, Charlie gave me a ring with six perfect diamonds, engraved, 'To my Sister.' I kept it pinned in my underpants so that I wouldn't lose it when I was performing. We were in Chicago. I went to the bathroom and accidentally flushed it down the toilet." She looks at me as if we have an understanding of some sort, but I do not try to hide my perplexity.

"Wouldn't your finger have been a safer place to keep it? Why did Charlie give a diamond ring to you?"

"I told you! He stole jewelry."

"And you accepted it, knowing that they were stolen gems?"

"When my brother gave me something, I took it." Betty looks me straight in the eye. "Never ask questions."

~

"Was Rocky his real name?"

Betty shrugs her shoulders and gives me a quizzical grin. "I don't know. That was the name on our marriage license, so maybe it was. We were working a carnival. He ran the Ferris wheel. Seemed like a hard worker. Always stopped and watched my performance. After about a week, he told me that he liked me. I needed a rigger, so we got married. I didn't want people to say that I was sleeping with my rigger."

We have had an early lunch and have decided to continue interviewing. I should know better. Emma woke me continuously last night and I am too tired today to regulate my features and police my responses. It has already been a long morning for me. Betty, however, seems unusually self-possessed. She relates the story of her second marriage casually, almost flippantly, showing none of the concern that she revealed for her aborted marriage to Romeo.

"It lasted several weeks. One of Harry's girls had left, so I was filling in on the ladders as well as doing my sway pole. Rocky accused me of caring more for my father than for him. I got pretty sick of listening to him. One time I was sewing on my slippers and he started in on me. I stabbed my needle right into his stomach."

Rocky ran away in Ponchatrain Park, New Orleans, less than two months after his marriage to Betty. Betty relates that he left her sitting in a restaurant with two cold meals in front of her. She figured out that he was not going to return from a trip to the bathroom about the same time that she realized that he had taken all of her money. "One of the girls who was going with my father saw him buy a ticket to Pittsburgh—a one-way ticket. He had a suitcase and a little brown bag with him. He'd flown the coop," Betty quips nonchalantly. "He'd stolen all my jewelry but we celebrated anyhow."

"Why did he leave?" I prod her. I am very uncomfortable with this story. All of my instincts tell me that it has been severely cropped.

Betty gives me a close look. "He was gay."

"How did you know?"

"Some of the prop guys saw him doing things with the 'girls' in the gay show when I wasn't around."

"In the open? What kind of things?"

Betty bristles. "Never mind! You know what kind of things. He never wanted to touch me when we were together. Every other guy I had ever been with wanted to do handstands on my boobs."

Betty laughs to herself, shakes her head, runs smoothly through an account that I suspect she has told many, many times. She relates that several months later, she ran into a girl at another fair who was wearing the stolen jewelry. The young woman claimed to be Rocky's wife and said that the jewels had belonged to his mother. "She loved him. I told her that I would divorce him, then I took my jewelry off of her," Betty states, and it occurs to me that Betty was a woman whom other women probably did not cross unnecessarily. "Rocky came later and begged me to take him back. He knew how much money I was making with my sway pole act. I told him that I would think about it."

Triumphantly, Betty explains how she tricked her husband into signing the divorce papers. "I called my lawyer right away and told him to send me two identical sets. I put one in a secret compartment in my purse. Then I played along with Rocky for a while. I bought him a nice leather jacket, spent money on him. I told him, 'You can't sleep with me now because my brother is staying in my room, but on the last day, when we tear down, you and I will drive off together.' He believed me! One day we were in town and I got real silly. I said, 'Here are the divorce papers I was going to give you. Let's go in the bank, sign and notarize them, then tear them up and throw them away.'" According to my subject, Rocky immediately agreed to this strange ritual. As they stepped out of the bank, he grabbed her purse, seized the papers, and tore them into tiny pieces. Betty relates gleefully, "My brother was standing across the street, watching. He just shook his head when he saw what had happened, but I knew what I was doing. The real papers were in the lining of my purse! I finished the date two days before closing. We tore down while he was on the Ferris wheel and pulled out without a word to him. And that's how I got rid of Rocky!"

"Why were you staying with Charlie?" I ask, genuinely perplexed. None of this story makes sense to me. In fact, it seems contrived.

"Because he was my rigger after Rocky!" Betty snaps. "I needed a rigger for my sway pole, so I wrote to Charlie in New York. He left his wife to come and work for me. I might as well have been working for Charlie, though. He lied and stole from me. He even got the guy at the garage to make out fake bills for fixing the truck. I couldn't trust him."

"So Charlie was divorced?" I ask.

"No, no, no," Betty responds, exasperated. "I told you. He left her back home. He didn't want her."

Something in my face must strike her as intolerable because suddenly she explodes, pulling all of her anger into a mean little rock to hurl at me. "You never pay attention! Half the time you're asleep and half the time you use the excuse that you're tired. That's your best excuse!"

"Take a look at me. Do I look peppy?" I offer, mustering what I hope is a disarming smile, but it does no good. Betty's body remains rigid, her eyes hard and fierce. "But I do listen, I just don't always understand what you're talking about," I plead.

"You never do!" she fumes. "Then you have go to Fritzi and ask her to explain it to you."

"Leave me out of this."

Relieved beyond words, I turn to see Fritzi standing in her mother's doorway. The cavalry has arrived in the nick of time. I have never seen Betty so irate, never been so directly the target of her unease. "She's picking on me," I say with a laugh, giving Fritzi a grateful Come-on-girlfriend-help-us-out-here look.

Fritzi ignores me and walks quickly into the next room. "I'm tired. I'm going to lie down," she mutters.

Betty becomes suddenly solicitous, as if deliberately demonstrating how differently she views her daughter's fatigue. "Go lie down, honey. Close the door so you won't hear us." Then she turns sharply back to me. "Now you listen this time."

I push back my chair and glare at her. "Stop being nasty to me or I'll go home," I announce, using the authoritative tone that my children call my "teacher voice."

Betty regards me closely, seems to be studying me. Finally, in a milder voice, she entreats, "Don't go home."

Betty offers me another cup of tea. I follow her from the kitchen, guarded, my nerves raw. I am ready to end the interview, uncertain of whether we can proceed productively, but I know that she will be hurt if I leave now. We return to the dining room with steaming cups, poise ourselves on our chairs. She looks at me for a long moment, then says, "You know, Charlie used to pass me in the street like he didn't know me." Startled, I realize that she has just "read" me quite accurately and is offering this story to bridge the gap between us.

"He was ashamed of his family," Betty tells me. "He changed his name from Parroff to Parr—Charles Parr III. When he went into the service, he listed some ritzy Park Avenue address instead of Woodside, Long Island, where Mama lived. He didn't want anyone to associate him with the circus. He didn't want his family." My subject shakes her head ruefully. "He would pass me on Fifth Avenue as I was walking to the rehearsal hall and say, 'Oh, hello there, Miss Patrick.' He'd be all dressed up, walking with his swanky friends, and they would all laugh at the little showgirl. Acknowledging me as his sister would have given away his new act."

∼

Betty's voice on the other end of the line sounds genuinely concerned. "Are you mad at Fritzi? There seemed to be something wrong between the two of you yesterday."

I do not want to have this conversation with Fritzi's mother. "We haven't seen each other in a while," I fumble.

"That's not true! She told me the other day that she was having breakfast with you. You just saw her."

"No, she canceled that breakfast—again. Except for the other day at your house, I probably haven't seen her in two months." Silence.

"Fritzi has been very busy, you know," Betty offers tentatively. I say nothing. "Well, all right then. Bye. I love you."

≈

I am rushing home from a longer-than-expected afternoon at Betty's, one eye on the little clock in the van's radio panel, the other scanning the long stretch of tree-lined country road ahead of me for hidden troopers. I want to get back before the elementary school bus turns the corner and drops my youngest son off. I know how Kurt hates to walk into our shadowy woods and find his house silent and motherless, the front door locked. Today I am going to be waiting cheerfully for my little guy with a platter of after-school snacks and all the time in the world.

I notice the dark pile at the end of our driveway long before I understand what it is. Oscar, our black Labrador retriever, always waits at the bus stop for Kurt in the afternoon—or perhaps he simply waits for the dog biscuit that my eleven-year-old tucks into his knapsack each morning. I roll into the driveway and turn off the engine, already feeling nauseous, and force myself to get out and walk slowly back toward the carcass of our pet, then I remember that Kurt's bus will soon stop right at the spot where that motionless mass is lying and I begin to run.

Oscar's sleek body is intact and there is mercifully little blood. Tracks show that whoever hit our dog swerved widely onto the curbless shoulder to do it. He is not stiff yet, and I realize with a pang that he has only just died. I want to touch him, see if he is still warm. I cannot. The tears roll down my face as I stare at the dog's beautiful head lying in the dirt, his mouth slightly open, his tongue hanging limply over sharp canine teeth. The one eye that I can see is glazed but still moist. He was here waiting for Kurt when I was not.

Kurt's face is thrilled when the bus door opens and he sees me waiting for him, arms open wide. Then he sees Oscar's body. The abrupt transition from joy to horror is harder to witness than his pain. I cover his eyes and lead him to the house. Call my husband and ask him to come home. Sit on the couch, rocking my child. Another bus arrives; my eldest son, Carl, bursts into the house shouting "Mom, Oscar's been hit! Did Kurt see?" He and Al have buried the dog in the garden, surrounded by begonias, by the time Kurt and I return from a drive. Kurt still has not spoken.

Over the next few days, I do everything that I can think of to ease my son's distress. We have a little service for Oscar, hint that there can be another dog when Kurt is ready to choose one. We talk and offer to listen, invite his friends over and take him out, remember and cuddle and care. Nothing works. Kurt's face is a mask of misery; he seems to believe that allowing himself even a second of relief might constitute a lack of respect for his lost friend. He ignores his homework, simply stares at his meals, cries himself to sleep. Finally I suggest that I might have to take him to the doctor if he does not perk up.

"What would help, honey?" I beg him. "Tell me what I can do."

He twists in my arms and lifts his freckled face to mine. "I want Grandma Betty," he pleads tearfully. "She'll know how my heart feels."

I have seen the tiny "shrines" that Betty has made to Nikki's memory, the pictures of her deceased pet hanging in places of honor on the wall, the plaster dog that she has positioned in a basket in the corner. I pick up the phone. "Call your mother and feel her out," I beg Fritzi. "I'm not sure. This may be too hard for her. I don't know what to do."

Two minutes later Fritzi returns my call. "Mom says to bring Kurt right over."

It is dark when we pull up. Grandma Betty is waiting in the light of the doorway. Kurt runs from the car to her waiting arms. She enfolds him and pulls him into the house. I sit in the cool darkness for a moment after the door has shut behind them, then drive to the plaza across the street and stroll nervously around a video store, killing time. Forty minutes later I return to Betty's house.

Kurt is in the kitchen, his arms full of gifts. His face is tear-streaked, but he is smiling. Betty's eyes are red and swollen. She hugs my son tightly before she sends him out the door, takes one look at me, and pulls me close against her chest as well. Kurt climbs into the front seat of the van, tenderly cradling the plaster puppy that Betty has taken from Nikki's little bed and placed in his arms. He carries it gently upstairs when we get home, puts it on the floor next to his bed, falls asleep with his arm draped over the edge of the mattress and his hand resting on its head.

The next morning Betty calls early. "How is he?" Her voice is thick with concern. I tell her that our little guy ran out of the house to catch the bus looking like a happy child. He did not turn to me on the porch, unnerved by the absence of a welcoming bark, a wagging tail. He did not reach for a dog biscuit as he packed his knapsack, then remember and shatter. Upstairs in his room, his gift from Betty sits beside his bed, an object to which he can transfer affection without guilt, a gift that represents both loss and support. "When I pet my dog," he explained at breakfast, "it's like I'm loving Oscar and Grandma Betty at the same time. I feel better, Mommy."

~

"That looks dangerous!" I exclaim, and Fritzi and Betty collapse into laughter.

"Well, gee! Do you think so?" they tease.

I have purposely invited them to my home together, hoping to heal the recent tensions between us, and we are watching Fritz Huber's home movies, two full cassettes of patched-together fragments that Bobby, Betty's son, has skillfully pieced together from piles of rotten and forgotten filmstrips. I snuggle into the couch, amazed at what I am watching—not only performances that audiences saw but the rehearsals that only other performers could scrutinize.

"That's Terrell Jacobs," Betty tells me. "I took care of a baby lion with rickets for him once. And the Valentines on the trapeze. We bought our property in Houston from Bill Valentine. Those Antelecks had a wonderful perch act. There's the Zacchinis—you know, the cannon act. Everyone knows them."

"Look! There's the Strawberry Festival in Ohio," Fritzi screams, then adds, grinning, "They had the longest outhouse I'd ever seen—forty holes! I've never forgotten that. Awww—look. That's Bobby and me teasing Roy Rogers and Dale Evans."

"Watch!" Betty interrupts. "This guy broke his leg." A rider on a bucking bronco flashes across the screen, arms waving and fringes flying. A moment later the movie captures the commotion as he is lifted off of the ground and carried away by anxious cowboys. "We heard the crunch," Betty remembers. "That's Gene Autry there. Remember how Ostermaeir combed his horse into a check pattern? What was the name of that jeep? Jezebel?"

"No, Mom." Fritzi laughs. "Nellybel, wasn't it? Something like that."

After a while, I stop trying to absorb names or understand how the acts were accomplished and simply listen to mother and daughter as they reminisce and critique: "That plange is incredible. She had amazing upper body strength. Watch this break away. Is that Mel Hall on his unicycle? Look—it's Ruby and her dogs. One dog was blind, wasn't he? No, that's Camille and her dogs. She was a real gypsy. Every morning she would let the dogs out and they would run right to me. That helicopter is actually a neck spin—they spin you out parallel. Proske had a fabulous rapport with animals, didn't he? There's Fritzi's godfather. Remember how he used to come to the dressing room for a Kotex to pad his supporter before he bounced on the wire? His wife, Musetta, could fling herself forward from the trapeze and catch on her heels. Look! There—she's going to do it! God! Just incredible."

"Circus people never get tired of watching circus movies," Fritzi explains apologetically. "We would go to performers' parties when I was a kid, and they would eat and show reels all night."

"You should see how other families take home movies," I warn her, laughing. "Just cakes with candles, and endless turkeys."

Fritzi explains that her brother had to splice numerous reels together before they fell apart, without knowing how they might be dated. The clips keep skipping backward and forward in time between Betty's early acts (Roman Ladders), her later routine with

Fritz, and other performers, scenery, monuments, parties, babies and toddlers. "That's a sway pole," Betty suddenly comments, and I spin around to face the television, grab the controller, and press the 'pause' button.

My children would call it "awesome"—not an inaccurate term. The silver pole is perhaps two hundred feet high. It is swaying back and forth in a huge arch while a lone man performs acrobatics while clinging to the very top—seemingly by his heels.

"That's Selden," Fritzi tells me. "Doesn't he have a great sway? He was a metallurgist. He came up with a metal alloy that allowed his pole flexibility without the risk of snapping. He wouldn't share the secret though. He had his rigging destroyed when he died."

"Some people are like that." Betty humphs. "We sold our rigging to the Carrillos after Daddy died. I like knowing that it's still circulating. There's Vern Orton on his pole. See the difference in the sway?"

"God, he's right against the roof!" I cry.

"Yep. The ceiling wasn't high enough for his rigging. He practically had to duck his head when the pole came up. He died on his sway pole. It wasn't guyed out properly."

"Is that the funeral we went to on the road?" Fritzi questions.

"Uh-huh," Betty responds, already intent on the next clip. However much she may have liked the people she has lost in this way, the possibility of dying while performing was something that they all understood.

"There's my pole!"

I pause the tape and Betty launches breathlessly into another angry story. Betty generally becomes agitated when she talks about Harry, but I can tell by Fritzi's expression that he is not a popular subject with her either. "I wanted my own act, so my father built that sway pole for me. I had no say in it. No one else would try it out. Harry told me, 'Get up there,' so up I went." I push the play button and watch the little speck that is Betty performing on the top of her pole as it carves a wide arch in the sky.

"Harry put a steering wheel on the top for me to stand on, but there wasn't a loop to hold my feet, so I had to spread my toes and hold on with them. That's why I never got a big sway—I was always scared that my toes might slip," Betty explains. "My father wanted me to do a headstand on that wheel, but it was too narrow. He stuck two little iron things onto the rim so that I could hold on with my hands and turn upside down, but I still couldn't do it. After I fell, Fritz told my father, 'Take that wheel down. I want to see it.' When he examined it, he was appalled. He said, 'Harry! There are no safeties for her and the wheel is too small,' but my father insisted that he could do a handstand on that wheel. He tried and couldn't do one, so he said that he just wasn't in the mood. He would never admit it when he was wrong."

Betty pauses for a breath. She is thoroughly indignant—as if Harry were in the room with us, awaiting our verdict. "Fritz got me a big wheel—like a bus wheel—and then he built me slippers so that I could slip my feet in. When I fell, it was my father's fault. Harry hadn't guyed the pole out properly. Fritz warned him that it was too slack, but Harry thought that it would hold."

"Tell me about falling," I urge her. "Were you hurt?"

"I told Charlie not to tell Mama," Betty continues. "She always mistrusted that sway pole. Charlie told Mama that I'd fallen out of the truck again."

"Again?"

"Oh, one time Harry was singing while he was driving. He was kind of swerving the truck to the music and he turned a corner real hard. The door came open and I fell right out of the cab and landed on my behind. I passed out for just a moment. My bottom was black, I'll tell you. When I fell from my rigging, we just told Mama that I'd fallen out of the truck again. I didn't want her worrying about my sway pole."

Months ago I might have suggested to Betty that an unreliable parent is surely as dangerous as bad rigging. I know better now. After Fritzi and Betty leave, I watch the sway pole footage again, then look back through the stacks of newspaper reports and reviews that they have given me to photocopy. I have examined every note in Betty's route books—pocket calendars on which she recorded bookings—and know where she played, when she laid off, have even noted the birthdays and little personal comments that she has written in the margins, but nowhere does she mention having fallen from her rigging. It is a big event to have omitted. Finally I find a review dated July 13, 1946: "Near Tragedy Strikes Circus on Opening Night."

It happened in Evansville, Indiana, on a Friday night before a crowd of six thousand spectators. Betty had finished her highpole act and had climbed fifty feet down to the one hundred-foot level. From there she began her "slide for life," a fast descent on a diagonal rope that connects the pole to the ground. Fritzi explains the process to me over the phone: "You get on a piece of tubing and you slide down the rope. Somebody is at the base to break your momentum. You do a sort of Indian burn motion on the tubing and that locks up on the rope. So Mom came down the pole, started the slide, and the rope snapped. She fell most of the way down. She must have hit a guy line because she nicked her shin somehow and that broke her fall. People who saw her say that she fell about eighty feet onto an infield on the fairground, so it was a soft landing. She was very relaxed and she bounced."

The reviews tell me that Betty walked away, in spite of a sprained ankle, and returned forty-five minutes later, after having been examined at the hospital, to take her bows and reassure the audience—a mark of professionalism in any field.

Betty tells a good story, but if I want an explanation of rigging or the intricacies of how a performance is accomplished, I need to ask Fritzi. She uses a terminology that I understand: winch, clamp, pulley, stake, tress. Betty will refer to the same items generically as "metal things," making it almost impossible for me to visualize what she is talking about. I have begun to thank Fritzi for her help and to say good-bye when she adds one more piece of information: "You want to know something weird? Mom told me that as she was falling, she saw my grandmother Babette's face, and Grandma told her, 'Don't be afraid, baby. I've got you. It'll be fine.' So she just relaxed. Not long after that, they found out that Grandma was dead."

~

Babette died in August of 1946. Betty believes that her mother died of a brain hemorrhage. "Mama was a Christian Scientist and didn't believe in hospitals or doctors or dentists. She took a bad tooth out herself once by biting on marbles." I throw her a horrified look and we both wince. Betty explains that she was visiting Fritz in his trailer when Charlie stopped by and said that he had some news. "I thought maybe [Charlie's first wife] had had her baby," she recalls. "Charlie told Fritz, 'Her mother died,' and then walked away. He didn't say our mother. He didn't even tell it to me! I passed out."

Betty, Harry, and Charlie flew to New York for a single day to bury Babette and to dispose of her effects. In order to make room for her daughter-in-law, who was still living with her, Babette had packed most of her belongings into storage trunks. The giant steamer trunks that had held up the family's mattress when the children first arrived from Germany had long been insufficient for her needs. Sixteen trunks were stacked in the garage, stuffed with linens, glassware, souvenirs, costumes, and pictures. Harry ordered Betty to have them deposited in a storage unit, so she called a moving company, made the arrangements, and pocketed the key. Because the day was so hectic and rushed, no one thought to ask where the trunks had been taken, and Betty did not volunteer the information.

Betty maintains that after her death, Babette's home was thoroughly ransacked by her husband and son. "They were looking for jewelry and money. Mama didn't believe in banks. She kept her money on her and bought jewels with what she didn't want to carry—rubies primarily. Mama had a ring with three black diamonds. She used to show it to me and tell me that it would be mine when she died. I'd say, 'Oh, Mama! Don't talk about that.' Charlie took that ring. When I told him that Mama had meant it for me, he just laughed. Then he struck me. He said, 'Now you don't have a mother or a friend either.'

"My mother never had a nice diamond wedding ring," Betty says quietly. "I used to say that when I got my own act, I would buy her a big stone. Well, I did. A gravestone."

∾

"I was with my mama at the circus the first time I saw Fritz," Betty recalls with a girlish grin. We are sitting in my car, stuffed and content after a typical southern lunch of fried fish and coleslaw at Mike's restaurant. Betty clutches a grease-soaked napkin filled with leftover hush puppies on her lap and smiles to herself. "I looked up at that tall, gorgeous man on the wire and told Mama, 'I'm going to marry him someday.'"

Years later, when Fritz Huber informed Harry that he intended to marry Betty, Harry responded, "Well, it's about time. She's been in love with you since she first saw you."

We stumble into the house, grateful for its cool darkness on a blazing hot day, and Betty immediately fills her coffee cup with water and pops it into the microwave. As I putter about the circus-toy-cluttered kitchen, examining gadgets and trinkets, and admiring my children's photographs and crayon masterpieces taped to the refrigerator, Betty explains that she met her third husband in 1936 when his act booked the same dates as the Liazeed troupe. Her heart pounded as the Swiss wire walker with the fabulous build, brown hair, and dancing hazel eyes paused to watch her practice. That evening nineteen-year-old Betty reluctantly agreed to a blind date with a friend of a clown whom her girlfriend was dating. When the girls arrived to meet their dates, there stood Fritz—washed, shy, and irresistible. Betty was head-over-heels in love before the evening even began.

"We just talked," Betty explains with a grin. "At the end of the week, we parted for different engagements. It was a couple of years before we played the same bill again, and then, suddenly, there he was, just as perfect as before. I wanted to hug him but I just shook hands."

Once again, she remembers, the Liazeed gang was together, having fun. Fritz would practice in the morning with Betty's troupe, always complimenting her on her acrobatics. By the end of the engagement, the two had become genuinely comfortable friends, but there was no sign of romance. Fritz said good-bye amiably. They did not write.

Betty often found herself thinking of Fritz during the months that followed that summer almost-romance but had little reason to hope that she was in his thoughts. When the weather turned cold, the Liazeeds booked on to the New York nightclub circuit. On opening night at the Roxy Theater, a long, satin-covered box arrived for Miss Betty Liazeed. Surprised that her mother would send flowers, Betty opened the card and saw unfamiliar handwriting, each word printed clearly and carefully in large caps—then she noticed Fritz's name at the bottom of the card. He had written that he would meet her after the show and had something important to tell her. Betty spun and flip-flopped that night as if she were made of air. After the performance, she freshened herself and waited, heart pounding, for his knock at the dressing-room door. She waited for a long time.

When the couple were finally reunited on a circus date two years later, Fritz explained why he had had to cancel his plans abruptly on that long-ago night in New York. He had originally entered the country illegally and had had to leave America and then reenter through Canada in order to obtain some kind of visa. Betty understood little of what Fritz was relating, other than that he was not an American citizen and that his mother had been the daughter of a high-ranking public official in Switzerland and had lost her fiancé in World War I before he could give their child his name. Fritz had run away to join the circus as a young boy and had learned his trade through sheer will and a good instinct. He and two wire-walking partners had eventually stowed away on an ocean liner, hoping to begin a new life in Canada.

Little that Fritz said mattered to Betty that day. She cared only that she had found him again and that their friendship seemed as solid as ever. Betty had grown quite a bit prettier in the years since their first meeting. When Fritz came to her shyly one afternoon and announced that he had fallen in love with a girl whom he intended to marry, Betty was not without hope that he was referring to herself. "I thought to myself, it has to be me!" she remembers wistfully. "I asked him, 'Who is she?' and he replied, 'A performer.' I asked, 'Is she good?' He answered, 'One of the best.' 'Are her parents in the business?' 'Yes, both of them.'" Betty smiles ruefully. "I was certain then that he had to mean me. I could hardly contain myself." Unable to stand the suspense any longer, Betty teased, "What kind of act does this wonderful girl do?" Fritz responded happily, "Elephants!'"

When the Arabs found Betty sobbing in her tent, unable to articulate anything more than "Fr-Fr-Fr-Fritz" in response to their earnest entreaties, they grabbed up stakes and ran to his truck, resolved to beat him senseless. Betty rushed after the murderous gang, wailing "He didn't do anything to me. He's just going to get marrieeeed!" The boys stopped dead and stared at her, then burst into peals of laughter. "Oh, Tafunis! And so you cry?" Fritz stuck his head out of the trailer. "What's going on?" he asked innocently.

Betty gives me a plaintive look. "What could I say? Boy, did I feel awful. I didn't care about anything after that," she admits. "I figured that I might as well go out and have whatever fun I could. I had some fun, but it wasn't the kind I really wanted." She looks at me meaningfully. Suddenly her earlier regretful stories of cruel game-playing, rash relationships, and two impulsive marriages make much more sense.

Eight years later, in 1946, only days after her second husband had disappeared with her belongings and wages, Betty was setting up her sway pole for a new eight-week run when she spotted Fritz's truck and trailer pulling onto the fairgrounds. His marriage had ended in divorce, he had recently finished a tour of duty with the navy, and he was working with a male partner once again. "I was terrified that I would say something silly," she remembers. "I didn't know how to react. I performed on my sway pole, and as soon as I had set my feet on the ground, there was Fritz—hugging me and telling me what a fabulous performer I had become! He said that he was proud of me!"

Betty remembers that she drifted to her dressing room on a cloud of hope and met Fritz's partner, Otto, along the way. Otto and Fritz had started performing together in 1931 as part of the American Eagles. When Fritz got out of the service, he had called his old buddy and suggested that the two reunite and form an act. They had been working quite comfortably together for a year.

"Otto had seen that hug," Betty tells me flatly, "and he didn't like it at all. He told me straight out, 'Look, we are a couple of bachelors and we intend to stay that way. We don't need any dames hanging around.' I figured that I was about to get hurt all over again."

Betty went with a gang of friends to a nightclub after the 11 P.M. performance, trying unsuccessfully to forget Fritz. She returned to her hotel in the morning, weary and frustrated, and moodily asked the desk clerk if there were any messages for her. "There were four messages from Fritz! He had called every hour!" Betty relates, her blue eyes sparkling. "When I got to the lot an hour later, Fritz ran up and asked why I hadn't come over to his trailer to talk after the show. I repeated what Otto had told me. Fritz took me in his arms and whispered, "Don't worry about Otto. I'm going to marry you.""

Betty's face is radiant with joy. She looks positively youthful as she beams at me from across the kitchen. "It was a strange proposal, but honestly, Donna, those few weeks of waiting were the longest of my life—even though I was happier than I'd ever been before! And on the day that I married him . . ." She lets her sentence drop, at a loss for words. I look at her glowing face and feel the tears welling in my eyes.

SHOWTIME

"We thought that they couldn't see us from way up there on the wire"—Fritzi laughs—"but they could look straight down through the trailer's skylight and watch us bouncing on the beds and wrestling and acting wild. They never let on that they knew. Bobby and I were supposed to be in bed while Mom and Dad performed their late routine. We were on a circus kids' schedule—midnight to noon sleeping. But really, how could we sleep? What our parents did at night was magical."

The magic began around eleven o'clock. Betty and Fritz would suddenly begin teasing and laughing at one another, growing increasingly animated as the clock ticked down to their hour, communicating in an intimate and unfamiliar manner that both intrigued and delighted their children. The makeup would come out and the shiny costumes, the enticing smells and bright colors. Their little trailer would suddenly pulse with excitement, as if its walls had fallen and exposed all the brilliant fireworks, screaming rides, rollicking music, and overheated crowds on the fairground as a mere backdrop for the amazing performance that their parents were about to enact.

Fritzi's childhood wonder at her parents' verve and daring was shared by every adult who saw them perform as the Sensational Kays. Betty and Fritz's comedic high-wire act left their audiences both breathless with suspense and shaken with laughter. "You want to make the people relax," Betty explains. "We'd get up there and people would be covering their eyes, saying 'Oh, I can't look,' but then they would hear us laughing and they would look, relax and enjoy themselves. The comedy put the audience at their ease and let them be attentive."

The Hubers' routine was a variation of one of the oldest combinations in circus history—the difficult—if humorous demonstration of how *not* to do a stunt followed by a rigorous straight act. According to circus historian John Culhane, the presentation of physical feats interspersed with clownish antics was invented in 1768 by Philip Astley, the founder of what we today call circus, when he introduced to British audiences an equestrian act called "Billy Buttons, or the Taylor Riding to Brentford." This humorous gag depicted an inept tailor desperately attempting to mount his horse and ride to a customer. Audiences howled with delight as the foolish tailor rolled off his steed's back, straddled the horse backward, slipped over and was whirled about the ring clinging for dear life to the horse's neck, his feet flying as he struggled to manage the beast. Having done everything wrong to advantage, the tailor would suddenly astonish the crowd by leaping onto the horse's back and shedding his clownish garb, revealing himself to be a masterful equestrian. The act would finish with a thrilling display of skill before an admiring audience.[1]

∽

When Fritz Huber reentered Betty's life in 1946, he and Otto were performing a high-wire variation of the Taylor Riding to Brentford, delighting audiences with a two-part act designed first to entertain, then to astonish. Dressed respectively in an elegant, black-tailed tuxedo and mismatched, ill-fitting street clothes, Fritz and Otto would lurch onto the stage area looking like two buddies from opposite ends of the social spectrum who had just gotten drunk together and had ended up in the wrong place. They would happen upon the precarious high-wire rigging and would manage to push and pull one another up the rope ladder to a tiny platform high above the crowd where their antics became increasingly spectacular.

A portion of this routine is captured on the Hubers' home movies. Although I cannot hear their banter, I alternately laugh and gasp as I watch these two aerial clowns displaying their amazing skills. Fritz plays the straight man to Otto's fool, clutching him by the seat of his checkered pants as Otto suddenly realizes how high they have climbed and grabs for the ropes, slipping off the platform several times in wild contortions of mock fear. It is Otto who ventures onto the wire first, crawling and sprawling; Fritz manages to haul him back in repeatedly. Finally the two tiptoe tentatively out onto the wire together. When his partner eagerly strains away from Fritz's hold on his trousers, Fritz lets go and leaps back to the platform, allowing Otto to hurtle across the wire, slip off, and hang by his hands. Undaunted, Otto pulls himself back up and stretches out on the wire for a tipsy nap.

Back on the platform, Fritz resolves to save his pal. He grabs a balancing pole but does not know how to use it. After several hilarious attempts to reach Otto, he manages to race unsteadily across the wire and ends up flat on his stomach in the middle whence he must somehow coax Otto the rest of the way to the opposite platform. The two tussle, grabbing at one another's feet, pushing, slipping, and masquerading their expertise in a brilliant pantomime of "almost falling" far more difficult to affect than a straight crossing. Finally Otto scrambles upon Fritz's back and, as he hoots and whips his wobbly "horse," is carried "piggyback" to safety.

As soon as Otto is set safely upon the platform, the comic portion of the men's routine ends; they strip down to their "straight" satin costumes, and Fritz is back on the wire exploding with energy, dancing and gyrating to the tune "Hold that Tiger." Even with the film set in slow motion, his feet seem to be flying as he jitterbugs backward and forward, then returns for Otto riding on a bicycle. The now-"sober" partners must have awed the crowds as Fritz maneuvered a bicycle across the thin steel cable while Otto climbed over his partner's back, planted his feet carefully on Fritz's broad shoulders, and rose up to his full height, his arms held wide and the wind whipping his hair across his face.

Betty and Fritz were married in Miami in October of 1946, immediately after Betty divorced Rocky. In December Fritz ensured that they could never be unexpectedly separated again by becoming naturalized as an American citizen. The new couple bought a trailer and a home in Houston; Otto slept in the truck during the season and lived in their driveway in the trailer during the winter.

"How did you all get along?" I ask Betty.

She sighs heavily and shakes her head. "Otto tried everything that he could to break us up," she admits, "but nothing worked. After a while, he and Fritz hardly spoke except to do the act. After Otto's accident, he gave up completely on circus. He went to Florida, got married, and had lots of children. I don't think that he ever stopped blaming me for ruining his career. He died bitter."

Neither Betty nor Fritz had planned to work together in the air, but shortly after their marriage, during a relatively simple part of the performance, Otto lost his balance and plunged to the ground, slamming into a partially dismantled lion cage on the way down.

"You can get too confident," Betty muses, confiding that the nimble Otto was flirting with a woman sixty feet below him when he stepped on his pants and fell from the wire. Miraculously, he broke only a leg, but the act had been booked for a full season and there was no time for a shattered leg to mend. Fortunately, Fritz had married a dedicated performer who loved heights almost as much as she adored him.

They had only a few hours between the tragic accident of the afternoon and the early-evening performance in which to prepare. Although she could not walk the wire, Betty immediately agreed to replace Fritz's partner in a hastily revised version of the routine, trusting her new husband to carry her across the cable—on his shoulders, on the bicycle, and upside down as a "human wheelbarrow." Fritz found a pair of scissors, set his wife down on a stool, and snipped her dark hair into a short "do" with bouncy bangs so that it would not fall across her eyes; then they climbed together up the ladder to the high wire.

"He told me not to look down." Betty chuckles. "I was an aerialist! Besides, I trusted Fritz completely." Fritz soon discovered, to his astonishment, that besides being a dynamic and agile acrobat, his wife was a natural clown, quite capable of fashioning her role into a signature comedy performance of her own.

Comedy acrobatics is one of the staples of the clowning tradition. Combined with a hilarious exchange that the audience could hear via a suspended microphone, the Hubers designed a routine that appealed to some of the most popular motifs of their day. Their performance, captured on a movie reel, reminds me of the antics of Lucille Ball and Desi Arnaz on *I Love Lucy*, and of Jackie Gleason's spats with his wise-cracking wife on *The Honeymooners*. Dressed in a flamboyantly flounced skirt that characterized the 1950s, Betty sprints up the ladder, leaving her husband to look for her on the ground. When he finally observes her high in the air, gesticulating wildly, calling to him to hurry up because their act has already begun, he clamors up the ladder, managing to slip at the very top. In this new routine, it is Betty who pulls an inept partner up to the platform by the seat of the pants; she cajoles him onto the wire, berates him when he gets his balancing pole caught between his legs, instructs him as he crosses the cable one foot at a time. "What are you lying down on the job for?" she yells when Fritz decides to take a nap on the wire. When he slips off the cable and hangs by one hand over the crowd, Betty becomes hysterical. I cannot help laughing at her frenzied antics; she throws herself over the guardrail and ends up swinging back and forth on a railing, frantically kicking her legs in the air while attempting unsuccessfully to hold her skirt down over her exposed fanny.

When Fritz finally returns to Betty on a lurching bicycle, she declares in exasperation, "Boy, I could do better than that!" Tired of her attitude, the long-suffering spouse grabs his outspoken wife and high-steps her across the wire while she screeches, "What's that foot doing up here? Why aren't they both on the wire?" Crowds must have enjoyed this comedy of marital comeuppance, so in keeping with the popular satires of the times. After a mock striptease on the platform, the routine finishes with Fritz dancing furiously on the cable in his "straight" costume while Betty does the Charleston on the platform, then smoothly accompanies him once more across the wire on the bicycle, perched on his back.

"The act was never exactly the same. We improvised each time," Betty recalls. "We would tell one another bad jokes before the microphones went on—to get ourselves laughing, you know. One night I shouted a dirty joke down to Fritz and the audience started to howl. That's when I knew that the mikes were already working. Geesh! The Shriners loved it, though. As long as we made the people laugh, they were content. One time a smart-alecky fellow came up to me after the act and said, 'I know how you stay up there. That guy holds you up with magnets.' He was referring to the rigger on the ground who regulated the microphone. I replied, 'Yup, that's how we do it. Magnets.'"

~

Post–World War II America was a nation eager to embrace domesticity, productivity, and, above all, fun. The Hubers did not realize that the 1950s marked the beginning of the virtual disappearance of circus, that the time-honored life that they loved was soon to become a casualty of motion pictures, television, and urban sprawl. Fritz and Betty were passionately in love and having the time of their lives.

The Sensational Kays found themselves showered with bouquets, gifts, and homage wherever they went. Free at last of her oppressive parents, loved by a decent and serious man, Betty blossomed seemingly overnight into a fun-loving, playful, warm-hearted woman intent on enjoying her life. During the days she practiced her act, gave soothing massages to muscle-weary performers, and told fortunes for her more favored female friends. ("It's hard to read for a man," Betty insists. "His mind travels too much while you're talking to him.") Evenings were filled with laughter, parties, barbecues; friends gathered together to play cards or instruments, to talk and tell jokes.

Betty never failed to make people laugh and often inspired the same playful tendencies in others. Soon her vivacity was appreciated all along the circus circuit. In St. Louis, one announcer constantly teased her, introducing her as the "Gypsy Rose Lee of the High Wire" because of the part of the routine where she stripped down to her straight costume. One night Betty looked down from the platform and saw someone standing below with a huge bouquet. She thought, Can those gorgeous flowers possibly be for me? When the Kays had taken their bows on the ground, Betty was presented ceremoniously with a huge bouquet of vegetables. The colors that she had admired from so high in the air were carrots and broccoli and cauliflower! The card read, "To the Gypsy Rose Lee of the High Wire."

Reporters quickly learned that the sociable Hubers would talk courteously with them no matter how tired they were. There would be no wisecracks, none of the impatience that they sometimes encountered from other weary performers. When the Hubers were the first to arrive in a new town, they would hook up their lights and water, then prepare a little picnic for colleagues still on the road behind them. "We worked once with Ricky Nelson and his brother; they did a flying act in Milwaukee," Betty remembers. "They came in late and had to put up their rigging in the cold. I made coffee and another act made sandwiches, and we brought it all over to them. Ricky never expected that. They were probably treated like kings on TV and movie sets, but I guess that they figured circus would be different. We knew that they would be tired and hungry. All circus performers have that in common. We weren't waiting on them; we were just being family." At night, Betty relates, most everyone would gather together to roast hot dogs and hamburgers, swap tales and jokes, enjoy one another's company.

Betty loved to hand out free passes, pictures, and autographs to children in every city that she visited. Each little face reminded her of the small girl who had once scrubbed convent floors for her meals. Miraculously, Betty still remembers the countless children to whom she offered kindness and who loved her in return. On a fairground in Canada, a child heard the Kays announced as a "free act" and fretted that the couple were not getting paid. "That little thing came up and offered us a quarter," Betty remembers, her eyes crinkling in a tender smile. "I didn't take it. I told her, 'Honey, we are well paid.' When I fell from my pole, the circus children took up a collection and gave me three cents to get me through the winter. I did take that. They would have been so hurt if I had refused. One child gave me a little drawing with real butterfly wings taped on. I still have it."

In Houston, Betty became a regular customer at the Goodwill. Throughout the year, she collected small stuffed animals, buying them for a quarter, then cutting off the tags. "They had to be clean," Betty tells me. "I had some powder to clean them with. There was one secondhand store that sold practically new dolls for fifty cents. I didn't want any with spots. They saved the nicest ones for me."

Each year, just before Christmas, Betty chose an especially dark night on which to drive to the local orphanage. The grounds were fenced but never locked. She could slip quietly through the gates and arrange dozens of freshly washed and dressed little dolls and animals on the doorstep. "They never knew when I was going to come, so they never knew who I was," she relates happily. "I wanted those children to have a bright Christmas. In the convent I had a doll, but the sisters would only let me play with her for one hour on Sunday afternoons; I wanted to hold her so badly. All children need something to love."

In Houston the Hubers were home folk. When the circus paraded through Houston streets, the Kays were always showered with flowers and applause. "Some of the other acts wondered why we got all the attention, but it was our home," Betty recalls. "We always tried to be friendly." Their reputation for courtesy and generosity followed them far from Houston, though. When the Hubers finished a tour of Hawaii, Fritz arrived at the airport carrying sixteen shirts and Betty toting sixteen muumuus—gifts from many new friends.

Both Fritz and Betty knew what it was like to feel stranded in a foreign country among strangers and never failed to offer help to new performers who did not understand American ways. "Immigrant performers often came to America thinking that the streets here would be paved with gold," Betty relates. "They ended up with a rotten trailer, no pots or pans. Fritz and I helped many a new act with food or money for a hotel until they could get paid. Not many people would offer money to strangers. They'd say, 'Go draw.'

My quizzical look reminds my subject that she is using a terminology that I do not understand. "If you are booked for six weeks, you get paid at the end. That way it's certain that you'll work through the contracted period," she explains. "If you draw on your pay early, the agents will know that you need the job and they will book you for less money the next time around, or keep a greater percentage for themselves. Some agents were notorious for that. You never want to ask for your money up front. Better to starve for a week than to let an agent know that you're broke."

Betty shakes her head emphatically. "We never drew, even when we were hungry." She smiles rather sheepishly at a sudden memory. "You know, we were so broke once that when a fellow bought Fritz a beer, he didn't have fifty cents to buy one back. He was ashamed to admit it. I said, 'Wait a minute, Daddy,' and ran into the bathroom.

I kept a half-dollar piece pinched into my navel; otherwise, my kind of belly button sort of pops out, you know? We used my tummy money to buy a beer!"

Many performers spoke no English. Some had no work papers or social security numbers and wanted to remain invisible in America, their identities protected by costumes and assumed names. The circus was a world into which newcomers could easily disappear, erasing their histories, separating themselves from the "outside" culture almost seamlessly. No one asked about the past other than to inquire whether the performer's family had shared the tradition. Acts that could boast a circus legacy were family immediately, but performers who were newcomers were not always so fortunate.

"A newcomer was called a 'First of May,'" Betty remembers. "If he was a good person, nobody would bother him, but sometimes other performers would play little jokes. They would send the new guy for a skyhook."

"What's that?" I ask.

Betty grins. "Nothing." I shake my head and laugh, realizing that I might have swallowed such bait easily.

"It wasn't funny." She sighs. "Someone would send the poor fool to the high act. The high act would say, 'We gave the skyhook to so-and-so in the concession stand.' Sometimes the new act would be sent to the ticket seller for the key to the fairground. He would run all over the lot asking everybody in broken English for the fairground key until somebody like me or Fritz took pity on him. It was a form of initiation."

"Like buying the Brooklyn Bridge?" I suggest.

"Well, yes"—Betty laughs—"but no one got hurt."

Betty relates that show people seldom had to fear other performers, but many an immigrant artist learned to be wary of townspeople. "We were practically outside the law, so we had to be cautious," she remembers. "We had our own language. Most circus people know 'gypsy' language. The Germans and Hungarians know the terms; the Italians have their own little codes. People would whisper 'The eagle is flying,' which means that they are paying off in the office. The term 'Hey Rube' originated with the carnival. It's an insider warning that a game is rigged, or that a carnie has been robbed, or that a fight is starting. Just spread those words and everyone will gather together fast to help out."

"So it is like a vigilante sort of law?" I ask.

"Well, we could force a thief out. He would be ostracized," Betty explains. "We didn't get too many Hey Rubes in the circus, but we had to protect ourselves. We were outsiders in strange towns. We took care of our own."

~

Within their protected circus circle, the Hubers felt nurtured, valued, and respected. Both partners had been disconnected completely from their relatives in Europe, and neither had a loving family in America. Perhaps because they lacked close relations, the couple grew to regard other performers and the circus itself as an extended family. Without nurturing family backgrounds on which to model their marital relationship, Betty and Fritz drew on every type of love that they could imagine—familial, parental, romantic—in order to create a union that could satisfy their needs. The Hubers became extremely close as a couple, playing together like siblings, sharing like friends, and calling one another "Mommy" and "Daddy"—terms of affection and implicit trust that neither had ever applied to a biological parent. Still, something vital was missing. Incessantly followed by other performers' children, Betty told fairy stories, baked cookies, saved scribbled drawings and little gifts, and yearned for infants of her own.

The Kays were on a circus tour of northeastern Canada in 1948 when Betty miscarried their first child. They had been driving deep into the night on a remote expanse of road that seemed to run to the icy pole of the earth. She had been sleeping for a while, but suddenly Betty sat bolt upright. She told her husband that she thought she needed to go to the bathroom. Fritz brought the truck to an abrupt halt, hundreds of miles from civilization. Fritz gazed in awe at the infinite pricks of cold light spread across the unfamiliar sky while his wife stumbled toward the back of the truck, her hand clutching a wad of tissues.

Fritz had begun to doze when the dim beam of Betty's flashlight quivered across the windshield. Betty leaned heavily against the truck. "Daddy"—she gasped—"I think that I lost my left lung." Fritz slid across the cab and grabbed the flashlight from his wife's hand.

"This I've got to see," he responded, frightened by the smallness of her voice but forcing reassurance into his own. He disappeared into the cold blackness but reappeared instantly, his broad chest heaving with deep emotion. "You were pregnant, Mommy," he said, sobbing, "and we didn't know it. I couldn't even look."

Betty trembled. "I had a baby?" she repeated. Fritz lifted his stricken wife very gingerly and cradled her in trembling arms. He leaned his face against hers and they wept silently together.

Hours later the Hubers neared the lights of a city, Fritz steering mechanically as Betty huddled against him, dizzy and nauseous. As their truck rattled into the dark lot of a little diner, Betty suddenly felt her spouse shaking. Fearing that he had begun to cry again, she pulled herself up and was shocked to discover Fritz's weary face convulsed with laughter. He leaned over and whispered, "Lost your left lung?"

Even in her pain, Betty could not help laughing.

"What am I going to do with you, Mommy?" Fritz whispered tenderly. Never stop loving me, Betty thought. Just love me forever.

~

The doctor grinned when Betty complained that she had pulled a muscle that would not heal. "It must be a pretty big muscle." He chuckled. "It's moving." A year after her miscarriage, Betty Huber still knew about her reproductive system only what the nuns and her sheltered mother had offered to teach her.

"My muscle is moving?" she responded, incredulous, and the doctor burst into heavy guffaws.

"Good heavens, girl. You're at least three month's pregnant!"

Fritzi Babette was born on February 7, 1950, on Betty's thirty-third birthday. Betty brought the infant home wrapped in a handmade blanket. At night she rocked her precious daughter, whispering all the little secrets of a mother's love into her tiny ear. At daybreak Betty would dance Fritzi through the trailer, crooning bits of showtunes or old German lullabies, dangling dazzling baubles of circus raiment in the dawning sunshine before her baby eyes. One morning Fritz awoke to find his wife standing fearfully beside their bed, her face sopped with frightened tears, the baby sleeping peacefully in her arms. "Please, Daddy, don't be mad at me. Our little girl is blind. I wave things in her face and she just stares. Are you mad at me, Daddy?" As if he were consoling a frightened child, Fritz explained gently that babies are born unable to see and that their daughter would develop stronger sight within a few weeks.

Little Fritzi seemed to realize almost intuitively that her inexperienced mother was watching her, eager for proof that her parenting skills were not inadequate. "She skipped steps," Betty remembers proudly. "She never crawled. One day we left her asleep in the crib for a few minutes. We didn't think that she could even sit yet. When we returned, Fritzi was standing up, shaking the railing. She had already taught herself to walk. We figured that we'd better not leave her by herself any more."

Fritzi was a deceptively quiet baby. She refused to flatter her parents with the gibberish for which they longed. When Betty coaxed her little daughter to say, "Ma Ma" or "Da Da," the child pursed her lips defiantly, but when she began to speak, Betty insists, she startled her parents by voicing complete little sentences. Adults would stop over and chat in the very simple, cute terms that people use with babies, Betty recalls. Fritzi would stun everyone by responding clearly "I understand" or "I don't understand."

"Oh, come on," I plead. "That's impossible for a one-year-old."

Betty merely shakes her head, amused. "I never knew what she was thinking or how much she knew. She was always learning."

Fritzi was fifteen months old when Bobby was born. When Betty unwrapped the new infant to show his curious sister, the toddler's astonished first response was "It's human!" Betty had often brought baby monkeys and animal cubs into the trailer wrapped in blankets. "The child knew the difference!" she remembers, still flabbergasted at the memory. "Daddy said, 'Well, Mommy, you're always playing with lions. What did you expect?'" Where Fritzi had learned the word "human" and how to apply it remained a mystery to both parents.

The slim little girl with the serious eyes assumed a parental affection for her baby brother almost immediately, almost as if she mistrusted her parents' ability to raise a "human." When she got tired of the smell of his diapers, she pulled the red-haired toddler into the bathroom and toilet-trained him. Together the two tykes wandered around summer-warm fairgrounds hand in hand, rolled in fresh mounds of fragrant sawdust under newly stretched "Big Top" canvases, played endlessly in their favorite toy—a large cardboard box—while their parents rehearsed complicated maneuvers high over their heads. Betty seldom worried that the children might roam too far. She knew that her little daughter was both practical and fiercely protective of her chubby-cheeked brother, but also understood that her children would be safely guarded by every performer within the boundaries of the fairgrounds.

So reliable was Fritzi's constant solicitude for Bobby that the Hubers sometimes forgot that their firstborn was only a year older than her baby brother. One afternoon, as he rehearsed on a freshly rigged cable, Fritz paused to watch his children playing near the edge of the ring, far below. He could see them sprawled on their tummies beside the bleachers, heads together, intent on creating roads in the sawdust for their matchbox cars. Fritz rubbed rosin on the soles of his slippers, bounced on the cable for a moment, then strolled to the center. He did not normally look down during a routine, but when he heard a lion's startled roar beneath him, he allowed himself a glance into the giant cage directly below. The metal door of the enclosure hung wide open. Three-year-old Bobby had toddled inside and was fingering the mesh around the interior perimeter; a huge jungle cat slowly followed him, curiously sniffing his unfamiliar scent.

With his heart pounding, realizing that a single misplaced step would not only plunge him into the cage but might also startle the beast into attacking his child, Fritz crossed the wire carefully and raced down the ladder. He did not dare to approach the cage himself but ran for help; he knew that the lion could react aggressively to anyone other than its trainer. Bobby was rescued from the lion's cage well sniffed, but otherwise unharmed. Little Fritzi returned minutes later with a cool drink clutched between two small hands; the four-year-old had been worried that her baby brother was growing flushed in the Midwestern heat and had left to fetch him refreshment.

It was by rare chance that Betty discovered what would become the longest leash any child could hope for. One afternoon, tired of searching for her wandering puppy, Smokey, Betty decided to try out one of the fashionable new dog whistles whose high-pitched blast could supposedly be heard by canine ears alone. She sat on her trailer steps and exhaled repeatedly into the black plastic mouthpiece, but only a thin rush of air hissed through the other end. Disgusted, Betty blew one final, silent blast, threw the whistle to the ground, and was about to set off to search for Smokey when Fritzi raced around the corner of the trailer, sweating and angry, with Bobby in tow. "What was that terrible sound?" she demanded as Bobby whimpered and sniffled. Doubtful, Betty felt in the grass for the tiny whistle, raised it to her lips, and let her breath out softly. She heard absolutely nothing, but both children immediately screamed and slapped their small hands to their ears. Smiling, Betty cleaned the pipe off and carried it into the trailer. "Time for lunch," she told her children.

~

"We were lucky. We had the luxury of a childhood," Fritzi insists, earnestly watching my eyes. "Most circus kids start working as soon as they are able, but Mom and Dad didn't want to train us from childhood. Their act was too dangerous."

The "childhood" she is relating seems completely alien to me. Over a large breakfast in her quiet suburban home, Fritzi tells of having grown up practically without schoolrooms or neighborhoods, friends or girl scouts, library cards or birthday parties, running water or a stationary floor.

"My earliest memories are visual ones of being outdoors when I was prelinguistic," Fritzi states solemnly, then suddenly stops talking and stares at me anxiously. "Before language. What? Didn't I use the word correctly?"

I struggle to control my giggles, swallowing so hard that I give myself the hiccups. "Fritzi, you have to understand what an abrupt transition it is to move from interviewing your mother to dealing with you."

Fritzi smiles, aware that I am complimenting her eloquence. "I thought that maybe I had used the wrong term." She laughs. "The look on your face was priceless. I am sitting in what I now know was a small table that had a seat dropped into it and a varnished railing of wood around the edge," she continues. "The surface was masonite, but it had been turned over so that it felt rough. There's light coming through leaves overhead and the leaves are moving in the breeze. I am spreading my fingers and playing with the shadows on my hands."

"How old are you? About four?"

"No. Mom has a picture of this. I am completely bald."

"That could have been age four."

"Oh, stop! I wasn't much more than one." Fritzi laughs, trying to frown at me. "Those are my first memories. My next strong remembrance is of lying in my bunk in the back bedroom of the trailer. It's about an hour after the late show has ended and my parents think that we are asleep. I can hear the door to the living area opening and shutting as other performers come in, adult voices talking, and occasional quiet laughter. Mom and Dad are sharing a late-night European-style supper—bread, cheese, a beverage—with friends, and they are all telling jokes and enjoying one another's company. It's a good memory. I feel safe and surrounded by happiness."

"Can you recall what the trailer was like inside?"

"It was all blond wood," Fritzi reflects softly. "There was lots of wood in those trailers. They were well made. There was a communal dining and living area that had a contoured cabinet with a hide-a-bed inside, and a sofa and collapsible chair. The kerosene heater was up front near the kitchen. Then a hallway with a closet on one side for costumes, and a bathroom and shower on the other. In the back was our room. My dad had built us bunk beds with cabinets overhead and underneath so that we had lots of storage, and he had built a bookshelf on the wall for my books."

Fritzi lowers her eyes for a moment, as if she has just remembered a beloved friend. "I adored books. Mom knew that books were important, but she mostly read magazines. Even today she loves those romantic and sensational tabloid stories. My father had read the classics as a child in Switzerland. He gave me Kipling, *Heidi*, *Aesop's Fables*, Grimm's fairy tales. He explained the Bible to me. Every night he read to us in bed. Bobby would fall asleep right away in the top bunk, but I loved listening to Dad's voice telling irresistible stories. There are wonderful visual passages in *Heidi*." Fritzi's face glows softly. "Do you remember how Heidi slept in the hayloft looking out at the stars through the broken roof? I was an insomniac as a child, and whenever I really wanted to sleep and couldn't, I willed myself into that setting. It soothed me to sleep.

"I wanted a library card desperately but couldn't obtain one because we never stayed in one place. When I finally got a card in Houston, I checked out as many books as I could carry. I slept with them, smelled them. My relationship with books was extremely physical. I began constructing my own little books as a child. There was no room for a library in the trailer, so I had to manufacture them very small. Some had words, others only pictures. I still have two. The first is a book of designs made by taping fabric samples into a leather portfolio. It's rather pathetic now—little bits of tape and material, all falling apart. The second is a book of imaginary creature illustrations that I made by combining two different animals and blending their names. Each illustration is stitched to colored paper."

"You would have made a great monk." I chuckle, and Fritzi smiles slyly. "You mean that I am still experimenting in the margins?" She laughs, then grows thoughtful. "Isn't it funny that as an adult, I ended up fabricating my own 'illuminated manuscripts,'" she muses, "but I grew up surrounded by fabulous visual transformations—that's the nature of circus. My parents weren't historians or scientists. Physicality and visual transformation is how they taught me to understand the world."

Suddenly Fritzi's eyes begin to sparkle. "Okay. Here's a good example of a science lesson when I was a kid. I saw an African American family on the midway one day and asked my mother why they had such dark skin. She considered for a moment, then pointed to a freckle on my arm. 'They had those little spots too,' she told me, 'but theirs just grew and grew.' Well, after that, I naturally assumed that I would eventually grow up to be black. Whenever we drove past a group of dark-skinned people, I would lean way out of the window, wave excitedly, and point to my freckles so that they would understand that I was one of them but hadn't turned color yet. As we drove past, I would think, I don't even know my people."

Fritzi watches with glee as I try unsuccessfully either to stop laughing or to lower my half-raised cup of tea before I spill it. "You are making this up!" I accuse her.

"Nope." She chuckles. The best times, she relates, were road trips on which the family shared the truck and pulled the trailer, leaving the car behind rather than splitting up in two vehicles. They would sing and chatter, tell stories and play road games.

Not having had a childhood in America, Betty knew none of the popular children's ditties or nursery rhymes that most of her contemporaries were teaching their offspring. She taught her children her favorite Latin tunes and the songs that she herself loved to sing; one of their favorites was "The Able-Bodied Seaman," a piece that Betty remembers from her vaudeville years. The first time that I heard Fritzi and her mother launch into its suggestive lyrics, swaying and bellowing like pirates, I bit my cheek while laughing too hard.

> I'm an able-bodied seaman,
> and I've sailed the briny deep
> from the Barbary Coast to Singapore.
> Made love in every language,
> had a girl in every port
> with welcome written on her door.

> I was married in Chicago,
> divorced in gay Paris,
> had girlfriends in Alaska,
> France and Germany.
> But the tattooed lady down in Coney Island
> was the one that made the biggest hit with me.

> Oh, gosh! Oh, gee!
> The tattooed woman captivated me.

> There's a landing of the pilgrims on her shoulder.
> On her arm the sun is sinking in the West.
> Where she wears her lavaliere,
> there's a scene where Paul Revere
> makes his famous midnight ride across her chest.

> On her back there is the roadmap of Kentucky,
> and the Dixie Highway runs around her spine,
> and you'll find the Everglades right between
> [deliberate pause] the shoulder blades
> of the picturesque sweetheart of mine.

Now we both agreed to keep our love a secret,
and she wears my picture where no one can see,
and she swears by the stars above
there's no doubt about her love
for whenever she sits down, she thinks of me!

"That song was the reason why I began to draw body tattoos," Fritzi explains, reminding me of the funny and realistic tattoo (featuring my name in a heart) that she drew on my husband's arm last Halloween.

"Do circus performers generally have tattoos?" I ask innocently.

"No!" Fritzi gasps. "In fact, Babette told my mother that you give away your character when you get a tattoo. You see, it's a costume that you can never change, a permanent costume that becomes part of you physically. Who would want that?"

In keeping with her enjoyment of all things physical, Betty loved to sing and dance. Fritzi relates that no aspect of the Hubers' family life escaped the influence of these sensuous passions. Even as simple a chore as making orange juice could be turned into a rollicking morning ritual. Betty would put the frozen juice in a container with a lid, then dance about the kitchen with her laughing children, shaking the juice like pretend maracas while they jumped and twisted to the beat of imaginary Latin music.

"Let's see, what else can I tell you about the physical nature of my upbringing?" Fritzi muses. "We were permitted to wrestle baby lion and tiger cubs until they reached an adolescent age where they began trying to claw one another. Baby jungle cats are tough little balls of energy; they wrestle in an intensely physical manner. A good-size cub can knock you on your back. They give little love bites, too—sort of gnaw on your limbs. Their aroma is pungent and wonderful. If a cub was big, Bobby and I tackled her together.

"Of course, this led us to wrestling with one another." Fritzi grins mischievously, and I notice that she has the same naughty twinkle in her eyes as her mother. "I grew quite accomplished at scuffling, which became a problem when I began to like boys. I assumed that if I could beat them at wrestling, they would really admire me. Guys thought that it was cute when I would say, 'Wanna wrassle?' but they were never very impressed when I beat them into the dirt. I was pretty tough."

"I grew up in a Catholic girls' school," I remind her. "Whenever I met a guy I liked, I tried to bond with him in the same way that I would with a girlfriend—by talking, deeply and confidentially. It never worked."

Fritzi grins. "Heck, I would just throw him to the ground. That didn't work, either." She pauses to think for a moment, then continues slowly. "Learning to interact with young people who had not shared my background was difficult. I wasn't allowed to visit 'outside' children when we were young. When families would come backstage and invite us home, we would make excuses. They meant well, but we didn't know these people. We were novelties to them. It would have been another performance—explaining our lives."

Only once, Fritzi recalls, was she allowed to visit alone an "outside" child, a little Canadian girl who lived a life that had been, for years, Fritzi's secret fantasy. Her home boasted a garage full of bicycles, sleds, and tools, a fenced-in yard with a doghouse and a swing set, closets and drawers full of too many things to be packed, and a pink bedroom with a pillowed bed and ruffled curtains. "I was mesmerized," Fritzi remembers, "but I was also frightened. I came home and told my mother, 'Imagine, that girl has lived her entire life in the same little pink room—eight years in the same space,' and my mother replied, 'Honey, that's how most other people live.'"

The Hubers traveled constantly during the 1950s, crossing the country in their little trailer, laying off only during the winters. The children had been enrolled in Calvert's Correspondence School and had no schedule to keep that conflicted with their parents' work calendar. On the road, the family slept in the trailer, if they had brought it, or, if it was a short-term booking, in motels. The children often napped on top of the rigging in the truck when they were tired of singing or of fashioning a "cave" out of pillows and blankets. How, I ask, did a family of four live out of a trailer for so long without getting cramped? Why did a "little pink room" seem so claustrophobic to a child used to a rumbling cot behind the rigging? To answer my question, Fritzi tells a story that reveals the stark difference in our concepts of private space.

It was Halloween night, 1956. Betty had been accosted on a sidewalk several years earlier by a small person in a mask who had demanded a "trick or treat"; terrified, she had handed over all of her money. When bands of costumed children arrived at her door in Houston the following year, she assumed that they were part of a circus-type event and gave them all of her change, then bills. The tiny marauders returned again and again, not bothering to change their costumes or to perform the promised tricks. Flustered, Betty ran to a nearby home and asked to borrow money so that she could pay the tricksters. Her amused neighbors handed her a bag of bubble gum.

The Huber family had been driving since breakfast; the short Ohio afternoon had swiftly turned to darkness and they could no longer see the ragged fields and occasional barns that they passed. In the last town, carved pumpkins had flickered eerily in windows and tiny goblins had darted across lawns in the dusk, swinging flashlights and paper sacks. Six-year-old Fritzi pouted and five-year-old Bobby pestered. Whatever trick-or-treating was, they knew that they were missing it.

When their father pulled over onto a wide shoulder of dirt surrounded by shadowy fields and windy silence, the children resigned themselves to early sleep, but Betty lit a candle on the bolted-down table and fumbled in the box underneath for their down-filled coats. "Why don't you visit the nice couple next door?" she suggested. Without a word, the children yanked on their jackets, caps and mittens, and stumbled out into the darkness. The metal door clanged shut behind them. They trudged to the back door of their trailer, pounded hard, yelled "Trick or Treat," and waited to see how their parents would respond.

The young couple who answered the door had been having a party. They were elegantly dressed in evening wear; diamonds glittered in her hair. He brandished a half-finished drink—evidently not his first. They were delighted to see the children, asked their ages and interests, popped fruit into bags for them. If it were not too late, they offered, perhaps the children could visit the duchess at the other end of the trailer on their way home. The duchess had the flu and surely needed some children to cheer her up. Perhaps they would take her some fruit?

Hours later, their sacks laden with vegetables, macaroni, cans of soup, rubber bands, pencils, and dishes, the Huber children were told by an elderly couple in pajamas that they really ought to be getting home so that their parents would not worry. As they trudged around the side of the trailer to a door that had already opened for them several times that night, they glanced through the window and saw their mother calmly sewing in the candlelight and their father nodding off to sleep in his armchair. How surprised Betty and Fritz were when the children emptied their Halloween booty onto the wooden table and told of the exotic neighbors they had visited: the schoolteacher who could speak ancient languages, the rich widow who loved music, the young bachelor who had traveled the world on a ship. The exhausted children fell asleep to the distant rumble of trucks and the faraway caress of a train whistle in the night.

The loneliness and beauty of that candlelit night in a child's history are haunting to me. Fritzi explains that her childhood was a construction achieved with parents who were creating for themselves childhoods that they had never been allowed to enjoy. "When my parents needed privacy, they spoke in German." Fritzi reflects. "They used German to discuss adult affairs—business or love talk that didn't concern us. They felt strongly that we shouldn't be involved in such things if we were to remain children; they understood that childhood must be guarded and nurtured. Our family didn't need much space on the outside because there was such vast private space on the inside, waiting to be traveled. We had time and freedom that most people never realize. We were at home in whatever story we were sharing. Costumes and visual transformation were part of our everyday lives."

Fritzi sighs, seems to fall a bit deeper into herself, searching for images that defy words. "More than anything, I remember the light in Cuba," she muses, her voice almost too soft for my recorder to capture. "The natural light was lovely. In the cities, they must have used lanterns for illumination. A lot of bad things happened in the dark. A man was hanged from a tree one night. But mostly the memories are gorgeous. One of my best visual memories is of walking at night with my mother, our guide, and Bobby. It was pitch black. We passed the entrance to an alley. Yellow lantern light was pouring out of a tiny door. I could smell strong espresso. I heard men's deep voices and a distinct tinkling sound. Out of the darkness, a lone man appeared pushing a cart of those tricolored, conical lollipops, all inverted in a little shelf on the cart. They were tinkling, and as the cart passed the doorway, that shaft of light hit the lollipops and dispersed their colors everywhere. It's a beautiful visual image that I will carry with me forever."

∼

Encouraged by their imaginative parents to develop their full capacity for storytelling and fantasy, it was not hard for the Huber children to find ways to roam in imagination, even within the confines of a trailer on a fairground back lot. Fritzi and Bobby expanded the boundaries of their world by fashioning for themselves a private, imaginary one. In the dirt outside their trailer door, the two children built miniature villages. Long summer days were spent constructing roads and houses, stores and warehouses, a fire department, hospital, civic center, and university, out of any materials that they could scavenge.

The most glorious days of all were those following the end of a show. When the rides had been dismantled and the concession booths had been collapsed into portable trailers and driven away, Betty allowed her children to wander the deserted midway and collect remnants of the magic that had been. Bobby's scavenger hunts often produced fabulous material for the miniature city. Fritzi loved to weave tiny baskets from the multicolored lengths of electrical wiring that littered the grounds after the rides had been dismantled.

On rainy days, when the children had to play inside, their favorite pastime was to construct a miniature performance. Bobby laboriously fabricated tiny riggings while his sister designed fantastic little costumes, then the dolls put on their show. "Our toys always had jobs to do," Fritzi explains matter-of-factly. "We lived around people who drove and worked all day; we took it for granted that everyone should have a job. We emulated our parents in that way."

Suddenly Fritzi narrows her eyes and inhales a deep breath.

"What are you remembering?" I ask gently.

She shifts uneasily in her chair. "It seemed like constant play, but work colored everything. I remember that we were in Cuba when my Susie fell apart. Susie was a rag doll about my size. She was my dear friend, but she was so tattered that my parents decided to throw her out and buy me another doll. I went wild when I couldn't find her.

"One afternoon we rode through a village and I spotted a doll like Susie in the window of a store. I cried, 'Look! There's Susie! She's got a job.' Given the work ethic in our family, this seemed a plausible explanation to me for her having disappeared. After I had been tucked into bed the following night, my dad ran outside and honked the horn of the car. Mom looked out the window and exclaimed, 'Oh, here's a cab.' They walked Susie into the trailer. Her job was finished and she had come home."

"Any other parent would have said, 'Here honey, let's buy a new doll,'" I reflect.

"Exactly!" Fritzi exclaims. "But they collaborated with my imagination. They chose a routine that they knew I would understand and applied it to my doll."

"Susie left without saying good-bye," I add softly, peering at Fritzi over my cup to gauge her response.

"Yes, she did," Fritzi responds slowly, refusing to look up. "That was part of our world, too."

"With so much physicality going on, and such a constant emphasis on work, I am surprised that you kids didn't want to practice circus tricks," I offer quickly, aware that my last comment was more of a subtle personal challenge than I had intended it to be.

Fritzi gives me a look that I cannot quite classify; her tone of voice suddenly goes flat. "I tried to practice walking on the wire once, but Mom pushed me off. I hit the wire coming down and scraped the whole inside of my leg. It's a twisted bunch of cable, you know? I cried, 'What did you do that for?' and Mom replied, 'I don't want you walking.'" Fritzi raises her chin indignantly. "I didn't want to walk any more after that!"

"She couldn't have just said 'Fritzi, get down?'" I prompt.

"That's not Mom's way," Fritzi responds coolly.

My mind is racing. Betty had watched her own mother grow heavier and bitter, had seen Babette left behind while Harry toured the country with his daughter and Rhonda. I consider whether Betty's abrupt reaction to Fritzi's tentative attempt at wire walking might have been grounded in jealousy and fear. In that split second of aggression, did Betty see herself at the kitchen window one day in the future, watching as a much younger and more agile version of herself clowned on the rigging with her husband? It seems like a plausible explanation for what I assume was an unusual act on Betty's part.

"Were your parents physical disciplinarians?" I ask.

Fritzi considers my question, then launches almost resolutely into a story. "When I was very small, I got mad at Bobby and bit him on the butt—hard. Mom struck me across the face. She split my lip. Mom hadn't realized what a heavy hand she had; she was immensely frightened that I was bleeding. She ran straight to Dad. I remember looking up at the two of them and saying, 'I was a bad girl and God punished me.'"

"Oh, gosh, Fritzi." I gulp. "You really were a little monk!"

"Well, I believed it," she confesses with an abashed smile. "Dad was very tolerant. The most I ever got from him was a swat on the legs with a balloon stick. He tried to spank us once. It was pathetic. He took me into the bedroom and gave me three little smacks through my clothes with a hairbrush. I came back to the kitchen table thinking, Is that it? My brother went next. Dad gave him the same three smacks and Bobby returning sobbing his little eyes out. Mom just looked at the two of us and began laughing. Of course, Bobby thought that we were making fun of him, which wasn't good. I considered that an interesting experience."

Fritzi relates that she and her brother were together so much of the time that they became conspiratorial secret keepers. The children were not supposed to run in the trailer or to play roughly with sticks. When Betty caught them acting wildly, she would march them into a corner and declare, "You can't go outside or have your toys back until you learn to play properly." She would keep their books and play-things out of reach for several days. "We were stripped of self-determination and liberty," Fritzi recollects, "and the boredom was horrible."

"At least you didn't get hurt," I offer.

"Of course we did," she exclaims, smiling at my glib maternal rationalization. "We just stopped telling our parents. Once I tripped on a stick and jammed it under my kneecap. I pulled it out myself, and between the two of us, we kept the secret that I was injured. If I jumped off a swing and scraped all the skin off of both knees, I simply wore long pants for a week." Fritzi suddenly looks at me closely, and I realize that she is perhaps even more perceptive as an expression watcher than her mother. "In a household where you are overexposed, disapproval is a big deal," she declares emphatically. "There was no margin for accidents."

"Did Bobby have the same sense that there was a need for conspiracy, or did you teach him that?" I ask rather boldly.

"Sure, he did. There was a little period of time when he would blackmail me—I would have to pay him a nickel not to tell if I had gotten hurt—but we were extremely close. We discussed everything."

Fritzi suddenly raises her chin but lowers her voice slightly, speaking more slowly. "When Dad died, Bobby and I stopped talking about feelings. It was a huge rift because we both responded so differently. I was traumatized even before Dad died, so I felt very isolated afterward, deeply depressed. I was a child who had been told to keep a terrible secret; I didn't know what to do with those emotions. There were years of only taking a deep breath and saying 'I'll be okay' and feeling terribly alone. When I was thirteen, it hit me that there was no one left to help me."

We stare at one another for a moment, then I rise and click off the recorder. "We had better leave those later memories for next time," I offer quietly, knowing even as I say this that my friend will now have reason to dread our next meeting and will probably postpone it as long as possible. Having waited so long for her to return, I have given her cause to distance herself again.

~

I now understand that parenting was an act in which the entire Huber family collaborated. The distinction between the "normally" exclusive roles of parent and child collapsed in a spontaneous family performance that was as magically wonderful as it was illusory, and ultimately devastating. While traditional "circus children" are incorporated into the family routine as soon as possible and are expected to carry on the family name as performers, the Huber children were unconventional within the circus world because they were not trained as performers nor expected to work with their parents. In this respect, their childhood was, indeed, a sort of "luxury." Their family's finest performances took place outside of the ring in tender, seductive private stories.

Perhaps Betty and Fritz hoped that generational patterns of abuse could be broken by the determined creation of new histories to replace them. Betty had long been used to parenting her parents; her current capacity for instantaneous, childlike joy was perhaps shaped during this intense period of collaborative innocence. Fritzi's natural creativity and fertile imagination thrived in the continuous family love affair that her parents were enacting; however, with a child's sharp intuition, she sensed its fragility and developed a keenly observant and prudent nature to balance her parents' carefree attitude. That an entire family negotiated between them a sustained idyllic adventure for a decade is, to me, as remarkable as change was inevitable.

~

Betty and Fritz were not the only members of Fritzi's world to wrap her in fantasy while stimulating her sense of self-reliance. Charlie did not disappear from Betty's life after she married Fritz; he simply became another chapter in the story that she and her family had been living. His character seems to have been alternately that of the dashing hero and of the villain, but meeting him was always an adventure.

Betty kept in close touch with her brother after she married her husband. After Charlie's second child, Christine, died of an accidental overdose of laxatives, Charlie sent his sister and brother-in-law a heart-rending note explaining "Our little angel is gone." Not long after that, Charlie left his wife and their toddler behind and began a new life.

Betty explains that Charlie decided to reinvent himself in order to pursue a lifestyle unconnected with the circus or his former family. "He performed in different ways," she admits. The stories that Betty proudly relates of her brother paint him as a consummate Pretender. Charlie taught real estate, worked as a plastics engineer, a management consultant, a publicity and public relations director; he started his own advertising agency, became a land developer and, eventually, a multi-millionaire. Betty cannot tell me how her self-sufficient brother learned to speak, write, and read English, but she insists that he was articulate, without any trace of a German accent. Although he had had only one year of elementary schooling in America, Charlie often claimed to have earned a college degree—usually from Harvard or Yale. "This was before computers," Betty explains. "They didn't check then like they do now."

"How did your brother become a millionaire—without a high school degree or an honorable discharge, without capital or training?" I beg.

Betty starts to giggle, then laughs out loud. "He had a photographic memory. Okay, here's an example: Charlie interviews with an engineering firm and pretends to be an engineer working for another company. The boss asks, 'Do you know anything about plastics?' Charlie looks at his watch, says, 'Oh, gosh, I forgot that I have an important business meeting, can I come back tomorrow?' By the next day, he has *memorized* everything that he can find in the library on plastics and repeats it all at his interview. When the boss acts impressed, Charlie replies modestly, 'I keep up.' Then Charlie offers, 'We have a new process on line right now that I'd like to tell you about when you have more time. If your plant could upgrade to this level, you would realize better returns almost immediately.' By the next meeting, he's read more, memorized more, and wows them all. Charlie gets hired as a salesman/engineer and gets sent all over the country with a fabulous expense account." Betty pauses, beaming in exactly the way that my mother does when she introduces me to people as "my daughter the professor." "He became whatever he wanted to be," she asserts. "Charlie was very smart."

Charlie's travels during the 1950s took him all over the country. When he called his sister in Texas from New York City one afternoon, offering to put her family up at the Park Plaza where he was currently staying and to treat them to a fabulous meal on his expense account, Betty accepted immediately. Although Charlie called later to explain apologetically that the hotel could not accommodate his guests, Betty eagerly convinced Fritz to make the trip.

"We stayed at the Belvedere, across the street from where my parents had had their restaurant," Betty remembers. "I didn't know what to wear for dinner, but Fritz told me, 'Just wear whatever you would normally be wearing.' I had bought a beautiful blue brocade suit for Fritzi and a little suit for Bobby. Fritz wore his bolo and a cowboy hat—after all, we lived in Texas. My brother met us in the lobby, looked us over. We knew that something was wrong, but we didn't understand what was bothering Charlie until we walked into the Park Plaza's restaurant."

Betty relates that everyone in the dining room was dressed in semiformal attire; the men sported dark designer suits, the women were elegant in evening wear and were conspicuously bejeweled. Charlie had reserved a table, but the headwaiter seemed hesitant to seat the party until their host laughed loudly, "These Texas oil men! They don't know how to dress in New York. This is his idea of a tie." The waiter's eyes opened wide and the Hubers were ushered to an elegantly set table in the center of the room.

As Betty tells me her version of this ill-favored evening, what strikes me most forcefully is that Charlie had much in common with the relatives whose instinct for fantasy had led to collaborative playacting on Halloween night. He also loved to tell stories, to pretend, to weave a fantasy world around himself, but he had to do this in the "outside" world, and without collaborators. On this particular occasion, Charlie was so entrenched in his pretense of being rich that he seemed genuinely embarrassed by the Hubers' real-life financial situation.

It is possible that Charlie merely resented their having arrived for his party without having donned the proper costumes, but Betty was hurt by his manner, suspected his sincerity. She resolutely refused to collaborate with the story that her brother was fabricating. When Charlie playfully asked Fritz how his oil wells were doing, obviously enjoying the sensation that his question provoked at neighboring tables, Betty replied stubbornly, "Fine, if we plant a bottle of oil in the ground." Before long Betty and her brother were hissing "Shut up!" and "No, *you* shut up!" at one another. Fritz sided with his wife, resenting the game-playing, perhaps resenting his brother-in-law's seemingly false generosity as well.

The menu was in French. Betty asked the waiter what the man behind her was having. With eyes discreetly lowered, voice expertly modulated, their server droned a succession of lyrical words that meant nothing to Betty. "That's what I'll have," she ordered. The server turned to Fritzi.

Fritzi had noticed none of the tension between the adults. She knew only that her amazing uncle was wearing a perfectly tailored tweed suit, that he had brought her to a brilliant fairy world, that she wanted to emulate the perfect posture of the ladies around her. Holding her small hands demurely in her lap, Fritzi turned to the waiter and repeated exactly the lines that he had just spoken to Betty. "Ah! She speaks French!" the waiter exclaimed. "And other languages, too," Charlie added with pleasure, beaming on his little niece. "I don't really," Fritzi murmured softly.

Charlie watched his sister's children throughout the meal, taking particular notice of his self-possessed niece. They sat quietly, ate politely. When a tray of tempting after-dinner chocolate mints was held under Bobby's little nose, he tactfully took only one. "No, thank you," Fritzi stated majestically, when the tray of sweets was offered to her. Betty stared at her husband in disbelief. As the family rose to leave, a prim matriarch sitting close by leaned over and touched Betty's arm. "Lovely children," she complimented, smiling graciously. Charlie followed his stiff-lipped sister to the lobby, hugged his niece and nephew, regretted that his work would not allow him to spend more time with them, said his good-byes and excused himself.

"My children didn't care for Charlie," Betty tells me with evident satisfaction. "They saw right through him."

"Fritzi told me that she had a tremendous crush on Charlie," I respond honestly.

Betty is quiet for a minute. "Well, I don't think he could have made much of an impression," she replies. "When Charlie claimed that he had to get back to work, Fritzi immediately said that she wanted to go home."

≈

Betty sips her McDonald's cappuccino appreciatively, leans across the table, and reaches for another breakfast burrito.

"Life is good," I tease her, and although she cannot answer me with her mouth full, her eyes twinkle mischievously. "When last we left our heroine, she was the mother of a precocious daughter and a fearless son," I remind her, laughing. "Tell me more about family life on the road."

Betty munches appreciatively on her breakfast. "Whenever I got into trouble, I knocked on the door of the trailer." She giggles. "Fritzi would call, 'Come in' and if no one did, she would yell, 'Dad, Mom's in trouble again.'"

The first trailer that the Hubers owned did not have a toilet, only a sink and shower. Fritz invested in what Betty apologetically calls a "slop thing," a tiny portable potty that resembled a covered bedpan. "It was all right for pee, but if we had to do anything else, we stopped at a gas station," she explains hastily.

Fritz generally waited until just before bed (about 2 A.M.) to carry the pot to the communal spigot at the back of the fairgrounds where he would dump its contents and wash it out. One night, knowing how her husband recoiled at the chore, Betty determined to take her turn. Grabbing a flashlight and the full potty pan, she tiptoed past the row of silent trailers and started to cross the field to the communal drain and dump. She had gone only a few yards when she stumbled into a hole, dropping the flashlight and sending the pot flying. "It seemed to be about five feet deep," she recalls, scrunching up her nose and forehead. "I figured that I was standing in everyone else's business. Yeach!"

When the hesitant knock sounded at the trailer door, little Fritzi hollered from the bedroom, "Mommy's in trouble again!" Fritz found his wife standing on the ground, several feet away, reeking of urine. "Well, Daddy, I emptied it," she whimpered.

Betty laughs heartily and takes a huge gulp of her coffee. "Fritz gave me a shower and put me to bed," she remembers, "but I smelled so bad that he pulled me back into the shower and washed me a second time, then dumped cologne all over me. The next day he went to rescue our pan and flashlight. He returned and grabbed my hand. 'Come on, Mommy. I want to show you how lucky you were to get out of there.' Betty hangs her head. "It was just a little hole, maybe two feet deep"— she sighs—"but it sure felt a whole lot bigger in the dark!"

Betty's nighttime exploits on the road were infamous. On long trips the Hubers often parked for the night beside a gas station, where they paid a few dollars for water and the use of the toilet. One freezing evening Fritz pulled the truck and trailer into a station and negotiated for bathroom privileges, then wearily told Betty to get the kids ready for bed while he took the car in search of a convenience store that carried eggs, milk, and bread—the few staples necessary for a quick, hot meal that would not cost restaurant prices. "You're tired, Daddy," Betty pleaded. "Let me go."

The sleet had turned slippery when Betty finally found a small store with its lights still on. She loaded her groceries into a plastic sack, scrutinized the treacherous drizzle icing the windows, then asked the notorious question that never failed to alarm her children: "Is there a shortcut back to the station?" Predictably, she was directed away from the highway with its lights, reliable traffic, and patrolling troopers, and onto a narrow back road that seemed to become increasingly private, until eventually Betty found herself on barely more than a path leading straight to a single dark house. This isn't right, Betty thought, and determined to turn around in the slick driveway. She began to back up slowly.

When the car skidded, Betty instantly slammed on the brake and sat still, thinking hard. What would Fritz do? She scrambled out into the bitter wind and wrenched open the trunk, found a board, and wedged it under the tires. Unfortunately, she placed the board in front of the tires rather than to the back, where it would have provided some traction. When the brake was released, the car instantly rolled three feet down into a ditch, but at least it turned around in the direction Betty had hoped to go. Once again Betty climbed out of the car, shaken and dismayed, stranded in the frigid night.

Within seconds Betty heard the heavy, crunching sound of approaching boots and sank down at the edge of the ditch to wait for whoever was searching for her. "Were you coming to see me?" a man's large voice called out through the darkness. With her own uncanny luck, Betty Huber had driven practically to the front doorstep of the local sheriff's home. He had seen her headlights approaching and had been pulling on his coat before the car even began to slide. He shook his head when Betty told of the grocer's faulty directions. "He does that to everyone." The sheriff chuckled, only half amused. "Sends 'em all over here, the fool."

The tow truck driver simply shook his head when he arrived and saw the car wedged deep into the snow-filled ditch. "Can't do nothing for you," he apologized to the half-frozen woman who stood beside the sheriff. "Hell, just hit it to sixty and maybe you'll fly out of there,"

204 WOMEN OF ILLUSION

he joked. Betty amazed both men by following the dubious advice, skimming her vehicle up a makeshift ramp and out of the ditch; she left them shaking their heads and waving as she maneuvered her broken car back down the narrow lane to the dark main road.

When she arrived back at the gas station, Betty drove a wide circle around the little trailer. She pounded on the door of the owner's small apartment until she had roused him. "Can you please get a new door for this car and fix it before my husband sees it in the morning?" she pleaded. The mechanic simply stared at her. "Lady, it's midnight! Are you nuts?" The door slammed unceremoniously in her face.

Like a child toting a bad report card, Betty shuffled doggedly through the snow, climbed the steps, and knocked loudly at her own door. From within, she heard her daughter pipe, "I bet it's Mommy and she's in trouble." When Fritz opened the door, there stood his wife, peering up at him with puppy-scared eyes. "Mommy! Are you hurt?" he gasped. "Jesus, you tore the door off!"

Betty tucked her chin and peeked at her husband, assuming a child's candor. "But, Daddy," she begged, "I didn't break a single egg."

Betty leans back, smiling ruefully. "People used to ask us, 'Don't you guys ever have any problems? You're always so happy.' Well, of course we did, but we kept them to ourselves. We didn't run around complaining and whining about car troubles or money troubles. Those things were no one else's business."

Betty sniffs sharply, glares at me as if to make her point, then relaxes slightly. I say nothing, knowing that she is mentally preparing another story. "I remember the worst trip—it was in 1959, because Fritzi was nine. We had to go from Springfield, Ohio, back to Texas. Bobby and I were in the car, following Fritzi and Fritz. I had cooked goulash and put it in the icebox in the trailer so that we could stop on the road and eat together."

Absorbed in singing and game playing, Betty and Bobby were soon far behind the trailer and truck, but Betty was not worried. She figured that she would simply drive until she came upon her husband waiting on the side of the road, ready for a picnic. Trouble came early in the form of two signs: "Truck Route" and "Car Route." Fritz would have taken the former, but Betty was driving a car and automatically followed directions. Eventually she came to a town and stopped at a restaurant, hungry and nervous. "Let's wait for Daddy," she soothed

Bobby, who had begun to suspect that they were lost as usual. Betty bought hamburgers and waited for an hour, then turned back onto the road. For the rest of the day, she inquired after Fritz at the police station in each of the little towns through which she drove, but she could not recall her husband's license plate number. Someone always remembered having seen a truck and trailer pass by earlier in the day.

Night fell hard on Bobby's empty stomach. Betty had driven past the dinner hour, knowing that she had only ten dollars and a Gulf card with her, hardly enough for a dinner, certainly not enough for a hotel room. Irritable with hunger and road fatigue, frightened at the thought of spending a cold night huddled in the car, Betty finally steered the car into the crowded parking lot of a busy lounge and restaurant. "You eat," she told her son, "but if they ask why I'm only having tea, say that I'm on a diet." While Bobby munched on a hot dog and chips, Betty walked through the restaurant to the boisterous lounge area. She managed to grab a few handfuls of peanuts from the full bowls dotting the bar before the bartender turned to take her order. "Do you have a room that my son and I could use tonight for five dollars?" she whispered. "We've lost my husband and have nowhere to stay." Betty's eyes must have spoken her full distress and the sincerity of her soul. When the bar closed for the night, the kind manager unfolded two army cots on the floor between the tables. He refused the five remaining dollars that his weary guest offered and even fixed the two travelers a hearty breakfast before they left in the morning. "Don't feel guilty, lady," he argued when Betty pressed him. "Return the favor to somebody else one day." Betty promised that she would.

The next day mother and son started out early and drove again throughout the day. The car broke down in Memphis, Tennessee. It was late in the evening when a frustrated Betty pocketed her Gulf card, pulled away from the gas station with an engine full of mysterious new parts, and sped toward the Texas border. In the backseat of the car, where it had spent the last forty-eight hours, the family parakeet lay still on the floor of a cage that Betty had long forgotten to uncover. Betty tried hard not to think about her dead pet as she careened down the dark interstate, but when she remembered how she had loved waking to the tiny songbird's joyful warbling, her eyes flooded with tears.

Several hours from home, Betty pulled into a familiar twenty-four-hour restaurant where the staff had come to know the traveling family over the years. She and Bobby had eaten nothing but a few candy bars during the day and had only some change left. "Order anything you want for fifty cents," Betty instructed her little boy and rushed toward the ladies' rest room, too exhausted to contain her tears any longer.

Ten minutes later, Betty returned red-eyed but with a washed face and renewed courage, only to discover a staggering feast spread across the booth in front of a wide-eyed Bobby. Sick with the shame of knowing that she would not be able to pay for the steaks, baked potatoes, and loaded salads that her well-meaning child had apparently ordered, Betty shuffled back to the kitchen and found her waitress. She drew a deep breath and prepared to apologize, but before she could speak, the waitress recognized her; the woman's tired face suddenly burst into exaggerated smiles. "Congratulations!" She beamed. "You are our five-hundredth customer and our honored guest this evening. Your dinner is on the house."

Back in the car, her full stomach aching, Betty turned to her sleepy eight-year-old. "Bobby, did you talk to that lady?" she pressed urgently. "Yes, Mommy," he murmured. "She asked why you were crying, so I told her that our little bird died and we lost Daddy, too."

Betty shakes her head, reaches for my teacup, and pushes back her chair. "Are you hungry?" she asks. "Would you like a cheese and tomato sandwich?"

I rise and follow her quickly into the kitchen. "So your waitress assumed that Fritz was dead?" I persist.

"What? Oh, yeah." She laughs. "We couldn't ever go back to that restaurant, and it had been one of our favorite places to stop." Betty turns away from me, bustles in the refrigerator, emerges with a bag of sandwich bread and four cheese slices. "The funniest thing was," she adds, "that I had three thousand dollars hidden in a cookie jar in the trailer but no money with me." She shrugs and reaches for the plastic tub of margarine and a bread knife. "Oh, well. Everything worked out all right."

≈

The Hubers had to become savvy as travelers before embarking on their half-year tour of Cuba during the height of that country's revolution in 1957. The dates seemed like an irresistible deal at the time: The circus would leave from Miami in December, a slow period when the family would normally be forced to lay off, and would tour the island until late spring. The Sensational Kays would be able to work in tropical heat throughout the winter, would enjoy gorgeous new scenery, and would be paid in American dollars.

Betty and Fritz had been warned of the potential dangers of traveling to Cuba as entertainers. Another circus had recently tried such a tour, arriving with all the performers' rigging and equipment loaded onto a single boat, and the Cuban authorities had confiscated the entire cargo. "Don't take your rigging over with you," the Hubers were warned. Accordingly, Fritz allowed the poles and cables to be packed up with the equipment for a concession [carnival] that would accompany the circus along its planned route. "The customs officials knew that concession," Betty remembers, "because it crossed the border every year at the same time and then returned to the States. No one questioned them or inspected their equipment. They had to pay duty on liquor but nothing else."

The Hubers passed easily across the border by declaring themselves tourists. In this manner, they escaped having to pay income tax to the Cuban government. "We once worked for six weeks in Canada," Betty recalls resentfully, "and at the end of the dates, a revenue agent made us pay Canadian taxes on those earnings. Nobody bothered us about income in Cuba because they thought that we were merely sightseers. When it was time to return, we rolled up our pay and stuffed it into tampon applicators."

The Huber family arrived in Cuba on December 6, 1956, and drove by caravan to Havana, not realizing that only days earlier, the *Granma* had landed on the beach at Las Coloradas on the other end of the island. Victoria Ortiz and Che Guevara have both written of the rebels' horrendous first days on the island, and their words guide me as I try to place the Hubers' experiences within the momentum of the revolution. Led by Fidel Castro and Che Guevara, eighty-two rebel combatants had reached their destination, sickened and desperate. For seven nights they had endured hunger, thirst, and constant seasickness while crowded onto a stripped-down fifty-eight-foot yacht built to accommodate eight passengers. Spotted by a coastguard vessel even before their arrival, the exhausted, vomit-covered revolutionaries staggered into the marshy swamps, pursued by Batista's army.

On the morning of December 5, after painful days of wandering through the tropical marshes, their blistered feet caked with fungus, their supplies lost in the swamps, the small band of guerrillas were spotted in a cane field by government planes and immediately showered with gunfire. The few demoralized men who escaped from the blazing fields into surrounding woods wandered all night through mosquito-bitten darkness, tortured by thirst. Aided by sympathetic peasants, tiny bands of rebels continued to scavenge and trudge throughout the week, finally regrouping on the rugged Sierra Maestra in southernmost Oriente Province. From there they would eventually amass a force of thousands to defeat Batista's well-equipped and internationally supported army.[2]

Betty and Fritz were about to embark on a five-month tour of the Cuban island that would take them through the very heart of Castro's growing stronghold in the south, but in sun-kissed Havana on December 6, no one realized that a revolution had begun. With its fabulous casinos, palatial country clubs, and hundreds of brothels, the glittering city was considered one of the most glamorous playgrounds in the world.

The Hubers arrived in Havana at a time when American business interests were at a peak and the dollar a most valuable currency. Ortiz relates that over 90 percent of Cuban utilities and half of the country's railroads were controlled by American investors. Roughly half of all profits from Cuban sugarcane were being funneled into the United States, as well, leaving the Cuban government with a decimated tax base and the Cuban worker with pitifully meager wages. Betty and Fritz were earning considerably more money each week in Cuba than the average worker could reap annually. By 1956 unemployment outside the city had reached epidemic proportions. Frustrated at the shortage of groceries, Betty had no idea that only 11 percent of Cubans in the countryside ever drank milk and that only 2 to 4 percent could afford meat or eggs.[3]

"We had a lovely Christmas and birthday over there," Betty enthuses when I ask her about the revolt. "The cities were beautiful, gold was cheap, and we made friends everywhere. After several months, though, things began to change. I wanted to go home. We couldn't buy milk. We had to drink that dried Carnation stuff that [the circus owner] would occasionally bring us from Florida. I hated that. Everything was getting so worrisome. There was no water or electricity. I had to give my wash out to local women and it would come back with things missing. I lost all my silk bras that way. Mothers brought children holding little paper bags to our trailer and tried to leave them with me. I couldn't make them understand that their kids would be taken away from me at the border. I was disgusted and having a good heart didn't help."

Unable to speak Spanish, unaffected by television or radio, Fritz and Betty could not have anticipated the turmoil that was simmering around them. Shortly after New Year's Day, Batista suspended civil liberties throughout the country and imposed widespread press censorship, but even without the aid of the media, it was not difficult to ascertain that the country was experiencing a major conflict. As victories emboldened the growing rebel forces, Havana became an increasingly popular target of insurrection. Militant electrical workers sabotaged the power cables that supplied the city with electricity, plunging Havana into darkness for days. Bombs frequently exploded in stores, factories, and places of commerce.

As I read through Guevara's diaries and skim historical accounts of this crucial period in Cuban history, I am amazed at the nonchalance with which Betty remembers having toured through a war zone. She seems to regard her six months in Cuba almost as a charming but rather inconvenient vacation. Puzzled by her casual stories of a revolution that apparently never piqued her interest, intrigued by the stark differences between her perceptions and her daughter's, I manage to arrange a rare interview between both women simultaneously. After an initial meeting more than a year ago, during which both women offered conflicting information, Fritzi informed me that she would not join me while I interviewed her mother; as we sit around Betty's dining room table on this quiet spring morning, I sense that she will soon announce that she has to leave. I ask very few questions, knowing that Betty's stories will, of themselves, provoke Fritzi's commentary.

"You never saw any revolutionaries in the cities, only in the mountains," Fritzi explains. "In the cities, we saw nothing but then suddenly something would explode." She relates grimly that her family walked out of a theater one evening just as a bomb blasted through a large luggage store across the street, hurling huge glass fragments toward them. Seven-year-old Fritzi ducked behind a car and watched the shards rain down on the sidewalk all around her.

"I started to run but Mike [the Hubers' hired rigger and local guide] held me back. He said, 'If you run, the authorities will assume that you set the bomb and will shoot at you,'" Betty says. "He also told us not to go swimming, that we might be found dead, but the beaches were so gorgeous that we did stop sometimes to take a swim."

"Mom was so funny," Fritzi interrupts. "She doesn't swim, you know. One afternoon she waded out into the water and was standing there, enjoying the breeze, when we noticed that the water seemed to be rising around her. Mom was standing on a little piece of driftwood that kept moving as the waves washed under it. She was slowly drifting out to sea. We jumped up and down on the beach, calling and motioning to her to come back in, but she thought that we were being playful and simply waved back. When she finally panicked and splashed back to the shore, her first words were 'Why did you let me get out so deep?'" Fritzi throws her mother a look of amused affection. "What could we do?"

"Why did you go swimming if you had been warned not to?" I ask, fascinated by this tale of forbidden pleasure.

"It was hot and the beaches were beautiful," Betty answers easily. "Things weren't all that dangerous. We made many friends. People would come and take us to their lovely cool houses." Betty looks over at Fritzi and the two women smile knowingly at one another.

"They are built for breezes." Fritzi sighs, indulging a pleasant memory. "A Cuban girl came to the circus one day and enjoyed the show so much that her family invited me over. Mom permitted me to go, which was very unusual. They lived in a large, one-room house with a palm frond roof. There was no electricity, only candlelight. They were warm and gracious. It was a huge family—lots of children. We slept in little cots in that one room. The food was simple but delicious. The entire lifestyle seemed extremely romantic to me. Of course, I could articulate only a few words in Spanish, but I had an ear for the language and said those few phrases so well that people assumed that I understood more than I did."

"You're still a bluffer," I tease.

"Nope. The first thing that I learned to say in Spanish was 'I don't understand.' I was telling it right up front, as usual." Fritzi laughs. "Mom's attempts at Spanish were even funnier than mine."

Betty chuckles and offers a story immediately to back up her daughter's assertion. "We had a boy who was supposed to interpret for us," she recalls. "I took him to the store and told him that I wanted a dozen eggs, but he didn't understand. I sat down on a chair, clucked, and laid an egg. I learned the words for all the food items that I needed that way. People began to line up each morning to watch me act out what I wanted. On the last date, we came back around full circle to that same town and I went into that store and ordered my groceries in Spanish. The man behind the counter answered in English! He had been having too much fun watching me struggle to admit that he understood."

"Weren't you at all nervous about what was happening in the country?" I press, even as I remind myself that I have had conversations similar to this with Betty before.

"We never thought anything of it," Betty assures me breezily. "You know, in front of the hotel, there were these old men who would sit in rocking chairs and rock back and forth all day long. I wore really tight pants in Cuba. Whenever I walked by, I would wag my tail and the rocking would stop. Fritz was watching across the street one day. He said, 'Mommy, I'm going to charge them fifty cents the next time you go by.'"

Betty pauses and smiles at me happily. "You flirt," I tease, hoping to prompt more stories.

"Oh, those Latin men like women." She laughs. "When we came to customs, the police always flirted with me. They would say, 'Oh, Señora, you have such beautiful blue eyes.' Then they would put a cross on the trailer and pass us through. I'd ask, 'Don't you want to look through our trailer?' but they would just laugh and wave us on. Fritz told me, 'They can look at you and tell if you are hiding things. You would have looked guilty, Mommy.' Believe me, we could have snuck so much across the border if I had wanted to.

"You know, we almost bought a house in Cuba," Betty confides, shaking her head indignantly. The family had been invited to the home of a wealthy expatriate who claimed that he was about to move to Europe and wanted to sell his house to a family that would appreciate it. "It was absolutely gorgeous." Betty sighs, recalling that the entire residence was constructed almost exclusively of glass. The downstairs living areas and kitchen circled a lush central garden with a swimming pool and shaded tile walkway. Upstairs, numerous lavish bedrooms boasted ornate balconies overlooking the garden. Every room was equipped with the most modern conveniences, including a spectacular tub in the master bedroom. The owner was asking only $10,000.

"We went back to Houston, thought it over, and decided to sell the winter house in Greenwood Lake to buy the one in Cuba," Betty remembers wistfully. "I could have lived there happily. We were practically ready to borrow the down payment when we heard that Castro had taken over the country and had confiscated all of the Americans' homes! He even took Errol Flynn's house! No wonder the guy had wanted to sell so cheaply. Thank goodness that we didn't send any money. Ahhh, I'd have loved to have lived in that house, though."

On New Year's Day, the Hubers began their leisurely tour of the island, moving from Havana to Santa Clara, a city farther to the south. Rumors of a rebel landing had already energized the many isolated insurgent factions that would soon be organized under Castro's direction, and although the government resolutely refused to confirm Fidel's presence on Cuban soil, the Hubers were halted by troops repeatedly as they made their way to the interior. "In every little town that we passed through, the soldiers would stop us and search through the trailer," Betty recalls. "They wanted to see if we had rebels or explosives with us."

The family arrived in Santa Clara without incident and set up for a three-day run. On the third evening, before the last performance, Betty was headed for the office to collect their salary. Her boss intercepted her and playfully shoved two hundred dollars into her hand, instructing Betty to run down to the casino area of the concession park and place some showy bets with house money in order to attract players. Betty was happily shooting dice when she heard a loud boom behind her.

"I didn't think much of it until I saw Fritz running through the midway, yelling 'Mommy! Mommy!'" Betty relates. "The bomb had blown off half of the boss's trailer. Fritz knew that I had been going there to collect our money. The guy who had thrown the bomb didn't get very far, though." Betty snickers. "He jumped into a jeep but couldn't pull out because it had flat tires. The lights went out suddenly; about ten minutes later the power came back on and he was hanging from a tree."

I stare at Betty in horror but her face displays no concern. "Was he a rebel?" I ask, and instantly realize the futility of my question.

"He was a rebel, I guess," she responds nonchalantly. "They were always blowing up anything they could. Every now and then Castro's men came out of the forest. You never could tell who was who."

"We were hearing bombs all the time," Fritzi adds quietly.

"One night the lights went out when Fritz and I were up on the wire," Betty relates, instantly growing more serious. "We were lucky because there was beautiful moonlight. It turned out that they were just after a pig."

Betty giggles and I look quickly to Fritzi. "The midway was always adjacent to some sort of agricultural area because there had to be a field in which to set up the show. Generally this was on the edge of town," Fritzi explains. "On that particular night there was lots of shooting and then a blackout. Apparently they suspected that someone was in the cane fields, but it turned out to be only a pig." Fritzi looks at me earnestly. "Lots of things happened at night in the darkness."

"Yeah," Betty agrees. "We didn't have bathrooms over there and I begged Daddy not to empty the pot in the field late at night. He always wanted to do that in the dark, but I was afraid that if the police heard rustling in the field, they would shoot. Fritz asked Mike to teach him how to say 'Stop, don't shoot' in Spanish, just in case he got stopped. Mike warned, 'No! Take a flashlight instead. Rebels never carry illumination. If the police see a flashlight, they will check before shooting.' Daddy felt better then, but I decided not to take any chances. We started dumping the pot in the woods before dark."

As I listen to her stories, I decide that Fritz and Betty benefited greatly from their typical good luck and perhaps even from their oblivious good humor during this period. On one occasion, Betty recalls, Fritz had purchased a fine pair of boots and had left the leather goods store carrying them in a large bag. He set the bag down for a moment and was immediately approached by two policemen with drawn guns. At this critical moment, Fritz spied his wife emerging from a shop on the opposite side of the street. "Mommy, look! New boots!" he yelled, pulling his purchase from the sack and crumpling the paper hurriedly. The police shook their heads and moved away quickly, seemingly disgusted with the "dumb Americans." "Fritz said that it was a good thing that I came out when I did." Betty smiles. "You couldn't set down a package and walk away for even a minute or the police would assume that it was a bomb."

"It sounds like you got lucky," I respond noncommittally.

Betty makes a tiny gesture of impatience but Fritzi picks up the conversation. "We did. I remember one occasion when we were very lucky. We have film footage of this," she assures me. "You'll see this in our home movies. We had left the convoy and were driving through the jungle alone. We came to a wide river of mud and rainwater. The local people all helped to push us across. What you won't see on the film is what happened after we came up on the other side of the river."

Fritzi pauses and looks straight at me, then continues. "Out of the jungle came guerrillas in khaki uniforms. One stood on the running board of the truck and pointed a machine gun to Dad's throat. Another ran to Mom's side and aimed his gun at her head."

Fritzi lowers her voice, speaking very earnestly. "What they saw coming were long hollow poles for making a sixty-foot rigging. This means that we had one hundred twenty feet of four- to six-inch in diameter steel poles loaded on top of the truck in fifteen- or twenty-four-foot increments. It looked like weaponry. The guerrillas demanded to know what the poles were for. It was a very touchy situation. Of course, none of us knew how to speak Spanish, so Mom, with her big blue eyes, smiled and began to gesticulate, attempting to convey that we were with the circus. Suddenly they understood. They instantly stopped interrogating and backed right off." Fritzi raises her chin and continues to explain as Betty nods approvingly. "The circus has traditionally been nonbiased politically. We are not aligned to any government, have no sworn alliances. We were artists, there to entertain. Harmless. They recognized this."

"But you were scared?" I urge, for what seems like the millionth time.

"Well, wouldn't you be? If someone pointed a gun at your parents?" Fritzi demands to my satisfaction, her tone shifting quickly away from the rather worshipful one that she generally assumes when she attempts to romanticize circus as a transcendent, universal culture. "We were very lucky. We were in a dangerous position, all alone, and quite frankly, if we hadn't been with a circus, I don't think that we would have gotten away."

Fritzi leaves soon after this story, and Betty returns to it almost purposefully. "Fritzi made so much out of that. No one would have hurt us if we had obeyed them," she insists. "Fritz always said that we should just be sociable with everyone we met. They only wanted to look through the trailer."

"She was seven," I remind Betty quickly. "Being accosted at gunpoint was surely rather scary for a child that age."

Betty shrugs. "Well, I guess so. I didn't think much of it."

Betty and I end our morning by poring over photographs of Cuba. There are numerous pictures of the family standing on patios, posing before monuments, and teasing one another. Mike appears in almost every picture, sometimes horseplaying with Fritz, often with Betty; occasionally beside a slim, dark-haired woman. "Mike was supposed to interpret for us," Betty explains, her voice growing noticeably softer. When we arrived, we needed somebody to help with the rigging. The owner told us, 'I have one boy available,' and let us use Mike. He was traveling with the show at the time, selling tickets and helping out. He always rode with his own people but helped us to unload and hit stakes. The first time that we tore down, Fritz tipped Mike ten dollars. He refused in a hurry. The circus was paying him only two dollars, and he didn't want his boss to accuse him of taking advantage of Americans. Fritz insisted though. After all, Mike was working for us, not the show. We always tipped our riggers according to how much we ourselves were earning."

Mike apparently repaid Fritz's generosity with good advice, sound warnings, and very tangible aid at the end of the family's journey. By March the Hubers had reached the farthest end of the island and were touring Oriente Province, now the openly acknowledged stronghold of Castro's revolutionary army. They performed in Yara, a short drive from the beach where Che Guevara had landed three months earlier, and in Palma Soriano and Guantanamo. On March 13, while the family were in Palma Soriano, the Presidential Palace in Havana was attacked in a failed attempt to assassinate Batista.

Several weeks later, while the family performed in Matanzas, the last city on their return route, four rebels leaders who had survived the palace attack were shot in nearby Havana. By the time the Hubers reentered the city, Castro had been interviewed in the Sierra by U.S. journalist Robert Taber in the historic exchange broadcast on CBS. The revolution was no longer a carefully avoided rumor; it had become an often violently disruptive fact.

Betty had given her boss notice several weeks earlier, arguing that her children were growing nervous and that she was eager to return to America. "He begged us to work for another two weeks," she remembers, "so I told him that I would only remain in Cuba if he gave me a gold bracelet—nothing cheap, but fine, heavy gold." Several days later the circus owner tossed a thick cord of twisted gold into the window of Betty's trailer. "Is that satisfactory?" he snapped. Betty accepted the jewelry, but her boss hastily fired Mike, fearing that the boy's warnings had been responsible for the Sensational Kays' growing desire to leave the country.

The Hubers arrived back in Havana in late April but were forced to wait for their rigging, which had been strapped to the concession train far behind them. Alone and without a guide, they drove to the train station, where they had determined to park for the next few weeks. Betty almost cried out in shock when she saw that the huge yard was closed and guarded. The night was feverishly hot, the children sweat-streaked and thirsty. Betty panicked. "What will we do without electricity or water?" she cried to Fritz. "Where can we go now?"

The Hubers' uncanny good fortune arrived suddenly in the unlikely form of a limousine, which slowed to a crawl as it passed their trailer, a mere outline in the night. A window rolled down and Betty heard a voice as seemingly miraculous as it was welcome call her name. Mike yelled to Fritz that he should follow the limousine, led the tired family to a nearby hotel, and arranged for them to park on the patio where lights and water were available. The hotel proprietor handed Fritz the key to a room with showers and a toilet that the family could use for two dollars a night.

"What was Mike doing in a limousine!" I exclaim, and Betty leans back and grins.

"His father was one of Batista's men," she explains. "After Castro took over, Mike was sent to Russia to work in the salt mines. Eventually he returned to Miami and set up an air-conditioning business. He kept my address and wrote to me for years."

Something in Betty's voice catches my attention. I tilt my head back, narrow my eyes, and murmur suggestively, "I see," wondering how she will respond. To my dismay, Betty immediately shows signs of nervous excitement. She fidgets uneasily in her chair but begins to speak hastily, almost eagerly. "After Fritz died, Mike wrote that he'd been in love with me in Cuba, but I had only liked him, but not physically, just as a friend. There was no idea of sex. I didn't want to cheat on my husband, but it was getting so that I wanted Mike around me all the time because he danced with me in the trailer and I loved that. I told Fritz, 'I like him, Daddy.' I asked my husband, 'Is it possible to love two men at once?' Finally I said, 'Take me home. I don't want anything to happen.' Mike never pushed himself on me. It was a danger zone, but I wouldn't have given myself to him. He loved the kids. He wrote for a long time."

That evening I call Fritzi. "What was the deal with Mike?" I ask boldly.

"Mom really liked him," Fritzi explains, "and we all had fun together. Mike took Mom out to clubs to dance. I think that it was pretty innocent, although I remember that when we got home, my dad found a picture of Mike taped inside a cabinet in the trailer and tore it down. Mike's girlfriend was with him most of the time anyway."

"Is she the dark woman in the photographs?" I ask.

"Yup." Fritzi laughs. "Mom always refers to her as 'What's her name.'"

I hang up the phone and go to my desk where I sit pensively for several minutes. Finally I open the box in which I keep Betty's records and carefully leaf through her tiny route book for 1957, hoping to discover personal comments that can serve as clues to her feelings during this time. In stark contrast to the increasingly narrative character of her route books for previous years, the notations for 1957 are strictly factual: dates, places, travel instructions. Disappointed but not surprised, I lay the little booklet aside and pick up a route book with 1956 on its cover. As I begin to skim its pages, I realize in growing amazement that its entries are identical to those in the 1957 book. On the inside front cover, the year 1956 has been scratched out and rewritten as 1957. Every factual entry in the two records corresponds exactly, but across the pages of this more private copy, Betty has penciled personal comments and impressions. I examine the entries, for the first time in the course of my project feeling like an intruder: "Palma Soriano: Mike, no good," "Banes: Mike, so-so," "April 15: MIKE GOT FIRED. Mike kissed me goodbye," "Leaving Remedio: No Mike here, so lonesome," "May 1, Havana, Mike," "May 12, Florida, Fritz got rigging in West Palm Beach. Mother's Day. Mike ???"

No wonder Betty did not pay attention to the political revolution brewing in Cuba, I think tenderly, when there was such a complicated revolution raging within her. I close the little book and lay it gently aside.

~

Bobby Huber settles back into the driver's seat, guiding the steering wheel with imperceptible movements of one hand as we fly down I-40 toward Raleigh, two hours ahead.

"My husband warned me that a man is only comfortable with a long talk when he's driving," I explain, smiling.

"I do like driving"—Bobby laughs good-naturedly—"and I really appreciate the lift to the airport."

"It's great to have a chance to interview you," I assure him. "I knew that I would never get out to L.A.."

I make a quick study of my companion as he experiments with our capricious cruise control. Strawberry blond, nice-looking, Bobby at forty-six still resembles the round-faced, inquisitive little boy in Betty's photo albums. I reach between the seats to turn on the tape recorder that I have propped behind us. "You see, I have so many stories about the 1930s and 1940s, but relatively few about the 1950s," I begin. "That is the period in which I am most interested, the time when your parents were performing, but your mother does not talk as much about those years."

Bobby nods quickly. "I think that she has good and bad memories, and she would rather block out that whole period than try to separate them," he muses.

"Well, she takes it for granted that I understand that way of life," I continue, "but I have to ask about such simple things—like how you managed without electricity."

Bobby throws back his head and laughs. "To this day, it thrills me to walk into my garage, turn on a switch, and see three or four things go on at once! I always have that little doubt in my mind that nothing may happen." He grins sheepishly at his admission, then offers an explanation. "My parents kept a drawer full of different types of fuses because they never knew what sort of box we would be plugged in to. There could be four trailers down the line plugged in to the same little 15-amp breaker. Our trailer had a gas stove with propane bottles underneath, but many others were smaller and needed electricity for cooking. Someone would flick on an iron or an electrical frying pan and Bam!—off to the fuse box. This went on all night long."

"That would drive me nuts," I confess.

Bobby smiles. "We didn't mind. So what else don't you understand?"

I quickly scan the list in my lap. There are so many topics about which I want to inquire, and so little time. "I have been learning about the dangers of circus life," I begin, but I don't get a chance to say another word.

"The real danger was Mom's driving!" Bobby blurts out. He looks at me earnestly, and suddenly, both of us are shaking with laughter.

With deep relief, I decide that I do not need to tiptoe around this subject's feelings, to watch eyes warily or ask carefully phrased, guarded questions. "Fritzi told me that she usually chose to ride with your father," I say, forcing myself to grow serious. "She never understood why you preferred to take chances with your mother."

Bobby's face grows thoughtful as he considers my implied question. "Mom was fun to drive with," he states frankly. "She never got tired of talking and singing; I would fall asleep while she was still playing games with me. Eventually, though, she would ask, 'Where's Daddy?' We would slow down; cars would pass us. I cannot tell you how many times this happened. I would cry, 'Mommmmm,' but she would assure me, 'I know where we're going. It's all right.' Then the map would come out. First, Mom would try to read it while she was driving, but it would be too big, so we would have to pull over. She would study the map and mutter, 'Oh, gosh. Maybe I should have turned back there,' then she would turn the car around and start back. That was always the first mistake."

Bobby pauses and looks at me dramatically, and we both start laughing again. "Once we got lost for two days," he recalls. "Mom had no money. She had put it all in the trailer. A little town that we passed through had a goldfish pond in front of the police station, so we stopped. I found a good tree branch, stuck some bubble gum on the end, and started fishing in the fountain for change so that we could eat. Mom kept watch; if a policeman came too near, she would distract him by speaking rapidly in German while I picked more pennies out of the water. I thought that I was doing the right thing."

"In that situation, you probably were," I muse.

"Well, a man's gotta eat, you know," Bobby agrees, laughing heartily.

"I still don't understand why you wanted to ride with your mother if she got lost constantly," I say, genuinely curious.

Bobby hesitates for a moment. "Mom used to let me lie in the back window, up on top of the seat back," he says softly. "I loved to watch the road go away from us, to see where we had been." He glances over at me, almost shyly, I think, and I nod encouragement. I am very familiar with this family's acutely visual orientation. "I also loved to listen to Mom sing. She had a terrific voice. She could have sung for a living, it was that good, but she was sensitive about it." Bobby lowers his head and grins mischievously. "One day I don't remember which one of us said, 'Mom, can you not sing that song?' and it just hit her wrong. She yanked the car over and cried, 'Get out! I'm going to kill myself!' Fritzi and I went hysterical. We were crying. Of course, Mom didn't mean any of that, but we had hurt her feelings."

"I would say so," I remark, enjoying my sense of freedom to make subjective comments.

"Yeah. Boy, we never said anything about her singing again." Bobby chuckles, shaking his head over what he obviously regards as a silly childhood misunderstanding far in the past. Again, I cannot help reflecting on how casually this subject is treating his storytelling, a marked and somewhat welcome shift from the intense immediacy with which his mother and sister recall past frustrations. "See, that's the way we were raised; it was drilled into us that thoughts count," he insists, turning from the road to look at me seriously. "We lived in small trailers, so little things meant a lot."

"Most people who live in small spaces get cabin fever and end up fighting," I offer. "Did that ever happen to you?"

"Not really," Bobby says. "Outside, we never fought. When the weather was bad and we had to stay inside, we got cabin fever sometimes. It was too small of an area to do any of the things that I loved doing."

"What did you love to do?" I ask quickly.

Bobby stretches and grins, seems to be enjoying his memories. "Wrestling was my all-time favorite sport," he confesses, almost with pride. "I wrestled every kid and animal that I could find. I was invincible and very tenacious. If I got my arm around a neck, the match was over. My friends and I did nothing but wrestle all weekend."

"But isn't that a pretty typical little-boy thing? My two sons love to wrestle, too," I suggest.

Bobby smiles knowingly. "I don't mean just rolling-around wrestling. I'm talking about wrestling until your nose and your ears bleed. No punching, no scratching. We set up ropes and had all of those rules, but somebody would always break them."

"Did you wrestle with Fritzi?"

"Naw. She didn't stand a chance with me. I was so much bigger than she was that I hurt her just playing. I never meant to, and I always felt really bad when it happened. If I wrestled her, it was only because she lost control and jumped on me. Generally, we played games together and did our schoolwork.

"We had correspondence school. It was difficult for Mom because she wasn't a mathematical genius. She had learned math so differently in Germany. Half the time, she really didn't understand what she was teaching us herself. Fritzi was always the smart one." Bobby shakes his head, remembering his sister's precocity. "Fritzi read constantly. She amazed us. We would be just driving along and out of the blue, she would say something like 'Did you know that this forest is the last one with these kinds of trees and they are going to cut them all down?' This little girl would know all about it and could tell us in detail. She remembers everything that she reads. I had no patience for formal learning. I couldn't wait to be finished with lessons so that I could go play with my miniature cars in the dirt. That's the one thing that . . ." Bobby hesitates, then continues quickly. "I wish that I had been more of a reader. Whenever I started, if the book didn't hold my interest immediately, I would be right out the door, busy at building a bicycle or something."

My companion pauses, then smiles rather proudly. "I loved to gather parts. I would work for months, and eventually, I would have pieced together a bicycle without having bought a single part."

"Fritzi just does the same thing with ideas," I offer. "The two of you were probably much alike."

Bobby squints at me, considering my suggestion, then grins his acceptance. "That's right. Exactly!"

"Tell me more about your childhood memories," I press. "What stands out about life in the trailer?"

Bobby leans back against the headrest and stares far down the road, searching for memories. I watch as contented smiles surface and flicker across his face. "I slept in the top bunk and bugged my sister by dropping stuff down on her," he acknowledges cheerfully. "We had more fun in that room. We had to be in after dark. We would wait until my parents were doing the act because we knew that no one would come in that door and catch us. As soon as we heard the music start, we began throwing things. When the last routine came on, I would climb up on the top bunk and open the vent. 'Hurry, they're climbing down,' I would yell. We would clean up fast and be lying quietly in our beds when Mom and Dad came back. Of course, they always watched us through the vent but they never let us know. They knew that we needed to be wild. They were firm but lenient parents. They never argued in front of us. Very loving."

"What constituted bad behavior," I ask, "or weren't you ever bad?"

Bobby smirks at my ingenuous question. "Oh, I got in trouble a few times." He laughs. "If we played with our food, Dad would put our plates on the floor and make us fight Smokey for our supper. He would say, 'You eat like a dog, you eat with the dog.'

"That's one of your sister's most indignant memories," I interrupt.

"Yeah, she hated that," Bobby agrees. "I never minded. I would be laughing and Fritzi would be crying. On the other hand, I remember Dad spanking me. That really hurt and I got mad at Fritzi for not crying. Mom tried to spank us a few times, but she wasn't very good at it. I would be running in circles while she tried to swat at me. Eventually it turned into a game and she would have to laugh. Her backup then was always, 'Don't make me tell your father. He's going to take his belt off when he comes home.'"

"Did he?"

"Not often. Once in a while I would break a window. That was a spanking. And one time the shower in the bathroom was plugged up, so I got the ice pick in the kitchen and poked holes through the metal floor of the shower so that the water could drain out. That was a spanking."

I am laughing but Bobby shakes his head solemnly. "That was stupid on my part. I was destroying something that I could have fixed. I should have waited and told Dad or Mom, but instead I put holes in the shower." He sighs. "Bad was not coming home when it got dark."

"Was there a danger?"

"Well, it was safer back then than it is now, but we had to stay in touch. They wanted us in at night because there were strangers everywhere and we were just little kids. We were raised without any fear but also without prejudice or animosity towards anyone. One good thing about the circus was that it provided such a wide base of nationalities; we had a multicultural upbringing because we felt comfortable with people from almost every culture."

Bobby pauses suddenly, as if troubled by an unexpected thought. "Well, my parents did take offense at being called carnival workers rather than circus performers. It's not the same thing at all. We were forbidden to associate with carnival people. Mom and Dad had a few friends who ran booths, but we were cautioned not to hang around their trailers."

"Do you recognize that distinction now, as an adult?" I ask.

"Yes. See, carnival picks up day players in every town. These guys will take a few dollars just to put up and they might not even hang around to tear down. These are people who have no money and who knows what kind of pasts; there are no records of who they are. Some would steal. The whole point of the carnival is to make money off of people. Circus is an art form—a profession. You can't be a jerk in the circus because then everyone will shun you and you won't be invited to anybody's trailer. That's what we do to jerks—ignore them so that they get the point and try to change."

Bobby assures me that he never for a moment wished for any other life than the one he had when he was a child. The Hubers lived well, even by road standards. Days were filled with sunshine and amusement, evenings with continuous visiting and camaraderie. Private life was as relaxed as a vacation.

Although neither parent was very religious, the Hubers always celebrated the Christian holidays with enthusiasm. Betty especially enjoyed decorating and shopping for Christmas. The family would go to mass and open their presents together on Christmas Eve. "We didn't go to church on Sundays because Mom and Dad had to perform," Bobby recalls. "But one of the shows on each Saturday or Sunday was generally a benefit performance for crippled children or for the burn center or the babies' hospital. Performers always did those for free. When you see those kids sitting out in the audience in wheelchairs and bandages, you know that they are being given something special—that's sort of a way of going to church."

Fritzi and Bobby both prayed on their hands and knees at night before going to bed. They were secure in their little world.

"I never went to a friend's house by myself, but I always looked forward to seeing other people's homes because then I could find out how they lived," Bobby admits. "I would see big bedrooms full of toys and a garage with bicycles and think, God, how lucky these kids are, but then we would go back to our trailer and I was perfectly happy. A couple times we visited our Uncle Charlie. He lived in a mansion in Beverly Hills next door to Vincent Price. Tony Curtis lived across the street. It was a very nice place. We always had a great time when we played with my cousins, but I was still glad to come home."

"Do you remember your Uncle Charlie at all?" I prompt eagerly.

"We never saw him. Maybe three times." Bobby pauses and looks at me thoughtfully. "It's odd. I have a single memory of Dad and Charlie in the same room. I don't recall ever seeing them together. I remember that when Uncle Charlie visited us in Houston, after Dad died, he seemed shorter to me. That's when I first realized that I was growing. Charlie was gone almost immediately. We seldom saw him because he had left the circus."

"You loved circus, didn't you?"

Bobby grins. "It was a great life for a kid. When it came time to hit the road for a new season, Fritzi and I always got really excited. We hoped that there would be children our age on the route for the next thirty weeks. We returned to many parks year after year; Fritzi and I would remember the best things to do in a place where we had been before. As soon as we pulled in, we would run to that ride or attraction first. We could ride anything we wanted all summer for free."

"What stands out?" I ask eagerly, amused at finding myself experiencing an almost childlike thrill as my subject describes this Never Land existence of constant carefree amusement.

"Pacific Ocean Park was one of our favorites, and Kenny Wood Park on the Hudson in Pennsylvania. We could horseback ride there. The Texas World's Fair stands out. There was a monstrous Big Tex out front with a giant mechanized arm that went up and down. He would say, 'Hi, pardner, Hi, pardner.' Fritzi and I would just sit there and watch that thing in amazement."

"Could you eat whatever you wanted to?"

"Nuh-uh. People would offer us things, but we were taught never to eat other people's food unless Mom and Dad said that we could."

"Did you watch the acts?"

"Oh, yeah. The demolition derby was my favorite. Mom would tease, 'Guess where we're going tomorrow?' and I would start jumping up and down. We could sit on top of the trailer and watch. The Kimris' act always mesmerized me. Her husband was so into it. They had fireworks and the trapeze would drop from the airplane, then when they finished, there were more fireworks. It was an incredible act—the best in the circus, I thought. Hugo Zacchini and the cannon were fabulous to watch too. I liked the rocket and the motorcycles in the cage."

"Fast things."

Bobby grins. "Well, yeah—and high things. The wheel of destiny, the high dive, motorcycles on the wire. I liked explosions, too, and fire. I was good at setting fires. I'm an Aries. In fact, the whole time I was growing up, I had this little blue jean jacket—my dad never knew that I kept a little can of lighter fluid and matches in the pockets. I went everywhere in that. I loved to build little model cars and then set them aflame and watch them burn."

"How fitting that you started your career in the movie industry with *Firestarter*," I tease him, amused by how casually he refers to his childhood exploits. Bobby is now a key grip, responsible for moving and setting up complicated rigging and film-making equipment.

"Isn't it? *Backdraft* was even more fun. I couldn't wait to do that one. Fires are dangerous—you can't be reckless with fire, but I enjoy it. That's another thing that I have no fear of."

"I suppose that you liked firecrackers, too?" I ask. "Did that lead to an interest in pyrotechnics?"

Bobby grins broadly. "Absolutely. I used to get a big steel pipe and empty all the powder out of a bunch of those black cap crackers. I would stuff it with anything that I wanted to launch."

"You did this around your parents?"

"No," Bobby says flatly, "only in Houston," and I understand that he means "after Dad was gone." "Fireworks were legal within the city limits there. You could go a few blocks from home and buy giant roman candles with enough powder to construct a bomb."

"You did this at age ten?" I question incredulously.

Bobby nods. "It was a different life once we had gotten off the road," he says quietly. "Fritzi and I missed it very much. We had had security in that life. People never could figure out how we all could be so happy living in that trailer, but we were."

Suddenly Bobby stops talking and swivels his head sharply, looking after a shiny trailer that has just passed in the opposite direction. "You know," he muses, "I just realized something kind of amazing that I never thought of before. When we were little, we would see a trailer way far ahead and we would instantly know who it was, what they were going to do, what date they were going to play. We would honk horns and wave. No one had trailers but circus performers back then. If we saw somebody's trailer on the side of the road, we pulled over immediately, and other performers always stopped for us."

"So it really was like an extended family?" I ask gently.

Bobby smiles wistfully. "It was wonderful." He sighs. "The people were wonderful. I was in love with Princess Tajana when I was little. I wish I had a picture of her. We had so many friends, constant company and joking. It was a very civilized way of life.

"The best trip that we ever took was to Cuba though. I remember lots of sugarcane. Fritzi and I were crazy about it—we picked it fresh.

We ate oranges everyday and caught these huge lizards with strings on poles. Mom made little collars for them so that we could put them on a safety pin and keep them right on our shoulders. You would be surprised how many mosquitoes one little lizard can eat!

"I also remember the humidity. We were caravanning and the truck and trailer got stuck in deep mud. All these little naked Cuban kids helped to push us out of the mud. It was wonderful."

"There was a war going on," I remind Bobby gently. "Fritzi says that she remembers guerrillas jumping out of the jungle and surrounding your truck, pointing machine guns at your parents' necks, speaking in rapid Spanish that they didn't understand. She was terrified."

Bobby draws a deep breath and lets it out slowly. "It was no big deal," he says casually. "Mom told us that there was a war going on and that soldiers would need to check our things for weapons—it was like customs. We had nothing to hide. Our rigging usually caught their interest, but Mom would get out pictures of the act and speak in her broken Spanish and the soldiers would start laughing. Mom told us, 'Oh, they're just fighting about something,' and that's how we left it. Mom knew more than she let on, probably. I never felt any tension. Fritzi would argue, 'Mom, they must have something to fight about if they're fighting,' and she would try to figure it out, but my parents never seemed worried."

"What sort of things did you want to find out?" I probe.

Bobby's face grows pensive. "I loved watching people's rigging," he reflects. "I would wonder how they made it hang there. It intrigued me. Dad taught me how to do things safely—the knots, the angling. There's a logic behind how one man can put up two big poles and a high wire all by himself. When I got older, I remembered everything Dad had taught me, and eventually, I ended up supervising all the circus rigging; then later I transferred that knowledge to the movie industry."

"Rigging is the hardest of all for me to understand," I confess. "I never can visualize how everything works."

"You can learn; I did," Bobby assures me enthusiastically. "To this day, people just stand in amazement when I put up a complicated rigging alone, but there's a simple logic to it all."

"Where did your father learn to do all this?" I wonder out loud. "No one knows anything about him. Did he ever tell you who taught him his craft?"

"No, but it's simply a matter of being around something that you want to do badly enough. You learn instantly when you watch someone else do it," Bobby assures me. "Dad was sharp—very sharp. He spliced other people's cables, was always fixing or designing or building something. People came to him constantly for help. I would feel honored to be anything like my dad."

"Are you, do you think?"

"Mom always tells me that we're the same, that we both give away things that we work on, that I should make more money than I do. I guess that I'm like my father in that I have no fear. I didn't grow up with fear, so I've never been afraid of heights—or of people. I had only one worry in life—Mom's driving. That was probably why I always drove with her."

"You were being protective?" I laugh.

Bobby grins. "Actually, the real reason is that she let me drive." I stare at him and he begins to chuckle. "When we would get out onto the thruway, she would scoot over and let me hold the steering wheel. Those big cars always had a sway in the steering; my goal was to hold the car straight with as little movement as possible. Mom was impressed by how I hardly steered at all."

"You're doing that now," I exclaim.

"Yup." Bobby turns to me, his face beaming. "Thinking back, that was one of my favorite things to do; that's really why I drove with Mom." We have almost reached Raleigh and I inwardly lament that our interview will soon be over, but Bobby seems caught up in his train of thought. "You know," he continues, as if suddenly struck by a memory, "Mom never let me drive when Fritzi was in the car, though. She only let me do it when we were alone."

～

The 1957 tour of Cuba signaled a turning point for the Hubers, although they probably were unaware that this period marked a transition for them, a refocusing of energy and determination, a redefining of goals. In 1953 Fritz and Betty had bought a second home in Greenwood Lake, New York, right next door to Elvira and Haji Liazeed. Winters at Greenwood Lake became their most precious period of family time. The Hubers loved the peaceful months there, enjoyed the company of good neighbors, relished the long nights in the privacy of a full-size room, separated from their sleeping children. With time off from work, surrounded by good friends and blankets of wonderful snow, the Hubers played and snuggled, partied and planned through the coldest months of the year.

Betty's route books for this period show that the couple had relatively little work but did not mind at all; Betty has scrawled numerous admissions of joy across pages that would normally be filled with work information. The personal comments in her route books up until 1953 are limited to hasty notations about birthdays, penciled in almost illegibly small script and wedged tightly into corners. Immediately after the purchase of the Greenwood Lake residence, Betty's writing changes dramatically from brief business notes to very subjective narrative. Her lettering grows larger and is centered, filling several months' worth of space.

"Home in Greenwood Lake—spent a wonderful Xmas with Fritz and my babies," Betty scribbles in January of 1954. Her informal memoir continues: "Resting at lake—no work for road but plenty in home—sure love this peace and quiet—no work but so far content— had nice Mother's Day—practically broke but happy." The back of the book contains a postscript: "Spent entire winter in Greenwood Lake. Boy, it sure is grand. We are by ourselves—love it." This entry is followed by recipes for Chop Suey and Lou Ann Style Green Beans. Denied a comfortable home and the pleasure of domesticity for her entire life, Betty suddenly had found both; the house in Greenwood Lake was a place to love, a place where it was too cold to practice but where she had neighbors who understood her work.

Elvira was a grandmother to little Fritzi and Bobby; she made them mountainous strawberry shortcakes and allowed them to build an entire miniature city in her cellar. "I had my own little dirt area that she saved for me and never touched," Bobby remembers happily as we approach the outskirts of Research Triangle and its cluster of landscaped corporate parks. "I had my own world in that basement. And boy, could she cook! You couldn't wait for dinner. She was a wonderful lady. She wore the pants in that family, too. Papa Haji was a funny, funny guy who did whatever his wife told him to do. We loved it there."

When they returned to the United States in 1957, Betty and Fritz began to reassess their dedication to performance and decided that they were ready to consider leaving the circus for a more settled vocation. Betty knew that she would not be able to tutor teenagers in algebra or chemistry. It was time to get off the road and enroll the children in school. For months she and Fritz talked about it, then began seriously to plan. Fritz spoke first with Charlie Lucas, a Greenwood Lake neighbor who had invited the Hubers to stay at his own home when the family first arrived and found their new house without heat. Over the years Charlie and his wife, Resi, had become dear friends, partners in fun and prank-playing, second parents to the children. Now Fritz asked the former musician turned home builder to build him a log cabin, complete with a fireplace and room for the kids to grow. Together, the two men laid the groundwork for the Hubers' dream home.

Fritz had been a bookbinder's apprentice back in Switzerland and was interested in opening a full-time printing business. He and Betty decided that they would put together an act suitable for occasional nightclub performances during the winter and would do their wire act when the kids were out of school in the summer. After a lifetime of travel, both partners were more than ready to get off the road.

In 1958 the Hubers traveled to New York City to get Babette's trunks out of storage. Determined to settle down in one place, they no longer feared having to leave a home full of lovely family treasures unguarded for months at a time. On the ride to the city, Betty told her wide-eyed children of the wonders that they would find packed in grandmother Babette's hidden boxes: Tiffany glass and exquisite linens, gorgeous gowns and costumes, souvenirs from all over Europe. Babette had collected dolls, many of them now valuable, in particular a treasured set of porcelain quintuplets that Betty wanted for her own growing collection.

In addition to collecting antiques, sentimental Babette had cherished photographs and papers. Deep in her trunks she had hidden all of Betty's schoolwork from Germany, her uniforms and award certificates. Carefully layered between sheets of wax paper and wrapped in linen were the reviews and photographs commemorating each year of her daughter's early career in vaudeville and the circus. There were letters from sisters and brothers back in Europe, photographs of the family that Betty and her siblings had never known.

Betty warned Fritz that the boxes would be extremely heavy, that she had watched four hulking men shoulder each one and wince as they lowered their loads into the moving van. She was astounded when Fritz hoisted the first trunk easily; the second and third seemed almost weightless when Betty tried to lift a single end by herself. None of the padlocks on the trunks had been broken, yet when Betty opened the trunks with her master key, she discovered that each one was practically empty. It was a blow that she had not been expecting. Betty fell down on the ground and sobbed. Fritz cradled her tightly, whispering "Mommy, there's nothing you can do. It's gone, baby; let it go."

Later Betty would rationalize that the moving men might have ransacked the trunks. She knew that they had not taken them directly to storage; the huge boxes had waited in a New York warehouse until a unit became available. Harry had been a mover; he had told her how often movers claimed that what they had stolen had been lost in transit. On that bright winter day in 1958, however, Betty understood only that Babette's legacy to her grandchildren had been violated. She salvaged the few bits of embroidery and glass that remained and rode home in uncharacteristic silence, tears running freely down her face, lips pursed tightly together.

The rape of the trunks seemed almost a portent of worse things to come. The following two years brought little work. Circuses were closing around the country; manageable consecutive dates were harder and harder for free agents like the Hubers to book. Worst of all, Fritz was seriously ill with mylenoma. Betty's route book for 1960 is a harsh reminder of the stark changes that were taking place within her as her family's hard-earned happiness crumbled. The personal comments for that dismal year are written in tight little letters once again: "Fritz in for operation—still in hospital—still in bed—no work," then several months of uncharacteristically blank squares. In December of 1960, Betty and Fritz left their children with friends in California and accepted a rare six-week tour date of Hawaii; they considered it to be the honeymoon that they had never had. These sun-baked, friend-filled weeks were the last carefree times that the couple would enjoy together.

This is Betty's last route book, a mutilated record of her last full year with Fritz. I hope that Bobby will let me share a glimpse of what Betty refused to record on those blank squares. Bobby was ten years old when his father lost his long battle with cancer. In the autumn of 1961, Betty left her children with Elvira and Haji and raced across the country with her dying husband, hoping that doctors in Houston could save a life that the New York physicians had predicted would end within three days. Left behind, the Huber children began a new life almost immediately. Elvira enrolled them in public school, which they continued to attend after Betty's devastating return from Houston without their father.

"Mornings were good," Bobby remembers. "Elvira would have done anything for us. I can smell her cinnamon toast and hot chocolate right now. It was so good on cold mornings before we went to school." He sighs slightly. "After school, though, the New York kids used to wait outside for me. Two would grab and hold me while the other three kicked and punched. They beat me every single day."

Bobby relates that it was by mere chance that he struck up a friendship with an older student on the school patrol named Roger. One afternoon the curious patroller approached the red-headed, fatherless little boy who seemed to linger when school let out and questioned him about the regular black eyes and the constant fresh cuts on his face. When Bobby described the daily torture session that he was about to undergo, Roger insisted on walking the child home. The walk was uneventful until they reached an alley. Bobby barely had time to whisper "This is the place" before the raucous gang of delinquents materialized, hungry for his terror. They surrounded the two boys, but Roger was intimidating in his eagerness to protect, and warned that he would hunt and pummel to pulp the next boy who dared to touch Bobby. Bobby left the alley unscathed, but his triumph was short-lived. "The next day," he relates grimly, "they grabbed Fritzi, too.

"Five big kids had cornered me down by the lake," Bobby recalls. "It was frozen and covered with snow. Fritzi saw them punching me and raced to help. She jumped on one bully and pulled him off, but he easily tackled and began choking her. We were right across the street from our house; I got up and ran fast. When I got back with my mom, the biggest kid was holding Fritzi's head under the icy water. Her face was blue and her body was still. It was pretty bad."

Betty flew out her house with the fury of a tiger. She slammed into the gang of adolescent thugs with the full force of her strength, pulled the would-be assassin off her limp daughter, and punched him so hard that the child's father later threatened a lawsuit. "Mom was like a wild animal," Bobby tells me. "She ended up falling through the ice—the water was about three feet deep at the lake's edge, and Fritzi and I had to help her back into the house. No one ever touched us again after she hit that kid. They knew that Mom would kill for us."

~

"There's a lot that I didn't put in there," Betty admits, when I finally get up the courage to lead her to this still-painful topic. "I didn't keep a book for 1961. We only worked seven weeks altogether that whole year. Fritz was bloated and miserable. He was in the dumps and refused to work. I fixed meals but he wouldn't eat."

In February of 1960, on Lincoln's birthday, Fritz had a suspicious mole removed from his leg. A biopsy revealed that the tumor was malignant, and Fritz's physicians immediately recommended radiation therapy. For several weeks Fritz remained at home with Betty, healing his body and spirit. Neither parent ever mentioned the word "cancer" around their children; Bobby and Fritzi were led to believe that their father had been treated in the hospital for a leg wound and had recovered. They joked about the skin that had been grafted from Fritz's buttocks to his knee, tickled that their daddy's lower body now resembled the patchwork comedy pants that he wore in his act. In keeping with this collaborative story of casual recovery, Fritz was back on the wire less than a month after his operation, seemingly eager to perform. Only his wife understood how weak he really was.

The Hubers were on the road again the next year, but Fritz and Betty were carrying a heavy burden of anxiety. An examination had revealed that the cancer was rapidly spreading. After playing the Shrine Circus dates in Minneapolis, the Hubers drove to St. Louis and worked a ten day run for the Police Circus. Over the following three weeks, the Hubers traveled constantly, setting up and tearing down daily in numerous small towns throughout Oklahoma and Texas, but Fritz never revealed how draining the schedule had become for him.

In May the family sped from Texas to St. Louis to purchase a new truck that they had ordered during their dates there. Exhausted, Fritz drove the new vehicle straight to Romeo's sister's home in the next state. Betty's route book shows that they performed for a Strawberry Festival in West Virginia during the early days of May, but there are no further listings after that—only two words scribbled in tiny letters: "no work."

By July the cancer had spread to Fritz's groin. "They told us that he would need another operation," Betty recalls sadly. "I didn't write because there was always so much stress. Fritz was so discouraged. I pampered him. I told him, 'Daddy, it will be all right.'"

The Hubers managed to book a few dates for the last part of the season that year. In late summer they drove from New York to Puyallup, Washington, in only three days, and Fritz was so weak that he almost passed out on the rigging. The circus owner wanted to send the Hubers home, but they resisted the cancellation, viewing it as unprofessional. Fritz was determined to conceal his personal problems at any cost and to honor his contract to perform. After the dates, the family left Washington and immediately raced back across the country to play for another circus in New York. On the first night there, Fritz could barely walk the wire and the circus refused to pay the Sensational Kays.

The Kays' final date for the year was booked for October in Boston, the city that had, over the years, always proved to be Betty's nemesis. Determined to fulfill his contract through its final date, Fritz canceled a much-needed appointment with his physician, insisting over the phone that he felt fine. During his Boston performance, the once-mesmerizing wire walker lay down on the wire but could not get up again. Tortured with pain, he slowly managed to crawl across the cable on which he had so often danced.

Terrified by her husband's pain and obvious debility, Betty drove him back to Greenwood Lake, where she ignored his protests and demanded that he see a doctor. The young physician who attended Fritz at home took a single look at the jaundiced, bloated, hollow-eyed man lying on the bed and informed the shocked family that Fritz was "a dead man."

Betty had not had the strength to resist when eleven-year-old Fritzi demanded to be allowed to stay close to her father during the doctor's visit. "Is Daddy dying?" she asked her white-faced parents, voicing a reality that no one else seemed to be admitting.

"No, honey. I'm not dying," Fritz assured her. "We'll fool them and I'll come back for Christmas." Fritzi had always trusted her father. She squeezed his hand and asked no further questions.

Betty and Fritz's last joint decision was to leave their children with the Liazeeds and to race back to M.D. Anderson Medical Center in Houston, where both hoped that the home physicians might help him. Betty drove as fast as she dared down the Atlantic coast. Halfway to Houston, her car blew a crank shaft and the frantic couple were forced to spend a night in a hotel, knowing that they had absolutely no time to spare.

It was with deep relief that Betty saw her husband wheeled into the hospital and relinquished all responsibility for his care other than emotional support. "He wouldn't let the nurses undress him because his stomach and his thing were so swollen," Betty remembers tearfully. "He begged, 'Please, Mommy, don't let strangers see me. Will you dress me?' The circus was in town and I told all our friends that Fritz was in the hospital, knowing that they would visit, but Daddy begged me not tell people that he was ill. He only wanted me beside him."

Betty swallows hard, draws in a deep breath, forces herself to continue. Her eyes are brimming with tears but we both know that this interview must be completed, that neither one of us will have the heart to take it up again if we allow ourselves to put it aside unfinished. "He went into a coma. I sat beside him for days. I thought of every moment that we had shared. I prayed and begged God for his life, but I was angry, too. Why take a good man? What had he ever done to deserve such suffering?"

Betty tells me fretfully of the priest who tried to shake her husband out of his last coma so that he could confess his sins and receive the last rites. "He had confessed when he came into the hospital and had fallen into a coma almost immediately. How could he have sinned in a coma? I watched that fool shaking my poor husband, shouting 'Come back, man, you have to confess,' and wanted to strangle him. I demanded that he leave the room. After Fritz died, that same priest offered to comfort me at my home but I told him, 'Don't come near me! Never! I don't need you.'

"Fritz opened his eyes once. He saw me and smiled." Betty sniffs. Choking on her tears, she murmurs, "His last words were 'Mommy, you're the best thing that ever happened to me.'" Betty turns to me with an expression that I literally cannot bear, the look of a terrified child in deep pain. My own eyes ache with sympathetic tears. I wrap my arms around her, feel her soft white curls against my cheek. "It hurt," she whispers into my ear. "It hurt so much."

After we have collected ourselves, wiped our eyes, and blown our noses, Betty pulls herself up stoically, raises her chin. "Our friends the Kimris took up a collection and sent me a check for two hundred dollars," she tells me softly. "The rest of that year, every circus took up donations and sent me a check. I needed the money desperately. We had nothing left after all the doctors' bills." Betty shows me the letter that the Kimris Duo sent her on November 22, 1961. The letter is signed by forty-six performers, many of the names famous ones that I recognize. I read it slowly, pause over the tender words of sympathy:

> You will have to be both father and mother to your children now with poor Fritz gone. . . . We can still not believe that Fritz is no longer with us. Keep your chin up, Betty. I know it's easier said then done, but life goes on somehow or the other. One thinks the whole world should stand still when you lose someone dear and close to your heart, but it keeps on moving. . . . Love from us both, Henri and Lee Kimris

Betty sighs deeply. I know that this afternoon's interview has shaken her badly. "After that, I drove back to New York to get my kids. I sobbed all the way. I didn't go back to circus life. The kids needed to go to school with other children. I sold the Greenwood Lake house and moved back to Houston. I found new jobs. I learned to work a cash register. I cleaned houses and painted apartments and washed hotel windows. I even learned Sheetrocking."

Her voice grows softer as she stares through the wall, back through time, seeing something I cannot see. "It worked out pretty good," she states quietly, almost confidently. "I guess that it all worked out in the end."

MOVING ON

"What are you doing now?" I demand, my pencil poised in midair. Fritzi launches into a detailed explanation of her dicing, seasoning, and frying while I hastily scribble notes on a legal pad. I have practically badgered her for weeks to cook me this breakfast, but I simply must learn how to make huevos rancheros the way that she does. As my friend chops home-grown cilantro and peels papaya, however, I begin to realize that I will probably never master this dish. I am not witnessing a recipe in progress but rather a creation; Fritzi explains that the individual spices that she is sprinkling over frying onions have come from specialty shops. Her stone-corn tortillas and cheese were purchased in tiny Mexican family-run stores that can be found in particular little towns along the thruway. Into my recipe, I hastily insert road directions.

The kitchen fills with enticing smells, their steamy perfume mingling with that of huge bouquets of dried roses that hang upside down from the ceiling in her kitchen. Fritzi arranges the fried eggs, homemade salsa, pungent Mexican rice, black beans boiled in cumin, and cool slices of papaya in careful patterns on warmed tortillas, decorates the beans with chopped goat's cheese, pours sauce over the eggs, garnishes the colorful platters with fresh sprigs of cilantro. She sets the table in the dining room, carries in a pot of hot black tea, hands me a linen napkin. Delectable.

"Where did you learn to cook like this?" I ask as I savor a mouthful of magic that would surely cause any professional chef to feel threatened.

Fritzi laughs. "Mom wasn't much of a cook after Dad died," she admits. "She assumed that if we were full then we were fine, so she would plop a box of doughnuts on the counter and sometimes that's what we would eat all day. Bobby looked liked the Pillsbury Doughboy and I was passing out in the girl's bathroom because I was so anemic!"

"And yet you are such an amazing cook today," I murmur.

Fritzi grins. "I think that many good cooks probably started cooking out of desperation. The first time that you taste really wonderful food, you think, Wow! How can I eat like this everyday? You make a point of learning."

We laugh, and I use our current train of thought to lead us into the difficult interview that I have planned for this morning.

"I am getting a strong idea that you were always different from your mom in fundamental ways, but what I still do not sense is a growing relationship between a young girl and her mother, the sort of bonding that occurs between a woman and a daughter."

"You mean, did she give me life lessons?"

"Exactly."

Fritzi chews thoughtfully and stares across the long sunlit living room that spreads below the railing of her balconied dining room. "Mom wasn't helpful in that respect. I started my period in Florida when we were on vacation. All Mom said was 'Oh, we'll have to get you some Kotex.'"

"Did you understand what was happening?"

"Yeah, because I had talked to other girls. Mom never explained anything about it. She did tell me that if you had sex with someone, he would never marry you, never respect you again. Now here's a real contradiction: She took us to strip shows when we were little kids. She had no qualms about what she took us to see. I knew gay couples. I knew that sexuality was around me all the time, but God forbid that I should participate before I was married."

"And yet your mother had had her share of premarital sex," I muse. "Was she trying to protect you, do you think?"

"I don't know. She was always flirtatious, even in front of us. She told dirty jokes. I repeated one to a chaplain once, when I was little. He had asked if I knew any good jokes. Mom just about died."

"When did you first hear the stories about your mother's past? Did she use those stories to bond with you or to pass on a family heritage?"

"She never told stories about her childhood. I didn't know much until the trunks incident, and then it all started coming out. I recall very distinctly going to get Grandma's trunks out of storage. Mom was weeping, and that's when I heard the most about my grandmother: 'You should have seen the beautiful things that she collected, the china and lace and dolls.' The trunks were practically empty—almost everything had been stolen but linens and papers. I do remember being struck by the handworked linens; this person whom I had imagined as a huge, heavy strong woman had made prolific piles of fragile embroideries and fine needlework. I had always thought of Babette mainly in terms of her professionalism. Mom told me then about having hidden little trinkets for Grandma in her suitcases, and that she often defended Grandma to Grandpa. I seldom heard stories about Grandma coming to Mom's defense.

"I always had a tendency not to want to listen to youthful pain stories. Mom didn't usually tell them in front of my father. She was more prone to reminisce when Dad wasn't around. It was one of the reasons that I generally chose to ride with my dad and let Bobby go with Mom—that and the fact that Dad managed to arrive wherever we were going.

"When I was in my twenties, Mom and I took a trip to New York because I wanted to see Elvira once more. She was already in her nineties, strong and stubborn as ever, but we knew that we couldn't take her presence on this earth for granted much longer. It started out as a fun trip, but then Mom began telling her stories. That was the first time that I had the courage to say 'Unless you have something good to tell, I won't talk to you.' I couldn't listen to those stories any more. I guess that she needed to purge."

"I find some of her stories very hard to listen to, as well," I confess. "They do not seem to be really cathartic because she has been telling them for so long and is still angry. She reminds me of war correspondents who swap field stories and show their scars, brag about where they were and how scared they were and about how they came through. These are survival stories, actually."

"Well, in a way, I think that Mom was trying to warn me that life is tough. The only method that she has for giving a lesson is to tell a story. She was trying to teach me that bad things happen and that you can survive them. I heard the same stories, though, until I became numb and rejected them. Talking about her past was her roundabout way of trying to help me without directly addressing my problems. At the time, I didn't know enough to be able to bring that to her attention. I felt completely alone after Dad died. I knew that Mom would have defended us like a lioness, but I felt utterly alone."

"Do you know what I have realized over the last year, Fritzi? Your mother is a wonderful storyteller as long as her audience does not expect reciprocity, but unfortunately, that is how women normally bond together. Think of how you and I generally talk: You tell me a story and then I share a similar story; we bond over our sense of similitude or shared understanding. It sounds like your mother talked *to* you rather than *with* you. It must have been terribly difficult to hear the stories of her frustrated youth when she seemed to be oblivious to the fact that, as a young girl, *you* were suffering incredible pain of your own."

Fritzi nods slowly. "I understand now that there's a dichotomy to my mother's personality," she states carefully. "Half of her is incredibly savvy, the other half is as innocent as a little child. Mom's real charm is her innocence. She can get tickled by the silliest things. She still has that sense of wonder that any of us would love to hold on to. This is why children identify with her. She can become a child, but at some point, any child that she's extremely close to becomes her sibling. My childhood memories prior to my dad dying are primarily memories about him. I remember Mom vividly, but in hindsight, she was removed from me. Mom treated me a bit like a sibling."

Fritzi explains that she first began to consider herself merely a continuation of her mother's existence when she became old enough to notice that mother and daughter shared the same birthday. "The party always seemed to be for Mom," she remembers. "I got presents, of course, and the assembled guests always sang 'Happy Birthday, dear Betty and Fritzi,' but there were only adults present and the food was adult food. There was one cake, decorated for an adult, so I got the impression that I was an extension of Betty."

"Was she aware of it?"

"No, I don't think so."

"You don't mention your father's role. Wasn't the fact that the parties centered around Betty his doing?"

"Mom did the cooking, the getting ready and telling everyone to come over. It wasn't ever a surprise."

"Perhaps he felt that taking care of children was a woman's domain?"

"Sure, and he was a man who didn't know anything about such matters. That my father was passive, though, never struck me. His main focus was always her. His world centered around her. They adored one another, and I have no qualms about that."

Fritzi pauses, then smiles to herself, as if she is tickled by a sudden thought. She watches as I gobble my breakfast. "I suspect that my father realized that I needed a little more attention than I had from Mom because whenever we stayed in a town that had a soda fountain, he would take me on what we called a 'date.' We would ride into town, just the two of us, and he would buy me a cherry ice cream soda, let me play my favorite songs on the jukebox. Never Bobby—only me."

"The word 'date' is interesting. Perhaps your parents used the terminology of adult courtship with their children because they had not had childhoods themselves?" Fritzi nods. "Was there a triangle going on?" I ask pointedly.

"I was Daddy's little girl. Dad and I were Big Fritz and Little Fritz. We were aligned. When we drove together, Dad would tell me stories about his childhood. He would speak Swiss to me."

"There's no such language as Swiss," I laugh.

"German with a French accent, then," Fritzi clarifies, a bit testily, I think. "He let me play with his pipe. Mom insists that I taught myself everything, but the truth is that my dad taught me a lot. We would draw, color, do collages together. He made me little flashcards to use as bookmarks, read to me at night. He was a very good father. Bobby and Dad did rigging together, so it wasn't as though my father ignored one child in favor of the other, but I think he sensed that there was a distance between Mom and myself. Mom never took a day to spend with me as my mother. If she took us shopping, Bobby and I usually got new corduroy pants. In photographs of us taken when we were really little, I'm dressed almost like a boy. That's the kind of clothes that Mom bought for me. When I got older, Dad took me shopping for feminine things. He bought all of my dresses."

Fritzi begins to speak again, then checks herself. "In fairness, I should also tell you that after Dad died, once a year, before school started, Mom would take me to one really nice little dress shop in Houston. The fellow who owned it liked Mom, and he would let her put a group of clothes on layaway so that I could start school wearing something other than used clothes and hand-me-downs. Mom could barely afford that sort of expense, and it was probably frivolous given her means, but she understood how terribly important it was to me not to look and feel different from all the other children."

"Do you consider your mom to have been a good mother?"

Fritzi responds as if she has had the answer to this question memorized for a long time. "She did the best that she could," she states dryly but firmly. "I know that now, but understanding her wasn't easy. I don't think that it was any easier for her to understand me probably. In a way, it's maybe fortunate that my dad passed away when he did because I was just on the brink of adolescence and Dad and I were very close. I'm not saying that I'm happy that he's gone, but we were at that critical point. Mom and I might have had a very different relationship than what we have today had my adolescence been different.

"Mom and I were closer when I was very little. She knew that I wanted to be a ballerina when I was small and bought me a pair of pink toe shoes. Whenever we played a big city that had a ballet, Mom would go to the concert hall during rehearsals, introduce me, and offer the dancers circus tickets in return for tickets to the ballet. They would usually agree, show me their toe shoes, teach me a few steps. It was wonderful.

"When I was a preadolescent, Mom and I shared a love of dolls and of sewing, and we bonded over that. I had a sewing kit and scissors when other children my age would not have been allowed to play with needles. In my room in Houston, I had a three-tier bookshelf that was actually an apartment building for my dolls. Each story held different rooms, and I made pillows and rugs and art for the walls to match the manufactured furniture that I received each Christmas. I had some very nice things."

Fritzi recalls that when she turned thirteen, she underwent a transition that substantially changed the direction of her play. She lost interest in the doll apartment and suddenly grew far more interested in inventing and drawing clothes for paper dolls. "The costumes became the focus rather than the dolls themselves," she remembers. "I didn't want to play with dolls any more, so I told Mom, 'Please don't get me dolls or more doll furniture for Christmas. I've outgrown them.' There was something else that I wanted; I don't remember now what it was, but I absolutely did not want dolls."

Fritzi sighs and looks away from me, her face a collage of conflicting emotion. "On Christmas morning there were dozens of little gifts under the tree for me," she relates quietly. "I was ecstatic. I couldn't imagine what Mom could have gotten me. One by one, I opened them, and every single gift was a piece of doll furniture. Mom tried to get me excited about the pieces, pointed out to me how each item would work with the others. Dad was dead and we had no money then. I knew that she had spent every dollar that she had saved on this fabulous set of miniatures to surprise me, but my heart was just gone."

"You were growing into an adolescent. That's difficult for most parents to follow," I reflect softly. "It's harder to know what will bring happiness for adolescents than for little kids."

Fritzi exhales slowly. "Mom believes that happiness that comes after tears is more valuable, that if you have a little pain, then when something wonderful occurs, it will be ten times better. I first realized this when we were working in Cuba. It was very difficult having holidays there. I was in a foreign country where bombs went off constantly, and I didn't have any friends except for a couple of strange temporary ones like the Siamese twins. I was lonely."

I stare at Fritzi and she laughs briefly. "That's another story entirely. Anyway, I was six years old that Christmas, and I wanted one particular doll desperately. I had asked for only that one present. On Christmas Eve, Mom confessed very solemnly that she had not been able to find the gift for which I had asked, and I went to bed in tears. As I lay there sobbing and brokenhearted, a light went on in the hallway and my mother appeared, walking the doll toward me—the same doll that she had assured me earlier that I couldn't have."

"She was willing to let you cry . . ."

"Just so that she could see that little bit of extra happiness shining through my tears when I realized that she had been lying."

"What did your father think of her plan? He must have approved?"

"When Mom did stuff like that, Dad sort of became invisible. Neither one of my parents had had what you might call proper parenting themselves, so they invented the rules as they went along."

"Were you able to become closer to your mother after your father died? Did you begin to see yourself more individually when there was no one standing between the two of you?"

Fritzi draws a deep breath. I suddenly realize that my plate is empty while hers is still quite full and feel a pang of guilt. I had forgotten that probing interviews and friendly social visits cannot easily be mixed. I remind myself that in spite of my insight on reciprocity, this process is allowing me to share little of my own life while we are exploring my subject's most bitter memories and resentments.

Fritzi begins her story in what seems to me to be a tone of weary resignation, as if she were beginning a necessary but unpalatable journey. "I hated living in Houston. I didn't want to be there, didn't make friends easily. I was older than all the other kids in my class, but at least I was finally in the fourth grade; for the past two years, my parents had made me repeat third grade so that I could be with Bobby. I was twenty years old when I graduated from high school because my mother and father had insisted that we stay together.

"Bobby and I would have quit school and run away in a minute, but we stuck it out because we didn't want to break Mom's heart. We now agree that we more or less raised ourselves, other than that Mom made us be home before it got late. The happiest times were summers. Mom scraped all year so that we three could climb into the car and drive off as soon as school ended. We would visit old friends, stay with whoever would have us. These were very joyous vacations; we almost had our old life back for a short period but never the old security."

Fritzi relates that security was almost nonexistent in Houston, largely because Betty was confronted with responsibility at a time when she was severely depressed. She had signed and returned to an agent in New York papers agreeing to sell the house in Greenwood Lake "as is," not realizing that she was selling all of her family's furniture, dishes, clothes, and belongings. When Betty returned during the summer to collect her possessions, the new owners swore that they had sold everything and closed the door in her face before she could see whether they were telling the truth. In a daze, Betty returned to offer them the owner's manual for the new stove that she had unwittingly sold to them.

Betty was no stronger at managing affairs in Houston. She was at the mercy of anyone with whom she had dealings. Charlie arrived with his family for a single day, offering to pay bills, but left abruptly without helping at all; he offered only the vague explanation that a storm might be brewing and that he had to get his family to Florida.

Harry also arrived right after Fritz died, parked his trailer in the driveway, and informed Betty that he was now the man of the family once again and offered to train his granddaughter. Over the course of the following weeks, Harry built a maze of elaborate riggings in Betty's backyard: web, trapeze, and even Roman Ladders. Between two tall pines, twenty feet apart on opposite sides of the yard, he stretched a cloud swing (a canvas-covered rope, two inches in diameter). There were hand loops on either side and two on the rope, which allowed the children to straddle the cord, swing high, and, at the peak of their swing, hold the hand loops to spin into dizzying revolutions. "It's like swinging a button on a string, then yanking the string so that the button spins," Fritzi explains. "We were the button." The sway pole was only fifteen feet high, not a grand distance for circus-proud children, but a welcome touch of the familiar in a foreign place. "It eased the transition a bit," Fritzi recalls softly.

Betty's qualms about Fritzi's training for aerial work seemed to have died with Fritz. "Grandpa trained me gently, not at all in the way that Mom remembered having been trained," Fritzi recalls. "Only once did he get angry with me. I was trying a trick for which I wasn't ready and I didn't release at the right moment. He grabbed my braid and yanked it, shouting: 'You go *now!*' I was hanging upside down and fell hard. Grandpa was very contrite. To apologize, he spent the next two weeks building me a fabulous walk-in playhouse out in the yard, complete right down to the flower boxes in the windows."

I shake my head in disbelief. "Harry had really mellowed, hadn't he? How wonderful!"

Fritzi inhales sharply, glares at me, and exclaims furiously, "He was an obsessive compulsive hedonist—extremely selfish! He was only nice to me because I looked like potential income for support.

He called me his princess, but he never had a kind word for Bobby or Mom. I can't imagine what he saw in me."

I swallow hard and try to breathe deeply, realizing suddenly that the type of old anger surfacing in this interview is no different from that which I have confronted during discussions of Charlie with Betty—this is the hatred born of a frustrated desire to love. "Why do you have such harsh feelings toward Harry?" I ask softly. "You've related only pleasant memories."

Fritzi snorts. "Grandpa was courting me, not us. He hated Bobby. Grandpa declared that my playhouse was for my use alone and forbid my brother to go near it. We tricked him though." Fritzi recalls that Bobby dug a tunnel under the playhouse wall and covered it with a board. He would circle to the back of the structure, slip the board, and crawl inside to play with his delighted sister, unseen by his grandfather. When Harry discovered the subterfuge, the children devised a more permanent solution. Bobby poured lighter fluid around the little house and burned it to the ground. Harry left soon after that.

After leaving his daughter's home, Harry eventually formed a lasting attachment to a woman much younger than Betty. I listen in amazement as Fritzi relates how assiduously Harry nursed a feeble young epileptic whose parents did not want her living with them. "I think that it was a rare platonic relationship. He cooked, stayed with her during her violent seizures. These were unbelievable: Her jaws would lock down, her back would double up, and every muscle in her body would strain to break her back. Grandpa and this girl took care of one another. It appeared to everyone who saw them that they were an elderly father and sick daughter living together on very little. Perhaps he regretted how his own epileptic son had died and wanted to make some amends. Who knows?"

Fritzi notices my eyes softening and begins to speak hurriedly and coldly. "Don't be fooled. Harry was a bastard and a bully at heart. One afternoon he was telling Mom what to do in *his* house; she responded that she was under her own roof now—and so was he. That's when he hit her. It was like beating an injured dog. She wasn't at her best. I was furious. I was standing behind Grandpa when he struck Mom, and I immediately grabbed a wooden coat hanger and raised it over his head. Mom could see what I was doing. Over Harry's shoulder, she gave me a look that said 'It will be worse for me if you do this.' I lowered the hanger, but that message from her reinforced that I could no longer count on anyone to save my skin. Mom wasn't even going to defend herself."

"You had always been Bobby's protector, and now you were thrust into the role of protector of your mother, as well," I suggest gently. "A heavy burden for an unhappy twelve-year-old."

"I had known from the moment that Mom came back without Dad that there was no strength there for me and that I would have to take care of myself. I had no training. I wasn't very good at it, but I tried.

"The year after Dad died, for instance, when I was thirteen, I told Mom that I wanted a party of my own, and asked if we could have it that coming Saturday. Mom responded, 'Okay, honey, you go ahead and have a party,' but I had no idea how to make a party happen; I assumed that she would take care of the arrangements for me."

"What kind of party did you want?"

"I didn't know. I wanted a cake, I guess, and other kids around. I had no idea what 'normal' kids did for their birthdays. I was looking for a way to fill the void in my life. Dad was freshly gone and I was traumatized. I knew that I needed friends. There were girls across the street my age. I thought that probably Mom would invite them over, and perhaps our next-door neighbors, as well. At school I told my friend George, 'I think that I'm having a birthday party this weekend.' He promised to come.

"That Saturday morning, I woke up excited and got dressed up to the teeth. I still tended to wear things that were rather costumey. Mom was in the kitchen drinking coffee. I gave her her card—she loved those huge elaborate cards that you wouldn't possibly buy anyone today because they are so ostentatious. We had little money then, but I had bought her the biggest card that I could find.

"George showed up later in the day. There was nothing. We sat on the couch, drank a glass of Coca-Cola. No one came. Mom obviously hadn't told anyone, hadn't planned anything. It was devastating. I could only sit there all dressed up, embarrassed and miserable."

"You had been taught to expect that nothing could mean something, that relief could follow deliberate devastation," I suggest.

"Exactly. I assumed that no decorations or discussion meant that she was going to surprise me after I had been disappointed sufficiently."

"Oh, Fritzi."

"Finally George left. I decided, that's it. I will never let myself go through this pain again."

Fritzi sits quietly. "The following year I started smoking pot. I stayed stoned for the next ten years." This is a story that I had not expected and I have no idea how to respond. She looks at me intently and continues, "I have learned that if I really need something done, and don't want to have my feelings crushed, I must do it myself. That belief has gotten me in trouble sometimes, especially in relationships, because it may seem that I don't consider the other person's feelings to be important. That's not necessarily how I am now, but I know that it carries over. I'm partly prone to this."

I take a deep breath, uncertain of exactly what Fritzi is trying to tell me, but knowing that her admission has several layers of meaning and that at least one of them applies to our friendship. "For years I felt that I couldn't count on anyone but myself," she explains. "The truth is that I was an extension of Betty until my father died. Then I had to try to reinvent myself."

I have been growing increasingly uncomfortable as I listen to my friend. Now I make a hasty resolution. "Listen to how you have been answering my questions," I say. "No matter what we begin to talk about, the answer is always 'We did such and such until Dad died.' Your mom, you, and Bobby all speak in the same terms: It was magic, and then Dad died, and we were suddenly plunged into despair and confusion from which we each have struggled individually to recover. Fritzi, that transition, as difficult as it was, occurred almost forty years ago; since then there have been numerous marriages and divorces, jobs and classes, friendships and travel, and yet your father's death still looms as the only major demarcation in any of your lives."

Fritzi raises her chin in the defensive manner that I have come to anticipate. "Yes it does," she declares flatly. "There's nothing that I can do about it."

I continue carefully. "And yet those early days with your father were not entirely idyllic. They have surely become rather idealized and romanticized over the years?"

Fritzi considers my question in silence. I watch as her shoulders tighten, her eyes grow harder; suddenly she relaxes a bit, as if she has weighed both my perception and her own response and found them not incompatible. "Those times have become ideal and romantic in relation to what followed," she explains. "Remember that the transition was extremely abrupt and changed every aspect of our lives completely. After Dad died, Mom immediately sold the house in Greenwood Lake, left the circus, severed every tie with anyone who reminded her too much of Dad. She had to distance herself in order to survive emotionally, but the isolation that she created for herself was one that we had to share.

"I can't speak for Mom or Bobby, but in my own case, I know that it was a very complicated period. In fact, I have no memory of the time between the rape and Dad's death. In my mind, the two happened almost simultaneously, yet I now know that there were several months in between the incidents. That period is completely lost to me."

Fritzi relates that during her family's ill-fated visit to Washington State in the summer of 1961, she and her brother were left during the Kays' performances in the care of a man whom her parents trusted. While she is not specific, I get the sense that this individual was influential and that Betty and Fritz considered him reputable. He suggested that Bobby go out and play, then sexually abused eleven-year-old Fritzi. She will not explain the details of the assault. "I don't want you to be able to visualize it," she insists, "but we both understand what he did to me. I was traumatized. It only ended because his grown son walked in on us and I was able to break away and flee."

When Betty returned and was told that Fritzi had gone out to play, she searched the fairground and discovered her daughter hiding in a bathroom, catatonic. Betty's first thought was of her husband, of the intense pain and sorrow that she had seen in his face as he struggled to cross the wire. Turning quickly to Fritzi, she instructed the child to "pull up her bootstraps" and wipe her tears so that her father would not suspect what had happened. "Your father is very sick," she told Fritzi, implying that she would be doing her beloved father a grave disservice by admitting to him that she had just been violated. When Fritzi's rapist came to the Hubers' vehicle just before the family pulled away, leaned through the window, and handed Betty a cold drink for the "little girl," Betty calmly accepted the gift and thanked him with a smile, as if she knew nothing of his attack on her child.

"Did she explain what had happened to you?" I ask gently.

"She explained nothing, but I knew what had happened to me. Sex wasn't hidden from us."

"Did you see a doctor? Surely your mother understood about sexually transmitted diseases?"

Fritzi shakes her head. "My mother told herself that I had been 'touched,' not violated. After we left the fairgrounds, we stopped at a diner where other performers were having coffee before getting on the road. I remember my mother going over to a table of men about her and my father's age, some a bit younger, putting her hands on the table and speaking with them. They all looked at me and left shortly after. My mother told me later that they went back and beat this man to the extent of breaking his legs.

"Mom and I did not discuss or resolve our 'differences' and find a sense of closure until my mother was seventy-six and I was forty-three years old! I think that's why I have no memory of the months following the rape. It was beyond my ability to understand that so much time could pass by and yet there was no attempt on my mother's part to talk with me, to console me or help me to heal. I had to bury it all so deeply. I only remember feeling a huge distance between myself and my parents and missing my father even before he was gone."

≈

There was no preparation; Betty and Fritz could not help one another to anticipate the pain of separation, much less help their children to prepare for this transition. Right up until Fritz's final moments, both spouses firmly denied the obvious and inevitable. As Fritz lay on his deathbed, he pleaded with his physician not to tell Betty that he was dying. The doctor shook his head and replied, "Your wife begged me not to tell you the same thing."

"Everyone kept a good face," Fritzi recalls, "but at least I wasn't completely unprepared. I had had dreams."

Fritzi relates that months before her father's death, she began to have a dream that recurred night after night, identical in every detail, a dream so terrifying in its clarity that it continued to torture her during the days. Finally she shared her burden with Betty. "I keep dreaming that Daddy is in a hospital room," she told her mother. "Ella and Floyd [the Hubers' neighbors in Houston] are there, but you aren't. Daddy dies and you aren't there."

Years later Betty would admit to her grown daughter that she had feared her during this time because of these seemingly portentous dreams. As Fritz grew increasingly frail, however, she urged Fritzi not to worry about her dream and begged her never, never to share her nightmares with her father. "Daddy's going to be fine, but don't ever tell him," she warned. One month later, after having stood for hours beside her comatose husband's bedside in a hospital in Houston, Betty allowed Ella and Floyd Young to persuade her to take a few moments for herself. While she hastily visited the bathroom and purchased a cup of coffee, her beloved husband died, without knowing that she had left the room, just as their daughter had foreseen.

"I knew immediately that our lifestyle would be different as soon as Mom came back to Greenwood Lake to get us," Fritzi recalls. "Her whole head had turned white in those few weeks. She could not face his death, couldn't even talk to me on the phone when she called from Houston. She was a shattered woman."

Fritzi pauses, obviously tired, and I consider ending the interview, but I know that this difficult subject must be resolved completely and then left behind for good. "How did she tell you that he was gone?" I ask Fritzi.

"She didn't. She called Elvira and gave her the responsibility of informing us. Elvira came to me first. She said, 'Fritzi, I have something to tell you,' but I replied, 'My father is dead. Yes, I know.' I left the room quickly. I couldn't feel anything. Bobby went in next. I could hear Elvira speaking to him, and he responded as you would expect a child to respond. I knew then that Dad's death was a complete surprise to Bobby and felt sad for him, more so than for myself."

Fritzi relates that she stumbled out of the Liazeeds' house and went to Charlie Lucas's home. The phone rang as she entered and she knew that Elvira was relaying the news. When Charlie saw the little girl with the tormented eyes, he went quickly to her, arms out, eager to wrap her in a fatherly embrace. "He pulled me to him, hugged me," Fritzi remembers, "and suddenly I panicked. I had just been raped by a man who had squeezed me in his arms. Charlie's kind embrace just triggered something in me and I snapped."

Fritzi screamed like a cornered wild animal, fought her father's dear friend hysterically, broke away from his sympathetic arms, and fled from the house. "It had nothing to do with Charlie," she muses. "He was a wonderful, fatherly man who sincerely loved us all, but I was a child facing a crisis while overwhelmed by a terrible memory that I could not share. I couldn't let anyone touch me."

When Betty returned for her children, Fritzi ran to another neighbor's home and hid behind the couch. "I didn't want to leave." She sighs. "On first eye contact with Mom, I felt that there was nothing there for me. I was on my own from that moment. Dad was gone, our home was gone, our friends were about to be left behind— everything familiar that might have helped us to make that transition. Mom couldn't even save herself. I had to grow up instantly.

"In my heart, I had said my final good-bye to my dad just before they left for Houston. He was lying in the backseat of the car, and I sensed then that I would never see him again. I didn't mourn his death until I was almost fifteen, though. Mom was working hard and had little time for me. I had crying fits but couldn't place where they were coming from: loss, abandonment, anger, no one taking care of me. All of it, perhaps? I remember coming home one afternoon to an empty house and realizing that I was completely alone in the world. I ran down the street, fell into a ditch, lay there and sobbed. It hit me full force at that specific moment that Dad was never coming back and that I was on my own."

Fritzi turns to me abruptly, raises her chin. "So there's the demarcation. I was an extension of Betty until my father died, and then I had to reinvent myself."

I draw a deep breath. I know better than to play psychologist with this woman who has so long suppressed her pain, yet she is also my friend, a sister with whom I have been encouraged to speak candidly. It hurts me to hear of her suffering, to know that she continues to suffer because of events that took place so long ago. "You don't mention harboring any resentment against your father—only your mother," I note quietly. "You are obviously still very upset with her for abandoning you, yet your father refused medical care so that he could keep performing right up to the last minute. He knew that he was dying yet made no provisions, no preparations. He kept his illness a secret from you, lied to you, assured you that he would come back. Your rape had to be hidden from him so that he could better hide his own sickness. Do you feel now that he should have made a different choice, should have put his family ahead of his career?"

"It wasn't his career—it's something else for an artist. It's his life force!" Fritzi responds instantly. "Without my art as a foundation, I would be devastated. It's the source of your spirit. That's where your soul is. If you believe that God is in you, then abandoning what constitutes your soul is like abandoning God. Mom and I understand so well that need to express yourself artistically. That's why we respect Dad's choice. If you and Al were to lose each other, God forbid, at least Al would still have his art and you would have your writing. That's your deepest being."

Later, when I replay this interview, I will better recognize the context of Fritzi's declaration and of my overreaction to it, but at this moment I know only that she has just voiced my deepest fear for my children. Shaken by her harrowing story, I am poorly prepared for the suggestion that either my husband or I might react to the death of a life partner by turning to art rather than to our children's solace; surely neither of us would condemn our children to the loss of security and self-esteem that Fritzi suffered because of her father's supposed choice. I recall that Fritzi will stand as sole guardian to my children if Al and I die together, and suddenly feel exasperated and angry, so much so that I permit myself to say something that I have sworn never to say to my purposely childless friend: "If you had children, you would understand how much more important they are to your life force than anything you may do for a living, or even for personal fulfillment."

"Of course," Fritzi responds casually. "You have created them. They are the ultimate medium."

"We are not talking about creativity, Fritzi. We are talking about parental responsibility and the complexity of love!" I insist indignantly, thinking of Fritz Huber's death and of the pain that it caused his family—and continues to cause his daughter.

Silence hangs between us for an awkward moment, then Fritzi responds, "I know," with deliberate composure, surprising me. This subject does not have to "read" me like Betty does; she knows me well. She understands that she has activated all of my maternal and familial defenses, is suddenly intent on repositioning herself as a subject. "I'm trying to figure out, if I have anger, where it is. I feel no resentment toward my father, but I am still angry at my mother for things she did that I thought were unethical."

"Like what?" I ask quietly, once again regretting my unleashed subjectivity.

"Like making me keep a terrible secret, not dealing with it and being nurturing as a mother. I understand now why she didn't help me, but that doesn't mean that I'm not angry about it. It also means that I don't hate her. I did for a long time as a younger person, but that doesn't do anybody any good and it certainly doesn't help me whatsoever."

Suddenly Fritzi turns in her chair and glares at me, her face twisted in anger. "I'm not going to spin around like night and day and say, 'Oh, thank you for your questions, it was wonderful.' It wasn't wonderful and that's the truth of it."

She stops talking abruptly, holds herself stiffly in her chair, most of the lovely breakfast now cold in front of her. In an instant of stark self-assessment, I realize that I have not treated this woman as a hesitant or uncooperative subject, have not assisted her with the autobiographical process as I have done with Betty. I have consistently regarded Fritzi as a confidante and facilitator rather than as an uneasy subject in her own right. So much have I depended on the solidarity of our friendship that I have judged her lack of enthusiasm for self-revelation as a personal disregard for my needs, a deliberate refusal to honor her commitment to my project, a blatant disdain of our fellowship. While I have worked diligently to overcome the natural distancing strategies that Betty commonly embraces, I have not recognized those same strategies when Fritzi negotiates them.

Feeling miserable, I try to explain to Fritzi how difficult it has been for me to walk the thin wire between being an interested, supportive friend and an accurate, serious biographer. "I wish sometimes that I had never touched this project because it seems to have put such a strain on a friendship that is very valuable to me—and apparently more fragile than I realized. I sensed months ago that our friendship was undergoing some kind of transition, that we both needed time to separate and let our relationship take its natural course," I explain, choosing my words with care. "I could not allow you or myself that freedom because I had just signed my name to a book contract—with your encouragement—and I had exactly twelve months to uncover and record several generations of your family's history. The material that I need is in your head, but you are continually distancing yourself from me. Do you understand the position that this puts me in?"

Fritzi's chin is up, but her eyes are receptive. "We both knew that there were going to be some very sensitive stories that would demand distance after they had been revealed. That recovery period has been limited, and this has caused a strain between us."

"How can I record the life stories of this family?" I exclaim in frustration. "You and your mother avoid talking to one another about the past. I ask myself constantly why you would want a serious biographer to delve into your history when you are only just at the point of confronting it yourselves. You accuse me of being too analytical, of dissecting your feelings, but biography demands questions and analysis. Its purpose is revelation and reflection. I know that the process is an intrusion, but I didn't come begging. You suggested that I write this book."

Fritzi answers me coldly. "Mom has wanted it for years. I don't have a problem with that creative process on her part. When I approach someone else's creative endeavor, I tend to be wide open and receptive. That's part of the experience of being creative. Mom knows that her time is limited. She wants someone else to have her stories. As she shares them, her life force gets stronger and she knows it."

"You went with me to Savannah, Fritzi. You wanted this project, too; you encouraged and supported me, swore to a room full of editors that you were grateful to me for providing this opportunity, then changed your mind when it came to discussing your past."

Fritzi shrugs her shoulders. "A void can be filled with pain, or mourning, or angst over absence, or you can fill it with something that enhances your memory of the dead and brings them back to life for you. I fill my voids with images, not words. I came into the world with a gift and I can't turn my back on that. You are the writer. You tend to hyperanalyze and take everything apart. When I draw, I purposely work at not complicating or analyzing my work. I don't take anything apart. What I do is a matter of venting, like a pressure valve, you know?

When I'm creating, that act is my pressure valve; I release it and gain a sense of calm and well-being. Telling stories provides Mom with the same release."

I snort and Fritzi stares at me. "You haven't listened to the tapes of your mother's interviews. 'Vent' is an understatement. There are times when her life force can threaten to blow you off the planet. It's like letting a dragon out of a cave. You are not all that different from her, actually."

Fritzi grins. "Well, if your mode of expression can't heal you, what good is it?"

I smile in spite of myself. "I guess that understanding other people's needs and weighing them against your own is a hard balancing act," I offer finally, hoping that she will understand that I am acknowledging her struggle as well as mine.

"That's the business we were in," Fritzi responds with a mischievous look, reaching for her fork. She glances up at me, and I see that her eyes are tranquil.

Suddenly I hold out my arms, as if I were on a wire, and exclaim, "Oops! Watch out below!" She does the same, and we both dissolve into much-needed laughter.

Only later do I realize that our pantomime serves as a perfect metaphor for this arduous process that we have undertaken with its constant balancing of revealing and concealing, negotiating and confirming, competing and suspecting, defending and accusing, worrying and hoping. I wonder whether, when the book is finished and we find ourselves on firm ground again, we will have chosen to descend together rather than on opposite sides.

∽

"I was fourteen when I started smoking pot and drinking and getting involved with drugs," Fritzi states quietly. "Across the street were older boys—football players—who took me out one night and asked if I wanted to meet Mary Jane. When I replied, 'Sure,' they laughed and handed me a joint. It removed me from reality and I appreciated that."

She pauses and stares at me as if to say "You won't understand the rest of this story and probably won't like me after I have told it."

I share her concerns but know that we must continue. Understanding the personal obstacles between us should be empowering, but the rest of our interview is highly emotional in spite of every resolution that I make to remain dispassionate. Fritzi relates stories of her difficult teen years, of decisions concerning sexuality and drug abuse that she must know that I will be tempted to judge harshly because I have chosen her as my children's guardian. Her interview is thematically comparable to many that I have had with Betty, and I attempt to respond with reassuring comments, as I would with her mother, but it becomes increasingly difficult for me to remain a receptive listener.

My relationship with Betty has long accommodated our differences, but I have always seen Fritzi as a kindred spirit. As our interview progresses, Fritzi's unfamiliar stories collapse the long-cherished myth of my friend's fundamental similarity to myself—a repercussion of which she is, no doubt, acutely aware. Only much later will I come to understand the complicated dynamics of an interview that will abruptly compel two friends to interrogate and renegotiate the extent of their compatibility.

"I got involved with smokers, made some bad choices in boyfriends," Fritzi tells me. "I had a crush on one red-haired boy who wore black leather and rode a motorcycle. He stole a car and got caught. Things would probably have gotten much worse if Bobby and I hadn't suddenly discovered a physical outlet that allowed us to get through the rest of our adolescence without abusing ourselves."

Fritzi relates that she first saw a surfboard in a magazine ad. She ran straight to the library, read everything that she could find about surfing. Finally she borrowed a board, begged a ride to the beach, and tried to teach herself how to use it. "I was working as a candy girl in downtown Houston, saving all my money for a surfboard." Fritzi laughs. "Bobby came up with a used one, eventually, and I convinced Mom to cosign on loan payments through Household Finance so that I could buy one on time.

"When I was fifteen, Mom and Bobby pooled all their savings and bought me a specifically cut woman's wet suit, which was a very big deal in the 1960s. It was even fitted to me. I had started surfing then, and intuitively Mom knew that I had so much that was wild in me that I needed a physical outlet. It was the best gift that she could possibly have given me. On her days off, Mom would stick our boards into the back of the station wagon, drop us off at the beach, then go to some hotel and lay by the pool while we tried to teach ourselves to surf."

Fritzi smiles to herself. "We were very bad at first, but I learned eventually. By the time that I got out of high school, surfing was all that I wanted to do. I couldn't drive, but I figured that if I owned a car, someone would take me to Southern California. I bought a used car for $450, convinced an old boyfriend who was living on the coast to return to Texas and drive me back with him, moved in with him, and surfed."

"How did you support yourself?" I ask.

"Mom and I had been making costumes in Houston—that's how I had saved most of my money. We were working for a man who supplied costumes for Mardi Gras, strippers, and drag queens. We made a standard fifteen dollars a day. Handwork like beading, embellishing, and jewels paid extra. I got ten dollars a dress for cutouts and openings and eyelets. When I got out to California, everyone was wearing costumes on the streets. This was in 1970, remember? I had brought some exotic fabric with me, so I started doing independent work: crewel embroidery on doeskin for renaissance fairs, consignment work for people who didn't want to wear industrially produced clothing, and, finally, handmade bathing suits. After all, I lived near the beach."

"Were you still on drugs?" I ask curiously, trying to imagine how anyone could be stoned and still do fine handwork and survive surfing on Pacific waves. There can be little reciprocity with this story, I realize with a pang.

"We were all involved with lots of drugs," Fritzi says with a sigh, "but never heroin."

"How about your art? Were you making art at this point?"

Fritzi leans back and thinks. "I had always been making art," she muses. "My creativity was the only private space that I had. One of the things that I most resented when we moved to Houston was that I had no privacy. Bobby got the extra bedroom and I had to sleep in a boxy hallway between the kitchen and his bedroom door. I had a little bed there, and some shelves and a small closet. Anyone who wanted to go to Bobby's room or the bathroom had to walk through that hallway. I was extremely exposed in that space and resented it.

I was the girl, but when I would try to tell Mom how I felt, she would only respond, 'Life is harder on women so you have to be tough.'

"In my first year of junior high school, my art teacher, Mappie [Mathelie] Miracle, noticed that I was withdrawn and didn't associate with other kids. I responded to her class though; I would sit in a corner and draw furiously. Mappie was only twenty-three, a recent graduate of the University of Iowa, and this was her first teaching assignment. She latched on to me and became my best friend. On weekends we would go to her parents' house to draw or down to a shrimping port to paint. We worked with clay in her home; she threw pots and made all of her own dishes. Mappie made sure that I read and visited museums and galleries. She was the best influence that I could possibly have had. She was with me constantly for two years."

Suddenly Fritzi pauses and looks over at me, rather abashed. "This next story is to my fault, not my credit," she explains slowly. "Mappie was trying hard to encourage my mother to help me to earn a scholarship to the University of Iowa. They still have an excellent program in art. I recall specifically one night that Mappie and Mom were sitting and discussing my future. I remember having a telescopic experience suddenly—sensing a sort of physical removal. These women were across the table speaking about me in the third person. I didn't exist. I had had enough of that. I wanted control over my own life, for better or worse. I stood my ground and stubbornly refused something that ultimately would have been very good for me. Mappie got romantically involved with someone after that, I became interested in boys and surfing, and we drifted apart.

"In high school, my art teacher saw what I had done in junior high and arranged for me to receive a scholarship for after-school art classes for gifted children at the Museum of Fine Arts in Houston. These classes exposed me to the museum—which was good, of course, but they taught me nothing. It felt like unstructured babysitting more than serious art study. I was a pain in the butt by that time. I left early one day. When the instructor confronted me later about having left class, I complained that I wasn't learning anything; she informed me that many students would love to have the opportunity that I was wasting and threw me out. I apologized then, but she refused to let me stay. I had to go home and tell Mom that I had lost the scholarship.

"Mom knew how much my art meant to me, but she didn't know how to help me. She finally sent off for one of those 'Learn to Draw' mail order courses. I did the lessons for several months but finally I quit. I told Mom, 'The better I copy, the better they think I'm doing. It's so boring.' Later I discovered that the course had cost Mom $500—a great deal of money for her at that time. I paid her back though, little by little.

"When I got to California, I began taking formal art classes. I wanted to draw more, but I could see that I had limitations in my skills and understanding. I knew very little about the sequence of American art history. I had a huge pocket of ignorance, and to study all of that on my own seemed overwhelming. Once I had lived in California for six months, I was able to attend the junior college system for nothing. It's a fantastic system. I began to take classes in life drawing, graphic design, and printmaking. My energies were becoming focused. I was trying to make a decision about what I wanted to do.

"After a while, I began to realize that it had been a long time since I had seen Bobby and Mom together. Bobby had gone straight on the road after graduation and was working circus. Mom had gone back to do wardrobe. I hadn't seen a rigging in years, but I had kept my old trapeze and was very strong from surfing; I could do a web routine. I contacted an agent in Texas and booked myself for the Texas dates as a web girl—what might be called a chorus girl. Web is a choreographed number, generally an extravagant production. You're fitted for a costume, practice to music. All I had to do was go on spec [participate in the opening circus parade], then the aerial number—we would be birds in cages or something, then the finale. I lived in my brother's camper, in a Volkswagen bus with Mom, in a hotel room—whatever worked in each town.

"I knew that going back to circus would be a difficult transition because I had been doing drugs since I was fourteen. I couldn't perform in the air like that. I had to quit cold turkey. I had a friend who had been teaching transcendental meditation for a decade and he taught me techniques to help me through that experience. I needed a transitional tool. TM quiets the inner voices—there is no dialogue whatever in that blank space; time stops. It was a deep rest that allowed me to transfer my energies in a different direction. Ironically, it was also at this time that I met my first husband while I was surfing."

Fritzi tells me of her first three brief marriages. "I was hiding in other people while I hid from myself," she admits. "I had much growing up to do." She explains what each man taught her, what caused her to end each union. What strikes me most forcefully about these stories is Fritzi's marked emphasis on how completely she resisted her first two husbands' pleas to have children. Her tone is extremely defensive as she explains her choice to a friend whose life she knows revolves around three kids. "I never had the desire that other women feel to have a handful of children. The world is overpopulated as it is," she protests, staring at me as if in challenge.

When her third husband asked her to have her tubes tied, Fritzi relates that she did so quite willingly. "I married [my current husband] partly because he didn't expect me to have children," she tells me pointedly. "If I had children, I am sure that I would devote myself to them. I have friends who have children and they don't have time to work at their art."

I say nothing in response to her challenge, merely nod my understanding. I have had ample evidence that Fritzi is not without a well-developed sense of family loyalty. I have watched her with children and have marveled at how instinctively she seems to speak their language. I know that my friend's protests are probably, at some level, regretful and self-consolatory; her narration has also helped me to understand that, in order to survive, Fritzi has learned to let joy in her creative work and inner life replace the need for social or familial interdependence. I am grateful to her for allowing me this intimate understanding, and yet I also realize that her admissions have forced me to reconsider a difficult decision of my own. I know that I must find someone who will agree to love my three children more than anything else in the world if I should die, and then I will have to change my will immediately. Although Fritzi will assume that I have judged her stories with narrow-minded morality, those same stories have convinced me that I must never take my children's futures for granted.

Fritzi is watching me gravely. "You know," she says softly, "my father died of cancer when I was eleven years old. He was given a choice of undergoing radiation treatment with a fifty-fifty chance of survival or of having his leg amputated with a guarantee that the cancer would be removed. It hadn't spread yet. He gambled his life and died. He chose radiation because he was an artist, a wire walker. He preferred to risk his life rather than to lose a leg because his art was what made it worthwhile for him to be alive. For him there was no choice. Can you understand that?"

Silence falls over us. I want to understand, but all that I can think about is the stricken wife and two miserable children whom Fritz Huber left behind. Fritzi's explanation does not satisfy me. I cannot respect a young father's decision to gamble his life for art, much less consider that choice a noble one. The artistic dedication that she is honoring so intensely seems hollow and masturbatory to me unless the love that inspires it can inform the rest of one's life. It seems to me almost a tragedy that this brilliant and sensitive woman may have spent decades believing that her cherished father loved his work more than his children and that she has ironically embraced the same priorities as a means of honoring him and of protecting herself from sadness. Nothing that I can tell Fritzi will convince her that she herself is worth far more, at least to me, than any artistic "gift" that she might possess.

Startled, I suddenly understand how much I had hoped that my friendship with Fritzi would replace the colleagues, students, and even opportunities that I had lost. What right had I to expect so much? What, I wonder, did she hope for from me?

∼

Beyond the windows of Fritzi's sun-spattered studio, summer light sparkles on dancing waves. Crowded crab traps bob in the water of the Intracoastal Waterway—only a few steps beyond the screen door. I love the freshness of this space, the scented breezes blowing off the channel, the lapping of the waves lulling us as we talk quietly. I envy Fritzi her peaceful work environment, only a short walk from the ocean. I have volunteered to help her to prepare for a show of her artwork at St. John's Museum of Art. My job is to cut strips of Velcro into small squares and then hot-glue them onto the back of her paper pieces. Chatting over handwork in this breezy studio is deeply soothing after long weeks spent riveted to my computer screen in a dark room. Later we will sip iced tea on the outdoor veranda of a favorite seaside restaurant as we wait for our fish platters to be served up hot. I must admit to myself that when I first considered writing this book, I had hoped that my research would entail many lovely hours spent here with my friend. I am hoping that today will help to reaffirm our shaky friendship.

I have been telling Fritzi about my recent visit to the Clyde Beatty & Cole Bros. Circus, of the unexpectedly high cost of tickets and of the necessity of maneuvering into the circus encampment through a PETA [People for the Ethical Treatment of Animals] demonstration. In spite of these frustrations, I carted my children onto the fairgrounds almost giddy with enthusiasm; finally I was going to have my first chance since beginning my research to view actual riggings and watch live wire walking. I was prepared to be deeply appreciative.

My technology-spoiled children seemed bored at first, more concerned with purchasing drinks and treats than with watching the performances. Halfway through the program, however, a large family of flyers strode gracefully into the ring, dropped their lavish capes, and quickly scaled the rigging to the trapeze. Brilliant points of colored light shattered across the audience as the spotlights sprayed their sequined leotards. Kurt suddenly elbowed his brother hard. "Carl, look!" he gasped, pointing to a slim flyer who had just gained the platform. Clearly visible across the man's bare back, from shoulder blade to waist, ran the long, deep scars of jungle-size claws. As the flyer grabbed a trapeze and hurled himself into the dust-clouded expanse above us, Carl hissed in my ear, "There's no net! He could die! Should Kurt be watching this?"

I tell of my children's startled concern for the performers and of my own unease when a young woman allowed herself to be hoisted into the rafters by her thick hair and spun in a dizzying blur high over my head. My cranium was aching with sympathetic pain by the time that she was lowered to the sawdust-covered floor. I stared at her tightly stretched face, her stoic smile, and felt a disturbing sense of voyeuristic guilt, not unlike the sensation that I remember feeling on a playground long ago as classmates cheered a child who had just been paid to eat a bug.

Fritzi listens calmly to my story, her hands busily clipping and snipping as I speak. "You shouldn't feel voyeuristic. To her this is a skill. She has chosen it," she assures me. "There's a distancing effect that you are not acknowledging."

"But if I have paid to watch this act, am I not responsible for having supported it? I felt as though I were witnessing self-abuse. Where is the skill in that? I am certain that I was not meant to feel that way, but I did. At the same time, I felt indignant for the performers; people were climbing over the bleachers and screaming for ice cream and Cokes while flyers and animal trainers were risking their lives right in front of us. It was very disturbing to watch how little respect they were granted by the audience, in spite of the obvious difficulty and skill of the performances."

Fritzi's perfect posture, the result of an old back injury, makes her seem as unperturbed as the placid water surrounding us. "I've talked to people who told me that they loved the show. You may have seen a different performance, though. It's interesting that you had such distinct responses." She watches me for a moment, then reflects, "People are pretty jaded. That may be part of what you were picking up on. We have fabulous visuals all around us. We are overstimulated constantly by amazing computer-generated imagery. We have become used to having a buffer zone between ourselves and reality. Our sense of the fantastic is gone, and so the circus is a dramatic transition to an unfamiliar realm.

"You watched your boys make that transition. Aroma has something to do with it. Popcorn, sweat, elephants—all those animal smells. The air fills with sawdust and your throat gets dry; that's when it starts to register that all this is *real*. There's an intimate proximity in the tent: You can make eye contact, feel the physical presence of people around you, gauge their emotional feedback. In a theater, by contrast, you are in a dark cocoon."

"But in a theater, you know that you are watching actors who are playing roles," I remind her. "Circus performers live their profession."

"Yes, and that's part of the curiosity. You know that you are seeing the manifestation of a real way of life. It's not safe, either. The danger that you're witnessing is actual and immediate."

"Danger is real for a firefighter, too," I muse. "They go into burning buildings everyday and risk their lives because there is something at stake, but they don't choose to put out bigger and bigger fires three times a day simply to entertain the populace. There is no socially redeeming reason to risk one's life for an audience. I have been reading about Blondin in Culhane's book. You know, he was a superb wire walker, but once he had crossed Niagara Falls, he had to keep complicating that first feat; he threw somersaults and did tricks, walked it blindfolded and on stilts. I think that at some point, people ended up watching out of a morbid fascination, not enjoyment or appreciation. Is there a point where professional artistry can mutate into an exhibitionist compulsion?"

"You're trying to approach this in terms of audience reception," Fritzi points out. "From the performer's standpoint, it's quite different. Performers will certainly grow uncomfortable if someone is foolishly trying a trick that hasn't been prepared adequately; that reflects on the whole circus. The true performer is a professional artist. He has to challenge himself in order to grow. Of course, he hopes that the audience will be appreciative, but he is really performing for himself and for other performers." She pauses, searching for the right terms. "They are on a journey. They set their own fires and put them out. It's a spiritual fire."

"That's a nice way to put it, but to me it seems more like war games," I admit, irritation beginning to itch beneath the surface of my frame of mind. "Like those soldiers who brag that they train with live ammunition so that if there's ever a real war, they'll be ready. Their risk is real but the need is hypothetical. That's not an impulse that I would associate with the creative drive or the search for spiritual fulfillment. It probably has more to do with a need to feel associated with a privileged group, to define oneself as extraordinary."

Fritzi calmly reaches for another strip of cloth. "I don't see it that way. You're risking your own life only. It is an internal drive, almost hedonistic. Yes, there's a sense of narcissism about it. You're looking at yourself, following your own standards and goals."

"Your mother says that the performance is all for the audience."

"No! It's for oneself."

"When you focus on yourself so much, you can become self-absorbed," I hint, referring indirectly to the friend who has repeatedly informed me that her need to produce art leaves her no time for friendship.

Fritzi's hands stop. "Mom is self-absorbed," she responds slowly, mistaking my reference. "But she is also one of the most giving people

I know—that's the balance. She will give anything that she can afford to part with because she feels that she is wealthy. Others may not see her that way."

"Mom does love little things." I chuckle. "She will buy piles of toys on a whim but she will give those same toys away instantly if someone admires them. She has that sense that life is transient and that things are merely things—but she is extremely tenacious of life itself. Is that what you're getting at?"

"There are precious things." Fritzi wipes hot glue from her fingers and hands me a cloth to do the same. "My friend Karen (Cristiani) Peters inherited her mother Miriam's elephants and a trunk of fabric. Miriam had never worn anything but transient costumes. She had a huge trunk full of leotards and fabric and shiny things; for each performance, she dug into her trunk and invented a new costume. Performers would gather outside their trailers at showtime to see what Miriam would be wearing. So you see, Karen had no costumes to inherit.

"Miriam had been a ballerina with the San Francisco Ballet Company before she ran away with her husband to join the circus. Back in the seventies, she gave me a pair of her own handmade scuff-around ballet slippers. They had canvas bottoms with red corduroy uppers and little red satin ribbon on them. I loved those slippers because they were Miriam's, but it dawned on me one day that I might wear them out, so I sent them to Karen. I saw her several years ago when she was working Hanneford [Circus] and she was thrilled that a part of her past had been restored, that it hadn't just slipped away. I have my mother's wire-walking shoes. We let big things go because the little meaningful objects are the important ones."

"Why are your mother's shoes so meaningful to you?" I ask quietly.

Fritzi glances up from her work and smiles. "They are handmade and part of a creative endeavor. Think of women sitting in trailers decorating costumes around tables full of beads and lots of glittery things. You are creating for the future something that is going to be beautiful and transforming. You may not even be speaking. It's like a quilting bee; there's a sharing of some sort of spiritual joy going on."

"Today has been a little bit like that for me," I offer hesitantly, and we grin at each other.

"This is why I love those masks and tiger costumes that I have on my walls at home," Fritzi explains. "The transforming ability of a costume or a mask is spiritual. Putting on a costume is almost a ritual; you are preparing to transform yourself. It's like preparing a gorgeous table to accompany a special meal. Self-respect is a big part of it."

"Teaching is like that," I muse. "What I do in the classroom is always a performance, but it has to do with desire and self-respect and sharing something precious. There's a reciprocity to it that's hard to explain to someone who thinks that teaching is just a form of training."

"Being technically capable isn't enough," Fritzi agrees. "People ask me, 'How can you teach other artists to make paper? Aren't you giving away your livelihood?' My work isn't just technique or some secret glaze formula. You can give all your tricks away and remain unique as long as the core of what you're doing comes from a genuine spiritual center.

"Show people would look down on you if you came into the ring dressed just like me and did the same trick. The exciting question is how creative can you be in presenting it? When someone comes up with a new trick, word gets out. Pretty soon people are wandering into the tent to watch the practice. Dolly Jacobs was practicing a new trick once and let Pedro Carrillo, the wire walker, help her. He was with Ringling [Bros. and Barnum & Bailey Circus] and then went to Big Apple [Circus] because he fell in love with Dolly. No one knew the details but the two of them, but this big, exciting rumor spread: Dolly's working on something! When artists hear that a fellow artist is breaking boundaries, everyone's energy is heightened."

"How much privacy can you have to develop a new act?"

"Not much, but enough. A circus camp is like any other campsite. People have their own schedules. In between shows, you can go into the tent and practice. The public can't watch, of course, but other performers can. If word gets out that you are pushing your own boundaries, your peers will pay attention. It's part of that spirit."

"What about rivalry?" I ask. "Your mother and I were talking the other day about borrowing in the circus—traditions, patents, using other people's material. I was amazed that she agreed to teach her routine to Frank Cook's wife. What comedian today would offer another comedian her exact routine? Mom's argument was that nobody else could copy her act even if they tried. She swears that she shared every word and gesture but that her act just did not look the same when anyone else tried it."

"Right. It's like sports." Fritzi smiles. "No one will see a somersault and complain, 'That's my trick.' Ideally, you want to be the first or even the only person performing a certain stunt, but this is part of the reason why you push the edge—what you can accomplish, others will invariably achieve. Besides, acts are unique because the performers are individuals. Nobody could design an airplane act that exactly copied the Kimris. The tricks that they did were all established ones, but that look was theirs alone."

"Audiences never really see that deep, creative impulse," I muse. "Maybe if we were able to compare different acts regularly, or to watch a routine evolve over time, we could develop the same educated appreciation that performers have for one another; but the circus comes to town for a few days annually and then disappears overnight without a trace. The performers do not mingle with the general community after the performances. So is it any wonder that the average audience has less understanding of the circus performer's art than, say, of an athlete's?"

Fritzi shakes her head. "Circus doesn't work that way. Performers are very protective of their privacy."

"Protective or defensive?" I ask, recalling Betty's constant pretense of having lost addresses and phone numbers of other performers whom I have wanted to interview.

"Wouldn't you be wary of outsiders? You're traveling alone. You have women in your trailer. These women have just been seen in a ring behaving flamboyantly and doing gymnastics in very scanty costumes. Perhaps someone will think, 'These women are interesting and easy. They have shiny jewels on their costumes. They may have money with them.' You are in a strange place and you are perceived as being seductive and unusual. Think about it."

"I can understand all of that, but times have changed Fritzi. Circus performers do not live like nomads anymore. On the road, they are indistinguishable from millions of tourists. They have homes and go shopping and talk to other people. I have been to Sarasota, you know."

Fritzi chuckles, but I push my point. "I can't get a sense of that individuality, that spiritual core that you are talking about except by meeting performers, and your mother is the only one that I know. I hate to make her a metaphor for the circus."

"Mom isn't even like all people much less all performers!" Fritzi laughs.

"But your mother will not introduce me to other performers. When she visits a circus, she always goes alone and lets me know about it afterward. I do not want to be intrusive or to interview anyone necessarily, but I would like to meet some of her friends and get a firsthand sense of that world. She tells me that circus people will not talk to outsiders, and that if her friends knew that she was working with me on this book, they would consider her some sort of traitor."

"Mom's generation is more protective than mine. She's been accosted by circus fans all of her life."

"Oh, please! She tells everyone she meets about her background."

"She'll do it now, but she didn't always. When I was a girl, I never told people that I was a circus child. Immediately that history replaced my identity. I became 'that girl from the circus,' instead of Fritzi. I couldn't talk about it for a long time, even though circus is extremely pertinent to my work. The whole time that we were growing up, we were bombarded with fans. They look at you like you're some sort of curiosity, a strange animal just escaped out of a cage, an alien from another planet. Fans will come to your trailer just to look at you. Everything you touch or use in your act is amazing to them. It's horrible to feel that you are on exhibit in your own home! Performers are exposed enough when they are performing. That's why they respect one another's privacy tremendously."

"So this isn't so much about outsiders as about not being obnoxious or insensitive?"

"Exactly. If Mom brought you with her to the circus and you started asking questions, her friends would think, 'God, I'm going to be dissected again. Betty should know better.' Circus fans are, by and large, a pain in the ass. Would you want someone barging up to you and saying 'Oh, you're a writer! Can I see your notes? What does this little mark in the margin mean?'"

"Your mother tells me that she always appreciated fans; surely there are some people who have a genuine interest in and respect for her profession? You are confusing writers with reporters. There's a big difference."

"Circus people are not used to hearing the truth about themselves," Fritzi muses. "Books about circus are generally written by an outsider who hangs out with a single circus long enough to write a juicy story that sensationalizes it. Performers are like Native Americans—accustomed to being either villianized, romanticized, or adulated without understanding."

"But isn't that precisely the reason to voice one's own story?" I urge. "Wouldn't it be to the circus performers' advantage to dismantle that mystique a bit by talking to audiences and biographers and interviewers? By telling their own stories and revealing themselves to be hardworking human beings? The mentality that you are describing sounds unnecessarily cultlike to me—that need to mistrust the outside world. Cult members must believe that they are supermundane, that they will be misunderstood or persecuted by the rest of the world."

"If you grow up in the circus, you know that you will be treated as an oddity. It's inevitable."

"Well, really, Fritzi. If you are going to spin by your hair until it falls out, you should expect to be considered unusual. That doesn't mean that you cannot find a means to communicate with other people," I plead indignantly.

Fritzi gives me a hard look. "When a stranger asks you what you do for a living, how often do you say 'I'm a critical theorist'?"

I open my mouth, then shut it quickly. "I don't. I say that I teach English and expect to hear, 'Oh God, I'd better watch how I speak.' I see your point. Often, if I admit that I am a university professor around people who have not gone to college, they either look at me as though I am bragging or say something scathingly anti-intellectual. Even other professors treat theorists like aliens."

I ponder Fritzi's analogy for a while, certain there is a flaw in it. "One of the reasons that you so intrigue me is that you have managed to live in both worlds and to be comfortable in both," I offer finally. "Doesn't that provide hope that others can achieve the same understanding?"

Fritzi's face suddenly contorts with impatience. "Circus performers have an understanding that no one else can really share. No one in the circus would ask a colleague, 'Why do you take that risk?' A performer doesn't want to be asked that," she responds coolly. "Circus people stick close together not only because they derive creative strength from one another but because they speak the same language. They don't need to explain to one another what can't be explained in words. An artist has been given a gift. Not everyone has that gift. My father chose to gamble his life rather than to lose his art. Any circus performer would understand that, but an outsider wouldn't."

My friend stares directly at me, seeming to stop just short of saying that she is referring to ungifted outsiders like me, people who insist on dredging up the unspeakable and trying to confront it with language. We continue our work, but a subtle change in mood is as apparent as it is intangible. Mistrust hangs in the silence between us. I feel as if I have been slapped repeatedly by an invisible little hand, but I have a perplexing sense that I have somehow been returning the blows. Later, in transcribing this interview, I will note how defensively the conversation has relied on generalizations: what artists feel, what performers must do, how apparently unbreachable is the spiritual barrier between these beings and "outsiders." Betty's most direct personal censure has never unsettled me in the way that Fritzi's indirect essentialist terminology has today.

I want so much to assure my friend that she has a worth that far outreaches her creativity as an object maker, that her worth as a friend is priceless, but she seems unconvinced of this herself. I feel powerless to alter her perceptions and values given my responsibilities as an interviewer—a responsibility so at odds with the impulses of friendship. Sensing my personal desire to question her priorities, Fritzi has apparently developed a need to posit me as an intellectual, a verbally oriented "outsider" who cannot appreciate the spiritual depth of a creativity that she feels defies words. How can I defend myself without compromising the integrity of our interviews? How can I worry about interviews when a valued friendship is being dismantled?

As we work in silence, I recall the expression on Fritzi's face several nights ago when I cornered her at an opening and informed her, as casually as I could, that I have changed my will. I thanked her profusely for her willingness to accept my trust when I had no one else, then explained that a newly married young nephew and his wife have offered to act as trustees for my children since they hope to become parents soon and already regard my kids as family.

Telling Fritzi of my new choice was the last step in a process that has brought me great relief as well as pain. My initial decision to include Fritzi in my will seemed, to me at least, incontrovertible proof of deep and everlasting friendship, a bestowing of trust tantamount to a sacrament. Changing my mind is equally symbolic, I know, yet how can I make peace with the knowledge that my precious children might someday be parentless and left in the care of a person who considers her own childhood happiness and security well lost for someone else's art?

I have just decided that we have reached a merciful breaking point in our interview when Fritzi stuns me with an unexpected reflection on herself: "On this last trip to California, I was feeling, God, I don't have any long-term friend. Am I not capable of long-term relationships?"

I stare at her. "You're a complex woman, Fritzi," I respond cautiously, and she laughs.

"This is a real dichotomy about the person that I am. I am not like my parents. They thrived on overexposure. Rarely were they separated. They loved living in close quarters and working together. I am willing to be cloistered with someone that I love for long periods of time, but when I feel the need for transition, that time is finished. There were periods of time when Rochelle, my friend of twenty years, and I were out of touch with each other for months. We were both going through transitions that we couldn't communicate to one another because we had nothing in common during those times."

I am considering the implications of her admission for our own friendship when Fritzi adds, "I still feel sorry that I lost Rochelle."

Fritzi has told me the story of the pretty blond girl whom she met while studying art at Palomar College in California. Although they looked nothing alike, professors consistently confused the two because their demeanor and carriage were so similar. During a critique for a life drawing class, Fritzi and Rochelle discovered, to their amazement, that they were the only students who had not drawn a nude. Both had drawn the model in the flamboyant kimono that she had worn into the room and discarded during the drawing session. Intrigued, they introduced themselves and eventually became very close friends, sharing an apartment and interweaving themselves into one another's life.

Fritzi has shown me the beautiful book of ongoing collages that she has created over the years to celebrate Rochelle's life, tragically cut short by cancer. She has told me of how difficult it was to watch her treasured friend dying, of Rochelle's gorgeous visual hallucinations under the influence of morphine, of her painful last request that Fritzi divorce her own husband, marry Rochelle's spouse, and become a mother to her two small children.

Shortly after Rochelle's death, her husband was also killed in a car crash. Realizing that he was dying, this incredibly self-possessed father spent his last few minutes talking calmly to the little boy at his side, determined to fortify and prepare his child for the imminent loss of his remaining parent. I remember Fritzi's desire to adopt her two godchildren after the crash. She tells me that she has been persistent in writing to them.

I find myself softening rapidly as I reflect on Fritzi's loss of a friend, her eagerness to mother someone else's children, her reference to transitions. Across the table, Fritzi has begun to clear her pile of Velcro away. I know that in a few minutes we will be tramping down to the beach for lunch, laughing over some harmless topic, purposely avoiding any serious discussion. With a pang, I realize that we are no longer the happy girlfriends who once enjoyed serious debates and discussions of principle. It has become painfully obvious to me that the process of recording this subject's life will be incompatible with that of nurturing our friendship unless I can restrain my protective maternal instinct, but I suspect that I might as well try to stop breathing.

～

Charlie Lucas settles comfortably into Betty's well-cushioned sofa and sizes me up amiably. "Have you met Charlie's angels?" He laughs, referring to his friends Grace and Ruby Zeigler, who have accompanied him and whom I guess to be only a little younger than himself. At eighty-four, Charlie is energetic and quick-witted, funny and warm. His handsome face is wrinkled with laugh lines. Following a phone call from Fritzi (for which I am very grateful), he and "the angels" have generously driven a full day's round trip from Santee,

South Carolina, to Wilmington, North Carolina, in order to be interviewed. I am hoping that Charlie can give me a man's insight into the character of his friend Fritz Huber. I have listened to Betty and Fritzi talk about this man for almost two years now but still have little sense of Fritz as an individual. All of their memories revolve understandably around Fritz's relationship to them.

I sit quietly for a while and listen to Betty tell many of the same stories that she has told me so often. Eventually Charlie turns to me and asks me about myself. When I mention that I have three children, all three seniors lean forward and begin pressing me with eager questions. For the next hour we talk animatedly about children, grandchildren, kids today, school violence, television shows, the Internet. By the time that Betty suggests coffee and banana bread, I am enjoying myself immensely. I have begun to fall in love with these joking, affectionate grandparents who are so very much like my own parents and grandparents.

Finally I ask Charlie about his memories of Fritz. He relates stories that confirm much that I already know—that the Hubers were well liked, loved their children, enjoyed practical jokes. Charlie's eyes grow misty when he recalls the fun that the families had at Greenwood Lake, perhaps, I think, because these are memories in which his late wife played a part, as well. Betty seems a bit perturbed that I am probing somebody else about her husband. "You never ask me about Fritz! You only want to know about Harry and the bad stuff," she huffs unfairly, to my amusement.

Emboldened by Charlie's presence, I respond, "If you want to have your story told, Betty, then I need to know both the good and the bad because that's what makes each of us what we are."

"She's right!" the others exclaim, and Betty sits back quietly, apparently reassured by their supportive response.

It is an offhand remark that finally captures my attention and shows me a side of Fritz that I have been waiting to see. In the course of telling a broader story, Charlie casually refers to hearing Fritz holler for his kids. I am struck by this image and suddenly realize that in the histories that I have been given so far, Fritz always emerges as an extremely quiet, passive man, almost docile in his adoration of Betty. This submissive image has disturbed me greatly because it is irreconcilable both with the confident posture and mischievous, intelligent eyes that stand out in photographs of Fritz and with the dynamic performance that I have watched him enact on tape. I do not quite understand why, but the thought of Fritz hollering good-naturedly across the yard for his kids to bring more lighter fluid for the grill is absolutely refreshing.

As I stand in Betty's driveway later in the afternoon, hugging Grace and Ruby, promising to send them pictures of Emma, Charlie carefully writes down everyone's address for me and reiterates how welcome my family will be at his home should we ever pass through South Carolina—especially if we bring my golden-haired little daughter for him to play with. The women begin to tease Charlie about the tin of candy he keeps on the front seat, which is almost empty. I know that they intend to stop at Hardee's for fried chicken before starting home and bitterly regret that I do not have the provisions to invite them all to my house for a home-cooked supper.

I feel thoroughly hugged and renourished for the next few days after this interview but am also more mystified than ever. If you can tell anything about a man's character by his friends, then Fritz Huber was an exceptional person whose friendship still deserves to be actively valued almost half a century after his death. I am certain that Charlie did not drive hundreds of miles for any other reason than out of love for Fritz and Betty. I cannot imagine the person who could inspire such timeless friendship putting his profession ahead of his family. It just does not make sense.

∿

There are two videocassettes left of Fritz Huber's home movies, or at least of the portions that Bobby was able to salvage and piece together. Snuggled barefoot on my sofa in a darkened room, I replay both of them, allowing myself to imagine that I am behind the camera with Fritz as he films, sharing his thoughts as he focuses visually on some subjects and passes over others. Because these movies are my sole source in understanding this man, I must attempt to "read" his visual records as thoughtfully as I have considered Babette's notebooks and Betty's route books. Although I have often examined visual "texts" with students, scouring advertisements for culturally constructed semiotic codes, this text is far more subtle and private. It presents a new sort of "reading" for me. I try hard to cleanse my mind of all preconceptions and to imagine that Fritz is about to take me on a journey with him.

Considered in this way, Fritz's home movies suddenly become far more revealing than I had realized. Up until this point, I have enjoyed these films as priceless behind-the-scenes documentaries of midcentury circus life, fascinating views of performers practicing without their makeup and teasing one another; now, however, I begin to notice the wonderful aesthetics of the films, their stark focus on spatial imagery, distance, and perspective. I notice that the vast majority of each clip is dedicated not to people but to the space surrounding them. With few exceptions, shots of acts are almost secondary to the slow-motion panoramas that follow as Fritz pans gently up the grandstands, taking in first the stages, then the riggings, then the rows of bleachers reaching so high that the audience becomes merely a mass of crawling dots, then beyond the top of the audience into the clouds. The camera seems constantly to be drawn up, then down, then back up to the farthest limits of its view.

There are numerous clips of scenery and landscapes, evidently shot from the windows of cars, boats, and planes. These are invariably vistas of depth and distance, taken from the peaks of ridges or the crests of mountains. Craters, waterfalls, vast expanses of land are captured in panoramic breadth before the camera telescopes and closes with a shot of the same measureless space disappearing behind a brilliantly detailed blossom or branch of foliage. One long sequence in Cuba captures Betty, Mike, "What's her name," and the children climbing a huge pyramid of ancient steps. They disappear into the sky, then are silhouetted momentarily against space as Fritz captures them looking out over a wall; finally the camera massages the full length of the landscape spread out below them, as if the happy family were the blossom that constitutes the most immediate point of Fritz's unlimited perspective.

In California, Cuba, Hawaii, Fritz has captured long moments of shorelines and coastlines, but the emphasis seems to be on the *passing* of these boundaries as the plane slowly wings over them, almost as though it were movement itself that intrigued the film-maker. I remember that Bobby loved to sit in the back of the car and watch the road slide away, then I think of Fritz moving across a cable from one stand to another and wonder whether the crossing might have had for him a significance far beyond that of mere physical challenge.

The films are, of course, silent; I cannot imagine any more suitable accompaniment than silence as the camera moves briefly over children rolling in snow as their mother dances with a shovel, then gently slides up the trunk of a fir tree, pausing at each snow-heavy bough, climbing peacefully from branch to branch until, at the very crest, it pans in on the frozen needles silhouetted against a gray sky. There is no doubt in my mind that while his family whooped and frolicked around him on this blizzardy day, Fritz was in a world of his own, momentarily high above them where the only sound was the ageless whistling of wind against ice. As the camera slides down the tree and across the yard, resting briefly on the house, the car, and the snow-covered trailer before gliding far beyond the confines of the yard and settling on the distant hills, I realize that the wire walker was moving effortlessly through space, able at last to look down and around, perhaps enjoying the ability to cross at will from the immediacy of his children's laughter to the soothing darkness of the wooded mountains beyond the frozen lake.

Suddenly I spring to my feet, grab the VCR control, and pause the tape. A few favorite lines from Robert Frost's "Stopping by Woods on a Snowy Evening" are ringing loudly in my head. Fritz Huber, I realize with a jolt, was a poet. No matter that his poetry was nonverbal; generations of teachers have pointed out the same juxtapositions, nature imagery, hints of realism and transcendentalism, themes of mutability and human significance in lyrics to which these movies might easily serve as a visual equivalent. Fritz's cinematic vision could have occasioned a superlative poem had he chosen the medium of words.

Fritz's movies seem to me to be informed by a mixture of artistic and philosophical fascination with boundaries and borders, heights and oppositional relationships. To define his "work" and "life force" as merely an athletic dedication to performing on a wire now seems utterly simplistic to me. I suspect that wire walking was a career choice determined by a far broader vision, a far more complex discernment. In fact, the dynamics of Fritz's movies are almost analytical, in the sense that analysis is the ability to draw way back from whatever one is seeing in order to view it within larger contexts. In spite of Fritzi's plea that an analytic mind is the tool of an intellectual bent on anatomizing beauty, I know that beauty is redefined continually within the framework of shifting perspectives that analysis provides. Fritz Huber apparently felt this, and I smile when I remember that I was initially attracted to Fritzi because she seemed to share this perception, as well.

I watch the earliest movies last. These are intensely physical records, filled with Easter egg hunts and snowball fights, wrestling and playing, neighbors cutting lawns or lying on blankets while laughing children pile on top of them. In these segments, Betty always appears to be completely immersed in the moment, chatting and dancing, absorbed in the social world around her while her husband's cinematic eye sweeps over faces and waving hands, then moves gently away across wide expanses of grassy lawn.

One of the last and longest segments documents Fritzi's baptism. Strangely, the camera moves only cursorily over the church, pausing for a moment on a statue of the Blessed Mother, then focuses with uncharacteristic determination on Fritzi herself as she is handed back and forth between her mother and her godparents. It is she who is the subject of this fragment, not the scenery or surrounding buildings. Intrigued, I watch closely as the movies run backward in time until a final segment shows baby Fritzi at perhaps only a few weeks of age, lying on her back in an outdoor bassinet. Sunlight flickers across her face, her tiny fists wave and her little mouth puckers in concentration. Long moments pass, but the camera never leaves her face while the moviemaker circles slowly around the tiny crib, filming his baby girl from every angle. I wait and wait, but the film remains riveted to its single subject. Smiling, I realize that I have finally discovered a plausible clue to what constituted Fritz's "life force." His usual drifting between the eternal and the immediate is arrested as he contemplates his infant. Fritz Huber simply could not take his eyes off of his baby daughter.

∾

"I want to talk about the circus today. Your act was so dangerous. What did you use for safety?"

Betty throws me the half-indignant, half-charitable look that she reserves for dumb questions. It has been several weeks since I have spoken with her and I have begun our morning with very pointed questions—not the most fertile invitation for Betty's storytelling disposition. For the past few weeks, I have been reading circus histories and trying to reconcile what I know of my subjects with their insistence that they are typical of a "culture" that outsiders do not understand. Betty instantly responds to my just-the-facts tone of voice, seems to realize that I have a job to do today. She leans forward and begins to speak slowly, as if she is teaching important rules to a neophyte.

"We never worked with a net, although Fritz built one in case the insurance company asked if we had it. Of course, I couldn't use a net with my sway pole. When you did a trick in my day," she emphasizes, "you did it without a net or a belt and you went for it. I could put you in a mechanic, Donna, and you'd go for the trick because you would know that there was no risk. When we performed a stunt, we had to know for sure that we could do it. In some of the big circuses today, you'll see performers using mechanics and helpers. That's the law. They have to be insured. It's not an embarrassment to wear a mechanic if you are training, but for a real performer, as soon as you are capable of doing the trick, the belt comes off."

Betty grows quiet for a moment, then smiles at me rather sheepishly. "I went for a trick when I was almost seventy years old. This is a silly story. Whenever Bobby came to Houston, I would beg him to cut away the bushes around my fence. That way my neighbors could kind of watch over me. I was mad at him because he had left without cutting those scraggly bushes back. I went out into my backyard and got the crazy idea that I just had to do a flip-flop. I messed up bad. I thought that I had broken my nose, I went for it so hard. I looked around to see if my neighbors were watching and, boy, was I glad that Bobby hadn't cut those bushes. People might have wondered what was wrong with me."

"There's nothing wrong with you, Betty," I assure her gently. "You just miss doing acrobatic."

"Well, my mind is real alert, but my body won't cooperate." She sighs. "After I retired from performing, I worked making costumes on the Shrine dates. I looked out of the costume truck one day and saw a kid practicing somersaults on a trampoline. I think it was one of the

Farfan boys. I hollered that he was tucking wrong, and he yelled, 'Show me.' Well, I was way too old, but he put me in a belt so I did a few turns. As I climbed off of the tramp, the boy asked me, 'You used to do acrobatic, didn't you?' Even a child could tell that I had the background! Out of the belt, I'm just not sure of myself anymore. It's hard because that desire never leaves you."

I lean over and give Betty a little hug. She reminds me at this moment of my own mother, who has also told me of how difficult it can be to watch your body grow old when there are so many adventures that you still want to have. Perhaps it is the thought of my own loving parent that triggers my next question. "What would have happened to your children if you had had an accident performing?" I ask candidly. I hope that the word "accident" will be disarming, but Betty knows exactly where my question is leading.

"When you're working, you don't consider danger. You know what you're doing," she replies quickly. "When you get in your car every morning, do you think that you might die in a traffic wreck? You have more control over your safety on a high wire than on the average city street."

I apparently look skeptical because Betty leans forward and begins to talk very seriously, very earnestly. "Listen to me. Most accidents in the circus happen because of negligence or too much confidence. That's the truth. When Fritz fell in Houston, he had walked up a slack cable during rehearsal and it snapped—pulled right out of the ground. That cable should have been guyed out but there wasn't much time, so we just wound it around one of the poles. At showtime, it took Fritz almost half an hour to climb twenty-five feet up to the platform on that cable. When the act was over, I gasped, 'Daddy, you're not going to go down the slack cable again? Just use the ladder,' but Fritz wouldn't compromise on the act. He made it halfway down; the cable rolled and he fell. It should have been guyed out properly. That's how accidents happen.

"The second time Fritz fell was during a police circus for crippled children. He landed right next to the ring, a few feet from the children—which was lucky; he might have landed on top of them! They carried him out immediately. I'll tell you, I flew down that ladder and when I'd reached the ten-foot level, I could see that the straw beside the ring was sopped with blood! I was pregnant with Bobby, but I leaped from the rigging and one of the prop boys caught me."

My subject shudders and swallows hard, remembering her terror. "The medical staff didn't want to let me into the first aid tent, of course, but I insisted on seeing my husband," she relates. "I rushed in crying 'Let me see the blood,' and there sat Fritz, propped up on pillows, calmly smoking a cigarette! He had broken his tailbone. No blood at all. Turned out that somebody had painted the rings red during setup and spilled a whole bucket of paint. Wouldn't you have thought that it was blood? It was a lovely shade of red, too."

Betty grins disarmingly and I realize that she is trying very hard to reassure me. "Why did Fritz fall that time?" I ask her.

"It was his own fault. He told me, 'Mommy, I should have checked the guy lines and I didn't wear my gloves.' It can happen to anyone. I was sort of glad, actually. Whenever I was pregnant, I felt that I was to blame for our not having work. Now no one could blame me. The union (AGVA) got us Blue Cross and Blue Shield and paid us for laying off. We waited six months until Fritz was completely healed."

Something in my face catches Betty's attention. She stops talking, looks at me closely. "What?"

How can I explain to her what I am thinking without causing resentment? I am deeply moved by Betty's passionate longing, her sadness at the inevitable disruption caused by age. I admire her hard-earned skill and unshakable professional pride, yet my stomach twists when Betty relates that she performed on the wire pregnant.

The possibility that my children might witness a fatal fall or a horrific mauling is with me whenever I take them into a circus tent, but my concern has never extended to the performers themselves. I have generally dismissed the circus performer as a variation of the movie stuntman, a sort of daredevil who has chosen to perfect a dangerous trick for pay; I have never wondered if he or she has a family, never speculated about why young parents might risk their lives daily.

"We were professionals doing what we loved to do," Betty tells me confidently. "We had to perform, just like you have to write because you are a writer." I don't point out that my children will never be left motherless because of a grammatical error.

Betty is observing me very attentively. "Performers are skilled artists, Donna. We know our work. People think that we are just doing stunts. They don't realize how many years we have practiced. We practice constantly. You need strength to begin with and talent, but then you work at it until you have built up muscles and calluses and perfected your sense of timing and balance. We don't just work for money, you know. Circus performers develop a sense of closeness because they understand one another. It's a way of life—a mentality."

Betty frowns slightly, searching for some more concrete assurance. Suddenly she pulls herself straight up and leans forward, her face deadly serious. "We have one crucial rule. Never touch anybody's rigging! That rule is absolutely sacred. You must take perfect care of rigging because your life depends on it. I had my sway pole X rayed every year to make sure that it didn't crystallize and get weak and snap. If someone tells you that there's a problem with your rigging, you'd better pay attention." She stares at me insistently. A moment later I am amazed to see a hesitant smile tickling her wrinkled face. "I just remembered something funny," she admits with a grin. "Thinking about my sway pole reminded me.

"Back in the fifties, a French sway pole act showed up on the route, but his pole was too high to use in the auditoriums. The prop boys couldn't guy it out far enough. They told him, 'If you do your handstand, you're going to touch the ceiling—don't do it!' The guy went for the trick anyway and, sure enough, he hit the ceiling; the pole cracked and down he came. He wasn't killed though. As the medics carried him past us on a stretcher, he told Fritz and me, 'You know, I have deed dis once before.' Geesh! He should have listened to the riggers. It was his own fault." Betty shakes her head and chuckles.

I know that Betty is not merely trying to dismiss my concerns. Her reassurances are grounded in fact; I have come across similar anecdotes and explanations of risk taking in a number of circus history books. Culhane notes that the notorious daredevil Blondin was less afraid of a "calculated risk" than of a "spontaneous gamble." "Blondin crossed Niagara Falls . . . blindfolded, wearing a sack on his head, trundling a wheelbarrow, on stilts, and sitting down midway to make and eat an omelette," he writes, yet "the walk across Niagara Falls probably didn't seem as dangerous as his voyage from Europe to

America, when he had leaped overboard to rescue a drowning man."[1]
Similarly, Betty is trying to tell me that she and Fritz felt safe because
they were in a controlled environment and knew what to expect, yet
I still get chills when she talks about her love affair with heights.

"Weren't you ever frightened?" I ask. "What about unanticipated
problems like wind and rain? Did the show always have to go on?"

Betty leans back and smiles. "Do you know why performers say
that? You don't get paid if you don't work, so of course the show
goes on. After all, no one else is hurt. If you fall, everyone else carries
on, but they will come and ask about you after the show." She
pauses, remembering. "I've seen quite a few accidents. It's more
common than people think, but there's generally more neglect
involved than people realize, too. We were at the Police Circus in
St. Louis when The Great Peters died. Remember him?" I shake
my head apologetically, and Betty laughs. "I forget how young I am,"
she jokes. "Peters was billed as the man who hangs himself and lives
to tell. There was a trick to it. He held his hand inside the loop to
keep his neck from breaking. The apparatus was made of rubber, so
he wasn't really hanged. Well, during the war, he bought synthetic
rubber. The sandbag came down and the fake rubber had no stretch.
It broke his neck."

I watch Betty's face transform into a mask of concern and
disbelief as she relives that moment. I can tell that she is momentarily
back under the huge circus tent, sickened by the instant hush that
has swept over hundreds of shocked spectators. I can imagine frightened children beginning to whimper, horrified parents straining to
see the motionless body surrounded by performers.

"My father and another man tried to lift him down very carefully,"
Betty relates quietly. "Peters could talk. He said, 'Harry, I think my
neck is broken.' Everyone was watching. The firemen rushed up and
insisted, 'We'll handle this,' but they didn't understand how the trick
was done. Peters slipped right out of their hands and was killed. My
father told me, 'If they had let us take him down right, he might have
lived.'"

I am undoubtedly staring at Betty in horror because she squeezes
my hand and shakes her head in mock impatience. "You don't get it.
Peters didn't test his new rope. He just assumed that it was the same.
He should have tested it. The danger was in his oversight, not in the

trick. It was a similar situation in St. Louis when Henri Kimris's brother died. Remember the aerial act that you liked so much in the movie? The one with the little plane that spins around and the trapeze hanging beneath it? That whole apparatus has to be hauled up on a pulley. You finish pulling the rigging up and get your pulley blocked, then you make a chain stitch with the slack and lay it next to the pulley block so that it doesn't just lie around on the ground where people can trip over it. Someone pulled on the wrong chain. When you pull the end of a chain stitch, it unravels, right? The girders fell about fifty feet. He was killed instantly."

Betty remembers that she and Fritz were setting up their rigging before the show when they heard something crash behind them. They thought that a sandbag had fallen. Fritz was the first to realize that they had lost a friend. He grabbed his wife in his arms, warning "Don't look, Mommy. Don't look." Betty winces when she remembers that horrible afternoon but is quick to assure me that the death was an accident and that her story has a redeeming moral. "Here's the thing," she insists, "This happened in the afternoon and we had our first show that evening. When it came time for the Kimris Duo to perform, Henri and Lee just stood there. Lee said, 'I can't do it.' I asked her quickly, 'Lee, did you ever see a woman without teeth?' and flipped out my dentures. She gasped, 'Betty Huber!' and started to laugh in spite of herself. Their music went on and I pushed her—'Get going! You're on!' She was nervous but she did well. She told me afterward, 'I'd have never gone on without your help. Henri wouldn't have made me.' I didn't give her time to think, that's all. You do what you have to do."

My head is beginning to ache, but Betty is caught up in her subject and I do not want to leave this topic hanging. "Even animals aren't as unpredictable as you might think. People know their animals as well as you know your children; you just have to be careful because they can hurt you. Proske playfully smacked a lion once, then turned around and the lion swatted him back across the behind. Quite a love tap!"

Betty chuckles, then sits for a moment, absorbed in her own thoughts. "Some jobs we couldn't work because it was raining and the wire was wet," she admits, returning to my initial question concerning the unexpected. "You have to have traction. We did cancel the act under those circumstances. Once an owner complained that another high wire act would perform in the rain but we wouldn't. I told him,

'If you can give me back the same man if this one falls, then I'll perform.' We were risking our lives up there without a net! I didn't need to hear about other acts."

The room is silent. "So you were aware that you were risking your lives?" I offer softly. "It wasn't really the same as driving a car, was it?"

Betty leans away from me ever so slightly. I realize that my subject has no relish for this line of questioning. Her posture, her facial expression, her tone of voice all tell me that she is growing impatient, mistrustful of my opinion. I understand that she does not want this single aspect of her profession to be sensationalized, although circuses have traditionally exploited a rhetoric of superlatives to advertise their acts; the billing for many a performer has announced "death-defying feats never before attempted." I am growing annoyed, as well, although I cannot yet identify the source of my vexation. I am probably not the ideal recipient for these stories, I know.

I am far from considering Betty a daredevil, but I can tell that she is not comfortable with the rhetorical balancing act in which she has suddenly found herself. Betty wants me to accept that her performance was a serious career, no more dangerous than other professions that require skill, concentration, and expert training, yet her stories are suggesting rather the opposite. She knows that in spite of all their precautions and training, circus performers live with ever-present, sometimes unpredictable danger.

Danger and deliberate risk are topics that seem to evoke mixed feelings in even the most hardy of circus researchers. In his *The American Circus*, Culhane asserts that "circus excellence is human excellence, based on practice and perseverance, mastery and self-reliance. . . . Dangerous circus tricks are usually calculated risks in which the odds favor the skillful athlete who keeps his head"[2]; yet his study cites numerous deaths and quotes many performers who refer to circus performance as a compulsive or pride-inspired "gamble" rather than as a calculated risk.

Even as avid a circus fan as Culhane allows his enthusiasm to waver when he discusses the legendary wire walker Karl Wallenda, to whom he refers as a typical daredevil, "pursuing a compulsion." Wallenda was seventy-three years old when he was blown off of a cable in Puerto Rico and plummeted one hundred feet to his death. Friends had warned him that he would die on the wire, that far younger members of his family had already fallen to their deaths, that age takes a toll on reflexes and strength, but Wallenda insisted that nothing could keep him from wire walking. "A typical conversation with a great daredevil," Culhane notes in a not-quite-enthusiastic passage. "It is hard to get such people to think the unthinkable; to imagine what might happen if they had a bad day. They seem to focus their minds on thought of discipline and technique and to leave the rest to God."[3]

"You can't do it forever, but it's very hard to leave," Betty muses when I ask her about retirement. "In Poland and Russia, they have retirement homes for performers. I think that's a good idea. When the acts from Poland came over to work for Ringling, they made only a few dollars a day; all the rest went back to their government, but at least they knew that they would be taken care of for life. They couldn't go out with us back then. Their countries always sent somebody to make sure that they didn't disinfect like all the ballet dancers."

"Defect." I laugh.

Betty snickers. "Oh, that's right, defect," she agrees. She shakes her head in amusement, then grows serious again. "There are very few circus celebrities. We aren't treated like Olympic athletes or rock stars. You can work all your life in the circus, but when you're through, nobody recognizes you. No one stops you on the street and says, 'Oh, I loved your act!' You're forgotten—except by friends. I have one friend who has known me since I was a girl. Whenever I run into him, he begs, 'Betty, make your hair red again. I loved your red hair.'"

Betty looks at me almost shyly, and we share a tender smile. I whisper, "That's beautiful."

"Well, he can love me with white hair," she answers, suddenly thoughtful. "I had enough makeup on my face when I worked. Let me be natural now. I want people to see me like I am."

I give Betty a hug and rise to leave. She chatters as I pack up my recorder and the usual sack of cookies for the kids, but I am too preoccupied to listen closely to her. I am wrestling with a bold resolution. When Betty hugs me again at the door, I decide to put my mind at rest. "Mom, I have something that I must ask you," I begin uncomfortably. "Fritzi has told me that your husband could have been cured of cancer by having his leg amputated but risked his life with radiation instead because he wanted to keep performing." I pause, breathless, then peer at her face cautiously. "I have to ask you if that is true. It just doesn't make sense to me."

Betty draws a deep breath. "We were going to stop performing soon anyway," she assures me.

"Fritzi told me that her father never really intended to leave the business, that at the time he died he was working on that reticulated horse in her studio so that he could take out a whole new act. She says that you wanted to get off the road but that Fritz's act was his life."

Betty grins. "Sure, we were putting together a new act, but it was for nightclubs and summer tours so that we could get off the road during the year. Listen, Fritzi was a little girl back then. There was a lot that she didn't know." Her face crumples suddenly into a look of tenderness and sadness. "Fritzi has her own beliefs, but the truth is, there were never any guarantees. There was a girl in the hospital with Fritz who had her leg amputated. Her mother told us, 'Well, at least the cancer is gone now.' Three weeks later that child was back in the hospital with cancer in her lymph glands. We were told that we could try amputation or radiation, but there were no guarantees either way. Daddy said, 'Let's try radiation, Mommy. At least I can keep working that way.' It was the more practical choice. We needed the money."

Betty gives me one more hug and then holds me at arm's length. "You are a mother, and you know that any parent would give up his life for his children," she declares, her voice certain and strong and sad. "My husband loved us all very much. He would gladly have given his arms and legs to stay with his children. He didn't have any choice."

"I know. Thank you," I whisper as tears fill my eyes to match her own. "In my heart I knew, but I had to hear you say it."

∾

After-work traffic is just beginning to jam the secondary roads out of Wilmington as I pilot my old van across Betty's corner lot and pull into the main stream headed for the city limits. The boys are bickering in the backseat, disgusted by the "uncool" denim jackets that I have forced them to wear over their T-shirts. Betty nestles comfortably into the captain's chair beside me, happily munching on the nut-free chocolate bar that I picked up for her on the way over, her down-filled winter parka buttoned to her chin. Too many nights on a midway have taught her how quickly a fine, early-autumn afternoon can turn into a frigid evening. "Knock it off, you two," I order my wrestling teens as traffic grows heavier.

"Turn up the volume! We can't hear you!" Betty yells over her shoulder, winking at me. Sudden silence follows, and we grin at each other.

The New Hanover County Fair is held annually on a large sandy pasture bordering Carolina Beach Road, halfway between the port city of Wilmington and the ocean's edge. It is Thursday, opening night, and we intend to be among the first to enter the fairgrounds. A cloud of dust follows each car that veers off the newly widened highway onto the darkening field. Attendants in pumpkin-orange aprons wave us along roped lanes and into a tight row of neatly parked vehicles. "Take your jackets!" I insist as the kids tumble out, slamming their door and then reaching hands up to help Grandma Betty. Somehow the fair seems bigger this year, the lights more dazzling than gaudy, perhaps because at the far end of the lot, beyond the 4-H exhibits, midway rides, and carnival concession stands, I can see the giant canvas dome of a circus tent—this year's free attraction for fairgoers.

I have always liked fairs—their overwhelming sensory impact. I enjoy the gobbling, honking squalor of livestock, the cacophony of mechanical carnival music, the choruses of screams from the whirling, plunging, flashing rides. It is a temporary environment so immediate and stimulating that one simply cannot think, a welcome reprieve after a full day of mental deskwork. My little band roams blissfully until showtime. Betty ignores signs urging viewers to keep their hands out of cages and pets every animal in the livestock tent that will permit her to touch it. We examine melon-size yams and gardenias with blue ribbons clipped to their vases. I laugh as the kids whoop and wave at me from a spinning contraption with hundreds of blinking lights. Betty wisely steers them away from barkers, cautions them not to waste their money on rigged games or gambles. As the night grows colder, I buy hot chocolates and coffees and find myself waiting with motherly patience outside the painted exit of a shrieking funhouse with four half-full cups carefully balanced in my arms. Through the eye-shape openings in the flamboyant facade, I catch glimpses of my kids scrambling wildly across a knee-jerking mechanical sidewalk as Betty runs hooting after them.

~

The canvas flaps of the circus tent have been pinned back to allow crowds to enter for the 6:30 P.M. performance of the Liebel Family Circus. At 6:15 Betty sticks her head through the opening, looks over the sawdusty single ring, pulls back, and motions me to follow her as she tramps around the outside of the tent, ducking under lines, and stepping over stakes. A young woman with a crate of popcorn boxes strapped about her neck meets us hastily as we near the animal pens, annoyance and professional courtesy competing in her tight smile. "Can I help you?" she asks, but before we can answer, a large man in checkered pants is at her side, dark eyes flashing under painted red curls and clown makeup.

Betty's white hair is generally disarming, and as they size her up in the near darkness, both performers visibly relax. "I used to be in the circus. I want to see if there is anyone here I know," she explains gently, and the ringmaster's face suddenly opens wide.

"Who were you?" he asks, genuinely interested. I can tell that he has never heard of the Kays—after all, they stopped performing almost forty years ago—but he is obviously pleased that Betty has come back to meet him.

"Liebel—that's German?" Betty asks. It turns out that the family are Hungarian, but Mr. Liebel and Betty launch into a lively conversation in German.

Suddenly the talk stops and Mr. Liebel turns to me. "Is this your daughter?" the big man asks politely. I hold up my head, expecting Betty to introduce me, but she does not answer. Almost imperceptibly I feel her pull her arm away from mine. I search her face and see a tiny flicker of pain deep in her eyes. Fritzi is returning tomorrow from a two-week visit to California, and I know that Betty resents having been left behind. Throughout the evening, we have been running into her friends from the senior center and the movie studios; invariably they have assumed that I am Betty's daughter and she has had to correct this assumption repeatedly.

Betty falters for a moment when she is asked the dreaded question once more but collects herself immediately. "This is a lady who is writing a book about the circus," she announces rather formally, not mentioning my name.

"Does she speak German?" Liebel asks quickly, referring to me in the third person.

"No," Betty says firmly. He turns from me rather coolly and resumes his animated conversation with Betty—in deliberate German.

Betty's party is treated like honored guests for the rest of the evening. The circus owner proudly carries four comfortable chairs into the tent and positions them at ringside. "Do you recognize this?" He laughs at Betty, holding up a small white chair built rather like a crate with laddered sides and back.

Betty grins and turns the prop over to reveal two little nicks in the bottom wooden bars connecting the legs. "For balancing on the wire," she explains to me.

It seems as if the tent fills almost magically. Children are wiggling on packed bleachers, parents are wedging strollers behind the stands and lifting toddlers onto their shoulders. The young woman from backstage passes between rows selling popcorn and graciously drops a free box in my lap. Suddenly I feel a sharp pinch on my finger and gasp. Betty turns to me curiously. "What's the matter with you?"

I pull my wedding ring off of my finger and examine it under the bright ringside lights. The band has split neatly in two where the soft gold has worn thin from twenty years of rubbing. "Good thing the diamond didn't fall out," I murmur, then realize that Betty is being very quiet. Looking up, I see that her eyes are frozen on the ring, her face white.

"You don't think that this means something?" I whisper, frightened in spite of myself.

"No! Oh, no," Betty assures me hastily, but her alarmed eyes tell me that she considers my broken ring an ill-fated omen. My husband is working out of town; suddenly, I wish with all my heart that he were home.

As the music begins, I glance quickly around the tent, trying to distract myself from the uneasy feeling that Betty's reaction to my ring has caused. The performers' entrance is directly across from me.

Piled neatly beside the open flap are painted barrels, a unicycle, various props, a set of drums; nestled into the farthest corner is a baby's playpen in which a toddler bounces happily. The Liebel Family Circus is very much a "family" affair, it seems. Mr. Liebel enters noisily as a "one-man band," honking and pounding and clanging as he clowns around the ring. Over the course of the evening, he will play many parts, from clown to master of ceremonies. There are only four performers, so everyone juggles acts. The pretty popcorn seller appears dressed like a gypsy in a blazing red skirt and smart black jacket, sequins flashing as her pony canters around the ring. A trapeze artist performs with a mechanic; Betty humphs her disapproval but applauds generously anyway.

The performer who captures my attention, however, is Tony Liebel, the wire walker, a handsome young man with dark hair hanging down his back in a long ponytail. He is probably not much older than my eldest son, Carl, who sits beside me munching his popcorn, probably wishing that he could jump into the ring himself, and I wonder if this teenager also has a messy room and resents having to baby-sit on weekends. Tony proves himself to be a most agile and talented performer. He appears in the ring over and over again, as a tumbler, an acrobat, a unicyclist, an elephant trainer, and, finally, on the wire. As an acrobat, he impresses even Betty. His performance on the cable is, of course, nothing like the star-quality act that Fritz performs in the movies, but it is more compelling to me, precisely because the boy is close enough that I can watch the minute signs of hesitancy and determination in his footing. Each time that Tony falters slightly, Betty leans over and whispers triumphantly, "He did that on purpose to make the crowd think the trick is harder than it is." I don't contradict her, but the mother in me recognizes in this boy's posture the same furious concentration that I have noticed in my Carl as he is learning to drive.

As the circus unfolds, I find myself staring hard at the rigging, finally understanding the mechanical arrangements that Betty has tried unsuccessfully to demonstrate with pencils and rubber bands. This alone has made the trip worthwhile for me, but I am also fascinated as I watch Betty in her supportive role of spectator. Throughout the show, she is always the first to applaud each individual trick, goading the audience to follow her example, almost as if she were a performer placed in the audience to enliven them. She is probably the only person present who has any sense of the difficulty and risk involved in what we are seeing. I am struck by how ignorant the audience is of circus etiquette—and even of practical safety. I watch in amazement as parents encourage their children to toss peanuts at the elephant while she performs her stunts; an elephant is, of course, an unusual creature, but surely no parent would dream of allowing a child to throw fish into the tank at SeaWorld while the whale is performing.

Betty springs to her feet when Mr. Liebel takes a final bow, applauding appreciatively. The tent empties rapidly as the audience realizes that night has fallen and the riotous midway is now illuminated with flashing colors. I hand my kids enough money to ride a few of the tilting, twirling rides and sit down quietly in the semidarkness to wait with Betty for Mr. Liebel. After a long ten minutes, I rise and stroll around the ring, enjoying the delicious opportunity to make a visual examination of the rigging. Betty is beginning to look worried that she has been forgotten when Tony returns and sees us still there. He walks straight to Betty, graciously holding out his hand as if he were introducing himself to circus royalty. Unlike his surly father, the teenager also includes me in his well-mannered introduction and I am grateful for the courtesy.

We are led back to a table in the performers' entrance where Tony writes down Betty's phone number and enthusiastically invites her to share some of her circus photographs and stories with his family. Obviously pleased, Betty agrees. Standing behind her in the shadows, I feel my heart leap at the thought of hearing Betty and her new friends compare past circus experiences with current ones. "I would like to come with you," I offer, thinking that Betty may be grateful for a ride.

I am completely unprepared for the violence of her reaction. Betty spins around and glares at me with undisguised anger. "No you won't!" she practically yells. "My *daughter* will come with me. Not you!"

Shock and silence follow her outburst; I can barely breathe, but Betty seems unconcerned that she has hurt me cruelly. I know that she would rather have come to the circus with Fritzi, that she is feeling abandoned; I have tried to call or visit her daily over the last two weeks to help her through this difficult period. I accompanied her to a doctor's appointment and treated her to breakfast afterward, have driven her to stores and invited her to lunch, called or dropped by every other day at least. Never have I tried so hard to be daughterly to a woman not my mother. My stomach suddenly aches and I struggle with a childish desire to cry.

As Betty walks away, apparently expecting me to follow her, Tony turns to me. "I would like to talk to you about wire walking," I explain, making a hard effort to collect myself, and he hastily writes down his home address and telephone number inside the cover of a circus coloring book.

"So come back by yourself," he invites, smiling kindly. "You don't have to come with her." It occurs to me that the sort of outburst to which I have just been subjected may be an experience that he understands. I thank Tony with genuine relief, but I wonder if I will have the courage to return alone.

∼

Visiting the rear lot of a fairground at midday feels like strolling backstage uninvited between theater performances. On a sticky, sweltering Saturday, I force myself to drive back to the fairgrounds feeling almost ill with apprehension. I have waited until early afternoon, certain that no one who works a late show appreciates being visited in the morning. I tell myself that a truly professional writer does not balk at an opportunity to interview a subject; in fact, a "serious" writer should probably be opportunistic, but as I drive slowly across the huge empty field, circling to the farthest corner where an opening in the fence has been made for trailers, I feel less like a serious researcher than an intrusive reporter.

Tucking my note pad hastily into my purse, aware that even having a purse over my shoulder is a signal that I am an outsider, I walk uneasily through the makeshift encampment. In the blinding sunlight, the silent rides look like the fossilized remains of giants, their white ribs stretching awkwardly toward the ground. Heat-weary animals stomp impatiently in a wire enclosure while shirtless men toss hay from a pickup truck. Trailer doors stand wide open; occasionally a beard-stubbled face appears in a doorway and watches me closely. In spite of Tony's invitation, I feel out of place and extremely uncomfortable.

I pass a young couple who are kissing on the hood of a car while they share something out of a cup; they raise their heads to stare as I walk past. No one else seems to be outdoors in the pitiless sun, and I know that I will not be able to bring myself to knock on trailer doors. A sweat-streaked carnival worker emerges from behind a canvas partition and looks me up and down without expression. I begin to wish that I had worn a dress to make myself seem like a reporter. My husband warned me that in my jeans and T-shirt, an outfit that I thought would be inconspicuous, I might be mistaken for a "lot lizard," a term that I have never encountered before. Now I remember his warning, which I had thought to be a joke, and feel even more self-conscious.

The circus tent stands at the farthest end of the encampment, and I tell myself that the Liebels' trailers will certainly be nearby. I assume that they would want to stay as close as possible to their animals, especially the elephant—a more delicate creature than most people realize. Stepping hopefully around the corner of the tent, I duck under the raised flap and see with one glance that the place is empty. In the brightness of daylight, I can make out golden cracks in the canvas. A child's slide is set up in the middle of the ring, a sawdusty playground for a trailer-restless toddler. Around the back of the tent, I notice someone working in the horse pen and think that I recognize the trapeze artist. I back quickly into the shadows, wondering whether I should approach him for help and risk being sent away before I can find Tony.

I have almost made up my mind to knock on the door of a trailer nestled hard against the animal pens when I spot a familiar figure. About ten yards away a tall, slim boy kneels on the ground, carefully examining some sort of console in his trailer's side paneling. Hesitantly I approach, uncertain of whether I have discovered my subject. He twists slightly, and with unspeakable relief, I spot a dark ponytail. "Tony?" I call. He turns, peering quizzically into the sunlight. "I hope you don't mind my coming back. Do you have a few minutes?"

As soon as he recognizes me, my subject greets me politely, although I think that he seems just a bit uneasy. He opens the door of his trailer, urging, "Please, come in."

I have barely taken a step when the door to the trailer beside the pens bangs open and Tom Liebel, Tony's father, flies down the steps.

"Where is Betty?" the big man hollers loudly in his heavy German accent, apparently incensed that I have dared to return without her.

"Betty will be coming with her daughter later on," I answer as respectfully as possible, recognizing deep mistrust in his voice.

"What are you doing here then?" he shouts, his face growing red. "You're interested in my son, is that it? You want to be with my son?"

For an instant, I wonder if Liebel realizes that I am more than twice the age of his eighteen-year-old son and feel vaguely complimented that he has seemingly miscalculated my age. His words were obviously meant to be demeaning, however, and I wonder how Tony will react. I am deeply gratified when he disregards his father's rudeness and ushers me graciously into his trailer, hastily shutting the door behind us. Once inside, though, his composure vanishes and his face colors with embarrassment; he invites me to sit down at the kitchen table, then, to my amusement, scrambles about, grabbing up clothes from the floor and tossing them through a doorway at the far end of the kitchen area, all the while apologizing breathlessly.

"Don't worry. I have three kids and you should see their rooms," I hasten to assure him.

Tony stops in his tracks, genuinely interested. "How old are they? Where are they now?" he asks eagerly. I tell him a bit about my children, their ages and names. "Who is watching your daughter? What does your husband do?" Amused, I realize that he can no more imagine my daily life than I can his, and that he is just as curious as I am.

"I can't offer you anything," my young host worries, holding open the door of his empty refrigerator to prove to me that he is telling the truth. Again, I am struck by the teenager's command of good manners and the universal rules of hospitality. I begin to explain that I am an English teacher writing a book about my friendship with Betty and her stories of life in the circus. "English! Ack! I am a terrible speller," Tony admits sadly, a grimace of real concern creasing his face. I explain impulsively that the English language is a patchwork quilt of numerous other languages and that for this reason there is no consistent logic to the way in which its words are spelled.

Tony listens intently. "Whew!" he smiles, when I have finished the brief lesson. "So it's not me then? That's great! I'm good at math though. I went to regular school for a while but I didn't enjoy it."

Tony tells me that many of the other kids in the public school that he attended seemed irresponsible, mean-spirited, and unhappy, and that he was content to return to home schooling.

"Didn't you ever miss being with other children your age?" I ask.

"In the circus, you're with kids all the time!" He grins, obviously tickled by my comment. "My new mother has her teaching certificate. She tutors me now." I recall the pretty girl in the gypsy costume whom I had assumed to be his sister. Tony catches me thinking and smiles infectiously. "I've been telling Dad for years that I want a brother." He laughs.

"Betty has told me a great deal about circus life, but I have only her views. For all I know, circus is very different for you now than it was forty years ago for her," I explain, eager to begin the interview in case Tony's father should decide to interfere. Tony nods seriously. "How long have you been performing?" I inquire, drawing my pad out of my bag.

Tony sits up straight in his chair, ready to work with me. "I started training on horses between the age of two and three."

"Do you have lots of baby pictures of yourself standing up in people's hands?" I tease. "Betty has dozens of those."

"Every circus kid does. It's how we come into the world—working." He chuckles, then grows more serious. "That's probably what made me different from the kids at school. Circus kids grow up fast. We don't differentiate between work and play. When I'm on the drums or on the wire—well, that's work but I'm also enjoying myself. I never need to do drugs because I get a high from practicing."

I sigh inwardly, relieved to hear this boy speaking of a practical joy in his chosen field rather than of a "gift" that constitutes his "life force."

"Did your father teach you to walk the wire?" I ask.

Tony explains that his father worked out a deal with a hired act that included wire-walking lessons for his son. "My father knows the circus. He gives me excellent advice. He taught me not to drink because when you drink, you get brave. You want to feel confident on the wire but never brave."

As I listen to my young host speak, I realize that the opportunity to interrogate an actual wire walker has been well worth every bit of discomfort that I endured to get here. Betty was wheeled and carted across the wire many times but is rather defensive about the fact that she never learned to walk herself. I have gathered from her comments that Fritz tried to teach her but that the lessons did not go well.

"How hard is it to walk the wire, Tony?" I ask, hoping for some solid information.

Tony gets up and carefully walks an imaginary wire on the floor, demonstrating how to place one's feet, how to twist the body before landing after a jump, how to run without pitching the body forward to create unwanted momentum. He shows me how easily an improper posture or lack of focus can result in broken ribs or paralysis, tells me of other performers' accidents and reenacts what caused them. He is intensely serious while he gives this lesson, and it occurs to me that if I were to ask him to put me in a mechanic and let me try to walk myself, he would probably do it. I do not even want to imagine what his father's response to that plan would be.

"You start out low," Tony explains, "and then you work up to a higher wire. Lying down is pretty easy, and climbing up the slack wire is easier than going straight. The hardest thing of all to do is to climb down. You're right over the audience and there's nowhere to throw your weight but forward down or backward up. Sometimes I'm tempted to play with the audience when I'm coming down, but if you break your concentration and lose it, you're going to land right on top of them.

"Working with a pole is both harder and easier. It helps to have the weight, but if you fall, you have to throw the pole before you can catch the wire. I find that I can compensate more easily for a light pole. A heavier pole can pull you over and it's harder to lose if you fall."

Tony sees my confusion and pauses. "If you fall, you must catch the wire either with both hands or with a hand and a foot. If you can only catch with one hand, then you're going down for sure."

"Betty told me that all circus accidents are caused either by negligence or lack of concentration," I offer.

"It's true!" Tony exclaims. "I've fallen twice, each time because I was thinking ahead instead of concentrating on what I was doing at that moment. I practice at one hundred percent but only perform at eighty percent—that's the safest way. You have to be a balanced person to walk the wire. You must know how to control your feelings and focus completely—one foot at a time. It takes patience to become good; sometimes I want to jump ahead of myself."

Tony waits while I hastily scribble notes in shorthand. He shakes his head in dismay and sighs. "I could never write a book. I don't have that kind of patience."

I stop writing and smile at his wistful tone. "Of course you do," I tell him. "You have just told me how much patience is required to learn wire walking. A book is really no different. You start out low (I point to my notes), then write over and over until you feel comfortable with what you have written. Then you let others see what you have done. The final product is never as good as you want it to be, no matter how hard you work."

Tony considers my analogy and then nods his agreement.

"Working with live subjects is hard for me because they are unpredictable and uncontrollable," I confess. "It's hard to stay balanced when your subjects aren't. The name of my book should probably be *Walking the Wire*." I laugh. "I figure that's a good metaphor for just about everything in life, but especially for writing this book."

"Life is a wire-walking act," Tony agrees. "You have to choose something that you really want and stay focused on it." His eyes grow earnest suddenly, and he leans forward slightly, as if to impress upon me the importance of what he is about to impart. "See, I know that our circus is just a mud show, but it's serious. Some of the biggest names can end up doing mud shows. It's not about the size of the show; it's about loving what you do and taking it seriously. People will forgive a fall but not a bad attitude."

"What constitutes a bad attitude?" I ask innocently.

"You should never get cocky. Some performers just get so full of themselves, but my father taught me, 'Never think that you are the best because you never are.'"

"That's true in every field." I laugh. "Do you know how many professors strut around expecting the world to adore them because they know all about some obscure little thing that nobody else cares about?"

Tony laughs out loud at my irreverence. "That's like my drums," he muses. "I love rock, but if you play with a group you can't try to be the star, you have to be part of the band. Circus is the same. The show is a group effort so it should always be greater than any individual's act. Günter Gebel Williams shoveled up elephant dung when it needed to be done. A true performer isn't above anything. That's why when performers visit another show, they always expect to be treated with respect. There are three important rules for people in the circus: Never brag, never criticize, and *never* mess with other people's props. Those are the crucial rules. My father will tell you the same thing."

I look over the table at this articulate, solemn teenager and think what a pleasure he would be to teach in a college classroom—or to have as a professional colleague, for that matter. However much I resent Tom Liebel's attitude toward me, I must give him credit for having raised a very mature son. Almost as if he has been summoned by my thoughts, Tom Liebel slams into the trailer at this very moment and towers over the table where I am sitting, his annoyance at my presence raw and unconcealed.

"Are you related to her?" he demands roughly. Mr. Liebel evidently feels compelled to be protective of Betty as well as of his son, and my frustration is momentarily diluted with wisely concealed amusement. Given my present circumstance, the idea of Betty needing his protection from me seems almost ludicrous.

"No, but my children call her Grandma," I tell him truthfully. "She seems like a part of our family."

Liebel grunts, unconvinced. "What is your family?" he interrogates. I explain that my husband and I have German backgrounds but no circus roots, then show Liebel photocopies of some of Betty's pictures, hoping to convince him that I am here to work on a serious project. He flips through the pictures with obvious interest but dismisses brusquely my attempts at explanation.

Even though the circus patriarch is determined to be unfriendly and his interruption of a valuable interview is a genuine annoyance, I find myself beginning to like him. I realize that Tom Liebel does not understand my motives in the least, that I must represent something very threatening to him. He probably cannot comprehend that Betty would allow someone without a circus background to chronicle her life, and her introduction of me certainly was ungenerous enough to prompt his suspicion. Tony has told me that his father's past includes travel with circuses in Russia and Hungary; how I would love to listen to this man tell of his own history, but gaining his trust would take far more time than gaining Betty's has. If I were a performer, however, this is a man whose advice I would take seriously.

Tony's father throws the pictures down on the table and glares at his son. "You have work to do! You can socialize after the show!" he shouts, his long experience in a demanding physical profession leaving no room for the idea that talking can be part of someone's work.

More concerned for Tony than for myself, I say, "I will be leaving in just a moment," but Liebel refuses even to acknowledge my presence now. He stomps out of the trailer and slams the door behind him.

"Have I gotten you in trouble?" I ask, but Tony shakes his head quickly.

"We can talk for a few more minutes. It will be all right." The trailer feels ovenish and I look longingly at the closed door. I can tell that my shirt is sticking to my back and worry that in a few minutes the front of it will be wet with sweat, as well. Tony gets up and opens the windows but leaves the door purposefully closed. Fascinated, I realize that I am witnessing a very symbolic contest between father and son, a mapping out of the boundaries of each man's authority in terms of private space. Tom furiously pounds on the door once more before walking away, but it is obvious that ordering me from his son's trailer would constitute a breach of respect for Tony. He is making it very clear that he wants Tony to make me leave.

I take a deep breath and tell Tony honestly, "I do not know what to make of this. Betty and Fritzi keep telling me that the circus is a special 'culture' and that performers never trust or talk to outsiders. It is kind of insulting but maybe it is also true."

Tony shakes his head and regards me knowingly. "Maybe it was true for them—for their generation [he nods toward the door, indicating that he is speaking of his father], but for the younger set, it's different. We don't differentiate; sometimes it's just hard to meet people when you move around so much."

"People feel the same way about circus performers," I suggest. "We find what you do intriguing but do not understand it because we never get to meet you."

"I think sometimes people almost hope to see me fall," Tony confesses softly, looking as if he needs me to respond to this accusation on behalf of the audience. His uncertain expression is touching.

"Believe me, parents do not want their kids to see you get hurt," I assure him firmly. "You have to remember that when you are on the wire, you are not an individual with feelings to the audience; you are simply a representative human being who is somewhere that he probably should not be." Tony looks rather shocked, and I hasten to explain. "Think of what you look like up there from the viewer's perspective. The tent is dark. There is a spotlight on a figure way up high. You are a silhouette against the light. The audience cannot see your face or eyes. All they can see is the wire and that figure trying to cross it."

"Ahhh, that's true," Tony exclaims, his face brightening as he listens.

"Besides," I continue, "it is hard for the audience to believe that the acts are not rigged and that the danger is real. After all, the circus is publicized as a children's show and accidents are generally downplayed."

"Not by us!" Tony interrupts, his eyes glowing with earnest indignation. "It really gets me! A circus performer can die and nothing will be said about it, but if some football player hurts his knee, that's a big deal."

I smile and add, "No one seems to care that the Mir is running out of oxygen, either. How much have you worried about that today?"

"Okay." Tony laughs good-naturedly. "I see your point."

"Do you want to raise your children in the circus?" I ask pointedly.

Tony does not hesitate even a second. "Absolutely," he replies enthusiastically. "Circus life lets you keep your children near you while you work; you get close that way. Look at how most people live. They drop their children off in centers while they work all day, and they never even see them." He stops suddenly, embarrassed, and asks, "Where is your little girl?"

"In one of those day care centers, and she absolutely loves it there. If I pick her up early and she is having a wonderful time, she will tell me to come back later." I laugh, tickled by Tony's preconceptions. "My life is not as bad as you think it is," I explain, "just as circus is not the glamorous lifestyle that most people think." Slightly embarrassed, I confess, "I used to want to be in the circus when I was a kid, though. My brother and I used to practice walking fences and doing tricks on our swing set bars."

"Did you do acrobatic when you were a kid?" Tony asks quickly.

His innocent question temporarily confounds me. I am not used to having a subject ask about *my* life. It strikes me that this unlikely interview has been the first completely unguarded and reciprocal discussion that I have had while working on my project, and, ironically, it is taking place with the one type of subject that everyone warned me would be unresponsive and mistrustful—a circus performer. "When I was young, I took ballet," I murmur, and Tony teases, "Oh, come on now!"

I grin in spite of myself; this boy's charm would have captivated me twenty-five years ago. "I grew up surrounded by people who needed to be taken care of," I find myself explaining with unexpected candor. "My father was sick from a tropical disease he had caught during the war, my grandfather was dying of Lou Gehrig's disease in our house, one grandmother was paralyzed when I was four, the other grandmother slipped in and out of comas while I was growing up. My mother was a middle school art teacher and managed to take care of everybody else but herself. She was so overburdened that I wanted to help her as much as possible. Whenever I needed to escape, I disappeared into books. That was my refuge. It is probably why I became a writer."

Tony is listening intently. "What are your other books about?" he inquires. I explain that I have written a scholarly book on eating disorders, tell him briefly about my premise that voluntary hunger in adolescents is a form of language.

"Ha! They need to join the circus. We'd work them. They'd be hungry enough then!" He laughs.

A sudden pounding on the door causes us both to sober instantly. "You get out here and take care of this elephant or I'll dock you for a whole day!" Tom Liebel storms.

Rising, Tony silently holds out his hand to me and shakes mine firmly, a pledge between two people who lead different lives but have decided to respect one another—even under pressure to do otherwise.

Mr. Liebel waits impatiently near the pens as we step down from the trailer. Tony strolls toward his father, knowing that any show of saying good-bye will be taken as a challenge, but he shouts back to me over his shoulder, "Come tonight and bring your kids. We'll put them up on the elephant!"

As I retrace my steps through the dusty encampment, no longer ill at ease, I am suddenly struck by Tony's deliberate choice of pronouns:

"We'll put them up on the elephant." There is no doubt in my mind that if I return tonight as a member of the audience, both Liebel men will be courteous and pleasant to my kids, a fact for which Tony can vouch with absolute confidence, in spite of his father's blustering. Could it be that the commitment, strength, and desire that I associate with circus life are less the products of a professional code than the result of shared basic values handed down within families over the generations?

As I reconstruct our recent interview in my head, it occurs to me that Tony's emphasis throughout the morning has been on how comfortable and contented he is working in his family's circus, not because performing represents some glorified calling but simply because it allows him to be with his family. He obviously takes pride in challenging himself to do his best, but this pride in his own work is secondary to his respect for what his family is trying to accomplish: a "serious" show. "A fall is better than a bad attitude," I repeat to myself appreciatively. "Never get cocky, never criticize—stay balanced, work together."

Fritzi's warnings had prepared me to encounter on this visit an attitude of self-celebrating exclusivity and artistic elitism, but Tom Liebel and his son seem very familiar to me. Tony is committed to helping his family but has also staked out an area of private challenge and pleasure for himself; Liebel is a solid worker with firm standards and a concerned, if exacting, parent. Out of his presence, I have little trouble comprehending Mr. Liebel's outbursts. I remember my husband's father, a German immigrant, shouting with equal ferocity at his sons for relaxing instead of cleaning out the barn and tending to hungry animals; he knew that an apathetic attitude toward these crucial and never-ending chores would have immediate ill effects. This circus family is in no way different from farm families across America in their work ethic, and they share with families of corporate executives or military personnel the tendency to band together with others who understand the professional necessity of moving constantly.

My meeting with Tony Liebel has shattered the romantic myth of "cultural difference" that Fritzi and Betty have generated about circus performers. The truth, I decide, is far more practical: Circus performers are families of hardworking people who struggle to make a living, to overcome generational differences, and to maintain a "good attitude" toward their work—like most other people in the world. The sense of family loyalty that Betty discovered in the circus world and still associates with it probably preceded professional ideals; circus life most likely just allowed what was already there to flourish within a supportive environment.

As I pull out of the stifling hot dirt lot with the van windows rolled down and the air conditioner set at full blast, heading for the nearest McDonald's and the promise of icy tea, I find myself repeating over and over, "We, we, we . . ."

~

"They left yesterday on the train," Fritzi explains. "My husband has to be in New York City for the weekend, so he's taking Mom up to see Anne for a single day. Here's the number; they'll be expecting your call."

I hang up the phone, stunned. The idea that Betty has suddenly gone out of town is strangely unsettling, although I am not sure why it should be. The opportunity to interview her sister, however, is as exciting as it is unexpected; I am pleased with Fritzi for facilitating this long-sought interview. I cannot wait to learn how Harry arranged Anne's passage to America. I wonder if Anne shares Betty's deeply ingrained dislike of him.

I wait until Emma is tucked into bed for her nap and thoroughly asleep, then nervously dial the number that Fritzi has provided. When a raspy voice answers, I plunge hurriedly into my introduction but am stopped abruptly when the voice interrupts, "You are speaking too fast! Who is this?" I begin again, more slowly, but again the voice interrupts: "Speak up! I can't hear you. I'm eighty-nine years old, you know." Quickly I grab a pad and pencil and flee with the phone into the laundry room, shutting the door behind me. I raise my voice to the volume that I have become accustomed to use with my dad.

Once she realizes who I am, Anne immediately tells me all about the weather in New York and explains that the sisters are baking bread—without nuts, of course, but with plenty of the fiber that they both need at their age. I can hear Betty on the other end asking who is on the phone. The women chat with one another for a moment, and then I hear two voices burst into identical laughter. I can imagine that these ladies are quite a lively team when they get together.

My interview with Anne Roberts ends up being short but very helpful. I realize immediately that I will not be able to use this shouted interview to probe her memory about long-past emotional intricacies but that I can ask a few broad, straightforward questions. Anne talks lovingly of her late husband and of their son. When I ask about her parents, she explains that she first met her father at the age of sixteen and came to America when she was twenty. "I used my own money to come," she tells me. "Harry never helped at all. In fact, he didn't know that I was coming. I had a hard time finding his family once I got to New York." Betty and I will later exclaim over Anne's revelation; it means that Harry can no longer be given credit for having spent the missing 5,000 marks from the sale of his parents' home on anyone but himself. Betty will also find herself confronting a fact that might have diffused her jealousy of her new sister seventy years ago, at a time when their relationship was marred by Betty's certainty that her father had lavished on Anne money that he would certainly have denied his American family.

I am especially delighted to discover that Harry told Anne a few stories about his childhood in Germany. She relates that her father spoke of having taught himself to do handstands in order to help his family. I know from Betty that he sent money for his mother's care during World War I. "He loved his mother very much," Anne confides, and I struggle to reconcile this information with the stories that I have heard from the Hubers concerning Harry's cruelty to Betty and Babette.

Anne admits that she looks a great deal like her father but that she and her sister think alike because both were sufferers as children. She tells me of her detested life in Germany, of the mother who abused and exploited her, denying her even a bed. Remarkably, she has nothing ill to say of Harry. "He never argued with me and would never have hit me," she explains. "He was always very pleasant. I know that he wasn't that way with Betty. I guess that she had one problem and I had another."

I have been enjoying my talk with Anne and am sorry when she suddenly realizes that the bread has to come out of the oven, yells to Betty, and hastily explains me that she has to hang up and go to the kitchen. "I'm sorry that my sister and I couldn't spend more time together when we were younger," she concludes thoughtfully, referring, I assume, to the bitter years of rivalry and mistrust that Betty has so meticulously chronicled for me. "We got close after we both had children. We spent years apart but now we are a family."

~

"My eldest nephew looks exactly like my brother. It made me feel really"—Betty pauses, searching for the right word—"really weird. Sometimes I would catch a glimpse of him from the side and for a moment I was certain that Charlie was still alive. Seeing him and his sister together reminded me so much of how Charlie and I used to be." She shakes her head in disbelief and lifts her coffee cup slowly.

After decades of distance, Betty was flabbergasted when Charlie's youngest son, William (Willy) Parr, called to invite her to Texas to celebrate his graduation from law school. She has returned with stories and pictures and is more animated than I have ever seen her. I am scarcely less excited. At long last, I feel that a key has been provided to the single permanently locked door in Betty's history. Betty tells me that of all Charlie's children by his second wife, only Willy, the youngest, has generous memories of his father. Instantly, I decide that Willy is the one with whom I want to speak.

It takes awhile before I can get the number from Betty, and as I leave a long message on Willy's answering machine, I assume that he will be unreceptive to the idea of a telephone interview with a stranger concerning his late father. On a Sunday evening several days later, however, Willy returns my call and enthusiastically agrees to be interviewed; he has even arranged to have a grandparent baby-sit his infant daughter so that we can talk without interruptions. It is after midnight and my family has been asleep for hours when I finally put down the receiver and stare at my many pages of scribbled notes. I am not sure what I had expected from this new subject, but I certainly could not have hoped for a more open and amiable interview.

As a recent law school graduate and the father of a brand-new baby daughter, Willy has far more in common with me than any of my other subjects, and I find myself liking him increasingly as we compare our thoughts about Harry and Babette's children. "I have formed the impression that Charlie was a brilliant and tortured man," I confess candidly. "Can you help me to understand him as a complex human being rather than as some sort of villain? Betty has nothing good to say about him, and yet he still dominates her memories. She is both guarded and volatile when we discuss him. Their relationship was a mystery that I cannot quite get a handle on."

"All of us have wondered about it," Willy assures me. "Chuck spoke the same way about Aunt Betty. There was something strong between them, but we will probably never know for sure what it was. When she visited, my brothers and sister and I could not believe how much Aunt Betty was like him—the same gestures, the way he stood and always walked fast. Both were storytellers. They had the same build, too: short and big boned, *Strong*. None of us could get over it. Aunt Betty and Chuck could have been twins."

Chuck, I think. Not "Dad" or "my father." "Betty tells me that you have good memories of him," I say. "Was Charlie really the terrible man that she has made him out to be? Had he no redeeming qualities?"

"He was a violent drinker," Willy explains. "He could be sweet, funny, happy, but he also had snap rages when he drank. I have seen him grab my eldest brother and beat him in a blind fury like a wild animal. He could be extremely cruel. When I was little, he would call me a 'rat' and tell me that no one liked rats. He never struck me though. By the time that I came along, Chuck was older and more mellow. I do remember that he got really mad at me when I was about five and grabbed a drum stick to beat me with. I was so frightened that I wet my pants, but he actually stopped himself. My mother was a sweet Irish Catholic girl who spent many nights crying silently. In our house, when I was growing up, it was everyone for himself."

"Do you know why he was so angry?" I ask. "Did he ever tell you?"

"There was a cloud over him his entire life," Willy muses. "He was furious that he and his siblings never got to be kids. He spoke often of how his childhood had been stolen from him. He told us that he was beaten in Germany for missing school. He never spoke of his older brother, Harry Jr. I think that he may have been depressed about what happened to him, too."

"Betty claims that Charlie was terribly spoiled and that she got all the abuse," I prompt.

"And Chuck said the same thing about her," Willy exclaims. "Harry fought with him, too." Willy relates that Charlie particularly recalled waxing a car one day and accidentally scratching it with a ring that he was wearing. Harry was so angry, Charlie told the children, that he broke an ashtray over his son's head.

"Chuck was angry but also seriously depressed. He felt guilty all of his life for accidentally killing his baby daughter by his first wife with castor oil," Willy tells me. "We thought that it was strange that he left behind his first son, whom we did not know existed until after Chuck's death, and later gave my brother the same name. It was almost as though he wanted to commemorate the two children from his previous marriage whom he had lost."

"Do you know why he left that wife?" I ask curiously.

"He told us that she was greedy. He also said that he broke with Betty because she was materialistic. Chuck claimed that after his mother died, Betty and Harry ransacked the house and took everything. He always resented that Babette had lots of trunks full of valuable things but that Betty had taken them all. He bitterly resented that his children had nothing from their grandmother."

I tell Willy the story that I have been told about the empty trunks and we compare our separate versions. "The whole family was this way," Willy says thoughtfully, "incredibly mistrustful of anyone they thought might be manipulating them for money. Chuck had almost a split personality. Very generous on the surface, but if you scratched too deep, there was a stark contrast underneath. He was constantly worried about security, and he equated security with money. He always resented the lack of money in the music and show business. Chuck was a multimillionaire repeatedly; he lost it all and made it back several times. He knew how to start from nothing; in fact, I think that he even enjoyed that part of it, but maintaining a business on a daily basis and running everything correctly was very hard for him. In that respect, he was like a bull in a china shop."

As Willy describes his father's business career as a home builder and land developer, marketing executive, investor, and founder of his own ad agency in California, I reflect that Charlie deliberately chose the most notoriously unstable fields possible as he sought financial security; for a fearless player, these are fields in which the rewards are unlimited but complete ruin is always a single poor investment away.

It also occurs to me that as an entrepreneur, Charlie was probably able to hide the fact that he had not finished even elementary school, a secret that must have been deeply distressful to the clever and ambitious businessman.

"The first big loss came during the Arab oil embargo," Willy remembers. "Chuck began again with nothing and pulled us out, but it was bad for a while. We moved to Tampa when I was in the sixth grade, staying just ahead of the creditors. Chuck had to get out of Los Angeles before he was served, so we fled south in a trailer during the night. In Florida, I used my own name in school but lived in an apartment complex under the name of Edwards."

I remember Betty's frustrated story about Charlie's family arriving in Texas in a trailer after Fritz's death, her hope that her millionaire brother would help her financially, her indignation over Charlie's bizarre decision to leave abruptly. I tell Willy this story and he shares his side of it with me. "My father told us that the Hubers had moved to Europe," he remembers. "He alluded that Betty was trashy and only wanted money from him, and that our cousins had no interest in knowing us. We were amazed when we ran into Bobby a few years ago in a restaurant in Florida. We are realizing now that we cousins were all told the same stories because Chuck and Aunt Betty were so much alike.

"The second loss came right after my mother died, and I think that it was just too much at once," Willy tells me softly. He relates that after so many years of difficulty, Charlie and Madeline had finally begun to mend their marriage. Charlie had decided to hire a secretary to keep an eye on Willy so that he and his wife could spend more time together. When she collapsed and died of an aneurysm in 1979, a devastated Charlie waited patiently until his son came home from school to tell him of his mother's death. "He was absolutely furious that as soon as he had told me, I went out skating," Willy recalls. "I needed to do that, though."

After Madeline died, Charlie started dating again. "Like Harry reincarnated, he dated only younger women," Willy tells me. "He was sixty-three years old but never told them his age; he was extremely secretive about it. Chuck seemed very troubled at that time; he was terribly afraid of growing old, but he was able to talk, somehow, with me. He would ask me if it was okay for him to declare bankruptcy again. I would tell him, 'Sure, I will support you in whatever you decide to do.'

"It seemed like he wanted to get closer to me after my mother's death," Willy says, recalling that Charlie took over the role of mother with intense determination. He did laundry, managed the house, and, each morning before school, even served his son hot cooked breakfasts of eggs and SizzleLean bacon in bed. "He loved that Sizzle-Lean." Willy laughs. Charlie bought his son handsome clothes and was heartbroken when the teen preferred to wear the inevitable jeans and T-shirts that have characterized American adolescents for decades. "I would wear those fancy shirts not because I wanted to, but just so that Chuck's feelings would not be hurt," Willy recalls.

Charlie could apparently surprise even his children with his unpredictable moods. "I got in some serious trouble when I was in high school," Willy admits, "but amazingly, when Chuck learned what had happened, he went to the Department of Health and Human Services and handled it all for me. Then he handed me the keys to his car, just to show that he still trusted me." Years later, after Willy had moved to college, his financially strapped father would cook stews and eat them all week so that he could afford to treat his son to dinner in restaurants during his visits home. "He had an incredible spirit, incredible will-power," Willy muses. "He could pull himself up from anything if he wanted to. He could even stop drinking cold turkey when he really tried. There were times when we had to pull him from the car though; once he drove off the road into a ditch, yet he could also be really funny and creative and hardworking when he was sober."

For the next half hour, Willy delights me with happier stories of his father. Finally I can imagine Charlie as he would, perhaps, have liked to have been always. Like his sister, Charlie loved to perform. He would put on funny skits for his children with his long, thick brows combed hilariously down over his eyes. Also like Betty and Fritzi, Charlie loved to be creative with his hands. When the Parrs needed a new driveway, the restless millionaire surprised his family by hand-laying the entire drive himself, using colored bricks to form artistic patterns. When Charlie took Willy with him to do yard work for an elderly man who had been a German U-boat commander in World War II, he amazed his son by launching into long conversations with the veteran in German. Charlie had painstakingly taught himself to speak perfect English without a trace of an accent, yet he could still converse comfortably in a language that he had left behind at the age of nine.

Perhaps I am too sentimental about the tiny islands of affection and playfulness that this deeply troubled man so seldom was able to enjoy; I find that I am calmly resigned to the stories of assault and despair that Willy relates, yet the happy memories he has of Charlie leave me feeling almost shaken. So often during the past two years, I have found myself moved to tears not so much by stories of tragedy but by the corresponding realization of how wonderful my subjects' lives *could* have been. Harry, Babette, Charlie, Betty, and Fritzi all possessed extraordinary resources of intelligence, creativity, and tenderness that could have ensured remarkable and joyful lives right from the start, yet each one ended up caught in patterns of abuse, mistrust, and anger that probably stretch back over untraceable generations.

Perhaps the most interesting tale that Willy tells me is of his father's intense mistrust of doctors and dentists. Like his cousins, Willy learned early to hide injuries. He taped his own cuts and covered bruises. One day he accidentally knocked a drinking glass into the washing machine and reached down into the tub to retrieve it. Unfortunately, the agitation had already shattered the glass; the churning fragments sliced deeply through his hand before he could draw it out, instantly turning the soapy laundry a bloody red.

"I almost passed out," Willy remembers. "Chuck sat me down and told me that I needed a few stitches, then he calmly sewed up my hand himself."

Laughing, I share with him stories of his cousins' similar deceptions and tell him of his grandmother Babette's mistrust of doctors. As we converse, I suddenly remember that Betty neglected to take Fritzi to a doctor after her rape and for the first time am able to consider her decision as part of a long-standing pattern of physical self-sufficiency rather than as mere neglect.

As the hours pass, Willy and I enjoy comparing notes about these two estranged siblings and the many amazing similarities that they shared, right down to a love of Cuban cuisine. I have to laugh when Willy relates that his father took the kids for a ride into Watts to see riots during the 1960s. Fritzi has told me a similar story about her mother getting lost and driving through Harlem during a race riot; Betty pulled to the side of the road and asked for directions from a resident who seemed horrified by her very presence and begged her to leave quickly. "They were fearless," Willy agrees, laughing. "Because he had grown up in the circus, Chuck did not differentiate between races or cultures. He always had that I'm-one-of-you-at-heart attitude."

"I have been given letters that your father wrote back in the fifties that try to explain to Betty why he left the circus to seek a more secure life," I tell Willy. "These letters reveal a very different sort of man than Betty has described, but if I point that out to either Betty or Fritzi, I am told that Charlie was a grifter who was always lying."

"I would love to see those," Willy says, and I quickly offer to send photocopies. "They were a family of performers in every sense, but Chuck had a human side, too. I have seen him cry."

Although Betty has told me many times of her brother's disdain for the circus, his determination to erase that past by reinventing himself, Willy tells a far different story. He admits that his father claimed to be "classier" and "brighter" than the other members of his family, but insists that Charlie always felt guilty for trying to be "something he wasn't."

According to Willy, Charlie bragged about his circus background throughout his life and, like my other subjects, loved to romanticize and glamorize it. He maintained friendships with many of his old circus friends, visiting and dining with them as often as possible. "Chuck would have dinner with Eddie Zacchini in Tampa," Willy recalls. "He remained friends with Henni Luxem until his death."

The truth, it appears, is not that Charlie hated his family's circus background but that he bitterly resented what that background had cost him: a secure childhood, an education, a stable and dependable family. Ironically, these are precisely the gifts that life within a more traditional circus family probably ought to have guaranteed. While Harry and Babette were undoubtedly "circus," I decide, their neglected and exploited children were never part of a circus "family." Perhaps for this reason, each one drifted through life desperately trying to find or create what had been missing from his or her youth, with varying degrees of erratic success. The disruptions and betrayals, starvation and beatings, exploitation and abuse that characterized Charlie's childhood apparently tortured him throughout his life, poisoning even his financial successes, marriages, and relationships with his children. Unlike Betty, who maintains that she has survived her life by "not thinking too much," Charlie possessed and nurtured an astonishing memory, a gift that also proved to be a relentless curse.

Willy thinks that his father was contemplating suicide long before he apparently murdered his girlfriend and then killed himself. In the months preceding his death, Charlie made careful preparations. He changed his will, made out property transfers to Willy's name, wrote meticulous instructions concerning his financial affairs. "Chuck had learned that his girlfriend was cheating on him," Willy explains. "He had found a letter from the young woman's mother advising her to 'take the sucker for all he's worth.' After his death, that letter was discovered shredded and stuffed into a tuna fish can; amazingly, the detectives were able to piece it together. After Chuck found that letter, he began drinking heavily and taking Valium or some kind of depressant."

The details of his father's final days are hard to connect; Willy tells me that after he discovered the cruel letter, Charlie broke into a photography store and attempted to steal some specialty photographs of himself and his lover. He was arrested, the relationship with the girl rapidly unraveled, his finances fell dangerously low, a court case was pending. Struggling under emotional burdens and weighted down by substance abuse, Charlie lost his heart for business completely. "He hinted about going away," Willy remembers, "and worried about whether I would be okay if he left."

Willy was twenty years old when Charlie requested that he fly home from college for a father-and-son weekend in Tampa. Willy recalls noticing that his father had a gun in the car, an unusual sight. "Chuck completely blew me off the whole weekend," he remembers. "I could not understand why he had even asked me to come home. On Sunday night, though, he suddenly apologized and begged me to stay for one more day. We had a wonderful next day together, went out to eat, spent time really talking."

On Monday evening, Willy recalls, Charlie drank. "He gave me lots of strange advice—permanent advice, like 'Watch your weight as you grow older,' and 'Take care of your money.' After I had fallen asleep, Chuck laid out an envelope containing his final papers and some cash, along with detailed instructions for how to manage the business after he was gone. He was very anxious about my care and had apparently spent a great deal of time trying to ensure that I would manage after his death."

I hold my breath as Willy explains how, after a very pleasant day with his youngest son, Charlie waited until the young man was asleep in his room, then drove to Bradenton and shot his lover in the head. After he had killed the young woman, he removed a ring from her finger, drove back to his own home in Tampa, left the ring beside his still-slumbering child, returned to his girlfriend's body, lay down on the bed beside it, and fatally shot himself.

"We have always had a grim sense of humor in my family." Willy laughs after he has related this harrowing story. "When people ask questions, I say that my father died of lead poisoning."

I exhale hard and laugh with him. "That's immigrant humor," I warn him. "I grew up with it, too." I glance at the clock, realizing that in Willy's time zone, it is yesterday. I am exhausted but also have a pleasant, peaceful feeling of resolution. I can hear a baby crying on Willy's end of the line, and for a few relaxed minutes, we happily discuss our daughters. Willy explains to me how he is trying to break the cycle of generational unhappiness that has tortured his family for so long. "I had to grow up and learn that I cannot blame him for what happens to me," he says firmly. "I promised Chuck that I would finish law school and I have. From here on, I take responsibility for my own mistakes and my own happiness. I love my family, and I am going to remain positive."

~

The next morning dawns bright and cheerful, but I am still tired and I leaf through Charlie's letters with a heavy heart. They seem far more tragic now, read with the knowledge of what his life would become. Most are addressed to Betty and Fritz, but by the second paragraph are inevitably directed to Betty alone. Throughout the letters, the self-taught writer begs his sister to be patient with his grammatical and spelling errors. Spoken English was obviously far easier for

Charlie to master without instruction than the grammatical complexities of written English. Three topics dominate all the missives: concern for his broken relationship with Harry, concern that Betty not think that he hates the circus, and concern for his young family and growing business prospects.

These are very thoughtful letters written by a man in his thirties: musings on life and what it does to us, explanations and attempts to discover motivations. It is hard to reconcile their intimate tone with Betty's insistence that she and Charlie were enemies. Two letters in particular hold my attention: a letter to Betty, dated October 9, 1954; and a letter to Harry, dated August 11, 1958. Over and over, I read Charlie's messages to his family:

To Betty:

I can only think how he [Harry] winds up with nothing no matter how much he has because of dames and drink. I know that is his business. But I warned him many times that he would find himself in that position. He always said not to worry that as long as he spends it he will have the incentive to make it. I know even at my young age, as I knew at a younger age, that there is something that happens to all of us when we age that robs us of our strength to work and our will to be determined enough just to make a living. . . .

However, here he is getting older every day. More than anything I would like to renew our relationship. Financially I couldn't and unless I help him when I contact him, he will not accept it as a friendly contact. . . . When I stopped writing dad my last letter was that he has never written to me without telling me how much trouble he had, how many flats, the last blown tire cost him $72.00, etc. He never wrote merely to say that he liked his son, or was just writing to me because he was my father. . . .

All this is very unimportant considering that he is aging by the day. How does one go about it when circumstances are as they are? Is there anything you can suggest? As hurt as he may feel about things, surely he can recognize that he too has hurt all of us deeply. And in spite of the lack of contact there is a bitter parental love tearing at my heart. Madeline and I have discussed this often. In not contacting him though, I hurt him less. I could only have told him what I say to you above and I don't want to take the heart out of an old man unable to fight back. . . . *With the bitterness he has felt because I did not contact him, he had strength, and I did not have to hurt him by being truthful.* But time is too far gone, I have a feeling that the strength gets less every day.

I fold this letter carefully and seal it in its bag. I wonder whether, in distancing himself finally from his widowed sister, Charlie might have thought that he was giving her, too, the strength that bitterness brings. Perhaps he resented her financial needs, mistrusting her motives as he did Harry's. This letter, however, suggests that Charlie understood that bitterness poisons over time. His letter to Harry, written four years later, apparently after a reconciliation, is even more poignant.

To Harry:

Fritz would be awfully smart to move before its too late to move but of course that is up to him. Show people are always talking about the dream to settle down. They would love to have money coming in weekly and make a lot of money. They talk about it and talk about it but when it actually comes to making the break, it is like trying to break the habit of smoking. Only will power can do it and looking ahead to the future. You know its a funny thing, just because I struggled to try to find a permanent business and security and forced my way out of show business, everybody thought that I didn't like show business. I loved the easiness of it, I loved the atmosphere and I loved the travelling. I disliked the insecurity and lack of work. . . . Naturally there is a frustration of being with strange people who don't understand show business at all and many memories of some wonderful days. You can't replace playing in Madison Square Garden with a big show and going over as one of the top acts . . . but you can't have everything. I am just gambling that security will take the place of all those things, or maybe in the end I will find it really wasn't important at all. At any rate all I can do is wait and find out.

∽

"You have a house full of death art," I remark jokingly as I wander through Fritzi's living room.

"Yup." She smiles. "I'm making friends with it."

I have purposefully asked Fritzi to spend the morning talking to me about her wonderful personal collection. Our friendship began over art, and it occurs to me that exploring our mutual love of art is perhaps the wisest way to reconfirm it. "It's a very cohesive collection and says a great deal about you," I suggest.

"I didn't plan them to go together; I picked each piece individually and ended up with this." Fritzi walks me around a living room that looks much like a comfortable private art gallery. Masks of all sizes fill the walls, large figures stretch from corners, cabinets are crowded with colorful clay objects. "Masks have a transformative quality," Fritzi explains, pointing to the scowling and grinning faces above us, many of them animal faces with human expressions. "We all have something primal in us that wearing a mask allows us to unleash. We are so conscious of being humans that we easily forget that we are also animal."

"Do you mean that we are overly civilized rather than carnal?"

"No, no. People are incredibly territorial in terms of the privacy of their homes. Animals are far more innocent in that they are less inhibited and can respond directly to nature. That's what we have lost touch with. I caught two deer in my headlights as I was coming home last night. They were playfully leaping toward the light. That's one of the beautiful things about animals that we have lost—joyfulness. Unencumbered, unburdened spirit. We've suppressed that but the safety of a mask can allow it to resurface."

I remember how I once frolicked at the Greek Festival with Betty and smile to myself. One does not need a mask, I think, if Betty is along and Latin music is playing. "These are rather monstrous faces— not playful or clownish," I point out.

"Yes, but not mean monsters! Emma loves these. Any kid will tiptoe up to these masks and touch them, then leap back and giggle. You mistrust the growling because it's too emphatic. It seems like a game. Clown faces, on the other hand, are that deathly white with garish, vampiric red lips. We've told ourselves that they are cute but I've always felt that they are frightening. They have to be a bit scary if they are going to be effective. The masks, on the other hand, are entertaining. If the beast is doing something fulfilling, you want to be a part of it."

"Unless it's masturbating," I tease.

"This is true." Fritzi laughs. "I haven't seen a masturbating one yet, but if I do . . ."

"Here we go!" I point to a brightly glazed ceramic piece on a nearby shelf. A clay figure of Adam grins up at me as he strokes his immense, erect penis, to the delight of the devil who hovers over him, apparently urging him on. Eve lies beside them amid flowers and crows, watching supportively. In spite of their eroticism, the figures seem playful and silly.

"That's a chiango from Ocumichu, Mexico." Fritzi grins. "These people used to be toymakers. Now they make these ceramic figurines. Little old grandmothers will hand them to you and giggle like children. To them, they're toys."

Fritzi explains that according to Tarascan legend, Michael drove the devil into the earth not far from the tiny town of Ocumichu. "The people believe that the clay is infected by the devil's presence and speaks through their hands, causing these objects to be formed," she tells me. "If you make a really good chiango, it doesn't mean that you are a bad person; it just shows that you are a great receptor. By ignoring the devil and facing him with humor, they gain strength."

"Like children dressing up as Nazis on Halloween?" I suggest.

"Exactly. What better way to dismantle the power of the past than to make fun of it? Keep in mind that these are extremely Catholic people, but they are saying 'Look, Satan, how silly you are. You're not scary; you're just a big goof.' This diablo figure here is a piggy bank. There are snakes crawling up him, and he has big teeth and black feathers, but he isn't in control of you. He's just clay and when he is full, you can break him and get your money back. It's empowering."

Fritzi tells me of her first trip to Mexico, a country that she has come to love, in 1972. She was struck by the incredible poverty. "People say that the countryside is so dirty, but these people were living in grace," she recalls. "I've never seen such pristine dwellings. They would wet the dirt and sweep it down. You could see from their posture, carriage, generosity, and dignity that they had a huge spirituality that meant more than money and a respect for what had been handed down to them through their culture and the clay."

"What about that fellow?" I ask quickly, pointing to a large, papier-mâché skeleton with tremendous teeth in a silly grin, a scorpion sitting on his head and colorful flowers erupting from his bones. "He makes me feel like we are playing a game. He is a beast who sneaks up and yells 'Arrgh.'"

"Yes, but look at what's happening to him. He's regenerating! He's giving life to all the other creatures in the forest. Matter never ends; it only transforms. These regenerating life skeletons are done by the Linares family. They are very well known in Mexico. I've seen only one of these figures who doesn't regenerate. During the revolution, there was a Hispanic woman invented by Posada, La Katrina, who was oblivious to the suffering around her. For her, the war was merely an inconvenience that meant she couldn't have the latest purse from Paris. They've done a few pieces of La Katrina, and she never regenerates life because she's void of life to begin with."

"It's wonderful," I admit, enthralled by the piece, "but I can understand why the salt-of-the-earth, Southern Baptist laborers who came in here after the hurricane took one look around at these grinning skeletons and animal masks and masturbating diablos and were scared out of their wits."

"They thought that I was a witch!" Fritzi exclaims, remembering the workers' confusion. "They didn't want to come in. I had to store all the art away until they were finished."

Laughing together, we both turn to the room's most prominent piece, a man-size, painted tiger costume mounted on the wall behind the dining room table. "In these villagers' Aztec past, it was believed that when a warrior died, he became a jaguar and his spirit roamed the forest. Eventually the tiger figure replaced the jaguar, and once a year now two men are chosen to become the jaguar warrior. They dress as the tiger and are banished from the village to live in the woods for two weeks. People leave out food for them, so they don't feel that the villagers are their prey, but they are free to explore the animal side of themselves and to interact with the villagers unexpectedly if they choose."

"So the villagers can experience their fear in a cathartic way in order to gain control over it?"

"Yup. Once these guys are in that costume, you don't know what may be happening in their minds. They might have gotten a little kooky in the woods. They might go a bit further than you want them to—maybe actually nip you to see what you taste like, maybe take you into the forest and roll you around for a while. This piece on the floor is a processional tiger figure; he represents one of the men who would be wearing the tiger costume." Fritzi points to a two- to three-foot painted statue of a man in a tiger suit, his face unsmiling and a too-small tiger mask pulled over his forehead almost to his dark brows. "A figure with a mustache, like this one, indicates Spanish blood, perhaps aristocratic blood," Fritzi explains. "The colonizer can become a jaguar, too, but you'll notice that the hat doesn't fit over his face so that he can fully disguise himself. This represents his attempt to blend coupled with an awareness that it's not really a part of his lineage. Look at those masks up there. Some are very animated, but the passive ones are all mustached Spaniards. They are lifeless, pasty-faced Europeans—just masks."

"It's an interesting way to view death. D. H. Lawrence used to call it 'death in life'—that zombie existence where you have only a false social consciousness and no sense of yourself as a living individual."

Fritzi nods. "Some of us are so susceptible to what's going on outside. What I love about Mom is that she has that internal sense of herself solidly established, and she doesn't care if you like it or not. When things shut down around her, she pulls up that inner strength."

"How do you find that inner spirit? How does one learn to depend on it, use it as a comfort, draw on it, and pass it on?" I prompt her.

Fritzi responds to my question very confidently: "I think you find it when you reach a point in your life where you've gone beyond it. That's how you learn where it is. It sounds weird, I know, but when absolutely everything is gone and you lose hope and are devoid of any sense of who you are, somewhere in the bottom of that is a spark of the gift you came into the world with. You can't go out and learn to be yourself. You are what is in you, and you have to learn to listen to that voice because it's a personal gift."

I bite down on my cheek. Up until a second ago, I was allowing myself to be soothed by our interesting discourse, happy in the company of my artistic friend. "I think that's an inadequate analogy," I suggest carefully. "I believe that we are all gifted, if you want to use that term, but hitting rock bottom does not mean that you have lost everything but some primal spark and must rise out of the ashes like a phoenix. Generally, what you lose in common crisis (not war or massacre, of course) is probably a part of yourself that you have focused on so completely that you have assumed that that was all there was to you. Then something destroys that avenue of self-realization—you lose yourself as a career person, or as a spouse, or as a parent. Your mother lost herself as a circus performer and as a wife, for example. Suddenly something that you never noticed before is free to exert itself, if you can find the heart to refocus your attention. Some people lose their careers and blow their heads off. Some people break up with a lover and go on a rampage. They cannot see possibility in that void."

"That's faith," Fritzi responds. "All you can do in that vacuum is to let go of control completely and let the natural flow occur."

"No, I think that most people have to work at developing the undeveloped parts of themselves," I maintain with growing confidence. "I don't believe that some of us are more personally gifted than others—by design. I think that *everybody* has new possibilities and unused strengths and can learn to be aware of them. Some of us have heavier burdens or more difficult transitions to deal with than others, that's all."

Fritzi says nothing but she seems to be listening. I continue, encouraged by her silence. "Your mother has taught me that change is central to life. In her paintings, people are always moving. She explained to me that we have to keep moving within ourselves, and we make that happen by being with other people or new ideas and by letting them challenge our perspectives. It doesn't mean that we have to change radically all the time. You don't think of the ocean as changing itself; it just keeps moving—that's what allows it to support life. Without that movement, everything would die. This is what regeneration is about, I think. A mask or costume is meant to be experienced through interaction with others. Wearing it alone would be useless."

Fritzi points to a ponderous totem near the front door, a primitive-looking and strangely soothing figure. "That's a Sepik River figure from New Guinea. It's indicative of an ancestral figure who has passed away and is alive in your memory. When you see the figure, you tell stories; as long as the stories live, that person's memory is alive. It doesn't matter if the stories change form over the generations; they just have to continue. When the stories stop and no one remembers any more, then the family parts with the figure and lets go of the spirit. Some of these are hundreds of years old. That's how long the stories last."

Yes, I think, narration is a form of movement because stories demand an audience. I realize suddenly that none of the pieces in Fritzi's collection are about death; rather, they all concern ways of dealing with the *memory* of death, even with the idea of oneself as a future memory. "What is real death then? What do you think happens to the spirit after the stories stop?" I ask her.

"That depends on what you believe happens after death," Fritzi responds softly. "To understand what happens after this world, you must look *at* the world. Look at how many different kinds of trees there are within the tree family, how many types of animals there are. These are all living things, unique and different from each other, and yet, at the level of physics, all are composed of the same particles, atoms, and molecules, and animated by life. Maybe that difference and similarity extends beyond the physical world."

"I'm not following you."

"There are variables after death, too. Whatever you *think* will happen to you happens. People who are devoid of belief and faith maybe go into this great pool of energy that gets dissipated in some way. If you have hope and belief in heaven and hell, there may be a heaven or hell for you. If you believe that you are going to be reincarnated in forty days, then you will be. The Godhead, if you want to call it that, is a great source of all energy, but it might take many forms. This is why I can never say that anyone else's beliefs are false or wrong—what they believe may actually happen for them because of the level of their faith. Perhaps there is even a level of regeneration beyond what any of us can imagine. What is important is to have faith in something far grander and more mysterious than we can ever understand."

"I don't think that I have ever heard anyone articulate a belief in the variable nature of reality so beautifully. How did you develop this theory?" I ask, genuinely touched.

"I grew up having hypnagogic hallucinations—those 'visions' that happen between the states of waking and sleeping. They are over-whelmingly detailed images and so 'real' that you are forced to start questioning what reality is. I mean, you know that you are seeing something 'real,' but you are also very aware that nobody else can see it."

I feel myself shudder. "I can vividly remember that happening to me when I was a young girl," I confess. "I sat right up in bed and saw a snake moving across my legs. I watched the sheets moving as the snake twisted back and forth. I was frozen; I couldn't even scream. Then its head went under the covers and my screams would not stop.

By the time my parents came upstairs and turned the lights on, I was hysterical, but I could still see those covers moving. My children have the same visions when they are feverish."

Fritzi listens quietly and nods. Her eyes grow sad. "Rochelle, at the end, was in a semihallucinatory state all the time from the morphine. She was participating in what was then an experimental project. They implanted a tank in her body with a digital readout and a continual feed tube that ran to her spine. Rochelle was completely lucid. She would tell me, 'See that bed pot over there? It looks so much like a zebra, I can't even tell you. And that zebra is grazing right now.' She would make direct eye contact with me, then look back to the zebra. Unbelievable."

"When I had Carl, they gave me morphine," I share, touched by the sadness in Fritzi's voice for her lost friend's suffering. "After three days of labor, I remember watching as the white walls turned to liquid and bubbled and ran like milk being poured down from the ceiling. I told the nurses, 'This is gorgeous but I can't even show you.' I know that I saw colors that don't exist to our eyes."

Fritzi suddenly gets an odd smile on her face, one that I cannot describe. "It's like taking LSD, Donna. That's why drugs are so popular. You lived a different life during the 1960s." Her tone seems to contain an insinuation that I have been sheltered from an experience that could have expanded my understanding. "There's a ton of bad drugs and designer drugs and chemicals that give you an effect like that," she continues. "Genuine LSD from laboratories in Switzerland is amazing. It actually made me stop taking drugs because once I'd tried it, I realized that everything that I had had up until then was crap."

I wait in silence until Fritzi's disturbing expression has disappeared; when she continues speaking, her tone is normal again and she seems aware that our discussion of spirituality has undergone a sudden change. "I know that some people wonder how I could have made such abrupt choices in my life," Fritzi states sharply, looking me directly in the eye, "but I was dealing with the issue of being in control of my own life. Where are those boundaries? Where do you stop? How much do you affect other people? How do you remain spontaneous and still be reasonable? It's really easy to hurt other people. I needed to find a balance between feeling alive and still not hurting anyone else."

I am dealing with almost the same issues, I think, realizing that we have come full circle to the questions with which we began this project; however, I have to find a balance between feeling alive and still being able to *help* others, a far more complicated formula. "What answers have you found?" I ask quietly.

"It's all about telling a story, creating a connectedness through writing or dance or making a visual object. We all have personal perspectives that other people can understand. That's a healing process. It keeps you from being lonely. It fills you. You know, Mom and I have always believed that whatever you do on New Year's Day affects what you will do the rest of the year, so you should do something that you want to do more of. On New Year's Day I pulled out some markers and paper and paints, and we made covers for some of the CDs that were soaked during the hurricane. Afterward, Mom told me, 'I'm really glad we did that. I want to draw this year.'

"The whole time that we were kids, Mom was doing little drawings—little dolls or women's faces—but she would put them in her pocket or throw them away," Fritzi recalls. "When she thought that her life was going to be short, after the surgery and the cancer, she began to do art in earnest."

Fritzi relates the discovery of her mother's tumor, the surgery followed by chemotherapy, the horrible day in 1991 when the oncologist admitted that blood work had just revealed that the chemo was not working any more. "Mom wanted me with her for all of her visits," Fritzi recalls. "I would talk to the doctor and then explain to her later what had been decided. On that afternoon, her physician simply told me, 'Let us know when she has discomfort and we'll do something for it.' I said, 'Are we talking about a preventative act or pain maintenance?' and he replied, 'Pain maintenance.' I asked, 'Are we talking about how long pain maintenance?' and he answered, 'Three months.'

"We walked to the car and stood there in the parking lot. Mom wanted to know what he had meant. I told her, 'Do you remember how Rochelle felt really good but there was nothing that they could do for her? Remember how they gave her a little pump? That's what he meant.' Mom just stood there for a moment, then she said, 'Oh boy.' We got into the car and for the first time she really began to cry. I told her, 'Look, here's what we'll do. I will speak to my acupuncturist. He knows a lot about women in China and herbal medicine. Now that you're not on chemo or being treated for cancer, he might suggest something for you. Let's start there. We're on an adventure!'"

I stare at Fritzi. "What a perfect way to put it for her," I compliment. "*We're* on an adventure," I repeat. "Very different from the way that your father's cancer was handled."

Fritzi smiles her thanks. "Yes! I won't ever live through that kind of complete denial again. It just extended the pain. I knew that if I didn't give us something to hold on to *that moment*, we would be in a terrible mess."

Fritzi relates that her acupuncturist immediately designed an herbal combination for Betty, which she took for three years, feeling better and better as the months went by. Finally, during a routine examination, the oncologist who had predicted her imminent death pulled Fritzi aside and admitted, "I have to tell you that I am questioning my diagnosis. Her lymph nodes are normal and so is her blood count." Fritzi explained, then, what her mother had been doing. "I don't know if it's the herbs or the power of her faith in them," the doctor mused, "but she is in complete remission. Congratulations!"

I draw a deep breath. "God, that is a wonderful story. It makes up for all the other stories you have told me."

Fritzi grins but she is wiping her eyes, as well. "That was six years ago," she says, "and look at Mom now." Suddenly we both start laughing, "What's *in* those crazy herbs?"

Growing serious, I explain, "I understand now why your mother told me something a long time ago. She said, 'I lost myself completely, but Fritzi is teaching me to know myself and to be strong.' She made it clear that she has learned to empower herself and to bond with women over just the last few years, and all through your influence."

Fritzi's eyes are shining. "We've worked at it," she admits softly, "both of us. For a long time she felt that she had given up all her control. I have to respect when she's stubborn sometimes and won't listen to me because at least she is standing up for herself."

"So how did she start making art?"

Fritzi grins. "Well, after she started taking the herbs, I suggested that she write down some of her stories, but she didn't want to write. Then I suggested that she start drawing. She asked, 'What could I draw?' and I told her, 'All the things that have made you happy.' Well, at first she wouldn't draw anything. I would bring her nice pads of paper and new art materials; she just put them up on a shelf. Finally I figured out what was wrong. She couldn't bear to mess up those nice clean, brand-new surfaces!"

Fritzi grins at me conspiratorially. "So I got a book of blank drawing paper, put a dust cover on it, scribbled on a few pages and ripped them out, carried it with me until it was kind of scruffy, then gave it to Mom. I said, 'Look at this! It's a perfectly good little book that I've been carrying around for weeks, but I just can't draw in it. It's not suited to me. I hate to throw it out. You like little things, don't you? Could you find something to do with it so that I don't feel terrible about wasting it?' Mom's eyes started to shine. She said, 'Oh, this is perfect!' and she filled every page. Now she works only on discards; I give her foam core, scraps, my matboard. She does like new pens and pencils, but her surfaces have to be used." Suddenly Fritzi begins to laugh. "You've seen that picture of the rehearsal hall that has a circle right in the middle of it?"

"With 'spot a no-no' written in it?"

"Yup. This is a great example of how Mom works. I gave her a piece of matboard without realizing that it had some resistance on it, so it wouldn't take paint or ink; it resisted the moisture. When Mom finished the picture, she simply drew a circle around the spot to call attention to the fact that it shouldn't be there. Her way of not wasting the matboard was just to circle the bad area and mark it 'no-no' so that the viewer knows to ignore it."

"And, of course, she believes that if she tells you to ignore the spot, you will." I laugh.

"Of course!" Fritzi chuckles. "Her work is completely untrained and innocent, but here's what really intrigues me. Even though she has had no formal training whatsoever, all of her drawings are perfectly balanced. Perfectly. Every single one. It blows my mind. If you look at her series painting of her pets, for example, there's a line right down the middle, like a tightrope, and every single element in the picture is exactly offset by some other element. I couldn't achieve that kind of balance, even with my training. It's uncanny. When Mom was young all of her balance was in her body, but her body has incredible limitations now. Somehow she has transferred all of that physical balance and it's expressing itself now through her work."

"She's like that with her story, too," I muse. "When she's handed me a memory that she likes, she balances it with something else that she wants to include. The logic of the connection is clear to her, but I am left to scavenge for some way to make all the fragments cohere."

"Scavenging for remnants is what Mom is accustomed to." Fritzi chuckles. "One of Mom's favorite things to do was to wander with me through the dressing rooms after the show closed. It was like being at a fresh archeological dig. Mom would exclaim, 'Oh, look! There's a feather from Princess Tajana's headdress. Wow! I could make a doll costume out of that. We would take these discards from the recent past and regenerate them—transfer them to a new form of life. It was a romantic gesture, I guess."

Fritzi falls silent for a moment, and I watch as little smiles flicker across her face. Suddenly she catches me observing her and grins. "This reminds me of something. We've been talking about death— did I ever tell you about [Romeo's sister's] funeral last Christmas? Mom and I went to Texas together. Many circus friends were there. Her son was doing the eulogy. I can't repeat it in his own exquisite wording, but he said something like, 'We all know how it feels when a show is over and you go back and walk the lot, see the holes where the stakes were, the peanut bags, the little reminders of the show that was there, and you feel very full and very empty at the same time.' This was his comment about his mother being gone.

"I was behind him up at the podium, and I could see all the faces. There were several generations of circus performers at the service, and there wasn't one person who didn't understand completely his analogy of having and not having simultaneously. It was extremely moving."

I shake my head slowly, appreciating the analogy. "I once referred to your mother's story as a 'scavenger hunt' without even realizing that it is one," I reflect. "She has been telling me for months, in her own way, 'Don't look for things; just see what's there and make something with it.' I get so annoyed sometimes with her hoarding of information. This is a good way to understand what is happening between us."

"Like the cancer incident," Fritzi suggests. "You're on an adventure together. What will you find?"

I think of the months of rambling interviews, the huge piles of notes and transcriptions that must now be transformed somehow into a cohesive story that makes sense *to me,* and heave a deep sigh. Fritzi stares at me, then bursts into sympathetic laughter.

∽

Betty's tone sounds guarded and falsely friendly when I phone to say hello. She answers my questions with the same coolly impatient courtesy that I reserve for telemarketers. I have been so occupied with writing for the last few weeks that I have not been as attentive as usual. We are not finished with the interviewing process, so I know that I have to determine what is bothering her and overcome it quickly. Betty has been betrayed too often by people she thought were friends to have developed a trusting nature. I understand that, if neglected for too long, she can easily allow an imagined slight to fester into permanent mistrust.

The next morning I stop by her home for a visit and bring Kurt along, knowing that his freckled smile can spread sunshine through even the murkiest mood. To my amazement, Betty greets us at the door with a grin that could thaw an iceberg. Something has delighted her so much that she can hardly contain herself.

"Look what I have!" She laughs as she leads us into the living room. I glance around at the familiar furniture and decorations but notice nothing out of the ordinary until Kurt suddenly gives a little gasp and falls to the floor with his arm stretched out. In a corner near the sofa, a tiny, hairless Chihuahua quivers on pencil-thin paws. Betty gently scoops the little thing up so that Kurt can caress it. I have never seen an animal quite like this one. She has a sweet face with huge eyes, the body of a shaved squirrel, and amazing strands of hair as long as whiskers growing out of her ears. She is appropriately named "Yoda."

"A lady called and told me that she had five big dogs and would have to give this little one away," Betty explains happily. "I wasn't going to take her, but Fritzi told me, 'Mom, do you realize how expensive those dogs are? People pay hundreds for them and you can have one for free. It needs a home. You understand how delicate she is; someone else might not take the right care of her.'"

I smile to myself. A "cast-off," I think, and wonder how Fritzi has arranged this. We have long known that Betty needs another dog.

There are already jars of baby food in the kitchen, I note as we leave, and wonder how long it will take Betty to perceive that this new pet, unlike the aged Nikki, has teeth and needs to chew. As I watch her clutch her precious new "baby," obviously beside herself with happiness, I think that no creature on earth will be as well loved as Yoda. I am very, very happy for Betty today.

We leave Grandma Betty cuddling a contented Yoda at the door, her face beaming, and I recall several similar mornings, now three years behind us, when I drove away from this house and left an equally radiant Betty standing on the threshold, my newborn daughter snuggled in her arms. Suddenly I comprehend that long before I ever asked Betty to trust me with her story, I entrusted her with something far more precious.

∼

It is almost seven o'clock in the evening when I finally pull down the driveway and come to a stop in a cloud of dust. Swarms of biting horseflies and mosquitoes are immediately attracted to the heat of the engine; I would wait them out if the inside of the vehicle were not almost as ovenish as the swampy forest outside. Straining against the padded bar of her booster seat, Emma sobs for her dinner, sweat and tears forming dirty streaks down her flushed cheeks. The boys wearily haul open the rear doors and load their arms with grocery bags. I plod back down the driveway, my howling daughter clutching my neck, to retrieve the mail. Al has to work late tonight—an unexpected commission, so I am alone with the troops. My one consolation is that in the process of whirlwinding to the high school, middle school, day care center, bank, grocery store, office supply, and photocopy center, I made it to the post office before they closed the window. All of the bills got posted on time, and I managed to send Willy the promised photocopies of his father's letters.

Indoors, I bustle expertly but numbly through the transitional chaos that inevitably marks the end of my "workday" and the beginning of my "other work" every afternoon. Emma is eventually soothed and distracted with raisins, milk, and a cartoon video that she has watched repeatedly for months; the groceries are put away and dinner started; the table laid and the boys settled into homework assignments due tomorrow; our phone messages checked and the mail sorted. Completely spent, I sift through a pile of papers that the boys have carried in from the car and thrown on my desk—school cafeteria menus, Emma's easel-size finger paintings, torn sheets of coupons; video rental, grocery, and postage receipts. On the bottom of the pile is a large brown envelope from the photocopy center containing Charlie's letters; these must go right back into the locked drawer in which I keep all of the Hubers' papers and pictures. I reach gently inside the envelope and pull out a stack of too-white, crisp copy paper. Sickened, I realize that in my hurry and fatigue, I have addressed and mailed the wrong envelope.

My first thought is to call Willy, explain my mistake, and request that he copy the letters and return the originals. I have no doubt that he will gladly do this. I pick up the phone, then slowly put it down again. After a moment of thought, I call Fritzi and explain the situation. "Do you want me to get the letters back or would you like Willy to have them?" I ask, already anticipating her response.

"Of course Willy should have his father's letters," Fritzi assures me immediately. "I know if someone had letters from my Dad, I would want them. I'll write my cousin and tell him that he's welcome to keep the originals. Just don't tell Mom. It took her years to let me have some of that stuff."

Relieved, I hang up the phone. My frayed nerves are telling me that I must complete this last item of business and get it off my mind right now or I will not be able to relax this evening. Glancing up at the clock, I estimate the difference in time zones, then leave a message on Willy's machine, telling him to expect original letters. I hang up the phone and take my first deep breath of the day.

The "transitional chaos" is never as bad on a Tuesday as it is on Monday. The next day, with the critical errands completed, I manage to make the rounds of after-school activities and arrive home with all three kids before six o'clock. There are enough leftovers from yesterday to assure an effortless meal, and I promise myself that this evening will be more humane. The message light on the phone is blinking insistently, but there is mercifully only one message. As I replay the long tirade, however, I feel my heart sinking.

Fritzi's frenzied voice fills the room, literally raving that I have "lost" her uncle's irreplaceable letters. She insists that I call her the instant that

I enter the house, warns that she intends to drive over immediately, explains that she has been extremely disturbed with me all day and will not rest until she has retrieved her family's photographs and papers.

I let the message run its long course, feeling in its unbalanced tone the futility of my hope for a simple forgetting of differences. Growing annoyed in spite of myself, I mentally argue that the reason that I have these papers is so that I can reproduce them in a permanent record for Fritzi's family. We both know exactly where Charlie's letters are, for heaven's sake. Picking up the phone, I call Fritzi and assure her that I will retrieve her "lost" letters from Willy instantly.

"Don't you dare call Willy!" she rants. "I just wrote him a gracious letter and told him to keep those letters. What choice did I have after you had *lost* them?"

As I listen to Fritzi's almost tearful voice, I realize that something is happening within me. I can almost hear a door slamming shut. Why isn't my heart pounding with indignant, wounded fury? Even a week ago, it would have been. Why am I no longer concerned about my friend's unhappiness? Her variable moods have taken me on an emotional roller-coaster ride over the past year, yet I feel strangely calm right now. I find myself listening patiently, with the same dependable composure that I use to weather Emma's occasional toddler tantrums, yet I am forming a resolution. "Of course you can have everything back whenever you would like," I assure Fritzi quietly. "Come over now if you want to. Now is just fine."

I hang up the phone and go straight to my locked desk drawer, retrieve carefully stacked folders and sealed plastic bags, put them together in a pile near the door. Next, I walk to the kitchen and pour myself a glass of wine. Al will be home soon to watch the kids, and I will not be needing my usual balancing skills for this meeting. Fritzi has given me far too many lectures on the importance of spontaneity and emotional immediacy while I have had to hide my personal feelings of frustration for fear of losing access to my subjects. Our last interview is finished. I do not need to be guarded or to choose my words with care anymore. I am no longer afraid to reveal that I also have emotions. Fritzi is going to be very surprised at how well I can reinvent myself.

∽

"You've been working with glitter, haven't you? Your face is all glittery. It's great. I love it." I gently brush at Betty's cheek with my fingertip.

"I'm a work of art, I guess." Betty smiles, touching her hand to her face. Outside, the first promise of fall has appeared, and Betty's front door is open to a tangy breeze. The vicious, scorching heat of Southern summer is finally behind us, and the hint of seasonal change seems appropriate for today's work. This will be our last interview, and I cannot help feeling a wee bit sentimental.

"I love these angels!" Betty exclaims, running her hand tenderly over the colorful AVAM (American Visionary Art Museum) brochure that I have opened before her. "This guy thinks Judgment Day is coming. Ha! His pictures look like tarot cards, don't they?"

Betty listens intently while I try to explain to her what "visionary art" is considered to be. I read her an excerpt from the AVAM Mission Statement: "Visionary art as defined for the purposes of the American Visionary Art Museum refers to art produced by self-taught individuals, usually without formal training, whose works arise from an innate personal vision that revels foremost in the creative act itself." The brochure continues, "Visionary artists don't listen to anyone else's tradition. They invent their own. They hear their own inner voice, so much so that they may not even think of what they do as art."[4]

"That's like me, I guess," Betty murmurs, smiling almost shyly. "When I did my act on the wire, I just followed my impulses. Nobody else could copy me, even when I tried to teach them. I was just having fun."

"What about in your visual artwork?" I ask, pointing to photographs of her paintings and circus scenes. "How do you decide what to draw?"

Betty's face scrunches up while she tackles my difficult question. "I don't think when I'm making art," she says, finally. "It just comes. Fritzi got me a little book to draw in. She told me to draw whatever I liked, so I decided I would try. I drew all the acts I had worked in, when I married Fritz, when we had the trailer at Greenwood Lake, what the kids did, and later I drew all the movies I was in."

Betty rises and retrieves a small booklet in which she has drawn herself in the many roles that she has played as a movie extra. "In that movie *The Ruby Bridges Story*, I played a very hateful woman. Before it came out, I warned the black people at the senior center, 'When you see me, remember that they didn't tell me ahead of time what I would have to do. They only said I would have a "special" part.' Imagine *me* holding up a black doll in a coffin and saying 'This is going to be you!' to a little black girl. I played with that child between scenes so that she would know that I wasn't really like that. The director told me afterwards 'Mrs. Huber, I know that was a hard part for you to play.' I didn't contradict him, but acting isn't hard for me. I love it.

"When I'm not working in a movie, I feel like a prisoner," Betty admits thoughtfully. "I used to love my free life when I could do whatever I wanted, go anywhere, be anyone I wanted to be. It's not like that now. This town is so small. In show business, if something happens to a performer, all the other performers know but the people in the audience don't. Now other people are always living my life. I don't enjoy it. It's harder to feel like me."

I page through a pile of black-and-whites, find a photograph of the comic-strip-like piece in which Betty has recorded her many pets. I notice that it is, as Fritzi remarked, amazingly balanced. "Tell me about this one," I beg.

Betty sighs and croons as she remembers each beloved pet. I watch her eyes wrinkle with alternating joy and distress as she points out the puppy that her father gave away when she was a child, the duck that followed her about at a barbecue, the police dog Harry gave her for a wedding present, then untied and drove away while Betty was performing. "We worked a fair and found a wounded baby chicken hawk in one of the barns," Betty remembers. "We called it Whiskey because Harry was drunk when he gave it to me."

"That's a bird of prey. Whatever did you feed it?" I exclaim.

"Chicken. It was a chicken hawk," Betty responds, her face as innocent as a child's. I burst out laughing.

"Well, they all ate whatever I fed them," she murmurs, unsure of whether I am laughing at her. "There's my bird Tweetie. Bobby left the cage door open and the cat took Tweetie away. Here's Fritz feeding Smokey. He was with us until Fritz died. Some woman in Fort Worth told me, 'I know you love dogs, so I'm giving you this one.' Well, I have a superstition that when someone gives you an animal, you can't give it away again. That's why I always beg people never to give me a pet.

"We found this dog, Cindy, with a broken leg. I made a splint out of a clothes hanger, but the kids put her up on a table and forgot about her. She fell off with that splint on her leg and broke her shoulder too. I held that dog all night until the vet opened. There was nothing he could do. I cried but Fritz said, 'Mommy, we can't let her suffer.' I buried her in the backyard. So we didn't have a dog for a while and then James Brown came on the television and I drew him. He has rhythm."

I smile to myself as Betty "scavenges" across time and themes. Today we seem to be traveling on the same road, right along side of one another. I understand that this drawing isn't about Betty's pets so much as about the way that they make her feel. The series is an exercise in associative thinking; each segment inspires the same pleasurable nostalgia. When James Brown popped onto her screen, Betty must have felt as good as if a favorite dog had just jumped into her lap, so she drew him into the series.

"One of Fritzi's friends found this cat screaming and brought it to me. It had been run over. The girl had been smoking marijuana, so she blew some in its face. The cat fell asleep and never woke up! We buried her out back."

"What's this 'pretty red fox'?" I ask, pointing quickly to the next segment of the picture.

"I found a little lost doggy at a fair. Fritz said I could keep it. Just then a man came with a stick with a loop on the end. He said, 'Drop it, lady! That's a wild fox!' It was growling at him but cuddling up to me. Fritz said that I had to put it in the box the man had with him. I went to his show everyday and petted the 'wild' animals. The guy always told me to leave if people were around."

Betty runs her finger along the tiny pictures in the series. "Hmmm, let's see. Bobby found this dog, but he ran away. I brought this blue jay into the house but I had to put paper down everywhere because it kept dropping," she muses, and I bite my lip so that I don't chuckle again. "This parrot talked dirty. I tricked a little stripper who lived down the street into keeping it."

"You didn't have a camel?" I gasp, looking ahead at the next segment.

"When we played the Shrine dates in Detroit, Smokey fell in love with that camel. He slept with her and even ate her camel food. They were always together. When they loaded the camel up at the end of the show, I had to dart in and grab my dog or I wouldn't have gotten him back."

"What's Bobby doing here with two dogs?"

"Learning about nature." Betty humphs. "I never told him anything. I guess Fritzi wised him up. Eventually that dog had puppies, but someone threw poison meat in my yard and killed them all. Here's a flying squirrel that Bobby found and brought in the house. It bit me. I'd never heard of rabies, but I did get a tetanus shot. I caught this chipmunk in Greenwood Lake. It would play hide-and-seek with me. I rocked over him with the rocking chair one day. We buried him, too. This last scene is in Peru, Indiana. Terrell Jacobs had a lioness there who had just had babies. He warned me to stay away from them, that the mother would get mad, but I put my hand in the cage and petted the babies and the mother just sat there and watched me. I was very careful."

"Animals love you, don't they?" I smile, thinking of how tiny Yoda stood protectively in front of Betty and yapped as I entered the house.

"They know that I love them," Betty responds matter-of-factly. "What else do you have there?" She begins to leaf through the pile of pictures and pauses at a three dimensional scene of a rehearsal hall, the very picture I had hoped that she would choose. Tiny figures twist and twirl, leap and stretch across the practice floor; across the top, Betty has written *WHATS BALLET.*

"I was watching the seniors exercise at the senior center," Betty muses, "and I got to thinking that these awkward exercises are what eventually turn into beautiful ballets. See, this guy is walking the bars. Here's a baton twirler. This fellow is trying to stretch that girl."

"What about the two guys at the top?"

"Oh, they're fighting with swords, like at those medieval fairs," Betty explains. "See, people take it for granted that all these performances just happen perfectly the first time, but they don't. This is what you don't see."

I remember a long-ago afternoon when Betty told me, "Before anything else, there's work, and even before that, there's just yourself." I smile, thinking that we have both worked hard since that day. "And this?" I tease, pointing to a circle in the middle of the photograph.

"That spot's not supposed to be in the picture. It's a 'no-no,' just like it says," Betty remarks casually. Yes, I think, those "no-no spots" happen all the time. Wouldn't it be wonderful if we could circle all our mistakes and label them in this way: "kindly disregard," "unintended insult," "human frailty." Betty's vision is starting to seem increasingly attractive.

"Tell me about this picture," I urge, pulling up what appears to be the most "visionary" piece of all. It is a beach scene. Fluffy clouds float in the serene sky, a striped umbrella is perched in one corner, sea creatures swim in the ocean. Beneath the water, however, flamelike lines stretch upward, entangling figures who raise their arms in supplication. A tiny child floats above the surface of the water toward a devil, complete with horns and a tail, who holds out his arms to receive her. Facing the devil, a winged angel, halo shining, stretches her arms toward the child, as if to intercede. Back on the beach, a lifeguard watches this struggle from high on his lookout stand, just as if he were helplessly witnessing a swimmer's attempt to outswim a shark.

"It was a project at the senior center. We had to do something about angels for angel week. See, the devil has thrown all these people into the water, and if they go down far enough, then they're in hell. This child's parents left her while they went to get something. They thought that she would be okay. She was just playing with her little sand thing, you know? The lifeguard can't help but the angel will rescue her. She will save the others, eventually, but right now she is saving the child."

"Betty, do you believe in angels?" I ask softly.

Her smile is gentle as she answers, "I believe more in angels than in the other thing."

"You mean God?"

"Yeah, I guess. I was raised in a Catholic convent but I have lost so much of my faith. I mean, if there is an almighty creator, how could he let so many criminals get away with hurting people? They keep telling me that Jesus will come back. Well, let me know when he comes. I'd really like to meet this person who has allowed such heartache for so many good people."

"Do you think that God makes bad things happen to us, or that we cause our own problems?" I prompt her.

"I think some force does make things happen. We don't really understand what that force is, but it is in us. Many people are good until they bump into something and it changes their lives entirely. They don't understand why themselves. Mother Nature has done a lot to us, let's put it that way."

"Mother Nature?"

I have never seen Betty struggle with such urgency to articulate her thoughts. She searches desperately for words that seem right to her, as if her future happiness depends on my understanding. "Life is very complicated," she tries at last. "A person can adjust, and then something happens and the force splits."

"Splits?"

Betty sighs. "It's there, and it needs something that we are not able to give it. It's like a hurt child whose mother has pushed it away. The child needs its mother's love, but the mother doesn't know how to give it to her, so the child doesn't trust anybody now. If she had a mother who could play with her and show affection, the child could behave differently, but without affection, she is filled with hate. She doesn't want to be hateful, but she dislikes people. If you love this child, she will love you back. We don't know how to give her what she needs, so she gets mad at us. It's not her fault."

My mind is spinning. I think of myself preparing to receive my angry friend by gulping down a cocktail. "So God is an abandoned child and we are the ones who must change the world by teaching her to love again?"

"That's right," Betty agrees. "They say that God is love, but I don't believe that. Love is within us. If we could learn to project that force outward, we could help so much. When you are angry with a person and don't want to talk to her, you are drawing away that force from both of you.

"It's like the Americans and the Mexicans," Betty explains, trying hard to be specific. "People here hated Mexicans, so they called us gringos to get even. Not because they hated us, but because they had been mistreated. Some people really do need to be pushed away, but you have to push only that one person, not the whole group. What happens with nationalities is the same with individuals. I push you, then you push me back. One person can put hate in you and it can spread, just like a bad apple can ruin the whole basket. Some people have been abused all their lives. When they get married, they abuse their children because that is how they were brought up. They never learned how to love their children, so their children learn to hate, too."

"I think that's true," I agree, thinking of all the responsibility and sacrifice that become inevitable when one is so attached to another person that his or her pain or pleasure become one's own. "Of course, the traditional Christian view is just the opposite," I muse. "Instead of God being the child who needs our love, we are the sinful children and God is a loving parent who teaches us to forgive."

"Yup. But what is he teaching us? It doesn't make sense. Look at where that first brother in the Bible slew his brother. If God had taken care of those boys right then and there, all this mess wouldn't have happened."

"So it was bad parenting from the start!" I laugh, amused by her wording but impressed by her reasoning.

"Yes," Betty insists. "Hazel [Betty's next-door neighbor] always tells me, 'Lay it down and ask God to take it from you,' but I did that when my husband died. I had no money. I didn't know if my children would forgive me for losing their father. I learned that God wasn't going to fix anything for me. I had to do it myself."

"So where do the angels come in?" I ask gently.

Betty sighs and relaxes. "You know how the flower blooms so beautifully? That's like the beauty that surrounds an angel. Soft colors and perfume. An angel is the spirit that makes you want to be good and helpful and protective. The weeds are this guy." She points disdainfully to her drawing of the devil.

"When you think about it," Betty continues, choosing her words with care, "whenever there's a beautiful flower, all at once these weeds come and kill it. The devil is like a weed that destroys what is beautiful, what you love. He tries to control everything, like Harry did. But flowers keep coming back. All winter long, they're gone, but in the springtime, they return, and they smell so pretty that people want to hold them and smell them and enjoy them. They draw you close like an angel."

"Children start out that way," I suggest, pursuing her analogy.

"Yes!" Betty seizes eagerly on my suggestion and extends it. "Then the weeds come and the child becomes angry and can't understand why it isn't loved." Suddenly she pauses and looks at me in the most grandmotherly way imaginable. "Donna, fighting is natural in life. Anger makes people lose faith, but angels are powerful. We can't believe in perfection because life isn't perfect. We can believe in beauty, though. It disappears sometimes, but you have to have faith that it will come back. Faith keeps beauty alive inside of you."

I had not expected this exquisite, touching lesson. Betty is looking deep into my eyes, as if she can read there the uncertainties that I have been struggling with for so long. I feel almost dizzy as Betty lowers her eyes and begins to browse through the pictures again. She holds up a photograph of a small doll that she has made. The tiny figure is garbed in an angelic costume of gauzy white petticoats. Two dark braids hang almost to her feet. A jewelry hook has been inserted into her scalp and she swings, suspended by her head, from a wire stretched tightly across a painted circus background.

"This makes me feel terrible," I murmur. "I want to shake her and tell her to stop. Won't she lose her hair?"

"They don't so much lose their hair as get migraine headaches," Betty responds. "I don't know why some women do this act, but they are very proud of it. The hook always goes into the braid so that the hair can't pull out. I made this doll to give to Fritzi."

"Why for her?" I ask quietly.

"I was thinking of all the different high acts. They get paid so little for the risk that they take. They will pull her way up high, but she wants to be up there. She has a full skirt so that when she comes down, her skirt will fly up."

I look closely at the little doll, noticing the loving details—the tiny necklace and pendant, the painted slippers. Slowly I begin to realize how many hearts there are in this piece. The circus ring is studded with hearts. The performers in the background have hearts on their costumes. Even the doll's lipless mouth is heart shaped.

"There's a lot of love in this," I offer. "She looks like an angel, don't you think?"

Betty chuckles. "Oh, gosh, I never think when I make art. It's a Fritzi scene. Fritzi's no angel, but she is beautiful. She can be an angel when she wants to be."

"She's been my good angel sometimes," I murmur, staring intently at the sharp hook embedded in the doll's proudly braided hair.

Betty smiles at me. "Have faith in beauty," she reminds me softly.

I draw a deep breath. "Do you believe there's a heaven where everything will be right again?"

Betty nods her head quickly. "I believe there's an in-between place," she assures me, "a state of complete relaxation. You will float above the world and admire its beauty but not need anything. You'll be just what you want to become because you'll be able to change yourself anytime that you wish. Everybody around you will be so friendly and nice. There will be no hatred, no jealousy. I think of it as sort of an adventure, like being locked into Macy's for the night."

I grin. "Try on all the diamonds, sample all the chocolates."

"Sleep in all the pretty beds," Betty joins in, laughing. "And nobody will care that you are there." She smiles and whispers, "Heaven is where we will finally be free to play."

SEVEN

CONCLUSION

As I sit in a quiet corner of my living room, relishing the silence of the surrounding woods, surveying the thick folders of notes piled high on an old desk where I have sat for almost two years writing this book, I cannot help but remember the faraway, hurricane-weary afternoon when Fritzi first urged me to "reinvent" myself, to discover a new "comfort zone" in which I could feel useful. I have spent thousands of hours since that day interviewing and writing, worrying and wondering; I have watched my daughter grow to preschool age and my dearest friend change into an almost stranger, but I have not reinvented myself. I believe that I have come to understand myself better, though, and to recognize that the foundation of my personal contentment can be built upon indefinitely and will survive transition.

I have learned a great deal from the Hubers. They have taught me to look inward for answers. I now understand that a comfort zone is not a place. The true comfort of fellowship cannot be searched for and found like a new job; it develops over time and perhaps must change naturally over time as well. My comfort zone at the university was created through the sense of fellowship that I felt with colleagues there. It ended when they became more publication-anxious than I was, when their desire for lengthy resumes and comfortable careers shifted the boundaries of our fellowship, leaving me an "outsider" within that particular value system. Had I tried to reinvent myself, considered myself flexible rather than firm in my own values and needs, I would never have survived the transition.

I must have understood this because through all my disappointment and frustration, the core of desire within me remained constant. It provoked me to cry over my books and the reciprocal learning that they represented, to search for a new friend who thrived on comparing thoughts, to share my little daughter with an eighty-one-year-old woman who understood that joy in children unites adults. It caused me to resent a lack of reciprocity both in the interviewing process and in the overwhelming details of domesticity that so often kept me needed but not fulfilled.

I clutched at the opportunity of a book contract because I thought that the project would turn Fritzi, Betty, and me into a nurturing, working "family," a new comfort zone of inquiring women to replace the colleagues and students whom I had lost. I did not understand that a comfort zone is found not in others but within oneself as one interacts with others. It is an extension of oneself through love, a foundation on which one can always build as long as one refuses to be isolated or emotionally distant. Ironically, I learned this hard lesson only when I embraced the isolation of a writer's lonely desk and the discomfort of a biographer's ill-fitting objectivity.

~

Grandma Betty remains beloved by my family. She calls regularly to ask how I am doing. I stop by with the children whenever they want to pet Yoda and be showered with almond cookies and grandmotherly attention. She still has moods, but I now regard her shifts in humor as transient breezes that must follow their own natural currents without regard for the stationary objects over which they blow. A cleansing breeze is, after all, invigorating, and a stiff wind can always be avoided.

It has been months since I have seen Fritzi. I have heard from Betty that she took a trip to Europe recently and returned excited and happy. I am stubbornly waiting for a phone call that I fear may not come because resentment has choked the tendrils of our once-trusting friendship. Fritzi has returned, through my husband, all of the books that I have lent her, a gesture heavy with symbolism.

Two years ago I would have felt bitter over the loss of so beautiful and brilliant a friend, but that was before I met Betty. Now I am able to regard this "transition of the heart" rather differently. Grandma Betty has taught me that just as weeds will eventually wither unless one waters them, permanent anger must be refueled, if only in memory. My memories of my friend are increasingly generous, and I hope that Fritzi also remembers the comfort of our laughter. I cannot help trusting that the resentment between us will turn someday, like the seasons. I received for Mother's Day a tiny card of handmade paper with Fritzi's distinctive signature, and while I could not yet bring myself to risk dismissal by calling her, I placed this symbolic sign of goodwill in my jewelry box with my other treasures.

Together, the Huber women have painstakingly taught a professor of language to pay sharp attention to the nonverbal and not to rely too completely on the haste of words. The last time that Fritzi and I stood face to face, our words to one another were blunt and cruel. We accused and rationalized, blamed and argued, made ourselves ill with tension. My last visual memory of Fritzi is of her standing on my threshold looking inwardly bruised, her face smeared with tears, her shoulders hunched miserably over her body. In that single moment, I loved my friend more than I have ever loved her. I temporarily forgot the jagged words that we had just hurled at one another, as well as the resentment that would keep me awake for many nights to come. Her tear-streaked cheeks and despondent eyes exposed the loneliness of an abandoned child and the misgivings of a proud woman.

Impulsively I wrapped my arms around my friend, felt how thin her shoulder blades were, how unsteadily her body was balanced. I felt also, in the rigidity of her spine, the relentless force of the anger that had settled between us. Fritzi returned my hug with an obligatory squeeze, but as I was resigning myself to this unsatisfactory parting, she suddenly tightened her arms around me. I could not see her face, no words passed between us, but in the fleeting insistence of that embrace I am sure that I felt the healing touch of an angel's wing.

◞

There can be no ending to a life story whose subjects are still living, no resolution to conflicts that are as seasonal as tempest and sunshine. I have learned that one does not resolve a transition, one chooses to view it with hope or with despair and then picks a direction in which to face. Tomorrow I will place my finished manuscript in the mail, pack up my family, and begin a new journey. I miss my mother's arms, my father's laugh. I will gather my parents and children together under one roof and let their love fill me. I will lie in my childhood bedroom and consider the possibilities of a midlife career change. Perhaps I will call Fritzi from my mother's house. As I have learned from Betty and Fritzi, we are on an adventure.

NOTES

*I have chosen to change some names: the first time a pseudonym is used,
it is followed by an asterisk.

CHAPTER 2

1. Meredith Etherington-Smith, *The Persistence of Memory: A Biography of Dali* (New York: Random House, 1992), pp. 240-241.
2. Ibid., p. 244.
3. Jean M. Humez, "'We Got Our History Lesson': Oral Historical Autobiography and Women's Narrative Arts Traditions," in *Tradition and the Talents of Women*, ed. Florence Howe (Urbana: University of Illinois Press, 1991), p. 130.
4. Linda Wagner-Martin, *Telling Women's Lives: The New Biography* (New Brunswick, NJ: Rutgers University Press, 1994), pp. 6-7.
5. Ibid., p. 12.
6. Victoria Glendinning, "Lies and Silences," in *The Troubled Face of Biography*, ed. Eric Homberger and John Charmley (New York: St. Martin's Press, 1988), pp. 49, 53.
7. Andrew Sinclair, "Vivat Alius Ergo Sum," in *The Troubled Face of Biography*, ed. Eric Homberger and John Charmley (New York: St. Martin's Press, 1988), p. 123.
8. Glendinning, "Lies and Silences," p. 54.
9. Wagner-Martin, *Telling Women's Lives*, p. 10.
10. Polly Rose Gottlieb, *The Nine Lives of Billy Rose* (New York: Crown Publishers, 1968), pp. 102-103.
11. Elia Kazan, *Elia Kazan: A Life* (New York: Doubleday, 1989).
12. Ibid., p. 482.
13. Ibid., p. 478.
14. Ibid., p. 481.
15. Ibid., pp. 478, 482.

CHAPTER 3

1. John Culhane, *The American Circus: An Illustrated Display* (New York: Henry Holt and Company, 1990), pp. 207, 186. Information in the following pages has been adapted from Culhane.
2. Ibid., pp. 203-205.

3. Linda Wagner-Martin, *Telling Women's Lives: The New Biography* (New Brunswick, NJ: Rutgers University Press, 1994), p. 12.

4. David Gelernter, *1939: The Lost World of the Fair* (New York: The Free Press, 1995). pp. 334-335.

CHAPTER 4

1. Richard Hubler, *The Cristianis* (Boston: Little, Brown & Company, 1966), p. 4.
2. Ibid., p. 66.
3. Lee Davis, *Man-Made Catastrophes: From the Burning of Rome to the Lockerbie Crash* (New York: Facts On File, 1993), p. 189.
4. Ibid., pp. 189-191. See also Hugh Clevely, *Famous Fires* (New York: The John Day Company, 1958), pp. 25-29.

CHAPTER 5

1. John Culhane, *The American Circus: An Illustrated Display* (New York: Henry Holt and Company, 1990), p. 1.
2. Victoria Ortiz, *The Land and People of Cuba* (New York: J. B. Lippincott Company, 1973), pp. 87-89, and Ernesto Che Guevara, *Episodes of the Cuban Revolutionary War* (New York: Pathfinder Press, 1996), pp. 88-100.
3. Ortiz, *The Land and People of Cuba*, pp. 72-75.

CHAPTER 6

1. John Culhane, *The American Circus: An Illustrated Display* (New York: Henry Holt and Company, 1990), p. 61.
2. Ibid., pp. 303-304.
3. Ibid., p. 358.
4. "The End is Near!" *Visions*, Vol. 3, American Visionary Art Museum, p. 20.

BIBLIOGRAPHY

Clevely, Hugh. *Famous Fires.* New York: The John Day Company, 1958.

Culhane, John. *The American Circus: An Illustrated Display.* New York: Henry Holt and Company, 1990.

Davis, Lee. *Man-Made Catastrophes: From the Burning of Rome to the Lockerbie Crash.* New York: Facts On File, 1993.

"The End Is Near!" *Visions.* Vol. 3. American Visionary Art Museum.

Etherington-Smith, Meredith. *The Persistence of Memory: A Biography of Dali.* New York: Random House, 1992.

Gelernter, David. *1939: The Lost World of the Fair.* New York: The Free Press, 1995.

Glendinning, Victoria. "Lies and Silences." In *The Troubled Face of Biography,* ed. Eric Homberger and John Charmley, 49-62. New York: St. Martin's Press, 1988.

Gottlieb, Polly Rose. *The Nine Lives of Billy Rose.* New York: Crown Publishers, 1968.

Guevara, Ernesto Che. *Episodes of the Cuban Revolutionary War.* New York: Pathfinder Press, 1996.

Hubler, Richard. *The Cristianis.* Boston: Little, Brown & Company, 1966.

Humez, Jean M. "'We Got Our History Lesson': Oral Historical Autobiography and Women's Narrative Arts Traditions." In *Tradition and the Talents of Women,* ed. Florence Howe, 125-144. Urbana: University of Illinois Press, 1991.

Kazan, Elia. *Elia Kazan: A Life.* New York: Doubleday, 1989.

Ortiz, Victoria. *The Land and People of Cuba.* New York: J. B. Lippincott Company, 1973.

Sinclair, Andrew. "Vivat Alius Ergo Sum." In *The Troubled Face of Biography,* ed. Eric Homberger and John Charmley, 123-130. New York: St. Martin's Press, 1988.

Stewart, Michael, and Cy Coleman. "Join the Circus." *Let's Go to the Circus.* Videocassette. The Walt Disney Company, 1994.

Wagner-Martin, Linda. *Telling Women's Lives: The New Biography.* New Brunswick, NJ: Rutgers University Press, 1994.